Listen to Your
Vegetables

Grilled Corn Salad with Dandelion
Greens, Cucumber, and Cilantro
Salsa Verde (page 121)

Listen to Your Vegetables

Italian-Inspired Recipes
for Every Season

Sarah Grueneberg

with Kate Heddings

HARVEST
An Imprint of WILLIAM MORROW

HarperCollins books may be purchased
for educational, business, or sales
promotional use. For information,
please email the
Special Markets Department at
SPsales@harpercollins.com.

FIRST EDITION

Design by Mia Johnson
Photographs by Stephen Hamilton
Illustrations by Andrew Jesernig
Vegetable icons © green-tea / Shutterstock;
agrino / Shutterstock; ctrlaplus /
Shutterstock; Olga Illi / Shutterstock;
Valadzionak Volha / Shutterstock

Library of Congress Cataloging-in-Publication Data
has been applied for.

ISBN 978-0-358-64711-9

22 23 24 25 26   RTL   10 9 8 7 6 5 4 3 2 1

To my mom, Trish the Dish.
Thank you for your love and
for teaching me as a young girl
to follow my dreams and career.

Contents

INTRODUCTION

I **have a little secret to share**: Fruits and vegetables are singing loudly around you, begging you to take them home and try something new. Are you listening? I am writing this book with one goal: to inspire you to rethink how you are cooking your vegetables. I want to change the way you shop and cook for your broccoli, mushrooms, and eggplant.

I believe the Italians are masters of listening to their vegetables. They cook whatever is most inspiring at the market day to day. If the asparagus jumps out at you, then you buy it! I first learned to embrace this way of thinking when presented with the beautiful abundance on my daily shopping excursions throughout the towns of Italy. Italians don't eat out of season, and every meal—whether it centers on pasta or meat or poultry or whatnot—is always accented by a variety of seasonal veggies. This is the way we like to cook at my restaurant, Monteverde, and the way that most chefs like to cook.

But first, I feel it's important to share where my deep love for vegetables began. It was—no surprise here—in the garden: my grandparents' garden in rural Texas, to be exact. I spent many happy summers escaping Houston for the country. My grandparents' house was off a country road, with pastures full of cattle and crops. They didn't have trash pickup, the water came from the well, and they had a septic system that the gophers always messed with. Meals were centered on what was fresh from their garden or their garden freezer. My grandmother would sneak almost any vegetable into her delicious casseroles, her dill pickles got folded into the tuna fish salad, wild dewberries studded her pies, and there was always a loaf of homemade bread at the table. My grandmother cooked by necessity, always deferring to what was in season and ripe for eating.

This was a dream for a young girl and soon-to-be aspiring cook. My earliest memories of Grandpa's broccoli were that the flowering buds were big and loose, not tiny and tightly grouped like what I saw at the supermarket. His homegrown corn was sweet, juicy, delicious and *two* colors—yellow and white, not pure yellow and perfect looking. In the winter we would pick satsuma oranges and Meyer lemons—I can tell you that a Texas Meyer lemon pie is hard to beat. My grandparents pickled or froze the ingredients they couldn't eat fresh and almost always had three deep freezers full of what they grew.

Fast-forward to a defining moment for me as a young sous chef at Brennan's restaurant in Houston. The chefs and I would drive to a farm just south of downtown Houston to handpick the produce for the week. The first time I went on one of those day trips, walking through the fields with the other chefs, it took me right back to my grandparents' garden. It was as if a light had been relit; it was a very special moment for me.

When I got back to Brennan's, I had to figure out how the produce from the farm visit would make its way into our nightly specials. I was stumped. This was a defining moment for a young cook: to make a dish, on my own, for the guests at the special kitchen table! My chef and mentor at the time, Chris Shepherd, gently nudged me into the walk-in cooler and said, "Listen around you. What ingredients are speaking to you right now?" I was intrigued by this idea. Who listens to the ingredients in the cooler? I found myself in front of a giant bucket of beets—and those beets *were* talking to me. They were saying, "Hey, pick us! We want to be more than just a salad—we're vibrant, sweet, and earthy, and our colors will grab the diner in a most intoxicating way. We are the real jewels of the walk-in!" (I bet you didn't know beets had so much to say, did you?) I grabbed some of those beets along with their tops and a few apples. I roasted the whole beets with salt, thyme, and a

splash of vinegar, then diced them with apples. I julienned the beet tops and sautéed them with butter and served them with a piece of fish and a beurre blanc sauce. The experience changed me. It was then that I was able to connect the idyllic summers at my grandparents' house with those long walks through the fields of produce with my chefs and start really *listening* to my vegetables. It changed how I cooked, how I saw food, and how I would create dishes for years to come.

Brennan's was a fast-paced kitchen—the restaurant had over 300 seats! The food was delicious but intricate, and all of the dishes were made à la minute (meaning they were made to order and not prepped ahead of time). I remember on my first day I got home and glowed about how cool the chopped edible flower garnish was on the shrimp rémoulade! I was put on the hot appetizer station and I had to make a beurre blanc sauce, which to me is one of the most important sauces to learn. It teaches a cook how butter emulsifies and how to reduce a sauce just the right amount.

I moved around the different stations at Brennan's. I would say that the game changer was when I got to work on the special menus for the ten-top table in the kitchen. Most chefs just pulled recipes from the main menu, but I created brand new dishes, and they were delicious. Everything started to click.

I became the first female (not to mention the youngest person, at the time) to become the sous chef at Brennan's. My exposure to produce under Chris's watch, along with the extraordinary training I got, helped solidify my love and appreciation of fruits and vegetables.

My deep love for Italian cuisine started after my time at Brennan's, when I went to work for Missy Robbins, who was then the executive chef at Spiaggia in Chicago. Frankly, I really struggled at Spiaggia at first. I was fully out of my league. The fine dining at Brennan's in Houston was very different than Chicago's fine dining scene. I was doing things I had never done at all, like cutting hamachi for carpaccio, making carne cruda (steak tartare)—even having to brunoise celery was new for me ("brunoise" means to cut into teeny tiny perfect squares).

Essentially, Spiaggia was a self-starting environment, which presented challenges—as well as wins—for a young cook. The upside was that I ended up bonding with other line cooks around me. That's the best part of the kitchen—that comradery, once it sets in, is unbeatable. That first week at Spiaggia I met great people who would play a key role in my life. I met my future husband, Jaime, and I also became friends with Meg Sahs and Rob Mosher, who would eventually open Monteverde with me.

After keeping my head down and working hard that first year, I grew fast. I worked all the stations, then Missy offered me the purchasing chef job. Some chefs say that's a cop-out job, but not at all. The purchasing job is so important—it's where you learn how to operate the business and how to buy and source the best ingredients. One of my favorite parts of this position was working with the local farmers and learning hands-on the seasonality of produce.

During my eight years at Spiaggia, my love for Italian food and Italy grew deep and wide, and I fell hard. The first time I ever went to Italy was when I got promoted to chef di cucina and chef and owner Tony Mantuano sent me for training, just as he had done himself prior to opening Spiaggia. I was so excited and scared—I didn't even speak Italian! In just two and a half weeks, I was fortunate enough to have staged in Rome, Florence, Parma, and Milan. On that first trip, I fell in love with traditional balsamic vinegar. So much so that when I came back to Chicago, I did a balsamic tasting menu, highlighting all the stages of balsamic. I also taught a few classes and events around balsamic tastings and pairings. I created regional menus, which taught me so much about the varied cuisines of Italy. I had

officially caught the Italy bug. I became obsessed and wanted to visit any chance I got and learn everything I could. I set a goal to visit every region of Italy in my lifetime.

Eventually I left Spiaggia because I was ready to go out on my own. Meg and I coincidentally reconnected at an event in California and knew at that moment that we were meant to partner on what was to become Monteverde. Meg, who worked in the kitchen with me at Spiaggia, was a genius with the business side of things. In fall of 2015, Monteverde was born. (*Monteverde* is "green mountain" in Italian, as *Grueneberg* is "green mountain" in German, and was the nickname given to me on that first trip to Italy.) Our vision was to open a restaurant centered on pasta, where I could cook my bold style of Italian food. To this day, Monteverde honors the Italian food and culture I know and love, weaving inspiration and learnings from my upbringing and other trips around the world.

Now, back to veggies. Vegetables can be the most rewarding thing on the plate! We can all take a rib eye steak, dust it with salt and pepper, throw it on the grill, and try to *not* mess it up. But it's the opposite for vegetables, which are almost always upstaged by that grilled steak or roast chicken. It's time for people to start thinking about their vegetables first. When dining out, I often read the menu starting with the sides or components of the dish, not the main protein. This is also how I approach what I'm cooking at home and how I get lots of healthy veggies in my day-to-day diet. What vegetables do I have in the fridge? How can I stretch that one head of cabbage into two meals? What vegetable can star on the center of the plate alongside a piece of simple roast chicken?

I've learned that it takes some imagination to make vegetables shine. For me, the process starts with asking myself a basic set of questions:

- ✣ What does this (mushroom/artichoke/radish/squash/tomato, etc.) want with it?
- ✣ What is the best method for cooking it?
- ✣ What ingredients do I have handy to pair with it?

Take tomatoes. You can make a classic tomato sauce, sure, but consider my arrabbiata, which is made with wok-fried cherry tomatoes; as such, it develops a rich, deeply caramelized flavor. Or perhaps you have an array of fresh vegetables from your local market or CSA. If so, try my Oma's salad on page 188. It may look like just any other salad, but I let the crunchy vegetables marinate for a while in a mix of olive oil, herbs, and seasoned salt before assembling, which makes it taste so good!

Instead of passing by the produce at the market, ignoring what might be calling your name for fear that you won't know what to do with it, I say, *Challenge yourself!* Don't be afraid to pick up whatever suits your fancy! Because from the farm stand to the grocery store, the best of the season is right there, just bursting with flavor, screaming "PICK ME, PICK ME!" and waiting to be whipped into something spectacular.

What I am trying to say is that we all have aha moments, and for me, that time in the walk-in with Chris was one of those moments. This was a new way for me to think about cooking vegetables and fruit, using my instincts. Later in my career, I learned to defer naturally to the Italian way with vegetables too. Italians have a special way of enjoying their veggies, whether it's topping them with an herby pesto, enrobing them in sweet and tangy tomato sauce, sprinkling them with great cheese, or simply dressing them with extra-virgin olive oil. They always take the vegetable to the next level. I mean, who else can turn an eggplant into one of the most craveable and soulful dishes imaginable: eggplant parm (ahem?!!)? Using instinct to make the most delicious vegetables is something I do almost every day at work but even more at home, where I crave simple

and special meals just like any home cook, and just like my grandma used to make. What I want to share with you is how to understand vegetables and embrace the myriad ways you can make even the most humble mushroom or potato shine.

Why Pasta Too?

You might wonder why a book about vegetables includes a pasta chapter. I absolutely love pasta, and it's a perfect blank canvas to showcase every single vegetable imaginable. Whether it's a box of dry pasta or fresh pasta made from the beautiful marriage of flour and eggs, there is a world of delicious and simply prepared dishes I want everyone to taste. From a luscious porcini Bolognese over fresh tagliatelle, to green olive–pistachio pesto paired with paccheri, to the most delicious roasted tortelloni with winter squash you've ever tasted, you will be over the moon with how perfectly pasta showcases your veggies.

And So . . .

I've learned so much at Monteverde, but one of my greatest takeaways is understanding that people love their vegetables. I am always pleasantly surprised that our guests request our seasonal vegetable dishes year after year. There is no question that vegetables present a golden opportunity to be creative and playful. Many of these recipes are deeply rooted in Italian cuisine because whether I'm at Monteverde or at home, I will always cook by the Italian way of simplicity and paying respect to the ingredients. I promise that *Listen to Your Vegetables* will make vegetables as craveworthy as any juicy steak and will leave you drooling over your artichokes and broccoli.

Dive deep into the produce aisle and have fun! You may be surprised at how it gives you so much more joy in the kitchen.

A Love Letter to Bees

Bees are one of the most important parts of our ecosystem, pollinating over 180,000 plant species. You can't have a book like this without talking about bees. In Italy, people are taught at a young age to revere bees, and I think it would be fantastic if we did the same here.

I've had many influences on my career, but perhaps one of the greatest people I've known was Andrea Paternoster, a third-generation nomadic beekeeper from Trentino. The very first time we met, I was sitting in a car on the side of a mountain near one of his hives. Andrea delicately reached into the hive and pulled out the queen bee for me to see. He had marked her each year to keep track of her age, and it was remarkable that he could so easily extract her from the hive—with no beekeeping gear at all! I knew then and there that I was witnessing something incredibly special.

He liked to call himself a bee shepherd, because he would shepherd his hives all around the hills, mountains, pastures, and plains of Italy. His nomadic style of beekeeping meant that he brought the bees right to the flowers, extracting nectar from blossoms at the peak of their growing season. Andrea was a big thinker, and he likened honey tasting to wine tasting. To best understand and appreciate its nuances, he would put honey into a glass, smear it around a bit, then sniff and taste to discern the aroma and the essence of a specific flower's nectar, as well as its terroir. Sunflowers, for instance, create a golden, rich honey; acacia honey is crystal clear and sweet; and chestnut flowers make honey with a bitter edge.

Andrea never called himself a honey maker. His job, as he saw it, was to care for and protect the bees.

We should all be trying to do this, though maybe not to the degree that Andrea did. Sadly, Andrea passed away in 2021, but his daughters carry on his wonderful company, Mieli Thun, selling myriad types of monofloral (single-flower) honeys from around Italy. If you can get some, when you taste it, close your eyes and just take a moment to imagine the flowers in the rolling green hills or sparkling pastures where the bees quietly went about doing their work to create that truly remarkable honey.

BEFORE YOU START

Please don't skip these pages. I love that you're excited to listen to your vegetables, but it will be even better if you can take a few minutes to read some useful info here. You'll find a lot of ingredient tips and information speckled throughout the book in sections called Get It Get It. That's my motto in the kitchen, and it's the act of taking a dish a step further or thinking outside of the box about it. At Monteverde we say, "Get it, get it, team!" as a way to push harder in the kitchen. But first there are some additional things I want to share to help make your food as delicious as it can be. Please also take a look at some excellent kitchen tools I think you should have handy for making the most amazing dishes!

A Few Cooking Staples

CHEESE

Pecorino

Pecorino is Italian for "sheep's milk cheese," as *pecora* is the Italian word for "sheep." There are hundreds of different pecorino cheeses made throughout Italy, but the best known ones come out of southern Italy. The most common is Pecorino Romano, or Roman pecorino. This aged cheese has a sharp, piquant salinity to it and a slightly funky, milky finish. Its firm texture makes it perfect for grating. I also love other aged pecorinos from Tuscany, Sicily, Calabria, and, of course, Sardinia! I find that these variations tend to have less salinity than the Romano variety, with more nutty, sweet, grassy notes. You really can't go wrong when exploring the world of pecorino.

Parmigiano-Reggiano

This is the Lady Gaga of Italian cheese, mainly because of its worldwide fame. A whole wheel of Parmigiano-Reggiano weighs roughly 80 pounds! Parmigiano-Reggiano is produced in the heart of northern Italy in three provinces: Parma, Modena, and Reggio Emilia. It has been made for over 2,000 years, and strict laws are in place to uphold the traditions of making it. Guidelines include the breed of cow that can be used, what the cow can eat, where the cheese can be made, and more. Do you know that this cheese is made with a mix of morning and evening milk? Here's another cool fact: Parmigiano-Reggiano is naturally lactose-free due to the aging process, which can take from 24 to 36 months. The aging process gives Parmigiano-Reggiano its incredible depth of flavor. There really isn't an American substitute—it simply cannot be re-created. Italian Grana Padano is its closest cousin, but Grana Padano has more flexible laws of technique and

tradition, and it can be made in several different areas of Italy.

I love to use Parmigiano-Reggiano in many recipes, and I often call for it to be grated. You can buy pregrated (just make sure it's Parmigiano-Reggiano), but it's so easy to grate yourself with a box grater or a food processor. Sometimes I call for using finely grated parm; all you need for that is a Microplane and a block of cheese. Another one of my favorite ways to use Parmigiano-Reggiano is to shave it. The shavings add an incredible flavor bomb to salads, veggies, or pasta. Essentially, I use grated parm to add flavor throughout a dish and shaved parm for specific boosts of parm goodness. I always stash both grated parm and block parm in my fridge, ready for a whim.

Parm rinds are a great thing to have on hand. After you've fully grated a chunk of Parmigiano, wrap the rind well and keep it in the freezer until you need it. Consider adding the rind to stocks, soups, and stews for a richer, umami-like flavor. When used in clear broths, feel free to remove the rind, rinse it, then freeze it for use in other recipes. I am definitely a bit obsessed when it comes to this cheese. In fact, I love it so much that our cat is named after it—we call him Parmi for short and he is a little prince of cheese!

Mozzarella and Burrata

Mozzarella is a fresh stretched-curd cheese made with cow's milk or water buffalo milk (then known as mozzarella di bufala). I'm going to start by talking about the cow's milk variety, which I use in recipes where the cheese will be cooked.

Whole milk fresh mozzarella is sold in its whey, which means it has extra moisture and a super-fresh, milky flavor. I love to use this whole milk mozzarella where I want the gooeyness of cheese, yet a slightly chewy and milky cheese bite. It's perfect for pizzas, topping eggplant parm, and for fillings and stuffings.

Low-moisture whole milk mozzarella (aka deli style) is available as a block, shredded, or sliced. It is a drier, compressed curd and not stored in its whey, making it less milky than fresh mozzarella but super for melting. I am looking for a stretchy, melty situation when I use this cheese. It's ideal in dishes like lasagna, where extra water is an enemy. I usually steer clear of preshredded mozzarella as it's packaged with starch to prevent caking, which, to me, dries out the cheese and prevents a melty masterpiece.

Mozzarella di bufala is a special DOP (protected designation of origin) cheese from Campania. It's made from the milk of water buffalo and is naturally almost lactose-free. *Wow!* This is the queen of Italy's mozzarella and what makes a margherita pizza a margherita pizza. I love mozzarella di bufala served as is—there is really no need to cook it. This mozzarella is *beyond* delicious, and I love to show it off in its pure, unadulterated form. It's really perfect simply enjoyed as an antipasto, salad, snack . . . you name it.

Burrata hails from the Puglia region, and it has taken the world by storm! It's made fresh by hand-stretching mozzarella curd and then stuffing it with hand-pulled stracciatella. *Stracci* literally means "rags" in Italian, and this cheese is made by hand-pulling teeny tiny strings of mozzarella curd and soaking them in fresh, sweet cream. (Think of stracciatella as the OG of string cheese.) Burrata showcases Italian ingenuity in its simplest form, taking something as delicious as mozzarella and making it possibly even better. Look for burrata from Puglia or labeled "Pugliese." There are other good burratas made here in the States, but I think they lack the uber creaminess of Italian burrata.

Ricotta

Buying ricotta can be a bit mysterious and illusive because the quality varies so much. "Ricotta" comes from the Italian word meaning "re-cook" (ricotta . . . get it?). Traditionally, ricotta was the second cheese that resulted as a byproduct of making the first cheese, most likely mozzarella or pecorino. Confusing? After making the first cheese, the whey would be boiled to extract any milky curd remaining, and voilà, ricotta! Well, nowadays we are all fancy and have decided that whole milk ricotta is the way to go, and I have to agree with that. If you have time, making your own ricotta (see Homemade Lemon Ricotta, page 173) is a semi-easy task that will tie you emotionally to a dish 'cause you actually made the cheese! However, if you don't have time to make ricotta, there are several brands I enjoy. One is BelGioioso Ricotta con Latte (whole milk ricotta), and Frigo—a throwback brand to my childhood—is now making a great whole milk ricotta. Both of these brands deliver on the creaminess front. Two of my favorite, more artisanal brands of ricotta are Bellwether Farms and Calabro. These are basket-formed or hand-dipped; these styles of ricotta are fine curd, uber-creamy ricottas. Some recipes call for ricotta salata, which is pressed ricotta that's salted, creating a firm texture that can be easily grated over dishes. You'll find a lot of flavored ricotta salatas too, such as those with herbs or chiles, and even smoked.

I have a few pointers when shopping for ricotta. Never, ever, ever buy part skim! It's grainy and will not give the creamy, luscious experience of whole milk ricotta. Look at the label and see what the ingredients are. Opt for ricotta that is made with just milk, cream, salt, and vinegar or lemon (just as it's made in Italy), and be very careful to avoid other ingredients, especially if you cannot pronounce them. You'll see that many ricottas contain gums, preservatives, and fillers. If by chance you find sheep's milk ricotta, buy it! It is totally incredible and what's mostly used in Italy. The quality of the ricotta is 100 percent why your pasta fillings are creamy, smooth, and delicious. It's such an important ingredient in Italian cuisine.

CHILES IN MANY FORMS

Chile Flake

I love using a pinch or two of chile flake in most dishes for straight-up heat. In some parts of Italy (mostly in Umbria), they serve tiny little dried red chiles that the diner crushes on their food. Much to my surprise, they are not too different from chile pequin, which I absolutely love for its spice level and fruity skin. For an all-purpose dried chile flavor, I usually use crushed chile de arbol. If you can find dried Calabrian chile flake, that's great!

Calabrian Chiles and Chile Paste

This is a variety of pepper from the Calabria region of Italy. Spicy, a little smoky, and even fruity, it's dark red and packed with flavor. You can buy whole or crushed pickled Calabrian chiles packed in olive oil. The whole chiles might be elongated or shaped like a Cherry Bomb pepper, and the good news is that they can be used interchangeably. I like using these jarred chiles for a pickled, umami flavor with a punch of heat. If you can't find crushed Calabrian chiles in olive oil, then opt for sambal oelek, an Indonesian chile paste made with chiles, vinegar, and salt. It has great chile flavor.

Paprika and Pimentón

"What is the difference between pimentón and smoked paprika?" you might ask. Both are technically the same: Spanish-style smoked and ground peppers. But think of them like truffles. Paprika is like the less expensive black truffle, whereas pimentón de la Vera is the white truffle of paprika! It's bright orange with incredible smoky, fruity notes. It's a great way to infuse smokiness into whatever you are cooking without having to use wood . . . or smoke!

TOASTED NUTS

I am in an exclusive relationship with nuts . . . well, that is with *toasting* nuts. I believe that the nuts are talking to us as they toast. In the oven, they are silenced. How many times have you said, "Oh shoot! I burned the nuts," as you pulled them out of the oven? (If you are a restaurant chef, I bet you don't have enough fingers or toes to count how many times!) The problem is that by the time you smell them, it's usually too late. This is why I opt for toasting stovetop. Use a nonstick or cast-iron skillet and a few drops of everyday olive oil—just enough to barely coat them. (The thin layer of oil encapsulates the nuts, helping them toast evenly; it also helps salt stick to them.) Toast on the stove over medium to medium-low heat, stirring or tossing often. You want to toast the whole nut, not just the skin. Times vary per nut, so listen for a slight sizzle, smell for that nutty delicious fragrance, and watch them as they turn golden brown. The toasting will continue in the pan off the heat, so it's best to transfer the nuts to a platter or bowl once they're toasted. Feel free to give them a pinch or two of kosher salt as they toast.

Now, there are some exceptions to the stovetop toasting method. I use the oven to toast larger nuts, and to toast whole nuts for a deep, dark golden toast when I want to achieve a super-rich, nutty flavor. You'll see this in my recipes for the roasted cashew parm dressing on page 47 and the almonds in the citrus salad on page 172.

TOASTED SPICES

I encourage you to take the extra step of toasting and grinding your whole spices because the resulting aroma and flavor are amazing—so much better than what you'll get from preground spices! Just toast your spices in a dry skillet over medium-low heat until they're fragrant. Once they've cooled, grind, crack, or crush them with a mortar and pestle. You can also use a spice grinder or coffee grinder.

OLIVE OIL

When it comes to cooking, I use relatively inexpensive extra-virgin olive oil, which I refer to in this book as "everyday olive oil." As with finer olive oil, I tend to look for bottles that are darker with an expiration date so I know that I'm getting a quality olive oil (see page 230). For finishing or drizzling on dishes, I use what I call "super-special extra-virgin olive oil" because just a drizzle adds incredible flavor to anything from salad, cheese, and seafood to pasta, meat, and even ice cream and chocolate desserts. If you're looking to buy some great oil for finishing dishes, Southern Italian olive oil (from Sicily or Puglia) will be light and fruity. Tuscan olive oil is super peppery, and Ligurian olive oil is fruity and a little spicy.

SALT

I have different salts in my pantry for different uses. I use kosher salt for cooking, layering, and seasoning items that need the salt to melt into them. I like using sea salt to add a *pow* or a little salt punch to liven up foods right before I serve them. It's perfect for raw ingredients and for finishing dishes.

For kosher salt, I like Diamond Crystal brand, which has fine flakes. Morton kosher salt is good too, but it's more coarse. The most important thing to consider is to stick to the salt you are used to seasoning with. Seasoning is a verb, a feel, a gut. You will eventually know when you have seasoned something right for you. My best advice is: When seasoning something, consider the surface area; be sure to sprinkle evenly over the top of the ingredient and not on just one little section. As you add an ingredient to a pan, consider seasoning in layers—that is, add a pinch or two of salt with each step.

As for sea salt, well, don't tell the Italians, but I love Maldon sea salt! I love the thin flakes of salt goodness that are so fun to crush with my fingers as I season.

When it comes to pinches of salt, a regular pinch for me is when I use my thumb, pointer, and middle finger to pick up about ¼ teaspoon of salt. A generous pinch is four fingers—I add the ring finger to the mix to pick up a little less than

Salting Pasta Water versus Vegetable Water

Oy, this is a big one. Let's start with pasta water. I used to be part of the "salty like the ocean" clan. But I found that my pastas at home were getting a tad too salty because I love the pasta marriage ceremony (see page 401). So I have backed off on the saltiness of my pasta water.

Salting also depends on if I'm using dry or fresh pasta. If I'm cooking fresh pasta that's going to spend less time in the boiling water and has a shorter marriage ceremony, then I season the water a little more heavily. If it's dry pasta, then I back off the salt a little more, as, depending on the shape, the pasta can cook in the water sometimes for as long as 10 or 15 minutes. And dry pasta loves the marriage ceremony! So having more delicately seasoned water is good. In short, for dry pasta I use 1 tablespoon of salt per 2 quarts of water, and I bump up that salt amount for fresh pasta.

Now, for blanching vegetables, I let the salt rip! Like, super rip. That water needs to be *seasoned*. Cooks and chefs I've worked with joke that the blanching water has to be so salty that you better choke when you taste it! I use 1 tablespoon of kosher salt for every quart of water. I know it sounds crazy. But the veggies are only in there for a few minutes, sometimes even just for a few seconds, so it's important that the salt works its way through the veggie. This makes a huge difference.

a teaspoon's worth. All of our fingers are different, of course, but I think this a good rule of thumb . . . well, fingers! Ha.

SESAME SEEDS

I like to buy pretoasted sesame seeds, but if you can't find them, just toast a thin layer of sesame seeds in a 225°F oven for about 5 minutes—watch them, as they brown quickly. You can also toast them in a skillet on the stove over low heat. If you are a sesame nut like I am, I recommend purchasing a Japanese sesame grinder, which gently cracks the seeds to release their fresh flavor and aroma.

Kitchen Tools

BOX GRATER

You need this for shredding and grating cheese, and also for tomatoes and root vegetables like carrots and radishes.

KITCHEN SHEARS

I love a good pair of kitchen shears. Joyce Chens are my go-to. The blades are small and help cut fine items like herbs and artichoke leaves.

MANDOLINE

Ideal for shaving or very thinly slicing veggies evenly. Be careful and use the guard, or buy a glove—even the most experienced chefs have a mandoline disaster story!

MICROPLANE

This is a rasp-like kitchen tool that I use all of the time. I like a fine Microplane for fluffy shavings of hard cheeses, citrus zest, and fresh garlic.

SALAD SPINNER

This will be the best $25 to $50 you spend for the kitchen—you'll easily save that much money by buying fresh lettuces and washing them yourself. (Not to mention avoiding the plastic waste from those clamshell boxes.) I spin all of my leafy greens and herbs, and tomatoes too!

SLOTTED SPOON OR SKIMMER

This is so helpful for transferring pasta shapes into their sauces! I love using a skimmer for small pasta shapes and tongs for strand pasta. This way, I always have pasta water to marry with the sauce.

Y-PEELER

I strongly urge you to invest in a sturdy Y-peeler to make peeling thick-skinned fruits and veggies like winter squash and eggplant a dream. They're not expensive, and I bet you'll never go back to a swivel peeler again! This is great for shaving cheese too.

WOK

Let's talk woks! Choose a wok that will best work for your stove. If you have a gas range, then a carbon-steel wok with a wok ring will be your best bet. Be sure to remove your stove grate so that the wok can be closest to the burner. If you have an electric stove or induction range, I recommend a flat-bottomed steel wok. If you do not have a wok, don't worry, you can use a 12- to 14-inch sauté pan or large cast-iron skillet. Get your wok super hot and have all your ingredients ready. It's fast and fun! If you get nervous that it's too hot, just pull the wok (or pan) off the heat to cool for a minute.

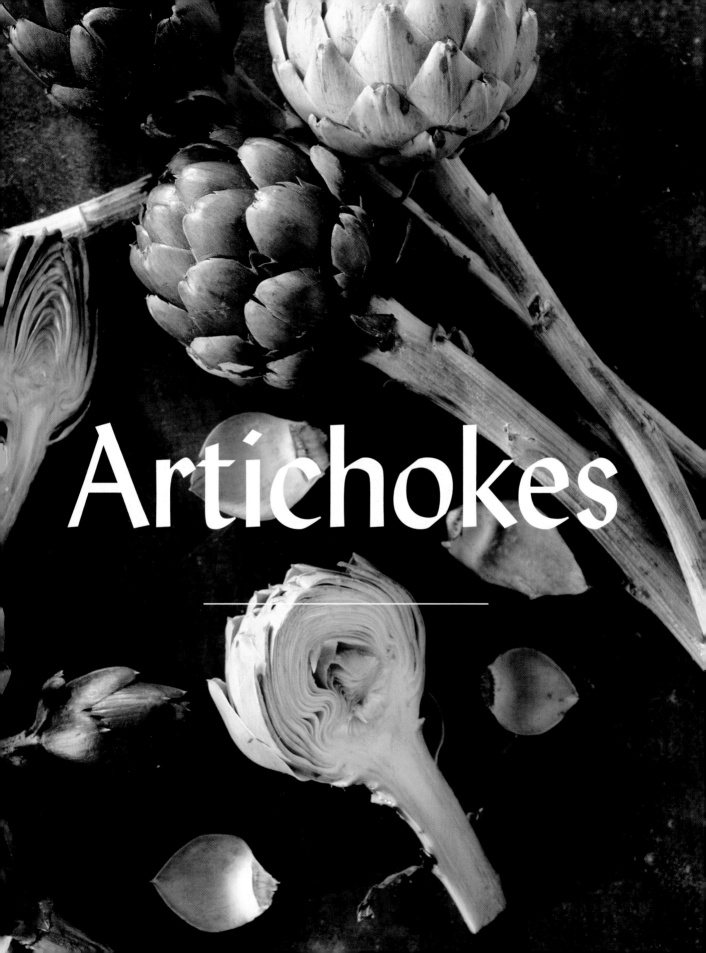

Artichokes

I have always loved artichokes, though my first experience eating them was from a can (which is actually all right if you've never tried a fresh artichoke before). Artichokes are available canned, jarred, frozen, and fresh, but from what I can see, most people don't seem to gravitate toward making the fresh ones. Even though they're a little difficult to clean and prepare, it's worth learning how. Fresh artichokes are supremely versatile—they can be braised, fried, roasted, stuffed, grilled, steamed, and even eaten raw. While artichokes of all sizes can be braised or poached, I like frying, roasting, and shaving (raw) baby artichokes. I opt to steam, stuff, and grill larger globe artichokes. It's a labor of love, so you just have to prepare mentally to tackle them!

Artichokes are, in fact, a flower—the immature bud of the thistle, to be exact. The outside of the artichoke is made up of sharp, pointy leaves, of which the base is edible (but more on that below). Inside the artichoke is a fuzzy, inedible choke, under which sit the heart and the stem. If an artichoke is left on the plant, it blossoms into a beautiful flower. This is truly a fascinating vegetable. There are over 50 varieties grown in the world, but the most common in the US is the globe.

Okay, let's take a step back. We, together, will master the elusive artichoke. When you're buying an artichoke, it should be firm, not soft, and its color should be bright green to army green and even purple. Don't choose an artichoke with brown spots, as this is an indicator that it's old and not worth the time to prepare. If you can find baby artichokes, they are much easier to work with than full-sized. Honestly, big artichokes can be a pain—they're a little like the mean kids in high school who you want to be friends with, but it's gonna cost you, and at some point you wonder why you even tried!

If you like to eat whole artichokes, I suggest slicing off the top 1½ inches and the stem. Pull the leaves apart a little, then drizzle the top with extra-virgin olive oil and some lemon juice and season with salt. Wrap in foil and roast in a shallow pan at 425°F for an hour to an hour and a half, depending on the size of the artichoke, until tender when pierced with a knife. To eat, pull off the individual leaves and scrape the meat off the flat edge of the leaves, using your teeth. Once you make it to the artichoke heart, scrape the hairy top off. Scoop out the meaty heart and enjoy every last bite!

I have just one last thing to add: You can buy incredible jarred Italian artichokes packed in olive oil. These are different from canned artichokes, which are packed in water and very soft. Oil-packed jarred artichokes have lovely texture and bite, and are great to keep in the pantry for salads, fish dishes, pastas, and more.

Gosh, artichokes can be a total pain! It takes a lot of work to get through their inedible armor, but get past that, and you'll reach the heart, where the most tender deliciousness lives!

Clockwise from top left: Artichoke and Celery Salad with Meyer Lemon and Pistachios (page 21), Artichoke-Sunchoke Crostini (page 20), Mediterranean Skillet Chicken Thighs with Artichokes (page 37), Manchego-Artichoke Cakes with Honey-Olive Tapenade (page 26)

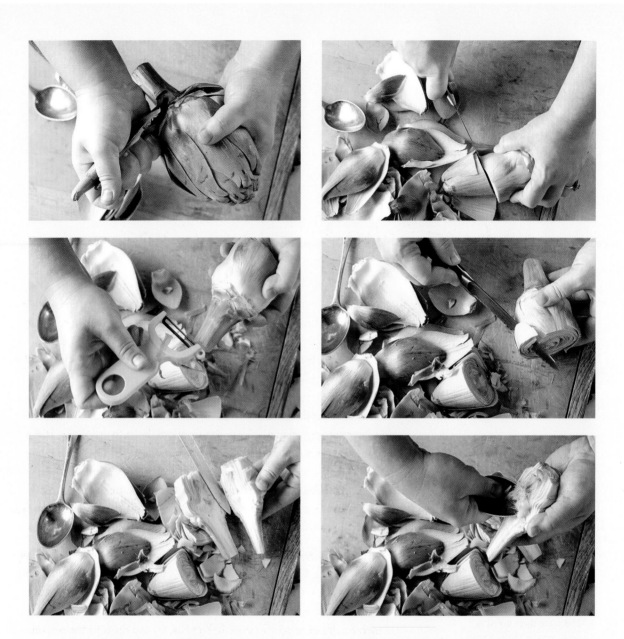

How to Clean and Prepare Artichoke Hearts

Start by filling a bowl with water and squeezing some fresh lemon juice into it—this prevents the finished hearts from oxidizing (browning) while you clean the rest. (Lemon juice is an artichoke's best friend as it keeps it from turning color when cooking too, so feel free to use it when steaming or boiling.) Working with one artichoke at a time, snap off the dark outer green leaves. Slice off all but 1 inch of the remaining leaves. Use a Y-peeler to clean the stem of the artichoke; I like to hold the artichoke in my hand with the stem pointed away from me, and peel the stem up toward the artichoke. Trim the bottom of

the artichoke with a paring knife. With your knife on a slight angle, trim and shave away the top outside leaves, so that what's left resembles a rose. This trims the green and more fibrous top part of the artichoke leaves. Halve the artichoke lengthwise and scoop out the furry choke, using a spoon. Add the artichoke heart to the lemon water; repeat cleaning however many artichokes are remaining. I suggest using them soon after they're cleaned. You also might want to wear a pair of kitchen gloves while cleaning the artichokes, 'cause they can make your hands a little yellow.

In Rome, one of the most beloved, must-have artichoke dishes is *carciofi alla giudia* (Jewish-style fried artichokes). These crispy whole fried artichokes are perfectly golden, and they are a true work of art! This version of fried artichokes is a bit more home-friendly, but still yields that crazy delicious crispy artichoke chip that you can't resist. Using 2 quarts of oil is key, as that helps you control the heat best while frying. Also, a mandoline is ideal for creating perfectly thin, even slices. These crispy artichokes will hold in your pantry for up to a week in an airtight paper towel–lined container. They are delicious and perfect as a crunchy topping on many things like salads, grilled fish, pasta, and chicken. I also love a simple baked or grilled snapper with crispy artichokes, lemon, and herbs.

Fried Baby Artichoke Chips

Makes 2 cups

Juice of 1 lemon

6 to 8 baby artichokes

2 quarts frying oil (I like to use peanut or canola)

Coarse sea salt (like Maldon)

1. In a medium bowl, combine the juice of 1 lemon with 4 cups of cold water. To clean the baby artichokes, I recommend wearing gloves, as they tend to stain your hands and have a few pointy thorns. Using a serrated knife, trim 1 inch off the top of each artichoke. Peel away 2 or 3 layers of the outer leaves until you reach the pale green-yellow leaves. Trim ¼ to ½ inch off the bottom of the stem. Using a Y-peeler, peel the stem until you reach the tender parts of the pale green stem. (Some of the stems can be very stringy, though this varies from artichoke to artichoke. If the stem looks too stringy, it might be best to remove it.) Place the cleaned artichokes in the lemon water until you are ready to fry them. You can refrigerate the cleaned raw artichokes in the lemon water overnight if wanted. I recommend placing a small plate on top to keep them submerged in the water.

2. Line a platter with paper towels. Place the oil in a 5- or 6-quart heavy-bottomed pot and heat over low heat until it reaches 275° to 300°F. Drain your artichokes very well and pat dry, then halve them through the stem. Using a mandoline, thinly slice the artichokes lengthwise to roughly ¹⁄₁₆ inch thick but not paper thin. In batches, fry the slices in the hot oil until golden, 3½ to 4 minutes. Gently stir the artichokes in the oil to keep them moving and ensure an even fry. Using a slotted spoon, transfer the fried artichokes to the platter and season with a pinch of salt. Let cool. The chips will crisp further once cool.

Get It

Please be careful and use the safety guard on your mandoline! It is okay if the artichokes are sliced slightly thicker; they will just take a little more time to fry. If you prefer to slice the artichokes and keep the slices stored in the lemon water, you can do that—just give them a good whirl in a salad spinner to make sure they're thoroughly dried before frying. Otherwise, it's best to slice and drop the freshly shaved artichokes right into the hot oil.

The key is slow and low when frying artichokes, as you want them to lose their moisture and caramelize in the oil. If the oil is too hot, they will develop a bitter aftertaste and run the risk of being soggy in the center.

Get It

My dear friend and sous chef, Patrick, and I created this crostini when we were first opening Monteverde. We put it on the menu as a special, but people loved it so much that we can't take it off! The double hit of sunchokes and artichokes is just the best. Sunchokes, if you're unfamiliar, are a root veggie also known as Jerusalem artichokes, but they in no way resemble a traditional artichoke. In fact, they look a lot like ginger! They're crunchy and mildly sweet when raw, and creamy and nutty when cooked. The restaurant version is a more complicated fonduta made with Fontina and ricotta, but this is a streamlined version that I think you'll totally love. I like to use a long rustic Italian bread that's a little wider than a baguette. If you have a round or oval loaf, you may want to cut the slices in half after baking. I love ciabatta, but if it's an extra-holey loaf, the cheese will sink through the bread.

Artichoke-Sunchoke Crostini

Serves 6 to 8

1 cup Homemade Lemon Ricotta (page 173) or whole milk ricotta (see page 8)

4 ounces Fontina cheese (preferably from Val d'Aosta), shredded (about 1 cup)

Kosher salt

4 medium sunchokes (about 8 ounces), sliced into ¼-inch rounds

2 teaspoons everyday olive oil

8 to 10 slices of baguette-style bread (about ¾ inch thick)

Roasted Baby Artichokes (page 23) or 2 cups jarred marinated artichokes (see Get It Get It), drained

Leaves from 1 fresh rosemary sprig

Fresh lemon juice, for finishing

Preserved truffle slices, truffle paste, or truffle oil (optional; see Get It Get It)

1. Preheat the oven to 425°F. In a medium bowl, stir the ricotta and Fontina and season with a few pinches of salt. In a small bowl, toss the sunchokes with the olive oil and a generous pinch of salt. Spread the sunchokes in an even layer on a foil-lined baking sheet. Roast for 20 to 25 minutes, until tender and slightly golden brown around the edges. Let cool.

2. Set a rack in a clean baking sheet, or line the sheet with foil or parchment paper. Schmear the ricotta mixture on top of the bread slices, about ¼ inch thick or so (think cream cheese on a bagel schmear versus buttered toast). Place 3 or 4 artichoke and 3 or 4 sunchoke pieces on top, gently pushing them into the cheese schmear. Sprinkle some rosemary between the artichokes and sunchokes. Bake on the prepared baking sheet for 15 minutes, or until the bread is toasted and the cheese is melty and warm. If you want your crostini to get a little color, you can toast them under the broiler for a minute or so. Finish with a squeeze of fresh lemon juice and a bit of truffle action—I will let this part be up to you. Enjoy!

Get It

There is also a shortcut to making these delicious crostini: Use jarred artichokes packed in oil instead of Roasted Baby Artichokes as a time-saving swap. Cut the artichokes into bite-sized wedges for topping the crostini.

Truffle slices go a long way, so if using, just top each crostini with 1 or 2 slices. If you're using paste, aim for ⅛ teaspoon. If you are using truffle oil, then I would suggest just a drop or two.

Get It

I grew up with a Meyer lemon tree in my backyard in southern Texas, and those lemons grew to be the size of small grapefruits! When I got to Chicago, most of the Meyer lemons available were the size of a regular lemon, though still packed with Meyer lemon flavor. If you don't know, Meyer lemons are a little sweeter than standard lemons, and their peel is super delicious. If they're not in season or are unavailable, you can sub regular lemons here. If you are confident and happy with your artichoke cleaning skills, you can make this salad with all artichokes, or just use more artichokes and less celery, though it could get costly. If celery isn't your jam, then you can also substitute shaved fennel for the celery. I think artichokes are incredible raw because they have very nice crunch. This crunchy, refreshing, light salad is such a great way to explore the vegetable in a different way.

Artichoke and Celery Salad

with Meyer Lemon and Pistachios

Serves 4

2 large globe artichokes

2 tablespoons fresh lemon juice

1 head of celery, large stalks peeled, thinly sliced on a bias (about 4 cups)

Coarse sea salt (like Maldon)

¼ cup everyday or super-special olive oil, plus a little more for garnish

1 tablespoon finely grated Meyer lemon zest (use a Microplane)

¼ cup Meyer lemon juice

¼ cup fresh flat-leaf parsley or chervil leaves

¼ cup toasted salted pistachios, chopped

½ cup shaved Parmigiano-Reggiano (use a Y-peeler)

Fresh cracked black pepper

1. To trim an artichoke, start by pulling off the outermost leaves until you get to the lighter green leaves. Then, using a serrated knife, cut off the top third or so of the artichoke and trim the very bottom of the stem. Use a Y-peeler to clean the stem of the artichoke; I like to hold the artichoke in my hand with the stem pointed away from me, and peel the stem up toward the artichoke. Cut the artichoke in half lengthwise through the stem. (Reserve the trimmings and leaves for future use, like in the artichoke stock on page 30!) Using a spoon, gently scoop out the choke or little hairs of the artichoke. (This is the only part of the artichoke that is not fully edible.)

2. In a medium bowl, combine the 2 tablespoons of lemon juice with 2 cups of cold water. Using a knife or mandoline, thinly slice the artichokes about ⅛ inch thick; don't shave them too thin or they will wilt in the salad. Transfer the sliced artichokes to the bowl with the lemon water. Reserve until you're ready to dress the salad.

3. When you are ready to serve, drain the artichokes, dry them well, and transfer them to a mixing bowl with the celery. Dress the celery and artichokes with a few pinches of coarse sea salt, the olive oil, and the Meyer lemon zest and juice. Taste for seasoning and adjust with a bit more salt if needed. Gently fold in the parsley leaves, chopped pistachios, and shaved parm. Drizzle with olive oil and garnish with fresh cracked black pepper. Serve immediately.

— Get It —

I totally recommend shaving the parm if you are able. The thin slices of cheese match the slices of celery and artichokes.

— Get It —

While you can use larger artichokes for the Roman Braised Artichokes on page 31, this is the place to use those adorable baby artichokes you see at the market. All they need is a simple roast and a toss with garlic and herb oil. Play around with the herbs and seasonings in the marinade. The key is to toss the artichokes while they are still warm to meld the flavors. This is a great all-purpose artichoke that can be added to many other dishes. The artichokes are so good I can't resist eating them right out of the fridge, but I also like them in salads, mixed with beans, or folded into eggs.

Roasted Baby Artichokes

Makes 2 cups

Artichokes

Juice of 1 lemon

8 to 10 baby artichokes

2 tablespoons everyday olive oil

Coarse sea salt (like Maldon) or kosher salt

Herb Marinade

¼ cup everyday olive oil

1 garlic clove, thinly sliced or chopped

¼ cup chopped mixed fresh herbs (like mint, oregano, and parsley)

2 pinches of chile flake

2 pinches of coarse sea salt (like Maldon)

Finely grated zest (use a Microplane) and juice of ½ lemon

Get It

Happy accident turned delicious mistake: I once reheated some of the roasted artichokes in a 325°F oven, but totally forgot about them. To my surprise, they had shrunk yet were crispy, crunchy delicious after about 45 minutes. If you like fried artichoke chips but don't want to use a mandoline to make them, this is your oven-fried answer!

Get It

1. **Make the artichokes.** In a medium bowl, combine the juice of 1 lemon with 4 cups of cold water. To clean the baby artichokes, I recommend wearing gloves, as they tend to stain your hands and have a few pointy thorns. Using a serrated knife, trim 1 inch off the top of each artichoke. Peel away 2 or 3 layers of the outer leaves until you reach the pale green-yellow leaves. Trim ¼ to ½ inch off the bottom of the stem. Using a vegetable peeler (I recommend a Y-peeler), peel the stem until you reach the tender parts of the pale green stem. (Some of the stems are very stringy, though this varies from artichoke to artichoke. If the stem looks too stringy, it might be best to remove it.) Quarter the cleaned artichokes lengthwise through the stem and place in the lemon water. You can refrigerate the cleaned raw artichokes in the lemon water overnight if wanted. I recommend placing a small plate on top to keep them submerged in the water.

2. When you are ready to roast the artichokes, preheat the oven to 450°F. Drain the artichokes and pat dry, then toss with the olive oil and a few generous pinches of coarse salt. Arrange them in an even layer on a foil-lined baking sheet. Roast for 15 to 20 minutes, until tender; feel free to taste one or pierce it with a paring knife.

3. **Meanwhile, make the herb marinade.** Combine all of the marinade ingredients in a medium bowl.

4. Turn the broiler to high and place the artichokes 4 inches from the heat source. Broil for 3 to 4 minutes, until the edges of the artichokes begin to turn anywhere from golden to a dark brown char. Remove from the oven. While they are still warm, toss the roasted artichokes with the herb marinade. Season with a few pinches of sea salt to taste. Serve warm, chilled, or at room temperature. These can be refrigerated in an airtight container for up to 1 week.

Man, I love baked feta so much. When you combine it with the crispy roasted
baby artichokes and sweet cherries, it's a true showstopper. Pick up some
of your favorite bread for scooping up all of the goodness here.

Roasted Baby Artichokes

with Feta and Sweet Cherries

Serves 4

Roasted Baby Artichokes and
their marinade (page 23;
see Get It Get It)

One 7-ounce block feta cheese
(I recommend finding a sheep's
milk variety)

½ cup fresh sweet cherries, pitted
and halved (see Get It Get It)

2 tablespoons honey

2 fresh oregano sprigs, for garnish

1 loaf of crusty Italian- or French-
style bread, for serving

1. Preheat the oven to 400°F. Arrange the roasted artichokes in a
casserole or baking dish that's just big enough to fit the artichokes in
an even layer. Top with the slab of feta and spoon a bit of the artichoke
marinade on top. Bake for 15 minutes, or until warm.

2. Turn the broiler to high. Remove the casserole from the oven. Top the
artichokes and feta with the cherries and drizzle the honey over the top.
Broil 4 inches from the heat source for 4 to 5 minutes, or until the feta is
golden and softened. The artichokes might char around the edges, which
goes great with the tang of the feta and the sweetness from the cherries and
honey. Garnish with oregano and serve with hunks of warm crusty bread or
toasted sliced bread.

Get It

I adore the recipe for Roasted
Baby Artichokes, but you could
substitute 2 cups of jarred olive
oil–preserved artichokes here.
First drain the artichokes and
spread them on a baking sheet.
Roast until they turn golden
and crispy. Add your garlic,
herbs, chile flake, lemon, and
salt to the reserved oil from the
jar. Then proceed from Step 1.

I love to sub the Candied
Lemon Slices from page 53
for the cherries; apricots also
make a great swap. For a more
savory note, you can skip the
cherries and use a mix of pitted
Castelvetrano or kalamata
olives and cherry tomatoes.

Get It

Listen to Your Vegetables

I love a good crab cake, so what you'll see here is very crab cake–esque . . . but with artichokes! The finely chopped artichokes give the cakes an almost crab-like texture. I also find that artichokes have a briny, sealike flavor. The combination of artichokes with Manchego, honey, and olives is truly outstanding. If you want, you can bypass pan-frying the cakes and use the mixture as a filling for all sorts of things, from chicken breast and twice-baked potatoes to peppers and mushrooms. If you can stuff it, you can use this filling!

Manchego-Artichoke Cakes

with Honey-Olive Tapenade

Makes 10 cakes

Two 14-ounce cans artichoke hearts in water, drained

2½ cups panko (Japanese breadcrumbs)

4 ounces Manchego cheese, shredded (1 cup)

¼ cup mayonnaise (love me some Duke's!)

2 small green onions, chopped (¼ cup)

2 tablespoons chopped fresh flat-leaf parsley

1 teaspoon Dijon mustard

Finely grated zest of 1 lemon (about 1 tablespoon; use a Microplane)

Kosher salt

1 pinch of chile flake

1 cup all-purpose flour

3 large eggs

6 tablespoons everyday olive oil

Honey-Olive Tapenade (recipe follows)

1. Line a baking sheet with parchment paper. In a food processor, pulse the drained artichokes 8 to 10 times, until coarsely chopped. Transfer to a medium bowl and add 1 cup of the panko along with the Manchego, mayo, green onions, parsley, mustard, and lemon zest. Season with a pinch or two of kosher salt and some chile flake. Using a ⅓ cup measuring cup, scoop up the filling and pack it down slightly. Invert each artichoke cake onto the prepared baking sheet. (You should get roughly 10 cakes plus a little tester cake, which is always a nice snack for the chef!) Refrigerate the cakes for 30 minutes.

2. Into three shallow bowls, separately place the flour, eggs, and the remaining 1½ cups of panko.

3. Lightly beat the eggs. Working one at a time, place a chilled artichoke cake in the flour, patting and flattening the cake a bit with your hands. Place the floured cake in the eggs, and using a fork, flip it to coat both sides. Lift the cake out, allowing any extra egg to drip off. Place the cake in the bowl with the breadcrumbs. Using both hands, pat the breading on it, pressing gently. Put the breaded cake back on the parchment-lined baking sheet. Repeat with the remaining cakes.

4. Line another baking sheet or a platter with paper towels. Heat a large nonstick skillet over medium heat. Add 2 tablespoons of the olive oil. Pan-fry 5 cakes until the edges begin to turn golden brown, 3 to 4 minutes. Using a pancake spatula, flip the cakes, adding another 1 tablespoon of oil to the pan. Continue to cook until golden, 2 to 3 minutes. Transfer the artichoke cakes to the paper towel–lined baking sheet. Repeat with the remaining cakes. Serve hot, with the tapenade.

Get It

You can amp up the artichoke flavor and texture by including fresh artichokes. Clean 2 globe artichokes (see page 16) and thinly slice on a mandoline. Mix the sliced artichokes with ½ cup of the panko in the food processor and pulse a few times. Use these artichoke breadcrumbs in place of the plain panko for breading. This gives the cakes a latke or hash brown–like texture.

If you want to make these ahead, place the pan-fried cakes on a foil-lined baking sheet and keep at room temp for a few hours. When you're ready to serve, toast them in a 400°F oven for 10 minutes, or until they have a light sizzle and are crispy.

Get It

Honey-Olive Tapenade

This tapenade is great on bruschetta, cheeses, and shellfish like roasted scallops or shrimp, and as a topping on grilled or roasted vegetables like summer or winter squash.

Makes just under 1 cup

¼ cup minced drained oil-packed pitted black olives (like Taggiasca, niçoise, or Leccino)

¼ cup minced pitted Castelvetrano olives

1 tablespoon everyday olive oil

1 tablespoon drained capers, minced

1 tablespoon chopped fresh flat-leaf parsley

2 teaspoons honey

Finely grated zest (use a Microplane) and juice of ½ lemon

½ small garlic clove, grated (use a Microplane)

½ teaspoon Calabrian chile paste or sambal oelek

In a small bowl, combine all the ingredients and stir well. The tapenade can be refrigerated in an airtight container for up to a week. (You can also place all the ingredients in the food processor and pulse together instead of mincing the olives by hand.)

Since you'll be making the Roman Braised Artichokes for this recipe, you can decide how you want them trimmed. You can opt to remove all the outer leaves, or leave them on and eat them with your teeth after grilling. Braising the artichokes first helps soften and flavor them, then finishing on the grill (with no extra oil) adds a deep charred flavor. It also helps crisp them up. The braising liquid acts like a vinaigrette here, and the gremolata adds a yummy herbiness at the end. Don't forget some good crusty bread for soaking up all of the delicious juices.

Grilled Artichokes

with Mint Gremolata and Extra-Virgin Olive Oil

Serves 4 to 6

¼ cup chopped fresh Italian flat-
   leaf parsley

¼ cup chopped fresh mint

1 small garlic clove, finely grated
   (use a Microplane)

Finely grated zest of ½ lemon
   (use a Microplane)

¼ cup everyday olive oil

Roman Braised Artichokes
   (page 31) with 1 cup of reserved
   poaching liquid, at room
   temperature

Crusty bread, for dipping
   (optional)

1.   Preheat a grill to high or heat a grill pan over high heat for 10 minutes, then reduce the heat to medium. Meanwhile, in a small mixing bowl, combine the parsley, mint, garlic, and lemon zest with the olive oil.

2.   Place the artichokes cut side down on the grill or in the grill pan. Grill for 6 to 7 minutes on each side, looking for nicely charred grill marks on the leaves.

3.   Transfer the artichokes to a serving platter and drizzle with the reserved poaching liquid. Top with the mint gremolata. You can serve these hot, cold, or at room temperature, with crusty bread for dipping, if you like.

At Monteverde, we don't serve whole artichokes, but we spend a lot of time cleaning artichokes to get at the hearts. At some point, I realized that we were tossing out so many leaves, and that broke my heart! Then it hit me to use the leaves in a vegetable stock, which would not only be super tasty but would also prevent us from wasting those flavor-packed leaves. I try to make this stock using green artichokes because purple ones turn the stock dark gray, which isn't so appealing. This stock is excellent used in lighter spring and summer recipes, wherever you might use chicken stock.

Light Artichoke Stock

Makes 2 quarts

1 tablespoon everyday olive oil

Green leaves and trimmings
  from 3 or 4 artichokes
  (about 1 pound)

1 lemon, halved and squeezed

2 garlic cloves

1 cup veggie trimmings (if you
  have them saved in your freezer!
  See Get It Get It)

2 cups white wine

1.　In a large nonreactive pot, heat the oil over medium-high heat. Add the artichoke leaves, lemon juice and halves, and the garlic and sweat for 2 minutes. Add the other vegetable trimmings and deglaze with white wine, scraping up any browned bits in the pan. Simmer for 1 minute, or until the liquid is reduced by half.

2.　Add about 2 quarts of cold water, to cover. Bring to a boil, then remove from the heat. Let sit for 15 minutes. Strain; discard the solids. Let the stock cool. The artichoke stock can be refrigerated for a week and frozen for 3 to 4 months. I recommend freezing it in pint containers so you can pull out just the right amount when you want it.

Get It

I keep a resealable plastic bag of peelings and trimmings in my freezer for making stock— I have everything from carrot and tomato peels to celery and leek trimmings in there. I encourage you to do the same.

Get It

This is a great all-purpose recipe for cooking artichokes, inspired by the Roman method of braising them in a mix of white wine, lemon juice, and olive oil with lots of mint. This braising liquid is my workhorse for almost every artichoke recipe 'cause it can't be beat. The artichokes can be served as is, drizzled with extra-virgin olive oil. If you like, they can be stored in their liquid for up to 2 weeks in an airtight container. They will soften up and become much more like canned artichokes. If you want them to retain their texture, however, store them separately from the liquid. Use the extra cooking liquid in soups, pasta sauces, or where a flavorful vegetable stock is wanted.

Roman Braised Artichokes

Makes 6 to 8 artichoke heart halves

1 cup dry white wine

½ cup everyday olive oil

½ cup fresh lemon juice (from 2 large or 3 small lemons)

5 fresh mint sprigs

3 unpeeled garlic cloves, smashed

1 tablespoon kosher salt

3 or 4 large globe artichokes

1. In a large nonreactive stainless-steel or enameled cast-iron pot, combine 2 cups of water with the white wine, olive oil, lemon juice, mint sprigs, garlic, and salt.

2. To trim each artichoke, start by pulling off the outermost leaves until you get to the lighter green leaves (see Get It Get It). Then, using a serrated knife, cut off the top third or so of the artichoke and trim the very bottom of the stem. Use a Y-peeler to clean the stem of the artichoke; I like to hold the artichoke in my hand with the stem pointed away from me, and peel the stem up toward the artichoke. Cut the artichoke in half lengthwise through the stem. (Reserve the trimmings and leaves for future use like Light Artichoke Stock on page 30!) Using a spoon, gently scoop out the choke or little hairs of the artichoke. (This is the only part of the artichoke that is not fully edible.)

3. Add the prepared artichoke halves cut side down to the pot as you clean them to prevent them from oxidizing. Bring to a boil over high heat. As soon as the liquid begins to boil, cover and simmer over low heat until the artichokes are tender yet firm—almost al dente in texture—10 to 15 minutes. Remove from the heat and allow to cool in the liquid.

4. Once cool, drain the artichokes and keep covered in an airtight container. You can reserve the cooking liquid (see the headnote).

Get It

When shopping, keep an eye out for artichokes with firm, dark green leaves.

How you plan to eat the artichokes will determine how far to clean them. If you want to eat the leaves by hand, scraping off the tender meat with your teeth, then you'll want to keep the majority of the firm green leaves attached. If you are looking for tender, fully edible artichoke hearts, then remove the outer leaves until you reach the yellow tender ones.

Get It

Get It

Don't skip the pecorino and black pepper, though the guanciale could be omitted if desired; substitute 2 tablespoons everyday olive oil for the guanciale drippings.

Get It

Rome is *the* city for artichokes. If you want to eat truly great artichokes, that is where you go. This Roman vignarola (fricassee) is beyond soul-satisfying, and a super dish to serve as a starter or side dish or a main course for lunch. Vignarola is a lesser-known dish here in the US, probably because it's time-consuming to deal with the artichokes, fresh peas, and beans. But while I love fresh beans, the season is short, and thankfully frozen peas and beans are quite delicious too! If you're looking to round this out with more protein, it's pretty tasty with poached eggs, though they're not necessary by any means. When in Rome, do as the Romans do, and eat this with great bread and lots of olive oil.

Vignarola

aka Roman Spring Vegetable Fricassee

Serves 4 to 6

Artichokes

1 lemon

2 globe artichokes

Fricassee

¼ cup diced guanciale, pancetta, or bacon (optional; see Get It Get It)

½ small red or yellow onion, thinly sliced

Kosher salt

½ cup white wine

4 cups Light Artichoke Stock (page 30) or store-bought vegetable or chicken stock

1 cup shelled fresh or frozen peas

1 cup shelled fresh or frozen lima, fava, or edamame beans

1 cup sugar snap peas, trimmed

1 cup shredded stinging nettles, spinach, or green leaf lettuce leaves (1-inch ribbons)

2 tablespoons fresh lemon juice

Super-special extra-virgin olive oil, for drizzling

¼ cup freshly grated Pecorino Romano

Fresh cracked black pepper

1. **Clean the artichokes.** In a medium bowl, combine the juice of the lemon with 4 cups of cold water. To trim the globe artichokes, start by pulling off the outermost leaves until you get to the lighter green leaves. Then, using a serrated knife, cut off the top third or so of each artichoke and trim the very bottom of the stems. Use a Y-peeler to clean the stems; I like to hold the artichoke in my hand with the stem pointed away from me and peel up toward the artichoke. Cut the artichokes in half lengthwise through the stems. (Reserve the trimmings and leaves for future use, like in the artichoke stock on page 30!) Using a spoon, gently scoop out the choke or little hairs of the artichokes. (This is the only part of the artichoke that is not fully edible.) Cut each artichoke half into 4 pieces. Place the cleaned sliced artichoke pieces in the lemon water. Just before cooking, drain them and pat dry.

2. **Make the fricassee.** Line a baking sheet with paper towels. Heat a medium saucepan over medium heat. Add the guanciale (if using) and let it render until golden and crispy, 3 to 4 minutes. Transfer the bits of meat to the baking sheet to drain. Add the onion to the rendered fat and cook until translucent and beginning to caramelize, about 3 minutes. Add the artichokes and sauté for 2 minutes; season with a few pinches of salt. Add the white wine and artichoke stock and cook, scraping up any browned bits on the bottom of the pan. Reduce the heat to medium-low and bring to a simmer for 20 minutes. Check the artichokes for tenderness; if they're not tender enough, give them another 5 to 10 minutes.

3. Add the peas, beans, snap peas, and nettles and cook for 5 minutes, until tender and the nettles are wilted. Season with salt and add the lemon juice. To serve, drizzle the fricassee with super-special olive oil and top with the pecorino and the crispy guanciale bits. Finish with lots of fresh cracked black pepper.

I could eat this pasta on a weekly basis, it is so dang delicious. It reminds me of my other favorite pasta, alle vongole (with clams), as the artichokes add a similar depth of flavor and level of satisfaction as the clams. The chef in me loves showing off an ingredient in a few different ways in a recipe because it demonstrates the versatility and complexity of that ingredient. Here, I love the artichokes in the sauce and also as a golden, toasty, crispy topping. If you are looking for a super-simple aglio e olio, you can make this pasta sans the artichokes; just reduce the starting oil to 2 tablespoons. I highly recommend making the fried baby artichoke chips for this—they're so unique and delicious. But if you just don't feel like it, you could substitute toasted breadcrumbs for that crunchy texture.

Double Artichoke Spaghetti Aglio e Olio

Serves 4 as a main or 6 to 8 as a side dish or starter

Artichokes

1 lemon

2 pounds baby artichokes
(10 to 12; see Get It Get It, page 36)

Spaghetti

Kosher salt

3 tablespoons everyday olive oil

1 medium head of garlic, cloves peeled and smashed (8 or 9 cloves)

2 or 3 pinches of chile flake

1 pound dry spaghetti

1 cup dry white wine

1 tablespoon finely grated lemon zest (use a Microplane)

2 tablespoons fresh lemon juice

1 cup fresh flat-leaf parsley, roughly chopped

Fried Baby Artichoke Chips (page 19)

2 tablespoons super-special extra-virgin olive oil, for drizzling

1.   **Clean the artichokes.** In a medium bowl, combine the juice of the lemon with 4 cups of cold water. To clean the baby artichokes, I recommend wearing gloves, as they tend to stain your hands and have a few pointy thorns. Using a serrated knife, trim 1 inch off the top of each artichoke. Peel away 2 or 3 layers of the outer leaves until you reach the pale green-yellow leaves. Trim ¼ to ½ inch off the bottom of the stem. Using a vegetable peeler (I recommend a Y-peeler), peel the stem until you reach the tender parts of the pale green stem. (Some stems are very stringy, though this varies from artichoke to artichoke. If the stem looks too stringy, it might be best to remove it.) Quarter the artichokes and place the pieces in the lemon water. You can refrigerate the cleaned raw artichokes in the lemon water overnight if wanted. I recommend placing a small plate on top to keep them submerged in the water.

2.   **Make the spaghetti.** Bring a large pot of water to a boil and season well with kosher salt. In a large saucepan or deep skillet, heat the 3 tablespoons of everyday olive oil over medium heat. Drain the artichokes and add to the pan; season with a few pinches of salt. Cook, stirring often, until the artichokes begin to soften and then caramelize, about 5 minutes. Add the smashed garlic and chile flake to the saucepan and cook, stirring often, allowing the garlic to toast, about 3 minutes.

3.   Meanwhile, add the spaghetti to the boiling water and cook for 4 minutes less than the package directions state.

4.   Add the white wine to the artichokes and cook, scraping up any browned bits in the pan. Add 1 cup of the pasta cooking water, reduce the heat to low, and simmer while the pasta finishes cooking, about 5 minutes. Using a pair of tongs, lift the pasta from the boiling water and transfer it to the saucepan. (If you prefer to drain the pasta in a colander, be sure to save another ½ cup of the pasta cooking water to have on hand if needed.)

recipe continues

Get It

If you can't find baby
artichokes, feel free to use 3 to
4 of the globe variety (about
2 pounds). Clean as you would
the baby artichokes, then cut
the cleaned artichokes into
quarters lengthwise through
the stem. Using a spoon, scoop
out the fuzzy choke of each
quarter-artichoke. Use your
hands to remove any sharp
point inner leaves near the
choke. Cut each quarter into
4 thin slices. Place the cleaned
artichoke slices in the lemon
water as you work.

In its essence, this is a simple
pasta dish, but the artichokes
make it pretty labor intensive.
If you aren't feeling like
cleaning the artichokes for
the sauce, I would recommend
substituting jarred artichokes
packed in olive oil. Shoot for
2 cups. Use the oil too, instead
of the everyday olive oil!

Get It

Gently shake the pan, allowing the pasta and sauce to become one. Let
the pasta and sauce marry, reduce, and thicken, about 5 minutes. Add
the lemon zest, lemon juice, and parsley to the pasta and stir to combine,
then remove from the heat. Taste the pasta for seasoning and doneness.
If you want it a bit more seasoned, add a bit more salt or pasta water. The
pasta should be al dente, with a nice bite, and the sauce should be clinging
to each strand. Yum. To serve the spaghetti, top generously with fried
artichoke chips and a drizzle of super-special olive oil.

I grew up making this easy weeknight dish—it was from my mom's favorite cookbook from the Junior League of Louisville. The original is made with chicken breasts and Spanish black and green olives. I like the brininess of everything in here—it ensures that this is no boring-tasting chicken dish! I have to say that I prefer using olive oil–packed artichokes from Italy, but I grew up eating canned artichokes so I won't hate on them here. If you're looking for a lighter meal, this can be made with chicken breasts too.

Mediterranean Skillet Chicken Thighs

with Artichokes

Serves 4 to 6

8 bone-in, skin-on chicken thighs (see Get It Get It)

Kosher salt

1 tablespoon everyday olive oil

1 small onion, halved lengthwise and very thinly sliced

½ cup Castelvetrano olives, pitted and sliced

½ cup kalamata olives, pitted and sliced

1 garlic clove, finely chopped

One 10-ounce jar or can quartered artichoke hearts, drained (see Get It Get It)

1 cup cherry tomatoes, halved

1 cup dry white wine

2 tablespoons fresh oregano, chopped

2 tablespoons fresh flat-leaf parsley, chopped

1. Preheat the oven to 400°F. Season the chicken with salt. Heat a large stainless-steel, nonstick, or enameled cast-iron skillet over medium-high heat. Add the oil and sear half of the chicken thighs skin side down until browned, 4 to 5 minutes; transfer to a platter. Repeat with the remaining thighs; transfer to the platter. Drain off all but 2 tablespoons of the pan drippings.

2. Place the skillet back over medium-high heat. Add the onion, both olives, and garlic and cook for 3 minutes, or until the onions are translucent and beginning to caramelize. Add the artichokes and cherry tomatoes and cook for another 2 minutes. Add the white wine and oregano, scraping up any browned bits from the skillet; cook for another 2 minutes. Nestle the chicken thighs into the skillet, skin side up. Transfer to the oven and bake for 20 minutes, or until the chicken is fully cooked. Garnish with the fresh parsley and serve. I love to serve this dish alongside steamed rice pilaf or Soft Polenta with Crème Fraîche and Parm on page 128.

Get It

You can substitute chicken breasts or boneless, skinless chicken thighs if you're looking for a lighter result here. You can really use any cut you like, but the cooking time will vary. Aim for an internal temperature of 165°F for fully cooked chicken.

Look for jarred artichokes packed in olive oil, which have a firmer texture than the water-packed varieties.

Get It

Asparagus

Asparagus is one of the first vegetables I remember eating, but sadly, it was not the fancy fresh kind. We used to eat canned asparagus seasoned with lemon pepper as a side dish at my mom's house. Canned asparagus cannot be more different from fresh asparagus. I remember when I first tried fresh asparagus in culinary school, it was a game changer. I began buying asparagus to make at home for my mom. It was one of the first "fancy" vegetables I bought to show off the skills I learned in school. The spears were crunchy, tender, and not at all like their stringy canned counterparts!

I've since reinvented my mom's canned delight by throwing raw asparagus on the grill or in a grill pan and dressing it with the zest and juice of a lemon, a drizzle of extra-virgin olive oil, and fresh cracked black pepper. This recipe is my go-to for most asparagus as it's simple without a lot of fuss. Asparagus doesn't play well with a lot of flavors in one dish 'cause it's a little snobby. It wants to be its own dish and is not usually excited to share the plate with other veggies, where it either loses its flavor or takes over the dish entirely. I also think that asparagus wants to be known as the elegant vegetable. It likes to be served on the finest of china!

Much of the asparagus we see here in the US comes from Peru and Mexico, so it's available year-round, which is a boon to asparagus lovers. But there is a huge difference in off-season, supermarket asparagus and locally grown and harvested asparagus, which is exceptionally green and fresh-tasting. In the Midwest, it grows wonderfully; our sunny, cool spring weather is an ideal climate for all shapes and sizes. It's so tender you can eat it raw. It's also a first sign of spring, and while its season is short, it takes over the restaurant menu as well as my home kitchen.

You will notice that asparagus is not a one-size-fits-all veggie. You are most likely to see skinny asparagus early in the season, since it grows first; then as those are cut, the bigger varieties come in. So keep an eye out for pencil-thin asparagus as well as medium, jumbo, and even colossal asparagus. There is a place for all of the sizes! I tend to like thinner spears for use in salads and pasta, where they can easily intertwine with other ingredients. The jumbo spears have more heft, so they're perfect for grilling and charring; they also won't fall through your grill grates.

Let's pause and talk about white asparagus. "Why is it white?" you ask. White asparagus is intentionally grown in the dark so it doesn't develop chlorophyll! Some people think it has a sweeter, milder flavor than green. My Oma ate it as a delicacy, and I think most folks still see it as something pretty special. I suggest peeling the bottom half of the stalks if you find yourself cooking white asparagus. Because the spears are thick, white asparagus should probably be boiled, steamed, or blanched but not grilled. It can also be thinly shaved into salads. As long as we're talking color, don't forget purple asparagus. It is actually quite similar to green in flavor, but take note that once purple asparagus is cooked, it turns green too!

Whether or not you peel your asparagus is mostly up to you. The thicker the spear, the more likely it'll want to be peeled. I find that peeling helps it absorb more flavor, so if you're glazing asparagus, for instance, peeling will give you maximum glaze flavor.

If you're going to be eating raw asparagus, good for you! The natural grassy flavor sings when it's raw. The thicker spears are best thinly cut on a sharp bias by hand, by angling your knife as you slice.

One word of warning: Don't overcook asparagus or it gets stringy. You only need to blanch it for 30 seconds to 1 minute, depending on the size. Grilling and roasting are the same: You want a beautiful light char with a mostly rare inside. The good news is that pencil-thin asparagus can get pretty well roasted and not get too stringy.

To store asparagus, put the stem ends in a small bowl or cup of water and put a little plastic bag over the top. The asparagus should keep for 1 to 2 weeks in the fridge.

Here they are, the supermodels and movie stars of the vegetable world. The first sign of spring in the kitchen, asparagus is elegant, pristine, sexy . . . and moody! Take note: Asparagus likes to take center stage.

Clockwise from top: Farfalle with Asparagus, Lemongrass, and Slow-Roasted Halibut (page 58); Raw Asparagus Salad with Roasted Cashew Parm Dressing (page 47); Grilled Asparagus with Charred Shallot Pepper Relish (page 54); Asparagus Fritti (page 46)

Stracci means "rags" in Italian, and in Rome this soup is called stracciatella for the rag-like texture the eggs form as they cook in the broth. This also happens to be the name of my favorite gelato flavor, stracciatella, in which the chocolate has the same rag-like texture. I love making this soup at home after work, when I want to have a light, homemade meal that is soul-satisfying and quick. I recommend keeping homemade stock in the freezer; take it out to thaw the day before you make this tasty recipe.

Asparagus Egg Drop Soup

Serves 2

4 cups Light Artichoke Stock (page 30) or store-bought vegetable or chicken stock

One 2- to 3-inch piece Parmigiano-Reggiano rind

Kosher salt

1 cup frozen English peas

½ bunch of asparagus, cut into small rounds (about 1 cup; save the tough stem ends for vegetable stock)

1 fresh thyme sprig

2 large eggs

Handful of fresh basil leaves, for garnish

Freshly grated Parmigiano-Reggiano, for serving

Super-special extra-virgin olive oil, for serving

Fresh cracked black pepper, for serving

1. In a medium saucepot, bring the stock to a simmer. Turn the heat to low, add the parm rind, and let steep for 20 minutes.

2. Remove the parm rind and season the broth with salt. Increase the heat to medium-high and add the peas, asparagus, and thyme sprig. Bring to a light boil for 5 minutes.

3. In a medium bowl, lightly beat the eggs with a fork. Using a ladle, spoon ¼ cup of the broth into the egg mixture while stirring with a fork to temper the eggs. Transfer the entire egg mixture to the saucepot and stir. Remove from the heat; discard the thyme sprig. Add the basil and serve immediately with copious amounts of grated parm (2 tablespoons per bowl is my preference), a drizzle of super-special extra-virgin olive oil, and black pepper.

Get It

It's delicious to finish this soup with fresh basil pesto, or consider adding a small pasta shape like quadretti or orzo. You should also feel free to experiment with other veggies in place of the asparagus. Spinach, carrots, or spring onions would all be great.

Get It

I first had breaded fried asparagus at Joe's Stone Crab in Miami and I was hooked. I begged Chef Andre for the recipe, but it's a secret. So I went ahead and made my own, and I think it's pretty darned good! Growing up in Texas, you fry anything and everything, and these supremely crispy asparagus are a testament to that philosophy. With an irresistible Parmigiano breadcrumb crust, these are a true crowd-pleaser. Just a little squeeze of fresh lemon, and you're good to go!

Asparagus Fritti

Serves 6 to 8 as a snack for aperitivo

2 quarts peanut oil or other good-quality frying oil

1½ cups all-purpose flour

3 teaspoons kosher salt

2 cups whole milk buttermilk (preferably organic)

3 cups panko (Japanese breadcrumbs)

1 teaspoon garlic salt

2 tablespoons chopped fresh flat-leaf parsley, plus ¼ cup leaves for garnish

1 teaspoon finely grated lemon zest (use a Microplane)

¼ cup freshly grated Parmigiano-Reggiano

1½ pounds jumbo asparagus, woody ends trimmed, stems peeled

Lemon wedges, for serving

Get It

I always recommend heating frying oil over low heat to best manage the rise in temperature. I also suggest using a frying thermometer that attaches to the side of the pot to keep an eye on the heat.

Feel free to bread all of the asparagus at one time and fry in batches, or you can bread each batch while you fry the others.

Get It

1. In a 5-quart heavy-bottomed pot, preferably enameled cast iron, heat the oil over low heat to 360° to 375°F. Keep the flame as low as possible to maintain a constant heat. You might find you will need to increase the heat slightly between batches of frying.

2. While your oil heats, set three shallow rectangular dishes (or any dishes long enough to fit the whole asparagus spears) on your work surface. Mix the flour and 1 teaspoon of the salt in one dish, and put the buttermilk in the second dish. In the third dish, combine the breadcrumbs, garlic salt, chopped parsley, lemon zest, 2 tablespoons of the parm, and the remaining 2 teaspoons of salt. Mix well.

3. Line a baking sheet with a rack and top with a layer of paper towels. Using your hands or a large two-pronged meat fork and working with 4 or 5 asparagus spears at a time, dredge the asparagus spears in the flour, rolling them around; shake off any excess flour. Transfer to the buttermilk and roll to evenly coat. Carefully lift the asparagus from the buttermilk and transfer to the breadcrumb mixture. Using your hands, gently pack the breadcrumbs onto the asparagus to coat. Drop the breaded asparagus into the hot oil and fry for 2½ to 3 minutes, until golden brown and crispy. Transfer to the prepared baking sheet to drain. Repeat with the remaining asparagus.

4. If you want to elevate your presentation, drop the whole parsley leaves into the oil to fry. (Be sure they are dry and be careful, as they splatter slightly.) Fry the parsley for 1 minute, or until it looks crispy and a dark green color, not brown. (I love fried herbs; you could add basil too.)

5. Let the asparagus cool slightly before serving (the spears can be very hot inside!). These are also delicious served at room temperature. To serve, stack the crispy spears on a platter and garnish with the parsley leaves and the remaining grated parm. Squeeze fresh lemon juice over the top and serve with a few extra lemon wedges. Yum.

The delicious, grassy green notes of asparagus shine best when it's eaten raw. This salad is crunchy and refreshing, and while I often say that asparagus doesn't play well with other veggies, the cucumbers and raw beets create the perfect balance in this dish. I think you'll really love the nutty parm dressing too, which has a nice roasted flavor from the cashews, as well as a hint of sweetness from the rice vinegar.

Raw Asparagus Salad

with Roasted Cashew Parm Dressing

Serves 4 to 6

1 bunch of pencil-thin asparagus (about 1 pound,) woody ends trimmed, spears sliced on a bias into 2-inch pieces

2 small (baby) golden beets, trimmed, peeled, and thinly shaved (about 1½ cups)

3 Persian or baby cucumbers, sliced into ¼-inch-thick rounds

½ head of radicchio, cored and shredded

Coarse sea salt (like Maldon)

Roasted Cashew Parm Dressing (recipe follows)

2 tablespoons salted cashews, lightly chopped

¼ cup fresh basil, mint, or flat-leaf parsley leaves

¼ cup shaved Parmigiano-Reggiano

Fresh cracked black pepper

In a large salad or mixing bowl, combine the asparagus, beets, cucumbers, and radicchio. Season with a few pinches of coarse sea salt. Toss the salad with half of the dressing to coat. Season again with salt if necessary. Drizzle a few spoonfuls of dressing over the top. Garnish the salad with chopped cashews, fresh herbs, shaved parm, and black pepper. Enjoy immediately, as the veggies are best when they are crispy.

Roasted Cashew Parm Dressing

Consider using this dressing on other salads in the book too. It would be awesome on the purple vegetable salad on page 93.

Makes 1 cup

½ cup raw cashews

½ cup vegetable or canola oil

One 2-inch piece fresh ginger, peeled and sliced

2 tablespoons seasoned rice vinegar

2 tablespoons freshly grated Parmigiano-Reggiano

1 tablespoon finely grated lime zest (from 1 to 2 limes; use a Microplane)

2 tablespoons fresh lime juice

1 tablespoon Dijon mustard

1 small garlic clove

½ teaspoon coarse sea salt (like Maldon)

¼ teaspoon fresh cracked black pepper

1.   Preheat the oven to 350°F. Place the cashews on a foil-lined baking sheet. Bake until they turn a deep golden brown, 10 to 15 minutes. Let cool.

2.   Combine the cashews, oil, ginger, 2 tablespoons of water, the vinegar, parm, lime zest and juice, mustard, garlic, salt, and pepper in a blender. Blend on high speed until chunky but combined, about 20 seconds. (I also like to use an immersion blender for ease and cleanup.) The dressing can be refrigerated in an airtight container for up to a week.

Get It

I recommend using skinny asparagus here because they are perfect when cut into 2-inch pieces, but use what you can get. If the spears are thicker, just cut them a bit smaller.

Get It

While it might sound fancy, this salad is not at all hard to make, and it uses standard pantry ingredients. I feel like people are accustomed to eating prosciutto off a platter, and they forget how good it can be when folded into a salad. Prosciutto isn't your thing? This salad would be great with smoked salmon in place of the prosciutto, or mozzarella di bufala for a vegetarian twist. Don't miss out on the frico—these crispy little pan-fried parm bits will make you swoon! Once you make (and eat) them for the first time, you will want to add the golden crunchy deliciousness to everything! They are perfect on their own as a snack for aperitivo hour.

Asparagus and Prosciutto Salad

with Crispy Parmigiano Frico

Serves 4 to 6

Everyday olive oil

½ cup grated Parmigiano-Reggiano (use the finest holes on a box grater, or use store-bought)

Kosher salt

2 bunches of asparagus, woody stems trimmed

Caraway Mustard Vinaigrette (page 93)

5 ounces baby arugula

4 red radishes, thinly shaved

6 slices of prosciutto, cut into 1-inch-wide ribbons

Fresh cracked black pepper, for garnish

1. Line a plate or platter with paper towels. Heat a small (8-inch) nonstick skillet over medium heat. Add a few drops of olive oil and rub it around with a paper towel. Gently sprinkle ¼ cup of the parm evenly into the bottom of the pan. Watch carefully as the cheese begins to sizzle and slowly turns golden brown, about 4 minutes. (The appearance will almost resemble lace.) Remove the pan from the heat for 1 minute, then using a rubber spatula, free the melted cheese from the pan and flip it over to cook for a few more seconds. Transfer to the lined plate. Repeat with the remaining ¼ cup of cheese (you shouldn't need to use more oil). The frico will become crispy as it cools.

2. Bring a large pot of generously salted (about ¼ cup of salt) water to a boil. Prepare an ice bath in a medium bowl. Blanch the asparagus until bright green; 30 seconds for pencil-thin asparagus, 1 minute for medium spears, or 1½ minutes for jumbo asparagus. Using tongs, transfer the asparagus to the ice bath until chilled. Once chilled, drain and pat dry.

3. Cut the asparagus into 1½-inch pieces on the bias and add to a salad or mixing bowl. Dress with ¼ cup of the vinaigrette. Gently fold in the arugula, shaved radishes, and prosciutto. Using your hands, gently crack the frico into bite-sized pieces and garnish on top. Drizzle a little more dressing over the top of the salad. Garnish with fresh cracked black pepper. Enjoy!

Get It

Use any size asparagus you like here; just watch the blanching time.

Get It

After a lot of roasting and grilling asparagus, I started cooking this dish to get myself out of an asparagus rut, even though this is really a very classic preparation. I like to peel the asparagus for this dish, as the color and tenderness make it so appealing, but if you're using pencil-thin spears, don't peel them. You can use a simple vegetable stock or even water to cook the asparagus, but making the stock is quick and easy, and it makes use of the whole vegetable, which I love. Just don't cook the stock too long or it'll get bitter—it's more like making asparagus tea. Once you try this asparagus, glazed so nicely with sweet butter and fresh herbs, you might not want to go back to grilling and roasting again!

Glazed Asparagus

with Fines Herbes

Serves 4

2 bunches of large or jumbo
   asparagus

1 teaspoon everyday olive oil

Kosher salt

2 tablespoons unsalted butter

1 tablespoon finely chopped fresh
   flat-leaf parsley

1 tablespoon finely chopped fresh
   chives

1 tablespoon finely chopped fresh
   tarragon

1.   Trim the tough stems of the asparagus, about 2 inches. Using a Y-peeler, peel two-thirds of the way up the stalk, leaving the beautiful tips. Don't discard the tough stems and peelings.

2.   Set a fine-mesh sieve in a medium bowl. Heat a medium saucepot over high heat. Add the olive oil and the tough stems and peels of the asparagus, and season with a pinch of salt. Add 1½ cups of water and bring to a boil. Boil for 5 minutes, then strain into the bowl. You should have roughly ¾ cup of asparagus stock. Discard the stems and peels.

3.   In a medium skillet, bring the asparagus stock to a simmer over medium-high heat. Add the asparagus, season with a pinch of salt, and cook for 5 minutes, stirring often. Reduce the heat to medium-low and stir in the butter. Cook until the asparagus is glazed and the sauce has thickened, about 3 minutes. Add the chopped herbs and toss the asparagus in the skillet a few times to coat. Serve right away.

Get It

This simple French recipe uses fines herbes, which normally includes chervil. Unfortunately, chervil can be tough to find, but if you can find it, definitely add a tablespoon here!

— Get It —

This simple asparagus and green garlic roast is a great base for you to let your creative juices flow! My go-to prep for asparagus is to grill it and finish with lemon juice and olive oil, but I wanted a way to achieve that roasted char flavor in an apartment or anytime that access to a grill is tricky. My solution is to roast the asparagus in a hot cast-iron skillet, then finish it under the broiler until it's blistered and charred. This takes it beyond al dente to a pretty well-done place—kind of like the asparagus I grew up eating and loving. The candied lemon is a bit of a surprise, but I think of it as a flavor bomb that adds a great pop of sweet and sour here. To further boost the flavor of the dish, you can also add sesame, za'atar, chile flake, fresh herbs, or a little freshly grated pecorino cheese.

Blistered Asparagus

with Spring Garlic and Candied Lemons

Serves 4 to 6

2 bunches of jumbo asparagus, woody ends trimmed, spears cut into 2- to 3-inch pieces

2 tablespoons thinly sliced spring garlic, or 2 garlic cloves, thinly sliced

1 medium shallot, thinly sliced

1 tablespoon everyday olive oil

Coarse sea salt (like Maldon)

Candied Lemon Slices (recipe follows)

1.   Adjust your oven racks: Place one in the middle of the oven and another about 3 inches from the broiler. Preheat the oven to 475°F and place a 12-inch cast-iron skillet on the middle rack to heat for 20 minutes.

2.   In a large bowl, toss the asparagus, spring garlic, shallot, olive oil, and a generous pinch of sea salt. Carefully add the dressed asparagus to the hot skillet in the oven. Roast until the asparagus look wilted and slightly browned, about 25 minutes.

3.   Turn the broiler to high. Scatter the candied lemons over the asparagus and carefully place the skillet under the broiler. Let the asparagus and lemon slices sear and char for 4 to 5 minutes. Remove from the oven. Drizzle 1 tablespoon of the syrup from the lemon slices over the asparagus and serve immediately.

Candied Lemon Slices

I love having these candied lemons in the fridge, 'cause they amp up so many dishes like fish, shrimp, chicken, and lots of different veggies. The lemon-scented simple syrup is also perfect for cocktails and iced tea, and I like to pour it over ice cream with blueberries.

Makes about 1 cup

1 cup sugar

1 large lemon, sliced crosswise on a mandoline (about 1/16 inch thick)

In a small pot, bring 1 cup of water and the sugar to a boil over high heat. Add the lemon slices, remove from the heat, and let cool in the syrup. Transfer the lemons slices to an airtight container and cover with the cooled syrup. The candied lemons can be refrigerated in the container for up to 1 month.

Does the world need another grilled asparagus recipe? The answer is: only if it's really good! When I grill asparagus at home, I usually just eat it with olive oil, lemon, and salt, but this is far more special. The punchy flavor of the charred shallots and pepper along with fresh citrus and cilantro dresses up the asparagus really well. It's also super versatile—it's just as good hot as it is cold.

Grilled Asparagus

with Charred Shallot–Pepper Relish

Serves 6

1 medium red bell pepper

2 medium shallots, peeled, with the root ends left intact

Kosher salt

¼ cup everyday olive oil

Finely grated zest and supremes of 1 orange (see Get It Get It)

Finely grated zest and juice of 1 lemon (use a Microplane)

½ cup chopped fresh cilantro leaves and stems, plus ½ cup leaves for garnish

2 tablespoons drained capers

2 teaspoons Calabrian chile paste or sambal oelek, or a generous pinch of chile flake

Fresh cracked black pepper

3 bunches of medium or jumbo asparagus

Coarse sea salt (like Maldon)

1. Preheat a gas grill to high heat for 10 minutes, until the thermometer reads 500°F. (You can use a charcoal grill too, or your broiler on high heat.)

2. Place the bell pepper and shallots on the hottest part of the grill and close the cover. This will allow them to char nicely. In 7 to 8 minutes or so, rotate the pepper and shallots. Grill until they have a nice thin black char all over, about 12 minutes total.

3. Transfer the bell pepper and shallots to a mixing bowl, cover, and let sit for 10 minutes. Your shallots might split where they have a natural split, and that's okay!

4. Trim the roots from the shallots, being careful to leave the charred skin on. Peel the bell pepper and remove the seeds. In a food processor, pulse together the bell pepper, shallots, and a generous pinch of kosher salt until chopped. Add the olive oil, orange zest and supremes, lemon zest and juice, chopped cilantro, capers, and chile paste and pulse until combined. Double-check for seasoning and add a bit more salt and some black pepper.

5. When you are ready to grill the asparagus, preheat a grill to high for 10 minutes, then reduce the heat to medium-high. Grill the asparagus until charred on one side, 3 to 4 minutes, then turn to char the other side for another 2 to 3 minutes. To serve, top the grilled asparagus with the shallot-pepper relish and season with a few pinches of coarse sea salt and the cilantro leaves.

Get It

To get the supremes from the orange for this recipe, after you've zested it with a Microplane, use a sharp paring knife to cut away the peel and bitter white pith. Working over a small bowl, cut in between the membrane segments to release the supremes into the bowl.

The shallot-pepper relish gets better the next day, so if you're looking to make it ahead, this is the way to go.

The relish can be refrigerated for up to 1 week in an airtight container. Because I like cooking the asparagus right on the grill—dry, no oil or salt—I make sure to season the relish well before serving.

Listen to Your Vegetables

Get It

The Dry-Grilling Method

There is simple beauty in a dry char. I believe in getting a char on my grilled vegetables. When using oil to grill veggies, the oil burns instead of the veggie. The idea for dry-grilling vegetables first came to me when I was eating grilled bread. I would oil slices of bread, then char them, and the result was burned oil—not deliciously charred bread! I realized that the whole idea behind good bruschetta is to char the bread, *then* add delicious fresh olive oil to it.

It turns out that this same method applies to vegetables. When you douse them in oil and put them on a hot grill, the result is burned oil and not nicely charred veggies. Instead, putting dry veggies on a hot, clean grill avoids flare-ups and allows them time to char and develop an intense flavor. To top that, drizzling the veggies with fresh olive oil after they're cooked gives you all of the benefits of the polyphenols, and you end up using less oil overall too! Some of my favorites to dry-grill are asparagus, peppers, eggplant, onions, tomatoes, zucchini, and lettuce.

If you're looking for a showstopping dish that shouts "SPRING!," then you have come to the right page. This gorgeous baked asparagus pasta is simultaneously light in texture and deeply rich in flavor. It highlights asparagus by rolling it up in a cannelloni "cigar"; be sure to leave the pretty tips peeking out so you can see them. If you are inclined to add some protein, you could include prosciutto or shredded chicken in the cannelloni, but trust me, you don't need it.

Asparagus Cannelloni

with Artichokes and Spring Onions

Serves 6 to 8

4 cups whole milk ricotta
  (see page 8)

1½ cups heavy cream

½ cup whole milk

2 tablespoons unsalted butter

1 large bunch of spring onions
  (scallions), green onions, or
  ramps, white and green parts
  separated and thinly sliced

One 14-ounce can artichoke
  hearts, drained and chopped

12 ounces semi-aged (6 to
  8 months) Manchego cheese,
  shredded (3 cups)

Kosher salt

Fresh cracked black pepper

3 bunches of medium asparagus
  (about 3 pounds total), trimmed
  and peeled

Fresh Pasta Sheets (page 259) or
  1½ pounds store-bought fresh
  pasta sheets, blanched

½ cup freshly grated Pecorino
  Romano

Everyday olive oil or olive oil spray

─ Get It ─

If you want to plan ahead,
make your components the day
before: pasta dough, filling, and
ricotta cream. Please note that
the ricotta cream could separate
slightly, so be sure to whisk it
to combine before assembling.

─ Get It ─

1. In a blender, combine 2 cups of the ricotta with the heavy cream and milk and blend until smooth, about 30 seconds.

2. Line a large baking sheet with parchment paper. In a medium sauté pan, melt the butter over medium heat. Add the spring onion whites and cook until softened, about 1 minute. Stir in the artichokes and cook until softened and melded with the onions, 4 to 5 minutes. Transfer to a large bowl and let cool.

3. Once cooled, fold in the remaining 2 cups of ricotta and 2 cups of the Manchego; season with a pinch of salt and pepper. Spoon 16 portions of the artichoke filling, a scant ¼ cup each, onto the prepared baking sheet. This will help speed along the rolling process.

4. Bring a large pot of water to a boil and season well with kosher salt. Prepare a large bowl with ice water. Drop the asparagus into the boiling water for 30 seconds, then transfer to the ice water. Once cooled, drain the asparagus and divide into 16 equal portions. I recommend using the same blanching pot from cooking the pasta sheets.

5. Preheat the oven to 325°F. On a large cutting board, lay out 4 of the blanched pasta sheets with the short sides facing you. Place a portion of artichoke filling on the center of each pasta sheet. Spread the filling horizontally across the center of each sheet. Lay the blanched asparagus on top of the artichoke filling, then roll the pasta sheet up around the ricotta and asparagus, like a cigar. Transfer to a baking sheet or work surface and repeat with the remaining pasta sheets, filling, and asparagus.

6. Lightly oil or spray two 9 by 13-inch lasagna pans. Spread 1½ cups of the ricotta cream evenly over the bottom of each pan. In each pan, arrange 8 rolled cannelloni pastas over the ricotta cream. Evenly divide the remaining ricotta cream over the tops of the cannelloni and sprinkle with the remaining shredded Manchego. Cover with foil. (I like to spray or lightly oil the foil that will touch the inside of the pan). Bake the pasta until hot and the cheese is melted, 35 to 40 minutes.

7. Turn the broiler to high. Remove the foil and sprinkle the top of the pasta with grated pecorino and the spring onion greens. Position the two pans about 4 inches from the heat source and gratinée (broil) until the cannelloni are golden brown and bubbling, 3 to 4 minutes. (If your broiler can't accommodate two pans at once, you can broil these one at a time.) Yum! Let cool for 5 minutes before serving.

I think asparagus wants to be known as green, grassy, and vibrant, and this pasta speaks of just that. I love the complexity the stalks give the sauce, while the tips add elegance and beauty. The lemongrass and ginger might not read as typical Italian ingredients for pasta, but the essence of this dish is purely Italian. I'd make this for a nice dinner party or serve it chilled for a lunch. Try it with a big salad and crusty grilled ciabatta.

Farfalle

with Asparagus, Lemongrass, and Slow-Roasted Halibut

Serves 4 to 6

Halibut

1 pound skinless halibut fillet, cut into 1½-inch pieces

2 tablespoons everyday olive oil

1 teaspoon finely grated lemon zest (use a Microplane)

Kosher salt

Asparagus Puree

2 bunches of asparagus (about 1 pound each), cleaned and trimmed

1 lemongrass stalk, end trimmed

1 tablespoon everyday olive oil

1 dried bay leaf

1 cup Light Artichoke Stock (page 30), store-bought vegetable stock, or water

¼ cup heavy cream

2 cups baby spinach

1. **Prepare the halibut.** In a small baking dish, toss the halibut with the olive oil and lemon zest and season with a few generous pinches of salt. You can refrigerate this overnight, if desired.

2. **Make the asparagus puree.** Cut the trimmed asparagus spears in half. Slice the bottom halves into ½-inch rounds; you should have 1 to 1½ cups. Cut the top halves (the spear ends) in half one more time, creating 2- to 3-inch pieces; reserve these for the pasta.

3. Using the back of a chef's knife, bruise the lemongrass by gently banging on the stalk. Finely chop the lemongrass. In a medium saucepan, heat the olive oil over medium heat. Add the lemongrass and bay leaf and cook until fragrant and lightly fried, about 2 minutes. Add a pinch of salt. Add the asparagus rounds, season with salt, and cook until they begin to release their natural water and soften, about 3 minutes. Add the stock and heavy cream. Bring to a simmer and cook until the asparagus is tender, 6 to 7 minutes. Remove from the heat; discard the bay leaf and let cool slightly, about 5 minutes. Add the spinach and stir to wilt; season with another pinch or two of salt. Scrape the mixture into a blender and blend on high until smooth and creamy, about 30 seconds. Transfer to a bowl and refrigerate for up to 4 hours or until you're ready to use it.

4. **Finish the pasta.** Preheat the oven to 250°F. In a small bowl, combine the ginger, garlic, and lemon zest and set aside. Bake the halibut until opaque and tender to the touch, about 20 minutes.

5. Bring a large pot of water to a boil and season the water heavily with kosher salt (about ¼ cup). Cook the farfalle for 2 minutes less than the package specifies for al dente.

6. While the pasta is cooking, heat another large pot over medium heat and add the olive oil. Add the shallot and cook until just beginning to caramelize, about 2 minutes. Add the ginger, garlic, and lemon zest mixture

---

Get It

I think you will adore the lovely, tender halibut flakes with the aromatic asparagus sauce—just be careful not to overmix the halibut or it'll fall apart.

Get It

Pasta

One 2- to 3-inch piece fresh
  ginger, peeled and grated
  (2 tablespoons)

1 tablespoon finely grated garlic
  (use a Microplane)

2 teaspoons finely grated lemon
  zest (use a Microplane)

1 pound dry farfalle pasta

1 tablespoon everyday olive oil

1 small-ish shallot, peeled and
  thinly sliced

½ cup dry white wine

2 tablespoons fresh lemon juice

Fresh cracked black pepper

¼ cup fresh dill sprigs, for garnish

and cook, stirring with a rubber spatula, until fragrant, about 30 seconds. Add ½ cup of the pasta water to the pot along with the white wine; use this to deglaze the pot, scraping up any bits stuck to the bottom. Remove from the heat.

7.   Add the asparagus spears to the boiling water with the farfalle during the last minute of cooking. Place the white wine mixture back over medium heat. Using a slotted spoon, transfer the farfalle and asparagus into the white wine mixture. (You can also drain the farfalle and asparagus in a large colander in the sink, if you prefer, then add them to the white wine mixture.) Stir the farfalle and asparagus, marrying them with the white wine mixture; the farfalle will begin to look glazed and the sauce will thicken, about 2 minutes. Gently fold in the asparagus puree and halibut and cook for 2 minutes, until combined and warmed through. Drizzle the lemon juice over the top, finish with black pepper and dill sprigs, and serve.

Follow Your Food

With so many words thrown around in the market these days—natural, organic, GMO, non-GMO, bioengineered—it can be pretty hard to know if what you're buying is healthy and has been raised responsibly. Everyone should be following their food, and by this I mean to find out where your food is from and who grew it. Don't you ever wonder about the back story to your broccoli or peach? If you knew it was grown with pesticides, would you buy it?

Whether you're at home or traveling, take some time to find a local farmers' market and seek out new and different things. Talk to the farmers. At some point during the 1950s, supermarkets became the de facto place to shop for everything, and our produce took a huge hit. Instead of buying from local farmers, folks just went to the market to buy the prettiest tomato and shiniest pepper. Those six perfect tomatoes that fit into the plastic clamshell? Come on now, you know

that's not how tomatoes grow. With the popularity—and convenience—of the supermarket, so many older varietals have been lost or forgotten. Thankfully, things have taken a turn back in the right direction, and we are far more aware of what we eat nowadays, with farmers' markets abounding across the country. We've even embraced "imperfect" produce—those gnarly carrot misfits and misshapen zucchini are just as tasty as their more perfect cousins!

This "follow your food" philosophy should apply not just to ingredients but to recipes and techniques—it's a great habit to dig into the people and history behind everything you eat. I love learning about great rice, flours, and varieties of heirloom beans and tomatoes and squash, just to name a few. And when I make a new recipe, it's always rewarding to know when and how it came to be. The more you know about your food, the better it will taste!

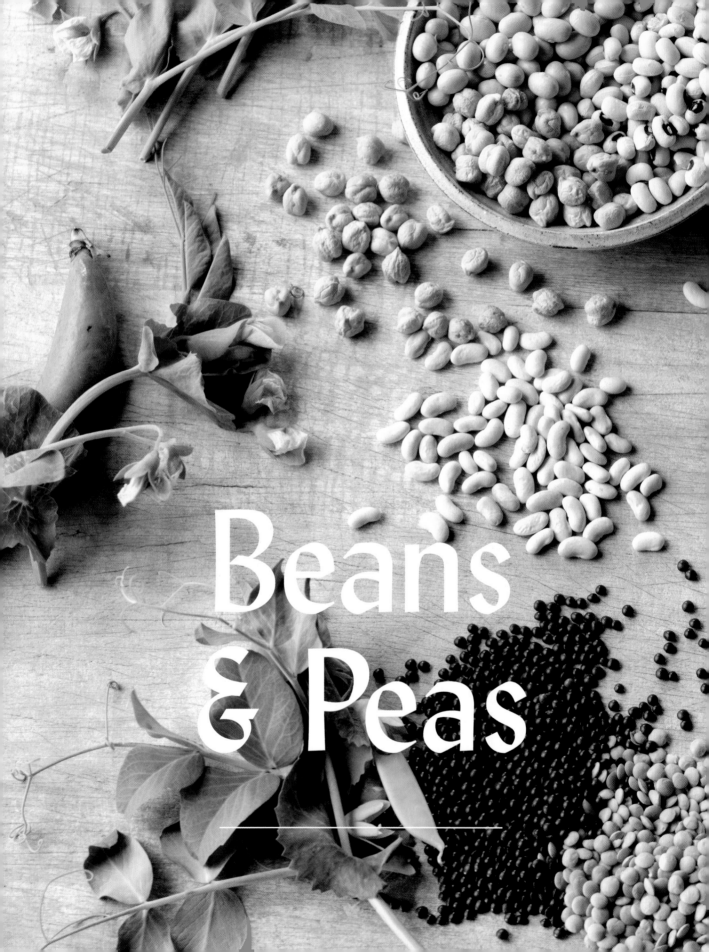

Beans
& Peas

You might not consider beans an Italian staple. However, many Italians eat beans two or three times a week in place of meat or pasta. Tuscans are known as the *mangiafagioli* (bean eaters) of Italy and have many great dishes like fagioli all'uccelletto, pasta e fagioli, and zuppa gran farro. The great white cannellini bean is king in Tuscany.

This chapter dives into both fresh and dried beans, but let's begin with dried beans. Packed with protein, super shelf stable, and easily transported anywhere, dried beans are truly little superheroes! I feel like they have a whisper of magic to them also, being the star of a few fairy tales (Jack and the Beanstalk, anyone?). Beans are one of the world's oldest cultivated plants, feeding people the world over and playing a huge part in the evolution of food and people.

I know making dried beans takes some time, but they are affordable and taste delicious when they're made from scratch. When you're buying dried beans, I suggest eyeballing the expiration date on the bag, because at some supermarkets they could have been sitting there for a while. Try shopping for "fresher" dried beans at a farmers' market or an heirloom bean supplier, where the beans are from recent harvests, not languishing in a warehouse. I will say that not all dried beans cook the same, but once you get the hang of cooking them, I promise you won't go back. (For more on cooking dried beans, see page 74.) As a rule of thumb, cooking dried beans is very much like braising meat. You can layer flavors in the pot, allowing the beans to slowly absorb those flavors while they simmer into rich goodness.

Now, fresh beans and peas. Holy cow! When fresh beans are in season, go snap them up! I tend to buy a whole lot and shell as many as I can, then whatever I don't eat right away gets put into resealable plastic bags and frozen for a cold winter night. Come January, there's nothing better than fixing a simple bowl of buttered peas for a taste of summer.

Fresh peas start showing up in spring. Some of the first ones you'll see at the market are sugar snap peas, snow peas, fresh green chickpeas, English peas, and favas, which are all incredibly flavorful and deliciously green-tasting. Later in the summer, look out for cranberry beans, limas, crowder peas, and black-eyed peas, plus all of the pole beans like yellow wax, romanos, broad beans, and haricots verts (green beans). These peas and beans cook in a matter of minutes, and they have a thin skin and creamy interior. Eating them fresh celebrates their sweet tenderness, and I feel like I am having a total delicacy. They are also less starchy when they're fresh, so they are great cooked into a light fricassee or stew.

It can be a task to shuck or shell the beans, and they can be a little costly, but I think they're worth it.

Not to be forgotten, pea tendrils and pea shoots are delicate and sweet, and so good in a salad. Larger pea tendrils can also be sautéed just like spinach. If you do end up buying fresh beans, all they need is a quick simmer or steam in a pan with a little water and butter, or you can blanch them and toss with butter too. Don't miss out on your beans!

The Peas Corps feeds the world! Delightful to eat both fresh and dried, beans and legumes are protein-rich and super nourishing. Beans and legumes are two peas in a pod that everyone should have in their pantry or freezer.

Clockwise from top: Pappardelle Pasta with Luck-and-Money Ragù (page 84); White Bean Bruschetta with Caramelized Shallots (page78); Lentil Salad with Pancetta, Soft-Boiled Eggs, and Chicories (page 72); Calabrian-Style Green Beans Braised in Tomatoes and Shallots (page 73)

In Italy, you can find perfect young little favas, which are delightful eaten raw (the favas aren't even double shelled!) with some fresh pecorino. Unfortunately, it's not easy to find young favas or that same fresh pecorino here in the US, but this bruschetta still gets at that incredible combination of flavor. The trick is to use an aged pecorino, ideally from Tuscany, Sardinia, or Calabria, where fava dishes are common and the pairing with sheep's milk cheese is a natural match. (These regions make a pecorino that's enjoyed more like a table cheese than Pecorino Romano, which is stronger and drier.) Mixing your aged pecorino with fresh ricotta creates the perfect schmear for your toasty charred bread. Don't forget the mint! If you don't already know, mint and favas are a match made in heaven.

Fava Bean and Ricotta Bruschetta

with Mint and Aged Pecorino

Serves 4 to 6

Kosher salt

1½ pounds fava beans in the pod, shelled (2 cups shelled)

2 tablespoons plus 2 teaspoons everyday olive oil

2 tablespoons minced pitted black olives (like Taggiasca, Gaeta, or Leccino)

Leaves from 3 fresh mint sprigs, torn

1 small, seedless mandarin orange, zest finely grated (use a Microplane), flesh segmented (see Get It Get It)

Coarse sea salt (like Maldon)

1½ cups Homemade Lemon Ricotta (page 173) or whole milk ricotta (see page 8)

Heaping ¼ cup very finely grated aged pecorino (ideally from Calabria, Sardinia, or Tuscany, plus more for garnish (see Get It Get It)

8 slices of Italian-style bread

1.   Bring a medium saucepot of water to a boil and season it well with kosher salt. Prepare a medium bowl with ice water. Blanch the fava beans in the boiling water for 30 to 45 seconds for small to medium beans or 45 to 60 seconds for medium to large beans. Using a skimmer or slotted spoon, transfer the beans to the ice water bath to stop them from cooking any further. To make sure they're done, squeeze a tender little green fava bean from the outer shell and taste; it should be al dente but not crunchy or mealy.

2.   Once fully chilled, squeeze the beans from the thick outer shell. Rinse the beans in very cold water.

3.   In a small bowl, combine the favas with 2 tablespoons of olive oil, the minced olives, mint, and mandarin orange zest and segments. Toss and season with a pinch of coarse sea salt. In another small bowl, mix the ricotta and aged pecorino with the remaining 2 teaspoons of olive oil; season with a pinch of sea salt.

4.   Preheat a grill to high or heat a grill pan over high heat. Grill the bread slices on each side until toasted and charred. Schmear the toasts with the ricotta-pecorino mixture. Spoon the fava bean salad over the top of the toasts (yum!). Use your Microplane to grate more pecorino over the top of the bruschetta and enjoy. So so so good!

Get It

If you don't have (or like) mandarin oranges, swap in ½ cup of quartered cherry tomatoes along with lemon zest and juice.

If you can't find an aged Italian pecorino, try Manchego, which is more readily available.

If need be, you can store the cooked shucked fava beans in the refrigerator overnight with ice on top. When you're ready to continue, pick up at Step 2.

Get It

Who doesn't love a Cobb salad? All those colorful rows of vegetables are so pretty! This particular Cobb is a love letter to spring, but don't feel like you have to use these exact veggies. Asparagus, cucumber, snow peas, and beets would be great! This is great as a lunch salad, and I also like to serve it at Easter or any other spring meal, especially alongside grilled lamb.

Sweet Pea Cobb Salad

with Green Goddess Dressing

Serves 4 to 6

Kosher salt

1 cup shelled fresh English peas (see Get It Get It)

8 ounces sugar snap peas, trimmed

1 heart or small head of romaine or Little Gem lettuce, washed well and chopped

4 ounces pea shoots or tendrils, cut into 2- to 3-inch sections

4 ounces blue cheese, crumbled (1 cup; I like to use Roth Buttermilk Blue)

2 medium carrots, sliced into ⅛-inch-thick rounds

5 red radishes, cut into eighths

1 avocado, halved, pitted, peeled, and diced

6 slices of crisply cooked bacon, chopped

2 large eggs, hard-boiled, peeled, and quartered (see Get It Get It)

½ cup fresh dill sprigs

Fresh cracked black pepper

Green Goddess Dressing (recipe follows)

1. Bring a large pot of water to a boil and season it heavily with kosher salt (about ¼ cup for 5 quarts of water). (It is important to blanch your vegetables in heavily salted water to flavor them and lock in their beautiful green color.) Prepare a large bowl with ice water. Blanch the English peas in the boiling water for 1 minute. Using a slotted spoon or skimmer, plunge the peas in the ice water. Blanch the sugar snap peas for 2 minutes, then plunge in the ice water with the English peas. Drain and reserve.

2. Put the chopped lettuce and half of the pea tendrils in a large serving bowl. Arrange the ingredients in rows on top of the salad. I like to start with the blue cheese, followed by the carrots, radishes, English peas, sugar snap peas, avocado, bacon, and eggs. Top the salad with fresh dill and the remaining pea tendrils. Finish with black pepper. Serve with the dressing.

Green Goddess Dressing

Makes just over 1 cup

¼ cup sliced green onions or fresh chives

¼ cup fresh tarragon leaves

¼ cup fresh dill, stemmed

¼ cup rice vinegar

¼ cup sour cream or plain Greek yogurt

¼ cup mayonnaise

2 tablespoons fresh lemon juice

1 garlic clove

½ teaspoon kosher salt

¼ teaspoon fresh cracked black pepper

Place all of the ingredients in a blender and blend on high until well combined. Transfer to an airtight container and refrigerate for 30 minutes before serving. The dressing can be refrigerated for up to 4 days.

Get It

I love fresh English peas and I can't get enough of them in season, but frozen peas are quite good too. If you can't find fresh English peas, I recommend giving frozen peas a quick blanch in salted water, only for 30 seconds.

If you have a small colander, place your peas in it after removing them from the boiling water, then plunge the whole colander in the ice water. This way, you won't be chasing peas around the ice water.

To make hard-boiled eggs, keep the water from the pea blanching pot at a boil. Gently drop the eggs in and turn off the heat. Let the eggs cook in the water for 12 to 14 minutes. Drain and run under cold water to chill. Peel the eggs, then quarter them lengthwise.

Get It

This is a standard chilled bean salad that Jaime and I have made for years. It's a low-key mix of great blanched beans with olive oil, lemon, onions, and almonds, and it never fails to be a hit on the table. It's a great way to showcase all kinds of beans, but you can keep it simple by making it with just one bean, if you like. This salad is great for the winter months too; you can use cooked dried beans like small white beans, chickpeas, flageolets, cannellini, or cranberry beans (see page 74 for how to cook dried beans). I love the pop of heat from Super-Toasted Chile-Garlic Oil, but you can skip that and just use some extra olive oil and a pinch of chile flake, or toss in a spoonful of spicy store-bought chile crunch.

Chilled Summer Bean Salad

with Super-Toasted Chile-Garlic Oil and Cherry Tomatoes

Serves 6

Kosher salt

1 pound assorted pole beans (like green, yellow wax, dragon tongue, or romano), stemmed and halved crosswise

2 cups fresh shelly (aka shelling) beans or frozen shelled summer beans (like limas, black-eyed peas, crowder peas, or green chickpeas)

1 pint assorted colored cherry tomatoes, halved or quartered, depending on size

½ small red onion, thinly sliced and soaked in ice water for 10 minutes

½ cup fresh basil leaves, torn

2 tablespoons super-special extra-virgin olive oil

Coarse sea salt (like Maldon)

1 tablespoon finely grated lemon zest (use a Microplane)

2 tablespoons fresh lemon juice

2 tablespoons Super-Toasted Chile-Garlic Oil (page 251), or feel free to use as much as you like!

¼ cup toasted slivered almonds

1.   Bring a large pot of water to a boil and season generously with kosher salt. This is blanching water (see page 10), and I like mine to be salty like the ocean, about 1 tablespoon of salt per quart of water. Prepare a medium bowl of salted ice water for shocking. Blanch the pole beans in the boiling water for 2 minutes, then transfer to the ice water.

2.   To blanch the shelly beans, place them in a small heatproof strainer or colander and set that in the boiling water. Using tongs, as the strainer will be too hot to touch, remove the strainer and dunk it in the ice bath. (The strainer helps when cooking and chilling the shelly beans so you don't have to fish the beans out of the pot or the ice bath.)

3.   Drain the chilled beans and spread them on a work surface lined with paper towels to dry, then transfer to a medium serving bowl. Add the cherry tomatoes, red onion, and basil and toss with the olive oil and a few pinches of coarse sea salt. I like to coat the beans and veggies with olive oil first, then mix in the lemon zest and juice. Taste again for seasoning, adding a few more pinches of salt if needed (beans can take more seasoning than you think!). Drizzle the chile-garlic oil over the salad and top with the toasted almonds.

Get It

If you don't have a small colander or strainer, then drain the beans into a colander and top with ice to chill them down.

By tossing the beans with the olive oil first, it protects the vegetables from absorbing the acid lemon, which leads to browning.

Think of it like a little protective layer of oil.

This salad holds well for several hours and up to overnight, but I recommend adding the cherry tomatoes, chile oil, and almonds right before you serve it.

Get It

On a trip to Lyon, France, I was really excited to eat classic Lyonnaise salad made with frisée, poached eggs, bacon, croutons, and potatoes. Funny enough, at many of the local *bouchons* (traditional Lyonnaise bistros), the salad was made with lentils, pork, onions, and herbs. For my take on the dish, I decided to merge everything I knew about Lyonnaise salad into one. Because I love radicchio and endive, I like using them instead of frisée. As for the potatoes, well, I find that a bag of sea salt kettle chips is really good on top to give the salad a great crunchy finish! If you'd like to omit the pork, use 2 tablespoons olive oil to cook the veggies in Step 2 and ¼ cup olive oil for the lentils in Step 4.

Lentil Salad

with Pancetta, Soft-Boiled Eggs, and Chicories

Serves 4

Lentils and Eggs

1 tablespoon everyday olive oil

4 ounces thick-cut pancetta or bacon, diced (optional; see headnote)

1 medium carrot, cut into small dice (about ½ cup)

2 medium celery stalks, diced

2 garlic cloves, minced

8 ounces French green lentils, rinsed and drained

1 dried bay leaf

4 large eggs

Salad

½ small red onion, thinly sliced

¼ cup sherry or white wine vinegar

2 teaspoons Dijon mustard

Kosher salt

⅓ cup chopped fresh flat-leaf parsley, plus a few leaves

3 heads of endive, trimmed, leaves separated and washed

1 medium head of radicchio, trimmed, leaves washed and torn

1 tablespoon everyday olive oil

1 tablespoon fresh lemon juice

Fresh cracked black pepper

Sea salt kettle-style chips, for garnish (optional)

1. **Make the lentils and eggs.** Heat a heavy-bottomed pot over medium heat. Add the olive oil and pancetta and bring to a sizzle. Reduce the heat to low and render the pancetta until golden and crispy, about 5 minutes. Using a slotted spoon, transfer the crispy pancetta to a paper towel–lined plate. Scrape the remaining pan drippings into a heat-safe medium bowl; reserve for the salad. If you don't end up with ¼ cup of drippings, add enough olive oil to amount to ¼ cup.

2. Add 1 teaspoon of the drippings back to the pot and bring the heat to medium. Add the carrot, celery, and garlic and cook until they just begin to caramelize, 4 to 5 minutes. Stir in the lentils, then cover with 3 cups of water. Add the bay leaf. Bring to a boil, then reduce the heat to low and give the lentils a stir. Simmer, uncovered, until tender, 35 to 40 minutes; add ½ cup more water if needed.

3. Meanwhile, bring a medium pot of water to a boil and fill a medium bowl with ice water. Gently add the eggs to the pot and boil for 6½ minutes. Transfer to the ice bath. Once chilled, peel the eggs and set aside.

4. Remove the lentils from the heat and let rest for 10 minutes before draining. The lentils can be served warm now or refrigerated for up to 2 days and served cold in the salad.

5. **Make the salad.** Toss the red onion, vinegar, mustard, and a few pinches of salt with the reserved pan drippings from the pancetta. Let stand for 10 minutes. Drain the lentils and add to the bowl. Add the chopped parsley, season with salt, and stir to combine.

6. In a large bowl, dress the endive and radicchio with the olive oil and lemon juice, then season with salt. Divide the leaves into four serving bowls. Spoon the lentil salad on top of the greens, then carefully cut the eggs in half (the yolks will be runny) and place on top. Add the crispy pancetta, parsley leaves, fresh cracked black pepper, and kettle chips, if using.

Southern Italians have a way of cooking things in tomato sauce that just makes them better! Here, there is no need to blanch the beans. Instead, the beans cook right in the sauce, like a quick braise. Many Italians prefer eating a fully cooked green vegetable over an al dente one. So here the beans become very tender and turn almost army green in color. Sometimes I make these green beans at home for an easy dinner with rice and a fried egg on top. My favorite beans to use are romano, a broad, tender green-to-yellow bean, or dragon tongue. The flavors are similar to a pole bean, but there is a total texture difference. The broad bean shape makes them a great choice for a longer cooking technique, like this quick braise. They don't get stringy like a pole bean or string bean! (Ha!) They are also iconic on Southern Italian tables. I really only like making this recipe when beans are in peak season, which coincides with tomato season in most places.

Calabrian-Style Green Beans

Braised in Tomatoes and Shallots

Serves 4 to 6

4 ounces bacon (about 4 slices), pancetta, or guanciale, cut into lardons or ¼-inch pieces

1 medium shallot, cut into ½-inch rings

1 tablespoon Calabrian chile paste or sambal oelek

1½ pounds green beans (any variety), trimmed

Kosher salt

2 cups Fresh Tomato Sauce (page 391) or your favorite jarred tomato sauce

¼ cup chopped fresh oregano

Super-special extra-virgin olive oil, for drizzling

1. Heat a large skillet over medium heat. Add the bacon and cook, stirring often, until rendered, golden, and crispy, about 3 minutes. Remove from the heat and transfer to a paper towel–lined plate. Leave 2 tablespoons of the bacon drippings in the skillet.

2. Return the skillet to medium heat. Stir in the shallot to coat it in the rendered bacon fat. Cook until translucent, about 2 minutes. Stir in the chile paste and green beans and season with a few generous pinches of kosher salt. Cook, tossing the beans with tongs, for about 2 minutes or until they have begun to soften slightly. Reduce the heat to low. Add the tomato sauce and ¼ cup of water. Toss to coat, then cover and simmer for 8 minutes, until the beans and tomato sauce have melded together.

3. Remove the lid and increase the heat to medium. Continue to cook, stirring occasionally, until the beans are tender and the sauce has thickened, about 3 minutes. Turn off the heat. Add the oregano and season with a bit more salt if needed. Toss to coat, then transfer the beans to a serving dish and top with the crispy bacon. Drizzle with a tablespoon or two of super-special extra-virgin olive oil. Serve immediately.

Get It

If you don't like things particularly spicy, feel free to reduce the amount of Calabrian chile paste to ½ tablespoon, or sub a pinch of chile flake. You can sub in a few other of your favorite green veggies too. A couple of my favorites are zucchini and asparagus.

Get It

Making a pot of beans can be a great way to spend a lazy afternoon. Sure, you can always sub a can of beans in a pinch. I do both! However, I am never as satisfied with canned beans as I am with a pot cooked from scratch. The potlikker (broth created when cooking dried beans) is unparalleled by the liquid you'll get from a can. Cooking dried beans can cause anxiety and frustration when the beans never seem to get tender or break apart when you want them to stay whole. It can be a wild ride. Once you make that first great pot of beans, it becomes somewhat addictive and a special challenge between you and the bean. Who will win?

Best Dried Beans

Makes 6 to 7 cups

1 pound dried beans (like cranberry, pinto, cannellini, chickpeas, white runner beans, or giant limas)

1 tablespoon everyday olive oil

1 small yellow onion, finely chopped

½ medium carrot, finely chopped

1 celery stalk, finely chopped

2 dried bay leaves

Kosher salt

Super-special extra-virgin olive oil, fresh cracked black pepper, and freshly grated Parmigiano-Reggiano, for serving (optional)

1.   Sort through the beans before you soak them, checking for any stones or rocks; discard those. Place the beans in a large bowl, cover with cold water, and soak for at least 4 hours or overnight.

2.   Drain and rinse the beans when you are ready to cook them. Heat a large heavy-bottomed pot over high heat. Add the olive oil, onion, carrot, and celery and cook for 2 minutes, or until slightly softened. Add the beans and bay leaves and cover with cold water, about 1 inch above the top of the beans. Bring to a boil and boil rapidly for 10 minutes. Skim the scum that floats to the surface of the water, if there is any. (This depends on the beans you're using.) Reduce the heat to low, cover partially, and let the beans "chill out" in the pot for 1 hour. For even cooking, try to not disturb the beans with a powerful simmer or any stirring.

3.   After an hour, check the tenderness of the beans to see how much they've cooked so far. Add a bit more hot water if needed just to keep the beans submerged. Continue to cook until tender. The cooking time will vary depending on the kind of bean, how long it has soaked, and how fresh it is. This can take anywhere from an additional 1 to 4 hours. I like to rotate my pot on the stovetop every 30 minutes or so to prevent a hot spot in the cooking process.

4.   Once the beans are tender yet slightly toothsome, season with several pinches of salt. Do this right before they are fully cooked, as this will allow them to absorb the seasoning so you're not just seasoning the liquid.

5.   Remove the beans from the heat and enjoy as is, with lots of olive oil, black pepper, and grated parm on top. You can also drain the beans or cool and save them in their liquid (see Get It Get It). The beans in their liquid can be stored in an airtight container and refrigerated for 1 week or frozen for 3 to 4 months. Then you can turn these delicious beans into a magical recipe like Couple Two, Three Greens Ribollita Soup on page 192 or White Beans all'Uccelletto on page 77.

Sourcing Great Dried Beans

1. Check for an expiration date on the bag of dried beans before purchasing. Not all dried beans are created equal. Chances are that if you've had some of those aforementioned dried bean dilemmas, it's not something you did or didn't do. It's likely that the beans you tried to cook were simply too old.

2. Order from heirloom bean growers! I *love* and am quite obsessed with Rancho Gordo in California. I have never been disappointed with their beans. They are on the pricier side, but the care they put into growing, sourcing, harvesting, drying, and storing is worth every penny. There are also great dried heirloom beans from Italy; try ordering from Gustiamo in New York or Ritrovo Italian Regional Foods in Seattle.

Get It

Finely chopping the onion, carrot, and celery allows them to meld into the liquid from the beans. If you are looking to cook beans without bits of veggies, cut the vegetables into large pieces so that they can be removed after the beans are cooked.

For the most part, you will know your beans are finished when they're tender and delicious. But if you're using the beans in a soup or a stew, you might finish them when they're slightly al dente, whereas if you're pureeing them, you should take the beans to complete tenderness.

I often drain the beans for other dishes and reserve the potlikker (the bean cooking liquid) to use as a vegetable stock; the starch from cooking the beans adds body to a soup or a sauce.

Get It

It is hard to believe that these beans are, in fact, vegan. They're so friggin' meaty and hearty that I think they could be a game changer for anyone on a plant-based diet. For me, these incredible beans signify what Italian cooking truly is: simple, ingredient-forward cooking. While these beans are soul-satisfying on their own, feel free to play around here. I recommend using cranberry, cannellini, white runner, or giant lima beans for this recipe. You can add bacon, pancetta, or sausage to the pot, or change up the herbs—mint and parsley would be great. You can also top the beans with freshly grated Parmigiano. I like to serve this as a main course alongside a great salad or vegetable dish. This recipe makes enough to feed a crowd or to have amazing leftovers for days on end!

White Beans all'Uccelletto

aka Tuscan Baked Beans

Serves 4 to 6 as a main or 8 to 10 as a side dish

Two 28-ounce cans high-quality whole peeled tomatoes (preferably Italian San Marzano or Bianco DiNapoli from California; see Get It Get It)

¼ cup everyday olive oil

8 garlic cloves, thinly sliced

2 tablespoons lightly chopped fresh sage, plus a few leaves for garnish

Kosher salt

Best Dried Beans (page 74), drained, or three 15-ounce cans beans, drained

Thick slices of toasted bread, for serving

Super-special extra-virgin olive oil, for drizzling

Fresh cracked black pepper

Get It

I recently fell in love with Bianco DiNapoli tomatoes, a brand that is the brainchild of the great Chris Bianco from Pizzeria Bianco in Phoenix and Rob DiNapoli. Given the super-simple nature of this dish, sourcing the highest quality tomatoes you can will make a big difference.

Get It

1. Set a colander in a large bowl and drain the whole peeled tomatoes. Wearing gloves or with clean hands, crush the tomatoes, allowing the juice and liquid to escape into the bowl. If you prefer, you can drain and lightly chop the tomatoes, but I love the rusticity that hand-crushed tomatoes give this dish. Reserve both the tomato juice and the crushed tomatoes.

2. Preheat the oven to 425°F. Set a foil-lined baking sheet on the bottom rack. Heat a 12-inch enameled cast-iron skillet or a cast-iron casserole over medium-high heat. Add the olive oil and garlic and cook, stirring, until the garlic turns golden brown, about 3 minutes. Add the sage and a pinch or two of salt and cook for a minute. Add the crushed tomatoes and a bit more salt and cook, stirring, allowing the tomatoes to fry in the oil; they will turn a richer red color and caramelize as they cook (this step makes me *so* happy), about 10 minutes. Add the reserved tomato juices and bring to a rapid simmer. Add the drained beans and gently stir to combine. Simmer, stirring often, until the sauce is slightly reduced and the beans have absorbed some of the sauce, about 10 minutes. Double-check the seasoning before putting in the oven. I suggest adding a few pinches of salt.

3. Transfer the pot to the middle rack in the oven and bake, uncovered, until the sauce has cooked down and been absorbed, 45 to 50 minutes.

4. Turn the broiler to high and broil the beans 5 to 6 inches from the heat source, until the top is a little roasty-toasty around the edges, about 5 minutes. Serve the beans piled onto the toasts. Top with whole sage leaves, a healthy drizzle of super-special extra-virgin olive oil, and black pepper.

In Tuscany, bean bruschetta is a common snack enjoyed with an aperitivo (at cocktail hour), but this bruschetta would also be good alongside a large green salad for lunch. This is a relatively simple bruschetta, but caramelizing the shallots takes a little time. The shallots are delicious, and they also deeply flavor the olive oil that the beans are mashed in. I can promise you it is well worth it.

White Bean Bruschetta

with Caramelized Shallots

Makes 1 cup white bean spread; serves 4 to 6

½ cup everyday olive oil

3 medium shallots, sliced into ¼-inch-thick rings

1 tablespoon fresh rosemary leaves (from 1 small sprig)

One 15½-ounce can great Northern or cannellini beans, drained and rinsed

1 dried bay leaf

Kosher salt

Fresh cracked black pepper

Italian-style bread or sourdough boule, sliced

2 tablespoons aged balsamic vinegar, for drizzling

1. In a medium saucepot, heat the oil over medium-low heat for 2 minutes. Add the shallots and allow them to bubble. Cook, stirring occasionally to separate the rings and help them to brown evenly; the oil should be at a moderate temperature, not too hot or cool, so the shallots are constantly bubbling. Once the shallots are nearing golden brown, add the rosemary leaves and stir until fragrant and softened, about 1 minute. Using a slotted spoon, transfer the shallots and rosemary to a paper towel–lined plate. (The shallots will crisp slightly as they cool. They can be kept in an airtight container at room temperature overnight.)

2. Add the drained beans and bay leaf to the oil in the pot and season with a pinch of salt and a few cracks of pepper. Cook until the beans soften, 8 to 10 minutes. Discard the bay leaf. Use the back of a spoon to mash the beans into a creamy yet chunky consistency. Add 2 tablespoons of water to help loosen the puree, then season to taste. Transfer to a small bowl or airtight container and reserve until you are ready to eat. (Can be made a day ahead and refrigerated. Bring to room temperature before using.)

3. When you are ready to serve, turn the broiler to high. Place the bread slices about 3 inches below the heat source. Toast until the edges are slightly charred, 2 to 3 minutes per side. Spread the toasts with a thick schmear of the bean puree and top with caramelized shallots and rosemary. Drizzle balsamic vinegar over the toasts, sprinkle with fresh cracked black pepper, and serve.

Get It

A quick note on bay leaves—they get stale! Some people probably have had the same jar of bay leaves in their pantry for years. I encourage you to toss those out and buy new ones. They can make all of the difference, especially in a simple dish like this one.

Don't be scared to burn the bread! Well, not quite burn . . . but a real bruschetta must have a char on the bread. If it's just toasted, then it would be known as a bean crostini. If you have a grill pan or a grill,

I recommend grilling the bread without oil so that you can get a good char without the burnt oil flavor.

Get It

Listen to Your Vegetables

This is a fun riff on traditional pesto, where peas take the place of herbs. The result is a rich, fresh, slightly sweet pea pesto that can be used with pasta and risotto and even simply schmeared on bread. Feel free to add fresh herbs like mint, parsley, and basil for additional flavor. I like to make this the same day I am going to use it, to keep it vibrant.

Pea Pesto

Makes 2 cups

Kosher salt

2 cups shelled English peas (fresh or thawed frozen)

¼ cup crème fraîche

½ cup freshly grated Pecorino Romano

Finely grated zest of 1 lemon (use a Microplane)

1. Bring a medium pot of salted water to a boil. This is blanching water (see page 10), and I like mine to be salty like the ocean, about 1 tablespoon of salt per quart of water. Fill a medium bowl with ice water. Blanch the peas for 1 minute for fresh or 30 seconds for frozen, then immediately plunge in the ice water bath. Once the peas are chilled, drain them in a colander.

2. Transfer the peas to a food processor and pulse a few times until finely chopped. Add the crème fraîche, pecorino, and lemon zest, and pulse until combined. This pesto is best if used the same day, but can be refrigerated in an airtight container for up to 2 days. I recommend sealing the top with plastic wrap to keep the air off the surface of the pesto.

— Get It —

I think crème fraîche creates a perfectly creamy and well-balanced pesto, but if you want, you can also use whole milk ricotta (see page 8). I suggest whipping it in the food processor until smooth before adding the peas.

— Get It —

I wanted to create a dish celebrating peas, so I didn't expect to include sausage when I first set out to make this. But as it goes, I had some sausage in my fridge, and when I saw it, I thought, "Yeah, sausage and peas will be delicious together!" Sweet green freshness is the perfect balance to the savory umami of Italian sausage. With plenty of pecorino and fresh cracked black pepper, this dish is reminiscent of cacio e pepe. I just love the sharp salinity of Pecorino Romano, and because of its robust flavor, I don't call for any extra salt here for seasoning besides in the pasta water. Even though I love it, the sausage in this dish can be omitted. Consider adding a little fresh lemon juice at the end for a pop of extra flavor, if you like!

Rigatoni

with Pea Pesto, Pecorino, and Italian Sausage

Serves 4

Kosher salt

1 teaspoon everyday olive oil

12 ounces bulk or link spicy or mild Italian sausage, casings removed

½ medium yellow onion, thinly sliced (about ½ cup)

1 pinch of chile flake

1 pound dry rigatoni pasta

2 cups sugar snap peas, trimmed

1 cup shelled English peas (fresh or thawed frozen)

Pea Pesto (page 79)

½ cup freshly grated Pecorino Romano, plus a little more for garnish

½ cup fresh basil leaves, plus more for garnish

Fresh cracked black pepper, for garnish

1. Bring a large pot of water to a boil and season generously with kosher salt (about 2 tablespoons). In a heavy-bottomed saucepan, heat the olive oil over medium-high heat. Add the sausage in small pieces and cook, stirring often, until the fat is rendered and the meat is lightly browned, about 4 minutes. Carefully drain the excess fat from the pan. Place the pan back on the heat. Add the onion and chile flake and cook until the onion is translucent and beginning to caramelize, about 2 minutes. Remove from the heat.

2. Boil the rigatoni in the pot of salted water for 2 minutes less than the directions on the package state for al dente, stirring occasionally. Add the snap peas and shelled peas to the pot with the rigatoni in the last minute of the pasta cooking.

3. Toward the end of the pasta cooking, return the saucepan with the sausage back to medium heat. Add 1 cup of the pasta cooking water. Drain the pasta and peas in a colander and transfer to the saucepan. Cook, tossing, until the pasta marries with the sausage and peas, about 1 minute. Off the heat, stir in the pea pesto, pecorino, and basil until creamy and the sauce is thickened. Garnish with lots of fresh cracked black pepper, a sprinkle of pecorino, and more fresh basil and serve.

Get It

Fresh peas are only in season for a brief time. If you have lots, you can shell them and freeze them in resealable plastic bags for later use.

Feel free to use a mix of peas—consider snow peas!—or just use all shelled English peas here, whatever you like best. If I have pea tendrils, I would fold those into the pasta for even more extra delicious pea flavor.

Get It

Did you know that to call something "marinara" in Italy, it should technically include something from the ocean? I love this spin on a traditional seafood soup. There is no right or wrong with the choice of seafood here. It's just about making sure you cook the seafood properly. The bulk of flavor comes from the slow-cooked *ceci* (chickpeas) in the vibrant tomato and olive soffritto. Soffritto is a layer of aromatics and veggies that is the base of a sauce or stew. The medley of seafood here gently cooks in that delicious base. In truth, the ceci absorb so much flavor that they are the sleeper hit in this rustic stew. Serve this with pieces of warm crusty bread and a garlicky aioli or butter. It can also be an incredible side dish for a crowd!

Ceci alla Marinara

with Tomato-Olive Soffritto

Serves 4 to 6

2 tablespoons everyday olive oil, plus more for drizzling

1 cup sliced or roughly chopped pitted olives (use a mix of varieties)

6 garlic cloves, smashed and chopped

½ medium red onion, minced

2 tablespoons capers, drained

2 pinches of chile flake

1 tablespoon plus 1 teaspoon dried oregano (preferably wild Calabrian or Greek)

One 28-ounce can whole peeled San Marzano tomatoes, crushed by hand

1 dried bay leaf

1 pound dried chickpeas, cooked (see Get It Get It), with their potlikker

Kosher salt

8 littleneck clams, purged (see page 326 for cleaning instructions)

8 mussels, scrubbed and debearded

1 pound large shrimp, peeled and deveined, tails left on

8 ounces calamari, tubes cut into 1-inch rings, tentacles cut in half if large

Finely grated zest and juice of 1 lemon (use a Microplane)

2 tablespoons chopped fresh flat-leaf parsley, plus a few leaves for garnish

1. In a large saucepan, heat the olive oil over medium-high heat. Add the olives and garlic and let fry and sizzle for 1 minute. Add the onion, capers, chile flake, and 1 tablespoon of the oregano and cook, stirring continuously, until toasted and caramelized and the olives are slightly shriveled, about 10 minutes. (Holy smokes, the kitchen smell is intoxicating.)

2. Stir in the crushed tomatoes and bay leaf and bring to a simmer, about 5 minutes. Add the cooked chickpeas and 2 cups of the potlikker and bring to a simmer. Cover and simmer over medium-low to low heat until the beans are tender and the broth and beans have melded together, about 45 minutes.

3. Season the chickpea mixture with salt. Add the clams and simmer for 6 to 8 minutes, until the clams open; discard any unopened clams. Add the mussels and simmer for a few minutes until they open. Add the shrimp and calamari and cook until opaque, 2 to 3 minutes; discard the bay leaf. Stir in the lemon zest, lemon juice, and chopped parsley. Drizzle with olive oil and scatter the parsley leaves and the remaining 1 teaspoon of dried oregano over the top to serve. Leftovers? I remove the shells from the shellfish before putting it away. Then I eat this as a chilled salad of sorts, with lots of arugula and a drizzle of olive oil.

Get It

To make the chickpeas, follow the directions for the Best Dried Beans on page 74, but cook for about 2 hours, or until tender but not mushy. I find that I don't need to presoak chickpeas before cooking them. This yields roughly 6 cups of beans and 2 cups of the potlikker. If you don't have the potlikker, you can use vegetable broth in its place.

Get It

This recipe title might sound a little cheeky, but it's too much fun not to use as a name! I love to make this pasta on New Year's Day, as it satisfies my family tradition of eating black-eyed peas for luck and cabbage—or in this case, Brussels sprouts—for money. As fitting as it is for New Year's, I assure you that this can be served on many days and nights, year-round. I love the texture of the shaved Brussels sprouts in here, as they just melt into the pasta. Plus, those extra leaves that fall off the sprouts can be thrown in for another layer of texture. The black-eyed pea ragù freezes really well for up to 4 months. Make a double batch and keep it on hand to use any time the craving hits.

Pappardelle Pasta

with Luck-and-Money Ragù

Serves 4

Black-Eyed Peas

8 ounces dried black-eyed peas (about 1½ cups)

1 teaspoon everyday olive oil

1 small onion, halved

1 small carrot, halved

1 celery stalk, halved

1 dried bay leaf

Kosher salt

2 fresh rosemary sprigs

Ragù

2 tablespoons everyday olive oil

½ cup finely diced carrot (1 small)

½ cup finely diced celery (1 stalk)

½ cup finely diced red bell pepper (½ small)

1 cup finely diced onion (1 small)

2 garlic cloves, thinly sliced or grated with a Microplane

One 28-ounce can whole peeled tomatoes, crushed by hand

One 2- to 3-inch piece of Parmigiano-Reggiano rind

1 pinch of chile flake

1 cup vegetable stock (try the Light Artichoke Stock on page 30 or the heartier Charred Onion Vegetable Stock on page 325)

1. **Make the black-eyed peas.** Sort through the peas, discarding any stones or rocks mixed in. In a medium saucepot, heat the olive oil over high heat. Add the onion, carrot, and celery and cook until just softened, 1 to 2 minutes. Add the black-eyed peas to the pot along with the bay leaf. Add water until the peas are covered by an inch or so. (To test this, dip the handle of a wooden spoon into the pot and measure from the top level of the peas.) Bring to a boil for 15 minutes, then reduce the heat to low. Cook, uncovered, for 20 minutes, stirring occasionally, until most of the water is absorbed and the peas are al dente. Season with salt and add the rosemary. Let sit for 10 minutes. Using tongs, remove the onion, carrot, celery, bay leaf, and rosemary, and discard.

2. **Make the ragù.** In a large, heavy-bottomed pot, heat the olive oil over high heat. Add the carrot, celery, bell pepper, onion, and garlic and cook, stirring occasionally, until softened and beginning to brown, about 5 minutes. Add the crushed tomatoes and their juice and cook down until thickened and the tomato begins to turn brick red, about 5 minutes. Add the peas and about 1 cup of their cooking liquid, along with the parm rind, chile flake, and the vegetable stock. Reduce the heat to low and cover. Cook the ragù for 30 minutes, stirring occasionally, until it has reduced and started to come together.

3. Check for seasoning. Remove the parm rind and discard. Remove the pot from the heat until you are ready to cook the pasta. The black-eyed pea ragù can be refrigerated overnight or frozen for up to 4 months.

4. **Finish the pasta.** Place the black-eyed pea ragù back over medium heat to warm it. Bring a large pot of water to a boil and season generously with kosher salt. Add the pappardelle and all of the Brussels sprouts to the boiling water and cook for 1 to 2 minutes, until the pasta floats to the top. Reserve ½ cup of the pasta water, then drain the pasta and Brussels sprouts

Pasta

Kosher salt

Hand-Cut Ribbon Pasta
(page 263), cut for pappardelle

8 ounces Brussels sprouts,
including any outer leaves that
fall off, thinly sliced (about
3 cups)

2 tablespoons unsalted butter

2 tablespoons snipped fresh chives

½ cup freshly grated Parmigiano-
Reggiano, for garnish

Fresh cracked black pepper, for
garnish

Super-special extra-virgin olive oil,
for finishing

and add to the pot with the ragù. Toss the pasta and ragù, then add the
reserved pasta water and stir in the butter; you are looking for the pasta and
sauce to marry together, which takes about 2 minutes. Remove from the
heat. Transfer the pasta to plates or bowls and garnish with chives, freshly
grated parm, and black pepper. Drizzle with super-special extra-virgin olive
oil and serve.

Wild Oregano

I almost always suggest using
fresh herbs in recipes, which
have the flavor most dishes
want. My one exception is dried
wild Calabrian oregano, which
might just be my favorite! Wild
oregano is hand-harvested in
the mountains of Calabria. It
has little flowering buds that
are bursting with amazing floral
aroma. You might be confused as
to how to use it, because it's sold
on the stem in beautiful bundles.
All you have to do is shake the
bundle, and leaves will fall over
the top of what's cooking or will
create a fragrant garnish for so
many things, from pizza and
chicken parm to simple pastas,
beans, and vegetables.

You can find wild oregano
at specialty Italian grocers and
online. I recommend storing
it in a large resealable bag and
pinching out whatever falls to the
bottom. Trust me, this oregano is
worth seeking out!

Get It

You can sub just about any
pasta for the pappardelle
with this ragù, like 1 pound
of fettuccini or broad egg
noodles. You can also substitute
shredded cabbage for the
Brussels sprouts.

Get It

Brassicas

Cauliflower, Broccoli,
Brussels Sprouts

Brassicas are part of a genus of plants that includes delicious healthy veggies like mustards, broccoli, cauliflower, cabbage, and Brussels sprouts. So many of these veggies are what I call my "fridge warriors." They are rock stars because they generally have a long shelf life in the refrigerator, making it easy to cook up a healthy meal without having to run out to the store. I always have something from this group in my fridge, whether it's broccoli, cauliflower, or a head of cabbage.

In case you were wondering, the Brassicaceae family contains over 3,700 species of flowering plants around the world. That's a lot of plants! Just to give you a sense of what this amazing family includes, here are some of the most familiar veggies: arugula, bok choy, broccoli, broccolini, Brussels sprouts, cabbage, cauliflower, collards, horseradish, kale, kohlrabi, napa cabbage, radishes,

Romanesco, rutabaga, turnips, and watercress. This is such a big group that I am focusing only on its heartier members.

Without a doubt, my favorite way (and the easiest way, I believe) to cook most brassicas in this chapter is to roast them in the oven with a little olive oil and salt. But they also love some garlic for company or getting finished with some acid. When it comes to the strong and hearty guys, I like to treat them a little bit like meat. "What does that mean?" you ask. These warriors take well to slow-cooking, which draws out their flavor, unlike so many other veggies. They can also be marinated before they're cooked (see how I dry-brine my cauliflower on page 101) and marinated after cooking too! The heartier brassicas can take the heat like meat, absorb flavor well, and can crisp and char on the grill or in the oven.

Brassicas do have a weird in-between situation that can happen when they're not quite cooked and they can be a little smelly; I'll call it "medium-rare" cooking. I try to avoid that zone. I suggest eating them raw or taking them to a good "medium" cook or beyond to coax out all of that flavor.

If I am eating brassicas raw, I like to thinly slice them, keeping them light while preserving their crunch. To highlight their fresh green flavor, opt for a quick blanch or steam. (This works for the hearty guys as well as for the more tender ones like rapini and broccolini.) And all brassicas can be roasted in the oven; just make sure they are cut in similar sizes so they cook evenly.

What I think you'll like here are some of the surprising ways you can use brassicas, like in my Lasagna Bianca with Roasted Cauliflower, Blistered Grapes, and Toasted Almonds (page 102), or Fully Loaded Broccolini Antipasto Salad with Peperoncini Vinaigrette (page 92).

Brassicas are nutritional powerhouses and they're inexpensive and easy to get. I encourage you to experiment with them and have some fun! ————————

The hearty bunch has arrived! These fridge warriors last a long time and are amazingly versatile 'cause they love to be eaten both raw and cooked.

Clockwise from top left: Lillian's Butter-Steamed Broccolini (page 95); Lasagna Bianca with Roasted Cauliflower, Blistered Grapes, and Toasted Almonds (page 102); Whole Brussels Sprouts with Dried Cherries and Pecans (page 94); Purple Vegetable Salad with Gouda, Walnuts, and Caraway Mustard Vinaigrette (page 93)

I liken this salad to the ultimate Italian salad bar salad. Jaime and I joke that this is a pizzeria salad—very old-school Italian American. In this salad, I wanted to show off the fresh, green, sweeter, more tender side of broccolini by blanching it. The combo of blanched broccolini, lettuce, carrots, bell pepper, and fennel ensures an abundance of fresh crunchiness, then adding the meat and cheese rounds it out so perfectly. But the real secret is the peperoncini vinaigrette, which is so addictively sharp and tangy. Be sure to have fun with the toppings. I love to add croutons, toasted seeds, artichokes, green beans, cherry tomatoes, and olives.

Fully Loaded Broccolini Antipasto Salad

with Peperoncini Vinaigrette

Serves 6

Kosher salt

2 bunches of broccolini, trimmed, florets separated, stems sliced

1 small head of iceberg lettuce, chopped into bite-sized pieces

½ head of radicchio, chopped into bite-sized pieces

2 small carrots, sliced into thin coins

1 small red bell pepper, cored, seeded, and sliced into thin rounds

1 small bulb fennel, trimmed, cored, and thinly shaved

2 ounces spicy soppressata or pepperoni, cut into ½-inch-wide ribbons

6 ounces fresh whole milk mozzarella, diced

½ cup freshly grated aged provolone or Parmigiano-Reggiano

Peperoncini Vinaigrette (recipe follows)

Fresh cracked black pepper, for garnish

1.   Bring a large pot of water to a boil with about ¼ cup of salt. Fill a medium bowl with ice water. Blanch the broccolini for 1 minute, then transfer to the ice bath until chilled, about 5 minutes; drain.

2.   In a large salad bowl, layer the ingredients. Start with the lettuces, followed by the broccolini, carrots, bell pepper, fennel, soppressata, mozzarella, and provolone. Right before serving, drizzle the dressing over the salad and toss. Garnish with fresh cracked black pepper.

Peperoncini Vinaigrette

Makes 1 cup

1 small garlic clove, finely grated (use a Microplane)

1 small shallot, minced

¼ cup chopped peperoncini peppers (about 6 peppers)

¼ cup of the pickling liquid from the peperoncini

2 tablespoons red wine vinegar

2 tablespoons fresh lemon juice

1 teaspoon dried oregano

1 teaspoon sugar

Kosher salt

½ cup everyday olive oil

In a medium bowl, combine the garlic, shallot, peperoncini and their pickling liquid, vinegar, lemon juice, oregano, sugar, and 1 tablespoon of water. Season with a few pinches of kosher salt. Slowly drizzle in the olive oil and use a whisk to combine. Taste and adjust the seasoning if needed. Refrigerate in an airtight container for up to 2 weeks.

I love this super colorful salad, which is a fun nod to my Germanic heritage. I always think of mustard, cabbage, dill, and caraway as iconic German ingredients. The tart, mustardy vinaigrette takes the cabbage to quick sauerkraut-like heights. It's really an elevated slaw that stands on its own as a hearty salad. It's a great accompaniment to meat or seafood dishes, especially the buttery crunch of schnitzel and fried fish or the richer flavors of pan-roasted salmon or cod.

Purple Vegetable Salad

with Gouda, Walnuts, and Caraway Mustard Vinaigrette

Serves 4 to 6

1 teaspoon everyday olive oil

½ cup walnuts

1 small head of purple cabbage, shredded or julienned

1 small head of radicchio, shredded

2 medium beets, peeled and shredded

1 tart apple (like Granny Smith), peeled, halved, cored, and shredded

2 cups cooked quinoa

2 tablespoons chopped fresh dill, plus sprigs for garnish

Caraway Mustard Vinaigrette (recipe follows)

Kosher salt

6 ounces aged Gouda, shredded on the large holes of a box grater (about 1½ cups)

Fresh cracked black pepper

1. In a medium skillet, heat the oil and walnuts over medium heat, tossing to coat the walnuts. Cook, tossing or stirring often, so the walnuts toast slowly and evenly, about 6 minutes. The walnuts should deepen in color and become fragrant. Remove from the heat and cool.

2. In a large salad or mixing bowl, toss the cabbage, radicchio, beets, apple, quinoa, and chopped dill. Drizzle with half of the vinaigrette and toss. Add a few pinches of salt and a bit more vinaigrette to taste. Top the salad with the Gouda, walnuts, and fresh dill sprigs. Finish with a few generous cracks of black pepper.

Caraway Mustard Vinaigrette

This vinaigrette is excellent on hearty salad fixings, but it's also so good drizzled over baked salmon or trout. When I use it that way, I add 2 tablespoons of maple syrup or honey and top the fish with toasted breadcrumbs and fresh dill. Yum.

Makes ¾ cup

1 teaspoon caraway seeds

1 medium shallot, minced

2 tablespoons apple cider vinegar or white wine vinegar

2 tablespoons fresh lemon juice

¼ cup spicy brown mustard

¼ cup everyday olive oil

Kosher salt

1. Place the caraway seeds in a small skillet and toast over medium-high heat, tossing, until fragrant, about 2 minutes. Transfer to a plate to cool.

2. In a medium bowl, combine the shallot and vinegar. Whisk in the lemon juice, mustard, and caraway seeds, then slowly drizzle in the oil until emulsified. Season with a pinch or two of salt. The dressing can be refrigerated for up to 2 weeks.

Get It

The salad can be prepped ahead of time and dressed just before serving. It is also delicious the next day when it becomes more like a slaw, which I love alongside a pastrami or turkey sandwich!

Get It

I'm bringing whole sexy Brussels sprouts back. I love cooking the sprouts whole because it helps them retain moisture and flavor and prevents the inside of the sprouts from getting oil-logged, creating little packages with big taste. To cook whole, you need to blanch the Brussels sprouts for longer than you think because they're tightly knit, with lots of layers of leaves. Once they're cooked, the sprouts get toasted with nutty brown butter, pecans, fragrant rosemary, and tart cherries. I think this is how sprouts want to be enjoyed: cooked whole and toasted with butter and crunchy stuff. It's definitely not rocket science. Having said that, you can totally cut the sprouts in half after they're blanched, especially if they are super big. They just might absorb more butter. Feel free to swap in any nut here, and mix up the dried fruit too!

Whole Brussels Sprouts

with Dried Cherries and Pecans

Serves 4 to 6

Kosher salt

2 pounds Brussels sprouts, trimmed

4 tablespoons unsalted butter

½ cup pecans or walnuts, chopped

Leaves from 1 rosemary sprig

¼ cup dried tart cherries, chopped

Fresh cracked black pepper

1.　Bring a large pot of water to a boil and season generously with salt. This is blanching water (see page 10), and I like mine to be salty like the ocean, about 1 tablespoon of salt per quart of water. Add the Brussels sprouts and boil until tender, 5 to 7 minutes, depending on their size. To check if they are tender, I treat them like potatoes: I stick a paring knife in one sprout, and if my knife doesn't get stuck, the sprouts are done.

2.　Drain the sprouts in a large colander. Place the pot back on the stove over medium heat. Add the butter and melt until foamy. Swirl the pan to check the darkening of the butter, about 1 minute. As soon as the butter turns golden brown, add the pecans and toast for 1 minute. Then add the rosemary and continue to cook, swirling the pan or stirring so the nuts don't burn. As soon as the rosemary is fragrant, add the Brussels sprouts and cherries. Cook until evenly coated and the Brussels sprouts are warmed through. Season with kosher salt and black pepper and serve.

Broccolini reminds me of the broccoli my grandpa used to grow in his garden—the official name for it is Waltham 29. His broccoli always had tender stems, with large florets and lots of green leaves. My Grandma Lillian would steam the broccoli and top it with butter. She almost always just steamed or boiled her vegetables, and sometimes that's all you really need to do to showcase great vegetables. In Italy, you don't typically find al dente vegetables, and I think in this case, a well-cooked piece of broccolini is just right. This is the way I like to cook regular broccoli too!

Lillian's Butter-Steamed Broccolini

Serves 4

4 tablespoons unsalted butter, 2 tablespoons cut into small pieces

Kosher salt

2 or 3 bunches of broccolini (1¼ to 1½ pounds total), stems trimmed

Finely grated zest of ½ lemon

1 tablespoon fresh lemon juice

Fresh cracked black pepper

Heat a large heavy-bottomed saucepan over high heat. Add the uncut 2 tablespoons of butter, along with 1 cup of water and a pinch of salt. Add the broccolini and stir to coat. Dot the remaining butter on the top layer of broccolini, followed by another pinch of salt. Cover and steam the broccolini for 7 to 8 minutes, or until soft. Remove the lid and stir the broccolini. Transfer to a bowl and top with the lemon zest and juice plus a few cracks of black pepper. Serve immediately.

Unlike broccoli or other hearty brassicas, rapini (also known as broccoli rabe) doesn't like an extended hard-core roast because it's very tender to begin with. I've learned this the hard way, essentially by dehydrating my rapini into a crisp! If you don't have time to make the peperonata, roast the rapini with a little chile flake and minced garlic, and finish with a squeeze of lemon.

Barely Roasted Broccoli Rapini

Serves 4

1 large bunch of rapini (broccoli rabe), ends trimmed, cut into 2-inch pieces

1 tablespoon everyday olive oil

Kosher salt

½ cup Peperonata and its oil (page 285)

Preheat the oven to 400°F and line a baking sheet with foil. Place the rapini on the baking sheet and toss with the oil and a few pinches of kosher salt. Roast in the middle of the oven for 10 minutes, tossing halfway through, until the rapini is wilted and the green leaves are just beginning to brown. Transfer to a platter, top with the peperonata, and serve.

Get It

Aged balsamic (six years plus)
is what I recommend using to
drizzle on the finished broccoli,
but if you don't have that, you
can use a standard balsamic too.
Just add a touch of honey to
give it a little more sweetness.

Get It

Super simple, I know, but this recipe is all about great ingredients and showing off their potential. You are probably thinking, "I don't need another roasted broccoli recipe!" However, I promise that this simple dish will be the rave at the table. I trim the broccoli stems so all I'm left with is the sweet interior part. Honestly, I'm obsessed with broccoli stems (and the leaves too . . . don't throw them away!), and I hope you'll love them as much as I do. Serve this broccoli right from the baking sheet and be sure to scrape off the bits of golden baked Parmigiano-Reggiano, which are reminiscent of Italy's famed cheese frico.

Oven-Roasted Broccoli Florets and Stems

Serves 4 to 6

2 bunches of broccoli (about 3 pounds total), tough stems trimmed

2 tablespoons everyday olive oil

Kosher salt

½ cup freshly grated Parmigiano-Reggiano

1 tablespoon aged balsamic vinegar (see Get It Get It)

Fresh cracked black pepper

1. Set the oven rack as close to the heat source as possible and preheat the oven to 425°F. Using a sharp knife, cut the broccoli stalk from the florets; separate the florets. Cut the stalk into 3 sections, then square it off by cutting the peel away. (This helps get to the tender center sections of the stem that are, quite honestly, more delicious than the florets.) Cut the stems into ¼-inch slices. Place the stems and florets in a bowl and toss with the olive oil and a few generous pinches of salt.

2. Lightly oil the baking sheet with everyday olive oil. Arrange the broccoli on the baking sheet and set in the oven near the heat source. Bake for 25 minutes, or until tender and the edges of the broccoli are a little browned.

3. Sprinkle the grated parm on top and place back in the oven for 3 to 4 minutes, or until the cheese is melted and a little golden. Remove from the oven and drizzle with balsamic. Top with fresh cracked black pepper and serve.

All-Purpose Sheet Pan Cooking

For a quick fix, most brassicas just need a toss of olive oil and a dry-roast on a baking sheet in the oven to caramelize and concentrate their flavor. Broccoli gets all crispy and crunchy-fried, and cauliflower becomes irresistibly sweet. Roasted chopped cabbage develops crispy, golden edges! So delicious!

For optimal roasting, cut your vegetables into similar-sized pieces, whether that's small or large. Line a baking sheet with foil (to keep cleaning minimal) and drizzle the vegetables on the sheet with extra-virgin olive oil. Toss with salt. Roast at 425° to 450°F and give the vegetables a stir once during roasting. Take them as far as you want—just keep an eye on them and pull the baking sheet out of the oven when the veggies are roasted the way you like them. You can serve them as is or drizzle with a simple vinaigrette. You can also top them with a crunchy nut topping or sprinkle with grated Parm and a little balsamic.

You can also keep some flavor boosters handy to rub over your veggies before they go in the oven. Some ideas include garlic confit, anchovy paste, or your favorite marinade, like the one I use for my smoky cauliflower on page 101. You could even rub on a mix of Dijon mustard, minced garlic, and bacon fat for a ridiculously delicious punch of flavor.

The root of the word "giardiniera" is *giardino*, which means "garden" in Italian. Giardiniera starts with brining the vegetables in a salt solution, which makes them super crunchy. Then they're pickled—and you can stop right here and just eat these vegetables pickled! But to make this into giardiniera, you then add olive oil, along with whatever else you like, such as capers and olives. You can definitely play around here. Sometimes I'll add carrots, fennel, and peppers and other unique favorites like chopped sun-dried tomatoes, Calabrian chiles, artichoke hearts, and fresh basil. Use this giardiniera as your secret weapon to liven up and add a pop of sweetness/acidity/ spice to your cooking. I love to use it as a condiment on a meat and cheese antipasto board. It's a dream tossed into salads like pasta salad or layered on sandwiches. And guess what? The giardiniera makes a great salad dressing in and of itself: Just pulse it in a food processor. Cauliflower is available in season in striking colors. My favorites are the orange and purple, and these would be gorgeous here. Despite the difference in color, the flavor is the same. I just try to stay away from green vegetables, as their color often turns brownish green.

Pickled Cauliflower Giardiniera

Makes about 4 cups

Brined Vegetables

1 small head of cauliflower (about 1 pound), cut into small florets

2 celery stalks, sliced on a bias about ¼ inch thick (see Get It Get It)

2 red finger chiles, Fresnos, or other fresh chile peppers, sliced into rings

2 tablespoons kosher salt

Pickle

¾ cup distilled white vinegar

½ cup sugar

1 dried bay leaf

1 teaspoon fennel seeds

1 teaspoon coriander seeds

1 teaspoon chile flake

1 teaspoon kosher salt

Giardiniera Marinade

⅓ cup sliced pitted green olives (like Castelvetrano)

2 tablespoons chopped fresh flat-leaf parsley

1 tablespoon drained capers

1 teaspoon dried oregano (preferably wild Calabrian or Greek)

½ cup everyday olive oil

Kosher salt

1. **Brine the vegetables.** In a large bowl, combine the cauliflower, celery, and fresh chile peppers. Toss with the kosher salt and cover with 4 cups of cold water. Refrigerate overnight.

2. **Pickle the vegetables.** The next day, drain the vegetables and tightly pack them into a large heatproof bowl. In a medium saucepot, bring the vinegar, sugar, bay leaf, fennel and coriander seeds, chile flake, salt, and ¾ cup of water to a boil over high heat. Pour the hot pickling liquid over the vegetables to cover. Cover and refrigerate for 2 days.

3. **Marinate the giardiniera.** Drain the pickles, reserving ½ cup of the liquid. Place the pickled vegetables in a medium bowl and toss with the olives, parsley, capers, oregano, and olive oil; season with a pinch of salt. Add the reserved ½ cup of pickling liquid and serve. Marinated giardiniera is best when served within a week and can be stored in an airtight container.

— Get It —

I've said it elsewhere and I'll say it again: I highly recommend lightly peeling your celery for the best texture.

— Get It —

Clockwise from top left: Peperonata (page 285),
Pickled Cauliflower Giardiniera (page 98), Lillian's
Pickled Beets (page 323), Porcini Sott'Olio (page 219),
Oven-Dried Cherry Tomatoes (page 393)

Get It

Spring and knob onions are the sprouting youth of regular onions. In the spring, as the onion bulbs begin to wake and sprout, they start off with small knob-like bulbs with green shoots. As the spring turns to summer, the green part of the onion begins to die, while the bulb in the ground grows into an adult onion. These onions are picked and cellared for fall and winter. Feel free to sub green onions if needed!

To toast seeds, I put them in a small skillet over moderate heat and toast for about 2 minutes, until fragrant, moving the skillet around so they cook evenly.

Get It

Since I'm big on treating cauliflower like meat, it came to me that I should salt-cure and marinate it. Salting cauliflower helps season it throughout and soften it slightly, so when it's grilled it develops a nice char as well as a nice texture: not too soft, not too firm. As I like to say, listen to your vegetables. They want to be treated like something special. You wouldn't think twice about salting or marinating a pork chop or steak, so why not do that for your veggies too? This marinade is smoky, sweet, a little spicy, and fragrant, and so great on cabbage, broccoli, and Brussels sprouts, not to mention how good it is on chicken and pork chops too. Consider making some extra and keeping it in the freezer for your last-minute veggie needs!

Spicy Red Chile Cauliflower

and Spring Onions

Serves 6

2 heads of cauliflower (about 1½ pounds each), cut into large florets

2 tablespoons plus 1 teaspoon kosher salt

2 bunches of spring or knob onions, trimmed, with some of the green stems still attached

6 tablespoons everyday olive oil

⅓ cup chipotle peppers in adobo sauce

2 tablespoons sherry vinegar

2 tablespoons honey, plus a little more for drizzling

2 tablespoons fresh oregano leaves

2 tablespoons coriander seeds, toasted

1 tablespoon fennel seeds, toasted

1 tablespoon pimentón de la Vera (Spanish smoked paprika), plus a few pinches for garnish

1 teaspoon finely grated lemon zest (use a Microplane)

2 tablespoons fresh lemon juice

2 tablespoons chopped fresh flat-leaf parsley

Coarse sea salt (like Maldon)

1.   In a very large bowl, toss the cauliflower with 2 tablespoons of salt. Transfer it to a colander and let sit for 1 hour.

2.   Slice 1 cup of spring onions and add to a blender or food processor. Reserve the remaining whole spring onions to grill. To the blender, add the olive oil, chipotles, sherry vinegar, honey, oregano, coriander and fennel seeds, pimentón, lemon zest, and the remaining 1 teaspoon of salt. Blend until smooth. (The marinade can be refrigerated in an airtight container for 2 days.)

3.   Shake the colander to knock off any excess salt or water from the cauliflower. Transfer the cauliflower and marinade to a gallon-sized resealable plastic bag and toss. (You can also use a large bowl.) Refrigerate for 2 hours or overnight.

4.   Preheat a grill to high for 10 minutes. (A charcoal grill gives the cauliflower the best char and flavor.) Place the cauliflower on the grill, cover, and cook, turning the cauliflower every 5 minutes, until charred all over, 20 to 25 minutes total. Place the spring onions on the grill about halfway through cooking the cauliflower. If you don't have a grill, I recommend roasting the marinated cauliflower and spring onions in a 425°F oven for 30 minutes, or until tender and golden brown.

5.   Transfer the cauliflower to a mixing bowl. Transfer the grilled onions to a cutting board and slice; add to the cauliflower. Toss with the lemon juice, chopped parsley, and a pinch or two of coarse sea salt. Transfer to a serving bowl and garnish a dusting of more pimentón and a drizzle of honey. Serve.

Are you looking for a rich and decadent showstopper for fall or winter? Look no further. I love making this white lasagna when cauliflower and grapes are in season. The roasted grapes act a lot like tomatoes, adding brightness and acidity. Roasted cauliflower also adds another layer of irresistible flavor here. I know this is a project, but you can spread the work out a bit. The besciamella can be made a day ahead and refrigerated. The fresh pasta can also be made ahead of time. And the dish can be assembled the night before to be baked the next day (just make sure to let it sit at room temperature for 1 hour before baking). Of course, if you want, you can use fully cooked dry lasagna sheets too, but I encourage you to take the time to make it fresh. There is something magical about thin fresh pasta, which is tender and soft with irresistible crunchy edges.

Lasagna Bianca

with Roasted Cauliflower, Blistered Grapes, and Toasted Almonds

Serves 8

3 tablespoons everyday olive oil, plus more for greasing

2 large bunches of red seedless grapes (about 2 pounds total), washed and removed from the stem

Kosher salt

2 large heads of cauliflower (about 4 pounds total), trimmed and cut into equal-sized florets (large florets cut in half lengthwise; use a mix of colored cauliflower, if you can)

2 tablespoons lightly chopped fresh rosemary leaves (see Get It Get It), plus sprigs for garnish

Parm Besciamella (recipe follows)

Fresh Pasta Sheets (page 259) or 1½ pounds store-bought fresh pasta sheets, blanched

2 cups shredded Gruyère cheese

½ cup freshly grated Parmigiano-Reggiano

¼ cup slivered almonds, toasted

1. Adjust the oven rack so it's 3 inches from the heat source and turn the broiler to high. Line a baking sheet with foil and lightly grease it with oil. In a large mixing bowl, toss the grapes with 1 tablespoon of olive oil and a few pinches of salt. Spread the grapes on the prepared baking sheet. Broil for 20 to 25 minutes, checking every 5 minutes or so. The grapes will begin to split and shrivel and their juices will collect on the sheet. In some areas, the juice might reduce and darken in color. (This is okay—the flavor of the grapes and their juices is concentrating.) You want the grapes to be slightly charred and blistered and the juices slightly reduced, darkened, and almost syrup-like. Remove from the oven and turn the oven temperature to 425°F. Let the grapes cool for 20 minutes.

2. Using a spatula, gently scrape the grapes and their juices into a small mixing bowl. You should have about 1½ cups of blistered grapes.

3. While the grapes are cooling, in a large bowl, toss the cauliflower with the remaining 2 tablespoons of olive oil and a few generous pinches of salt. Divide the cauliflower onto two foil-lined baking sheets and roast for 20 minutes; rotate the pans and roast for another 20 minutes, or until the cauliflower is tender, crisped, and caramelized. Remove from the oven and turn the oven temperature down to 300°F. Toss the cauliflower with the chopped rosemary while still hot. Allow to cool.

4. Lightly oil a 9 by 13-inch casserole dish. Using a spatula, spread roughly ½ cup of besciamella evenly in the dish. Add one layer of pasta sheets; feel free to cut a few sheets to match the size needed to complete the layer. For the next four layers, spread roughly ½ cup besciamella, followed by 1 cup of cauliflower, ¼ cup of grapes, and about ⅓ cup of Gruyère; top each layer with pasta. For the final layer (which is the top),

Parm Besciamella

My grandma always served (insert vegetable here) in a white sauce. I know that hers was much simpler, made with just butter, flour, and milk, but it still created my deep fondness for veggies in a white sauce. If you're the same, this besciamella is a great recipe for you! I would just cut the recipe by half, giving you a little over 2 cups of sauce for your veggie eating.

Makes about 5 cups

4 tablespoons unsalted butter

4 tablespoons all-purpose flour

1 medium shallot, minced

1 dried bay leaf

1 quart whole milk

1 cup heavy cream

Kosher salt

1 cup freshly grated Parmigiano-
    Reggiano

A few pinches of ground nutmeg

1.   In a medium saucepot set over medium heat, melt the butter. Slowly stir in the flour, then whisk until combined and slightly foamy. Add the shallot and bay leaf and cook for another minute, or until the shallot begins to sweat. Slowly whisk in the milk, cream, and a few generous pinches of salt. Allow the mixture to come up to a simmer, whisking often, about 10 minutes. (Be sure to whisk the bottom and corners of the pan to ensure that the milk isn't sticking.) The mixture should acquire a thick, sauce-like consistency. I like to test the sauce texture with a spoon: Dip a spoon into the sauce and look at how it coats the back of the spoon. If it runs off, it needs to cook longer, but if it sticks to the spoon with a nice even coat, then it is ready. Discard the bay leaf.

2.   Remove the besciamella from the heat and add the parm and nutmeg. Whisk continuously until the cheese is melted. Transfer the sauce to a mixing bowl and cover the surface directly with a sheet of plastic wrap to prevent a skin from forming. Your besciamella is ready for the lasagna.

Get It

Sometimes if your knife isn't sharp enough, you can wind up bruising instead of cleanly chopping your rosemary, which can make the rosemary taste bitter. Try to use a sharp knife, or just opt to chop instead of mince your rosemary to avoid the bitter result.

Get It

add the remaining besciamella, cauliflower, grapes, Gruyère, and the ½ cup of grated parm. (You will have a total of 5 layers of pasta.)

5.   Bake the lasagna for 1 hour to 1 hour and 15 minutes, until the top of the lasagna starts to brown. Remove from the oven and nestle the rosemary sprigs on top. Place back in the oven for 15 to 20 minutes, until toasty and golden. Let rest for 25 minutes before serving. Garnish with toasted slivered almonds.

Get It

If you're short on time, you can always cut the Romanesco in half. Place it cut side down in the baking dish and add ¾ cup of water. Roast for 20 to 25 minutes, until tender when pierced with a knife.

Get It

Beautiful Romanesco, a proud member of the brassicas, is sometimes called Romanesco
cauliflower and at other times Romanesco broccoli. I tend to cook and treat Romanesco
like I would cauliflower, but it's its own vegetable, with a distinct spiky texture and light
green color. I am mesmerized by the geometry of this incredible vegetable! Roasting and
presenting this whole shows off the shape of the Romanesco, and it also gives it a wonderfully
caramelized exterior. If you can't find Romanesco, feel free to substitute cauliflower.
When I was creating this dish, I was thinking of the Romans eating their vegetables
with garlic and anchovies, which is just so freakin' delish and flavorful. Slow-roasting
the garlic and anchovies creates a super-savory umami-rich schmear. I promise you
the anchovies are not at all fishy and a game changer when it comes to flavor.

Whole Roasted Romanesco

with Garlic-Anchovy Confit

Serves 4

Garlic-Anchovy Confit

8 garlic cloves, peeled
  (about ¼ cup)

6 oil-packed brown anchovy fillets

1 tablespoon everyday olive oil

Romanesco

1 head of Romanesco cauliflower

Kosher salt

2 tablespoons everyday olive oil

⅓ cup plain dry breadcrumbs
  (from Italian-style bread)

2 tablespoons freshly grated
  Parmigiano-Reggiano

Finely grated zest of 1 medium
  lemon (about 2 teaspoons; use a
  Microplane, and save the zested
  lemon for juicing)

2 tablespoons chopped fresh flat-
  leaf parsley

Super-special extra-virgin olive oil,
  for drizzling

1. **Make the garlic-anchovy confit.** Preheat the oven to 350°F. Lay two
10-inch square sheets of foil on top of one another. In the center of the foil,
combine the garlic cloves, anchovies, and 1 tablespoon of olive oil. Bring
the edges of the foil together to form a little pouch. Bake directly on the
oven rack for 20 minutes, or until the garlic is tender. Scrape the mixture
into a food processor and blend to combine.

2. **Make the Romanesco.** Increase the oven temperature to 425°F. Trim
the bottom of the Romanesco so that it sits flat, keeping some of the leaves
attached. Using a paring knife, pierce the Romanesco all over 6 to 8 times
for the most even cooking. Set the Romanesco into a small baking dish
or round pie dish. Rub with the garlic-anchovy confit and season with a
few pinches of salt. Lightly tent the Romanesco with foil, add ¾ cup water
to the dish—this allows the Romanesco to steam and roast at the same
time—and roast until golden, 40 to 45 minutes.

3. Meanwhile, in a medium bowl, combine the everyday olive oil,
breadcrumbs, parm, lemon zest, and parsley. Remove the Romanesco from
the oven and top with the breadcrumb mixture, allowing some of the
breadcrumbs to spill over into the dish. (The bits that fall off get all crispy
as they cook, which is one of my favorite parts of this dish!) Roast for
another 15 minutes, or until the breadcrumbs are golden brown. To serve,
squeeze fresh lemon juice and a drizzle of super-special olive oil on top and
carve into four wedges.

This is an old family recipe from my grandmother's mother, Emma. My grandmother, Lillian, taught me this recipe, and I have fondly named it after her. Of course, she didn't make it with allspice, aged balsamic, or Parmigiano, but the roots of the dish—cabbage, saltines, onion—are straight from the original. Funny enough, this is such a modern approach to cooking a vegetable. Stuffing it whole is an old technique that fell out of style but now seems new and modern, maybe because of the no-waste movement championing use of the whole vegetable. Whenever anyone sees this whole cabbage beauty, they are like, "Wow, that is such an innovative approach to cabbage!" You ask, "What does cabbage want?" It wants to be stuffed with itself and presented whole! This is definitely a favorite of mine for a holiday table, because it's such a wow dish.

Lillian's Whole Stuffed Cabbage

Serves 8

Kosher salt

2 small heads of savoy cabbage (roughly 1½ pounds per head)

1½ sticks unsalted butter, 4 tablespoons (½ stick) diced

1 medium onion, halved lengthwise, then thinly sliced crosswise

1 tablespoon fresh thyme leaves

1 tablespoon chopped fresh flat-leaf parsley

½ teaspoon fresh cracked black pepper

2 pinches of ground allspice (optional)

1 sleeve (4 ounces) Premium Saltine crackers, crushed

½ cup plus 2 tablespoons freshly grated Parmigiano-Reggiano

2 large eggs

2 fresh rosemary sprigs

2 tablespoons aged balsamic vinegar

1. Bring a large pot of generously salted water to a boil. This is blanching water (see page 10), and I like mine to be salty like the ocean, about 1 tablespoon of salt per quart of water. Meanwhile, using a sharp knife, remove the bottom core and stem of each cabbage. Gently peel away the outer cabbage leaves from each cabbage until you have 10 to 12 leaves total. (I use a paring knife to separate the leaves from the head of the cabbage.) Quickly rinse if there is dirt in the leaves. Set the leaves aside.

2. Fill a large bowl with ice water. Add the cabbage leaves to the boiling water and blanch for 2 to 3 minutes, until softened and pliable. Remove the leaves and submerge them in the ice bath to stop them from cooking further. (Don't empty the pot of water.) Drain the leaves and transfer them to a cutting board. Using a paring knife, shave away the thick core/stem section of the cabbage leaves so that it is the same thickness as the leaves. Place on a platter or baking sheet.

3. Thinly shred the remaining cabbage hearts; you should have about 6 cups. In a large saucepan set over medium-high heat, melt the 1 stick of the butter. Add the onion and cook until translucent, about 2 minutes. Add the shredded cabbage, season with salt, and cook until the cabbage is softened, about 10 minutes. Add the thyme, parsley, black pepper, and allspice, if using. Transfer to a large mixing bowl. Add the cracker crumbs, ½ cup of the parm, and the eggs and mix gently until combined; do not overmix. (I like to see different-sized cracker crumbs in the mixture.)

4. Line a medium (cabbage-sized) mixing bowl with a lint-free linen towel or cheesecloth. Begin layering the darker green cabbage leaves in the bottom of the bowl, positioning them so they drape over the rim. (I like to

recipe continues

start with the greener leaves on the bottom, as this will be the presentation side of the cabbage.) Continue layering all the leaves so they hang halfway over the top of the bowl.

5.   Place the cabbage-saltine filling in the center of the bowl, pressing down and shaping it into a ball. Then begin folding the leaves over the top of the filling, working up and around the filling to cover. (It should begin to look like a whole cabbage.) Lift up the sides of the towel and twist the towel, squeezing it and tying it into a knot, shaping the cabbage so it's round.

6.   Return the pot of blanching water to high heat and bring to a boil. Place the tied cabbage in the water and boil for 15 minutes. Using tongs, remove the cabbage from the water and allow to cool for 5 minutes. I like to tie the towel to a large wooden spoon or dowel so it's easier to lift the cabbage from the boiling water, but don't worry—tongs work well too!

7.   Preheat the oven to 350°F. In a round baking dish, cast-iron skillet, or 9 by 13-inch baking dish, place the diced butter. Untie the cabbage and place it seam side down in the pan. Bake for 30 minutes or until the cabbage and butter begin to brown and turn golden. Remove from the oven and add the rosemary sprigs to the butter. Sprinkle the top of the cabbage with the remaining parm and spoon the browned butter from the pan over the top. To serve, slice the cabbage in half and then into wedges similar to a pie; drizzle with the balsamic.

Quick Sauerkraut

Have you ever bought a head of green cabbage and realized just how much cabbage that is? Here's a great way to use that cabbage, and it makes an excellent accompaniment to fish or pork, or even hot dogs and sausages! Shred your cabbage and transfer it to a colander. Salt it lightly and let it drain; you're purging it of some excess moisture, like you do with eggplant. Once that's done, in a medium skillet, sweat a chopped onion in some butter, then add the cabbage and cook to soften it. Hit it with some rice vinegar or white wine vinegar and season with spices like caraway, fennel, and coriander seeds. (For a more Germanic flavor, try caraway, dried mustard, and a pinch of cayenne.) Eat the sauerkraut warm, or try it chilled. This keeps for 4 to 5 days in an airtight container stored in the refrigerator.

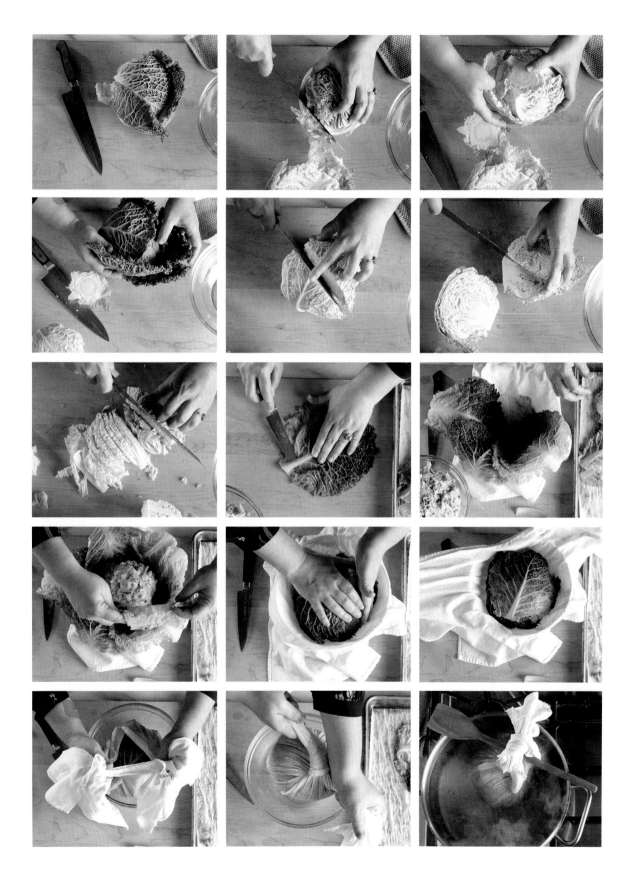

Corn

Eating corn on the cob is as about American as it can get. I love when summer comes because all I do is grill the ears in their husks until they're a little charred, then schmear them with some sweet butter and kosher salt. Corn is actually a New World crop, so fresh sweet corn is not a common vegetable for Italians. In Italy, most of the corn you see is dried, which is milled and then cooked for polenta. But living here in the Midwest, we have fresh corn for days. Even if it's not traditional, I have learned to embrace fresh sweet corn and incorporate it into my Italian cooking, but sometimes I can hear Chef Tony Mantuano telling me that there is no sweet corn in Italian cooking! He might be right, but I can't resist including it in dishes like grilled corn and cucumber salad (page 120), and corzetti pasta with sweet corn, shrimp, and herbs (page 126), both which scream SUMMER!

When buying fresh corn, pull the husks back slightly to make sure the corn is fresh with plump kernels. You also want the ears to feel heavy so you know there's tons of milky corn juices in there. You can keep fresh corn in the husk in the fridge for up to a week, but I find it rarely takes me more than a day to eat it up! I am passionate about my method for scraping fresh corn, so please check out how to do that on page 118.

In this chapter, I also include recipes using dried corn staples. There are two types of dried corn: Dent (so called because of the dent on the top of the kernels) is used for making cornmeal and grits. Flint, which is multicolored and very hard, is what's typically used to make polenta. Industrial polenta is made when corn is dried with fans and heat, then ground. Artisanal polenta, on the other hand, is made from corn dried on the stalk through winter, so it retains amazing flavor. I urge you to seek out well-made polenta. For more on this, see page 129.

Polenta is a great pot of deliciousness that you can easily multiply when feeding a small army. I often eat polenta with a hearty ragù spooned on top, or mixed with roasted vegetables, just like a pasta. Please have fun with polenta—it's a great base for so many delicious veggies, herbs, and cheese.

Corn and butter are the best of friends! Corn is also the "butter" of the vegetable world, bringing sweetness and creaminess to many dishes.

Calabrian Chile Cornbread with Whipped Goat Cheese Butter (page 117), Sweet Corn Caesar Salad (page 122), Oven-Steamed Corn on the Cob with Roasted Garlic–Porcini Butter (page 116), Polenta-Filled Tortelloni with Sweet Corn, Bacon, and Hatch Green Chiles (page 130)

One summer weekend a few years back, my good friend Chef Ashley Christensen showed up for the weekend with a cooler full of goodies from her restaurant, including a tub of porcini butter and another one of roasted garlic butter. After tasting both, I decided to combine the two into one dynamite, delicious, Ashley-approved butter that now is a staple on my summer corn! This roasted garlic–porcini butter is *fantastic*. It has such beautiful earthy notes and is the ultimate umami bomb. The butter would be great tossed with fresh tagliatelle, spread on warm bread, and used to top meats and fish. It will amp up the flavor on just about any savory dish that calls for butter! I love this method of roasting corn in the husk in the oven. Not only is it ideal for folks who don't have a grill, but cooking corn in the husks seals in the best flavor. Another bonus: The smell of the roasted husk while you're eating the corn just adds to the overall magic of enjoying sweet summer corn at its best.

Oven-Steamed Corn on the Cob

with Roasted Garlic–Porcini Butter

Serves 6

8 garlic cloves, peeled

1 tablespoon everyday olive oil

½ ounce dried porcini mushrooms (about ½ cup)

2 sticks unsalted butter (preferably European-style), at room temperature

½ cup freshly grated Parmigiano-Reggiano (use a Microplane), plus a little more for garnish

Kosher salt

6 to 8 large, plump ears of sweet corn, in the husk

1.   Preheat the oven to 350°F. Lay two 10-inch square sheets of foil on top of one another. In the center of the foil, combine the garlic and olive oil. Bring the edges of the foil together to form a little pouch. Bake directly on the oven rack for 20 minutes, or until the garlic is tender. Remove from the oven and allow to cool a little. Increase the oven temperature to 400°F.

2.   Meanwhile, in a coffee or spice grinder or blender, grind the porcini at high speed into a fine powder. Scrape into a food processor.

3.   Add the garlic, softened butter, parm, and a few pinches of kosher salt and blend to combine. Transfer the butter to a small bowl. The butter can be refrigerated in an airtight container for up to a week. (Be sure to pull it out of the fridge to soften before serving.)

4.   Place the corn ears in their husks directly on the oven rack. Roast for 30 minutes, until the husks have darkened and the corn kernels are tender. (They steam inside their husks.) At this point, you can turn the oven off and keep the corn warm until you are ready to serve it.

5.   To serve, peel back the corn husks, pulling them down to create a handle. Using kitchen shears, cut off the tops of husks, leaving 4 to 5 inches attached to the cob. Remove the corn silk. Schmear some porcini butter all over the hot corn, garnish with a little more parm, and serve extra porcini butter on the side for more schmearing!

Get It

This is one of those times when it's really great to use a Microplane for the parm. The fluffy, fine shreds of cheese melt just enough and help the butter adhere to the corn instead of sliding right off the kernels.

Get It

Listen to Your Vegetables

I know lots of people like their cornbread sweet, but I prefer a savory version like this one. The beautiful thing about cornbread is that it's such a good starting point for additional flavors. I like adding shredded cheddar cheese or crispy chopped bacon to the batter, or I cook 1 cup of corn kernels with the onions. I also love the crunchy texture that coarse cornmeal brings to the table, but this flexible cornbread can be made with finely ground corn meal too, which yields a more cake-like crumb. I sometimes like making my cornbread with a mix of half coarse and half fine cornmeal. Feel free to play around with the texture! No matter how the cornbread comes together, my favorite way to eat cornbread is the next morning for breakfast, toasted crunchy in the oven and spread with a little softened butter and honey! I grew up eating cornbread dressing, and this is a great basic cornbread for dressing.

Calabrian Chile Cornbread

with Whipped Goat Cheese Butter

Serves 6 to 8

1 stick unsalted butter

1 medium onion, finely chopped

2 tablespoons Calabrian chile paste, sambal oelek, or chopped fresh hot chile peppers (optional)

4 cups coarsely ground cornmeal

3 cups buttermilk (preferably organic or whole milk)

2 large eggs

1 teaspoon baking soda

1 teaspoon baking powder

3 teaspoons kosher salt

2 tablespoons lard or high-heat cooking oil

Whipped Goat Cheese Butter (recipe follows), for serving

1. Preheat the oven to 450°F. Place a 10- to 12-inch cast-iron skillet inside to heat up. In a small pot, melt the butter over medium heat. Cook the onion until translucent, about 5 minutes. Remove from the heat and add the Calabrian chile paste.

2. In a large bowl, whisk the cornmeal, buttermilk, eggs, baking soda, baking powder, and salt. Whisk in the onion mixture. Very carefully remove the hot skillet from the oven and add the lard, swirling it around the pan to coat. Pour the batter into the skillet and place it back in the oven. Bake for 20 minutes, or until a toothpick inserted in the center comes out clean.

3. Let the bread cool in the skillet for 5 minutes, then flip it out onto a cutting board. Serve warm with goat cheese butter, or transfer to a rack to cool for later. The cornbread can be kept at room temp for 2 days or refrigerated for up to 1 week.

Whipped Goat Cheese Butter

This creamy, tangy goat cheese butter cools off the spice in the cornbread.

Makes about 1 cup

4 tablespoons unsalted butter, softened

4 ounces fresh goat cheese, softened

Kosher salt

Place the butter and goat cheese in a food processor and process until smooth; add a pinch of salt. Transfer the butter to a serving bowl. The butter can be refrigerated in an airtight container for 2 days; let stand at room temperature for 20 minutes before serving.

Get It

I search out local farmers' markets for fresh heirloom cornmeal and grits. This is a great way to add a unique and amplified corn flavor to your cooking while using non-GMO heirloom varieties of corn and supporting your local farmers. Anson Mills is another great source for freshly milled cornmeal products!

Get It

This dish is about as easy as it gets. It's a fantastic side dish at Thanksgiving, but also makes a great accompaniment to shrimp (à la shrimp and grits). You can play around a lot with this, changing up the herbs or cheese, perhaps, or including bacon or hot chiles. Have fun with it!

My Oma's Creamed Scraped Corn

Serves 4

4 tablespoons unsalted butter

1 large garlic clove, finely grated

4 cups scraped corn (see box below)

Kosher salt

½ cup freshly grated Pecorino Romano or Parmigiano-Reggiano, plus a bit more for serving (use a Microplane)

Fresh cracked black pepper

1 fresh rosemary sprig, plus a few leaves for garnish

In a medium saucepan, melt the butter over medium heat. Add the garlic and let it sweat and sizzle for 1 minute, until just barely golden. Add the scraped sweet corn, 2 tablespoons of water, and a few pinches of salt and cook until the mixture begins to bubble, about 5 minutes. Stir in the grated pecorino and some black pepper, then add the rosemary and remove from the heat; let stand for 2 minutes. Remove the rosemary sprig. To serve, top with a bit more pecorino, a few rosemary leaves, and more cracked black pepper.

How to Scrape Corn

My Oma always made scraped corn, which was a staple of the Thanksgiving table alongside mashed potatoes and gravy. We loved making a well in our potatoes, filling it with scraped corn, then topping it with gravy. I figured scraped corn was a pretty common thing, but I discovered over the years that most people just cut the corn from the cobs and leave it at that. They're missing out, because scraping the corn ekes out every single bit of deliciousness from the cob, while leaving the corn pith on the cob and not in your milky sweet corn. The trick is to start by shaving the kernels off the cob, not too much or too deep. Then you use the back of your knife to scrape away every little last bit from the kernels on the cob. You'll see a big difference when you cut corn this way because you're getting all of the additional juices and milky starch that typically gets left behind and is loaded with amazing flavor. Be sure to save your cobs for making corn stock (see page 125).

Shuck 6 or 7 ears of fresh sweet corn, removing all of the silks. Place a large mixing bowl on the counter and set a smaller inverted bowl in the center of the large bowl. (The larger bowl collects the kernels and their milk.) Place an ear of corn stem end down on the smaller bowl, and using a sharp serrated or chef's knife, begin shaving the kernels from the cob. It's important to literally shave the kernels, even though you might feel like you are leaving too much corn on the cob. In essence, try not to cut the corn kernels deep into the cob, shaving just half of the kernel. This is absolutely what you should be doing, because next you will scrape the cobs to get at the remaining tender, milky corn germ, aka little corn vittles. Holding the cob firmly in one hand, use the back side of your knife (not the sharp blade) to shave and scrape down the length of the cob, pressing firmly to remove all of the goodness left on the cob. This makes about 4 cups of milky, sweet, delicious corn.

Note: Fresh scraped corn needs to be cooked or eaten within a day or two. Its high sugar content means it is prone to fermentation.

This recipe is not super Italian, I know, but it's freakin' amazing and I think corn wants this recipe in the book, so here it is. Despite my dry-grill rule for most veggies, I do like oiling corn for the grill because it helps char the kernels for the best roasty flavor. Just don't be afraid of the pop you might hear. The corn can also be broiled if you don't have a grill. Don't skip the dandelion greens, which add a nice bitterness that balances the sweet corn and refreshing salsa verde. I love this salad with avocado or grilled shrimp. It's a perfect match! Also, if you want, you can garnish this with fried shallots, chopped peanuts, or cherry tomatoes.

Grilled Corn Salad

with Dandelion Greens, Cucumber, and Cilantro Salsa Verde

Serves 4

1 English cucumber, peeled, quartered lengthwise, and cut into ½-inch pieces

Kosher salt

2 tablespoons everyday olive oil

5 or 6 large ears of corn, husks and silks removed

1 bunch of dandelion greens or other bitter greens, washed and chopped (about 4 cups)

Cilantro Salsa Verde, aka green sauce (recipe follows)

1. In a colander, toss the cucumber with 1 teaspoon of kosher salt. Drain for 30 minutes to an hour. (This helps crisp the cucumber.)

2. Meanwhile, preheat a grill to high (500° to 600°F). Drizzle the olive oil over the corn ears and season with a bit of kosher salt. Place the corn directly on the grill grates and cover the grill. Grill for 10 minutes or so, turning the corn every 2 to 3 minutes, allowing some of the kernels to char; you even might hear a few pop. Remove the corn from the grill and let cool for 5 minutes or so, until you can handle it. Using a chef's knife, scrape the corn from the cob, getting all the little nuggets (see page 118).

3. In a large mixing bowl or salad bowl, combine the corn with the drained cucumber and the dandelion greens. Toss with 1 to 1½ cups of salsa verde, and season with a pinch or two of salt if needed. Serve immediately. (This salad will collect a bit of water in the bottom from the salsa verde, but it is super delicious.) The undressed salad can be refrigerated overnight and dressed right before serving.

— Get It —

The level of spice here is up to you, but I recommend going a little bit on the spicier end of things with this salsa verde. Cut the serrano and give it a sniff. If it smells grassy, you can leave the seeds in, but if it smells very spicy, you might want to take some of the seeds out.

I like using turbinado sugar for flavor, as this salsa is typically made with palm sugar. White sugar can be used if that's what you have.

— Get It —

Cilantro Salsa Verde

This cilantro salsa verde is inspired by a recipe for nam jim given to me by Chefs Nick Wong and Chris Shepherd, a Thai green chile sauce that's a freakin' delicious flavor bomb! It's a staple in my kitchen, and I love it so much that I wanted to include it here. My take is more of an inspired version versus traditional, as it's made in a food processor and with more tomatillo. Chris and Nick's nam jim is made with palm sugar and blended smooth. I love to use colatura, which is a bit milder than Asian fish sauce, but I like both equally. My friends go crazy for it, and we now just fondly call it "green sauce." I love it on all grilled veggies, seafood, and rice.

Makes a little over 2 cups

- 1 pound tomatillos, husks removed, tomatillos quartered
- 2 garlic cloves, roughly chopped
- 1 bunch of fresh cilantro, chopped (1½ cups)
- 1 or 2 serrano chiles, stemmed and roughly chopped (see Get It Get It)
- 1 tablespoon finely grated lime zest (use a Microplane)
- ¼ cup fresh lime juice
- 1 tablespoon plus 1 teaspoon turbinado sugar (preferably Sugar in the Raw; see Get It Get It)
- 3 tablespoons colatura or 2 tablespoons Vietnamese fish sauce
- 3 or 4 pinches of coarse sea salt (like Maldon)

In a food processor, combine all of the ingredients. Process for about a minute to combine and chop into a smooth sauce. The salsa verde can be refrigerated in an airtight container for up to 5 days. The sauce will be vibrant green when you make it, but as it sits, the lime begins to "cook" the cilantro and the color will change a bit; it'll still taste great.

It's hard to improve on a great Caesar salad, but it's always fun to put a new spin on it that's just as tasty as the original. This twist on the classic adds a nice sweetness to the robust garlicky salad, highlighting sweet and creamy nuggets of corn, both in the dressing and in the salad itself. I love a Caesar and I like it cold . . . ice cold, so it's crispy and refreshing. I recommend you clean your lettuce and shock the leaves in very cold water, then drain and dry them well.

Sweet Corn Caesar Salad

Serves 6

2 to 2½ cups Italian-style bread, cut into large cubes (1 inch-ish)

2 teaspoons everyday olive oil

1 garlic clove, smashed and roughly chopped

3 ears of sweet corn, cut and scraped (see page 118); reserve ½ cup for the dressing

Sweet Corn Caesar Dressing (recipe follows)

½ cup freshly grated Parmigiano-Reggiano

Coarse sea salt (like Maldon)

Fresh cracked black pepper

2 heads of romaine lettuce, cut into bite-sized pieces (see Get It Get It)

Super-special extra-virgin olive oil, for drizzling

1.   Preheat the oven to 375°F. In a gallon-sized plastic bag, combine the bread cubes with the 2 teaspoons of olive oil and the chopped garlic. Seal the bag and shake the bread cubes well to evenly coat them with the oil and garlic. Transfer to a foil-lined baking sheet and toast in the oven until golden and super crunchy, 15 to 20 minutes. Let the croutons cool.

2.   In a large salad bowl (ideally a wooden one), toss the corn with half of the dressing and ¼ cup of the grated parm. Season with a few pinches of sea salt and some black pepper. Fold in the lettuce and toss. Add a bit more dressing so the salad is evenly dressed. Top with the croutons and the remaining ¼ cup of parm. Drizzle with super-special extra-virgin olive oil and (if you're like me) add lots of fresh black pepper.

Get It

This recipe also works well with the romaine cut into four wedges, topped with the corn and dollops of the dressing. If you have a block of Parmigiano-Reggiano in the fridge, garnish the salad with a few shaves of parm in place of more grated.

I love the raw corn in the salad, and I make it all summer. If I'm grilling outdoors and feeling like I want to change things up, I like to turn this into a grilled Caesar. Grill the ears in the husks, then shuck, cut, and scrape. Cut the romaine lettuce into

four wedges and quickly grill. It's also nice to keep the corn game strong and toast some leftover cornbread for a crumble or croutons.

Get It

Sweet Corn Caesar Dressing

*I love the creamy sweetness that corn adds to this dressing, allowing
me to boost the umami-ness with anchovy and miso.*

Makes about 1 cup

1 large garlic clove

½ teaspoon kosher salt

2 large egg yolks

½ cup fresh scraped corn
(reserved from the salad)

½ cup freshly grated Parmigiano-
Reggiano

2 tablespoons white miso

2 oil-packed anchovy fillets

2 tablespoons fresh lemon juice

1 tablespoon Worcestershire sauce

1 tablespoon Dijon mustard

1 tablespoon red wine vinegar

Coarse sea salt (like Maldon)

¼ cup everyday olive oil

Fresh cracked black pepper

Tabasco sauce

In a small mortar, using a pestle, or on your cutting board, smash the
garlic with the kosher salt. In a food processor, combine the egg yolks
with the smashed garlic, corn, grated parm, miso, anchovies, lemon juice,
Worcestershire, Dijon, and vinegar. Season with a few pinches of sea salt and
pulse to combine. With the processor running, drizzle in the olive oil. Add
several cracks of black pepper and 6 to 8 dashes of Tabasco. Taste and adjust
with a bit more salt and pepper, if needed. The dressing can be refrigerated
overnight in an airtight container. Due to the sweetness of the raw corn, it
can begin to ferment in a few days.

Succotash is a decidedly American dish, first introduced to colonists by seventeenth-century Indigenous Americans. It's the quintessential use of the three sister crops of corn, beans, and squash, which not only grow harmoniously but taste sublime when combined on the plate. I think of succotash as summer in a bowl. When it's properly layered with seasoning and each vegetable is thoughtfully added and cooked, the dish melds into an amazing fresh vegetable summer stew. It's superb eaten hot or cold and makes a great main or side dish. Consider doubling up on the corn at the table and serving this with the Soft Polenta with Crème Fraîche and Parm on page 128.

Sweet Corn Summer Vegetable Succotash

Serves 6

4 large, plump ears of corn, cut and scraped, cobs reserved (see page 118)

½ cup heavy cream

2 tablespoons unsalted butter

½ large red onion, diced

Kosher salt

2 medium yellow summer squash, quartered lengthwise and cut into ½- to 1-inch pieces

2 large heirloom tomatoes, chopped (about 4 cups)

12 ounces (about 1½ cups) fresh shelly beans (like limas, cranberry beans, lady peas, or black-eyed peas; see Get It Get It)

8 ounces green beans, trimmed and cut into 1-inch pieces

2 tablespoons fresh thyme leaves

½ cup freshly grated Parmigiano-Reggiano, plus more for garnish (use a Microplane)

Finely grated zest of 1 lemon (use a Microplane; about 2 teaspoons)

Fresh cracked black pepper

1 tablespoon thinly sliced fresh chives

1. Cut or snap the cleaned corn cobs in half and place in a medium saucepot. Cover with 5 cups of cold water and the cream and bring to a boil. Boil for 20 to 25 minutes, until the liquid is reduced by two-thirds; remove the corn cobs and discard. You should have 2 to 2½ cups of corn stock.

2. In a large skillet or saucepan, melt the butter over medium-high heat. Add the onion and a pinch of salt and sweat until translucent, about 2 minutes. Add the squash and sweat until softened, 2 to 3 minutes. Season again with a few pinches of salt. Add the tomatoes and cook until they break down and reduce, about 5 minutes. Add the corn and sweat until it softens slightly, about 3 minutes. Season with another pinch of kosher salt. Add the shelly beans and corn stock and simmer rapidly for 8 minutes, allowing the mixture to stew together, reduce, and meld.

3. Add the green beans and thyme and cook for a few more minutes so the beans cook slightly but retain their crunch and bright green color. Remove from the heat. Stir in the parm and lemon zest and season with a few more pinches of salt and lots of fresh cracked black pepper. Garnish with a sprinkle of parm, more black pepper, and the chives.

Get It

If you are using green lima beans, add them with the green beans, as they cook very fast and you want them to retain their beautiful green color.

This dish is amazingly versatile, so here are some thoughts on swaps and additions:

✤ If you have access to lemon thyme, I highly recommend using it! It is a beautiful, hearty herb to add to this dish as well as to your herb garden.

✤ If you can't get fresh shelly beans, you can use frozen beans, or you can cook dried black-eyed peas and use them here too.

Get It

I love shrimp and corn; they are truly a perfect match. I don't know how often people think about coordinating their pasta dishes, but corzetti (flat rounds of pasta imprinted with a stamp) hold on to the kernels so well, and the little rounds of green beans mimic the shape of the corn and corzetti. It might be a geeky chef thing, but I totally enjoy the way that happens! This dish would also be very good with thinner ribbon shapes, like tagliolini or tagliatelle. A dry pasta (for ease) would be great too; try paccheri, penne, or linguine.

Sweet Corn and Shrimp Corzetti Pasta

with Fresh Herbs

Serves 4

4 ears of corn, husked and scraped (see page 118), cobs reserved for the stock

3 tablespoons everyday olive oil

1 pound medium wild-caught shrimp, peeled and deveined, shells reserved for the stock

2 dried bay leaves

1 cup dry white wine

Kosher salt

2 garlic cloves, thinly sliced

2 or 3 pinches of chile flake

2 cups diced heirloom tomatoes (2 medium tomatoes)

Corzetti Pasta Coins (page 260)

1 heaping cup thinly sliced fresh green beans (sliced into rounds)

4 tablespoons unsalted butter

½ cup freshly grated Parmigiano-Reggiano, plus a bit more for finishing

2 tablespoons fresh thyme leaves

2 tablespoons roughly chopped fresh flat-leaf parsley

½ cup fresh basil leaves, plus a few handfuls for garnish

Fresh cracked black pepper

1. Cut or snap the scraped corn cobs in half. In a small stockpot or a large pot, heat 1 tablespoon of the olive oil over medium heat. Add the shrimp shells and cook, stirring, until softened and sweated, about 2 minutes. Add the corn cobs and bay leaves and cover with white wine and 1 cup of cold water. Bring to a boil, then simmer over medium-low heat for 30 minutes, until fragrant and the flavors have melded. Strain the corn-shrimp stock and discard the solids.

2. Bring a large pot of water to a boil and season generously with kosher salt. Meanwhile, in a large saucepan or skillet, heat the remaining 2 tablespoons of olive oil over medium-high heat. Add the garlic and chile flake and toast for 30 seconds, until fragrant and golden. Add the tomatoes, allowing them to sizzle and fry for about 2 minutes (the tomatoes will begin to break down and soften). Add the scraped corn and all of its corn milk and cook, stirring continuously to cook the corn, about 2 minutes; season with a few pinches of salt. Add the corn-shrimp stock and bring to a boil. Let cook until reduced by half, 3 to 4 minutes.

3. Add the corzetti to the boiling water and cook for 2 minutes, or until they are tender and begin to float; stir a few times to prevent them from sticking. Reserve ½ cup of the pasta cooking water. Using a skimmer, transfer the pasta to the sauce with the corn, and stir to marry. (You can also drain the pasta in a colander.) Add the green beans and butter. Reduce the heat to low. Check for seasoning. Fold the shrimp into the pasta and sauce and cook for about 3 minutes, until the shrimp are opaque. Stir in the parm, thyme, parsley, and basil, then stir in some of the reserved pasta water as needed to loosen the sauce (the corn has a natural thickening quality). Remove from the heat. Garnish the pasta with more basil, a sprinkle or two of parm, and some fresh black pepper.

If you buy well-made, freshly milled polenta, you don't want to change the flavor; you want to enhance it. Much like rice, polenta takes on the flavor of whatever is added to it. As a result, many restaurants serve polenta that tastes more like reduced heavy cream than corn. I find that dried corn wants to be hydrated before I introduce any fat to it, so I cook it in water, which allows the soft polenta to develop a creamy, porridge-like texture and retain its pure corn flavor. I love finishing it with a bit of crème fraîche, but butter, heavy cream, and milk work too.

Soft Polenta

with Crème Fraîche and Parm

Serves 6

1½ cups stone-ground or heirloom corn polenta (see box opposite)

1 dried bay leaf

Kosher salt

1 cup freshly grated Parmigiano-Reggiano, plus 2 tablespoons for garnish (use a Microplane)

¼ cup crème fraîche

2 tablespoons unsalted butter

2 tablespoons fresh rosemary leaves

Fresh cracked black pepper

— Get It —

When making polenta, start with a ratio of 4:1 water to polenta. Keep in mind that some polentas may take up to an hour to cook.

When I was in Friuli, I had a bowl of polenta served with diced nuggets of Alpine cheese, likely Montasio or Asiago. With the heat from the polenta, the cheese became semi melted and utterly delicious. If this appeals to you, swap out the parm on top of the polenta at the end of Step 4 for small pieces of a semi-soft Northern Italian cheese.

— Get It —

1.   In a medium saucepot over medium-high heat, bring 5 cups of water to a boil. Once boiling, slowly whisk in the polenta, then add the bay leaf and season with a few pinches of salt. Armed with your whisk, whisk the mixture until it begins to bubble. Reduce the heat to low and whisk continuously for 5 minutes. (This is one of the most important steps, as the little grains of corn need to absorb the water and hydrate. By whisking and keeping them moving, you help suspend the corn in the water; otherwise it would just settle in the bottom of the pot and scorch. Yuck!)

2.   Continue to cook for about 45 minutes, whisking for a good 30 seconds every 5 to 10 minutes or so. If you feel the bottom of the pot is getting a little sticky, use a spatula to loosen and scrape the sides as you whisk. Gradually add another cup of water if your polenta is too thick or seems dry as it cooks.

3.   Once the polenta is thickened and creamy and the corn granules have softened, stir in the grated parm and crème fraîche. Taste and adjust the seasoning with a bit more salt. Discard the bay leaf. Cover and remove from the heat until you're ready to serve. (The creamy polenta will stay warm for an hour or so, but place it back over medium-low heat to warm up fully before serving.)

4.   In a small skillet, melt the butter over medium-high heat, allowing it to brown, about 2 minutes. Once the butter begins to brown, add the rosemary and reduce the heat to low. Pour the creamy polenta into a serving bowl. (I like to use a terra-cotta or ceramic dish or another heatproof serving vessel.) Sprinkle some black pepper and the remaining parm over it, then spoon the hot brown butter and rosemary over the top. The parm will foam when the butter hits it. So yum!

Listen to Your Vegetables

What Is Polenta, Really?

Polenta is a special ingredient made from grinding dried corn, particularly dried flint corn, which is a beautiful corn with many colorful varietals. But not all polentas are the same—the corn variety, grinding method, and size of the grind are all variables to navigate. Grocery store polenta and grits are often the quick-cooking variety that have been preboiled and can lack true corn flavor when compared to heirloom varietals. Try to source artisanal polenta, and seek out heirloom or heritage corn, polenta that is milled to order, different corn varietals, or colorful ground corn mixes. Anson Mills from South Carolina and Barton Springs Mill in Texas are both great sources for corn, grains, and rice. Locally in Chicago, I buy from Marty Travis at Spence Farm; I love his Floriani polenta. You can order from him at mandk@thespencefarm.com. I also like the organic grits and polenta from Bob's Red Mill, which are found at many grocery stores.

Grandpa Ralph's Cornmeal Fried Fish

My Grandpa Ralph is amazing, and he and my Grandma Lillian are the reason this book exists today. My grandparents had a big farm, and their lives revolved around planting, growing, harvesting, raising livestock, fishing, hunting, and preserving. They truly lived off the land. One of my favorite memories is of going wade fishing with my grandparents, my Uncle Randal, and the whole family in the Gulf bays of Texas. We would catch redfish and speckled trout (still some of my favorite fish to this day), and the only way to eat it was battered in cornmeal and deep-fried in peanut oil. Nothing beats a crackly cornmeal crust. My grandpa mixed cornmeal with a bit of flour, seasoned it up, and then tossed fish fillets and oysters in the breading before frying. I love using a different basic breading method for green tomatoes too: a bowl of flour, a bowl of egg wash, and a bowl of cornmeal seasoned with a little bit of cayenne, oregano, and garlic salt. Then I pan-fry or deep-fry until crispy. You can also make seriously fantastic oysters, and you don't even need to bother with the flour and egg wash! Just dredge the oysters in cornmeal and deep-fry until crispy. Here's to my grandpa and Uncle Randal for teaching me not just how to fish, but how to fry!

Italy meets the American Midwest in this recipe, which showcases fresh and dried corn in a super-cool way. The polenta-filled tortelloni have amazing flavor and chew, almost like corn gnocchi. I like adding roasted New Mexican Hatch green chiles, which are smoky and just a little bit spicy, and a fresh peach for a pop of acidity, just like a tomato! I have always loved a roasted green chile. New Mexican Hatch chiles are the kings of the roasted green chiles, in my opinion; poblanos are a strong second choice. Sweet corn and Hatch green chile season peak around the same time, usually in August. If your grocery store carries fresh Hatch chiles, please do yourself a favor and buy several pounds, then roast and freeze them for future use. (In some places, stores roast them in their parking lot!) For tips on roasting your own peppers, see page 285. My favorite brand of jarred Hatch green chiles is Zia.

Polenta-Filled Tortelloni

with Sweet Corn, Bacon, and Hatch Green Chiles

Serves 6

Tortelloni

1 cup dried coarsely ground, quick-cooking polenta or grits (preferably Bob's Red Mill Corn Grits Polenta)

Kosher salt

1 cup freshly grated Parmigiano-Reggiano (see Get It Get It; use a Microplane)

½ cup mascarpone cheese

Fresh cracked black pepper

½ cup "00" flour mixed with ½ cup semolina (aka bench flour), for dusting

The Essential Egg Yolk Pasta Dough (page 256)

Finishing

6 ounces smoked bacon (5 or 6 slices), diced

½ small red onion, finely chopped

1 ripe large pitted peach or medium heirloom tomato, diced

3 ears of sweet corn, husked and scraped (see page 118)

1 cup roasted Hatch green chiles, chopped (from 3 whole or prepared)

1. Make the tortelloni filling. In a medium saucepot, bring 3 cups of water to a boil. Gradually whisk in the polenta and bring to a simmer. Reduce the heat to low and season with a few pinches of kosher salt. Cook, whisking and stirring often, until the polenta absorbs the water and thickens, about 10 to 12 minutes. Look for the polenta to thicken substantially and to begin to pull away from the sides of the pot. This is good—you want the filling to be as dry as possible. (Depending on the polenta you are using, you may need to adjust the amount of water needed or the cooking time. What is most important is to cook the polenta down until it is thick and pulling away from the pot.) If your polenta is not thickening up, consider adding a tablespoon or two of additional polenta. You may also notice that as you stir, the polenta holds its shape and doesn't rush back, so that you can see the bottom of the pot.

**2. Once your polenta is ready, using a wooden spoon, stir in the grated parm. Taste and adjust for seasoning. Transfer the polenta to a shallow dish and refrigerate to cool and firm up, about 30 minutes.

**3. Once the polenta has cooled, transfer it to a stand mixer fitted with a paddle. With the machine on low speed, mix in the mascarpone. This helps incorporate the mascarpone and enrich the filling. (If you add the mascarpone while the polenta is hot, the heat from the polenta will melt it.) Season with salt and lots of black pepper. Scoop the filling into a pastry bag or a sturdy resealable plastic bag; snip off the corner.

4. Shape the tortelloni. (See page 270 for photos.) Line a large baking sheet with a lint-free towel and dust it lightly with bench flour. Cut each ball of pasta dough in half so you have four pieces total. Work with one ball of dough at a time and keep the other pieces wrapped in plastic. Set your pasta machine to the thickest setting, which is usually 1. Flatten the

½ cup freshly grated Parmigiano-Reggiano, plus more for serving (use a Microplane)

2 tablespoons unsalted butter

2 tablespoons fresh lime juice

2 tablespoons chopped fresh oregano, plus a few sprigs for garnish

— Get It —

Have fun with the cheese here. I love Parmigiano, but I think an aged cheddar or Gouda would be awesome in the filling too.

This can be a great vegetarian dish! Omit the bacon and cook the onion and peach in Step 5 in 2 tablespoons of unsalted butter.

This pasta shape relies on the dough being freshly rolled and still damp so it seals shut. If the dough's surface has dried a bit and you notice a skin forming, I recommend having a small spray bottle of water handy to dampen the squares; a slightly wet pastry brush will do the trick too. Just be careful to not wet the dough too much, as it will become too sticky to handle.

— Get It —

dough slightly with a rolling pin, creating a rectangle shape; be mindful to match the width of your roller. This will create consistent-sized pasta sheets. Feed the dough through the roller. Continue to feed the dough through the roller on increasingly thinner settings; you might need to add a little flour to one side of the dough if it's feeling a little sticky or wet. If the pasta starts getting too long, you can cut the piece in half. You want this pasta thin, but it can be hard to work with, so once you've reached setting 5, run the pasta through twice and then transfer it to a work surface that's lightly dusted with bench flour.

5.   Cut the long strips of pasta dough into 12-inch lengths. Trim the sides to straighten the edges, then cut the pasta strips into 2½- to 3-inch squares. (You can discard the scraps or reroll them to use for another shape, like tagliatelle.) Place 1 scant tablespoon of filling into the center of each square. Fold the square into a triangle, gently pressing the edges to seal. Using your thumb, gently press the pocket of filling up toward the peak of the triangle, then pull the two corners downward and press to seal. Transfer the finished tortelloni to the prepared baking sheet. Keep it covered with a clean lint-free towel while you roll and shape the remaining pasta. If you're not using the pasta immediately, sprinkle a generous amount of bench flour on top of it, cover with a clean lint-free towel, and wrap tightly in plastic. The pasta can be refrigerated like this overnight.

6.   **Finish the tortelloni.** Bring a large pot of water to a boil and season generously with kosher salt. Meanwhile, in another large saucepot or large saucepan, cook the bacon over medium heat until golden, rendered, and crunchy, 3 to 4 minutes. Transfer to a paper towel–lined plate. Drain all but 2 tablespoons of the bacon drippings from the pan and place it back over medium heat. Add the onion and cook until translucent, about 1 minute. Add the peach and cook, stirring, allowing the peach to deglaze the pan, about 1 minute. Add the corn and roasted green chiles, and season with a few pinches of salt. Cook, allowing the vegetables to sweat together for a few minutes. Reduce the heat to low and keep warm.

7.   When the pot of water has come to a boil, add your tortelloni and cook until they begin to float and the edges of the pasta are tender to the touch, about 2 minutes. Using a slotted spoon or skimmer, transfer the pasta to the pan with the corn. Feel free to cook the tortelloni in two batches if needed. Add ½ cup of the pasta cooking water. Gently fold the pasta and corn together, adding another ½ cup of pasta water to loosen the sauce (you are conducting a quick pasta-to-sauce marriage ceremony). Stir in the parm, butter, lime juice, and oregano, and season to taste. Garnish the tortelloni with the crispy bacon, fresh cracked black pepper, and a few oregano sprigs. Serve with additional grated parm on the side.

Eggplant

I love eggplant because it's incredibly versatile and special enough to be the main dish at the table. But yikes! Who first tried eating eggplant? In thirteenth-century Italy, it was rumored to make people insane. And because it's a part of the nightshade family, many people also thought it was poisonous. (In truth, if you eat too many of the flowers and leaves, it *is* poisonous.)

This queen of the garden is also known as aubergine and brinjal. It has been a staple in Asian and Mediterranean cuisines for many centuries. Although we call it a vegetable, it's technically a fruit—a berry, to be specific. The meaty texture of eggplant lends itself to many preparations, and it's a good substitute for meat in so many recipes. It's absorbent and spongy with some bitterness, but when it's properly salted, that bitterness is eliminated and the eggplant turns all delicious and creamy. That's why I call salt eggplant's best friend.

While there are many kinds of eggplants, I most often use standard globe, Italian, graffiti (aka Sicilian), Rosa Bianca, Japanese, and Chinese eggplants. Japanese and Chinese eggplants don't have a lot of seeds, so they aren't too bitter, and they're particularly great for stir-fries and grilling because their flesh is more compact and holds up well with these cooking methods. The other eggplants are all pretty much interchangeable, but their shape will likely help determine which one is good for what. Globes, Italian, Sicilian, and Rosa Biancas are all great for slicing and breading, stuffing, dicing into sauces or caponata, and grilling too! How you cut an eggplant will vary, and whether or not it's peeled will depend on the recipe you're using. Try to choose the right shape and size eggplant for the recipe. For layering in casseroles or rolling *involtini* (roll-ups), for instance, use larger eggplants sliced lengthwise. When dicing into a pasta sauce or a marinated salad, Rosa Bianca or Sicilian eggplants are a good option.

When you're shopping for eggplant, always, *always* choose an eggplant that is smooth, heavy, and firm. Avoid eggplant that has wrinkles, soft spots, or browning of the skin. There are many varieties of eggplant to choose from, especially in late summer during peak season, though eggplant is readily available in grocery stores year-round. As a rule, eggplant should be stored in a cool, dry place (not the refrigerator) and used within a couple of days of purchasing.

Queen Aubergine representing
the royal court of the garden:
rich colors, a smooth and
creamy texture, and regal in
every way.

Clockwise from top: Grilled Eggplant Salad with
Balsamic Vinaigrette, Basil, and Pistachio (page 140);
Sicilian Eggplant Caponata (page 141); Rigatoni alla
Norma (page 151); Bay-Grilled Tuna Skewers with
Pickled Eggplant Agrodolce (page 144)

The first time I had a charred whole eggplant, I was blown away. I didn't know you could throw the whole thing on the grill and end up with something so magical. While the exterior chars and roasts, the interior becomes creamy and tender. Raw eggplant is spongy, but when it's cooked like this, it evolves into something entirely different. This creamy charred eggplant salad is great with grilled meats, seafood, and other veggies, and it's awesome with bread, raw veggies, pita chips, or crackers as a dip or a spread. You might have guessed that it's inspired by baba ganoush. I love the nutty sesame flavor from the tahini and the bright pop of sweetness from the cherries. This recipe creates a chunky salad or dip, but if you prefer a smooth dip, you can pulse the stemmed eggplant (skins and all) in a food processor or blender with the tahini dressing.

Creamy Charred Eggplant Salad or Dip(!)

Serves 4

3 medium eggplants (about 2 pounds total)

2 tablespoons tahini (I love Soom brand)

2 tablespoons everyday olive oil

2 tablespoons fresh lemon juice

2 tablespoons chopped fresh oregano, plus leaves for garnish

1 garlic clove, finely grated (use a Microplane)

Coarse sea salt (like Maldon)

1 cup fresh sweet cherries, pitted and halved (see Get It Get It)

2 tablespoons super-special extra-virgin olive oil, for drizzling

1 tablespoon toasted sesame seeds, for garnish

1. Preheat a grill to high (500° to 600°F). Place the whole eggplants directly on the grill. Grill for about 20 minutes, rotating them every 5 minutes or so. You will notice the eggplant skin darkening and splitting—this is okay. The interior of the eggplant is cooking and steaming right inside the skin. As an alternative to the grill, you can char the eggplant under your broiler. Place the eggplant on a baking sheet fitted with a rack. Broil the eggplant about 3 inches from the heat source, rotating, until the skin is darkened and splitting. Once the eggplants feel soft, transfer them to a baking sheet. Cool for a few minutes.

2. In a medium bowl, combine the tahini, everyday olive oil, lemon juice, oregano, garlic, and a few pinches of sea salt. Using a paring knife, cut a slit into the side of each eggplant, starting at the stem. Using a spoon, gently scrape and pull the eggplant flesh from the charred peels; discard the peels. Add the eggplant to the bowl with the tahini dressing and stir to combine. Taste and season with a bit more sea salt if needed.

3. Spoon the creamy charred eggplant into a shallow serving platter. In a small mixing bowl, dress the cherries with the super-special extra-virgin olive oil and a pinch of sea salt. Spoon the cherries over the top of the eggplant and garnish with the sesame seeds and oregano leaves.

Get It

If cherries are not your jam, or you're looking to avoid pitting fresh cherries, sliced peaches or halved cherry tomatoes would be lovely here too.

Have fun with spices and herbs. Cumin, coriander, sumac, and Aleppo pepper would be great additions. Basil and dill are nice herby swaps or additions too.

Get It

It bears repeating that eggplant is like a giant sponge. If you put oil on raw eggplant, it just absorbs it, and then you think you need to add more oil; by the time you grill it, it causes a giant flame from all of the oil! Much as I do with so many vegetables, I like to grill my eggplant dry. I believe in getting a char on my grilled vegetables, but when I use a lot of oil, the oil burns instead of the veggie. There is simple beauty in a dry char. After you grill, then you can add all of the delicious oil, vinegar, and salt. Young balsamic has tart, fresh acidity, not like an aged balsamic, which will be sweeter and richer and not as good in this eggplant dish. Here I cut the slender Japanese eggplants into 1-inch slices and grill them on their cut sides. Nestling these eggplant slices in the dish and pouring the balsamic on the top allows them to return to their natural sponge-like nature.

Grilled Eggplant Salad

with Balsamic Vinaigrette, Basil, and Pistachios

Serves 4 to 6

2 pounds Japanese eggplant, trimmed and sliced 1 inch thick

2 teaspoons kosher salt, plus more for seasoning

¼ cup young balsamic vinegar

¼ cup everyday olive oil

2 tablespoons Sesame Za'atar (page 395) or store-bought green za'atar

1 cup loosely packed fresh basil leaves

½ cup chopped unsalted pistachios (you can also use salted, if preferred)

1. In a large bowl, toss the eggplant slices with the 2 teaspoons of salt. Transfer to a colander to drain for 30 minutes or up to a few hours.

2. Preheat a grill to high for 10 minutes, then lower the heat to medium-high; if using a gas grill, you want it at about 500°F. While the grill is heating, in a medium bowl, whisk the balsamic and olive oil with the za'atar and season with a few pinches of salt. Place the eggplant on the grill cut side down, then cover and grill until charred, turning once, 6 to 8 minutes per side. The eggplant should be charred on both sides and tender to the touch. If you don't have a grill, use a well-oiled cast-iron grill pan over high heat to char and cook the eggplant slices. Transfer the eggplant to a wide, shallow serving bowl in a single layer.

3. While the eggplant is still hot, pour the vinaigrette evenly over it. Let stand for 10 minutes. Flip the pieces and let stand for 10 minutes longer. (You can cover and refrigerate the eggplant overnight at this point; it tastes even better the next day!)

4. Before serving, flip the eggplant slices one last time, then nestle in the fresh basil leaves and sprinkle with the chopped pistachios.

—— Get It ——

When it comes to grilling eggplant, it's crucial that you salt it ahead of time to eliminate much of the excess liquid. Don't skimp on the salting! It's also important to make sure your grill grates are clean so that the eggplant doesn't stick to the grates. If the grates are clean and hot enough, you don't need to oil them ahead of grilling.

—— Get It ——

To be Sicilian, you must love eggplant and you must love that sweet-and-sour life. When I went to stay with Katia Amore at her cooking school, loveSicily, I was on a quest to find "real" caponata, the sweet-sour Sicilian relish made with eggplant and other vegetables. I came across versions with cocoa, cinnamon, zucchini, artichokes, nuts . . . and no nuts. Well, it turns out that there really is no one way to make it! It's made from what you have on hand and what you like. But almost every single version included celery, as well as tomato in one form or another, plus a combo of sugar and vinegar for that signature sweet-sour flavor. People often complain about eggplant 'cause it's too oily or bitter, but using it in caponata turns eggplant soft and tasty and surrounds it with many amazing flavors and textures. I love to have caponata as an appetizer with crusty bread and mozzarella. It's also perfect with grilled seafood and meat and makes a perfect side dish on its own or served over sliced tomatoes. This is an incredible vegan and gluten-free dish that will wow everyone—don't miss out!

Sicilian Eggplant Caponata

Makes 4 cups

2 medium eggplants, diced (about 1½ pounds)

1 tablespoon kosher salt, plus more for seasoning

4 tablespoons everyday olive oil

1 celery stalk, diced

½ small red onion, diced

½ small red bell pepper, diced

½ cup sun-dried tomatoes, drained if packed in oil

¼ cup pitted Castelvetrano or green olives, sliced or chopped

1 tablespoon drained capers

1 garlic clove, chopped

One 14½-ounce can whole peeled tomatoes with their juice, crushed by hand

2 tablespoons red wine vinegar

2 tablespoons sugar

2 tablespoons pine nuts

2 tablespoons sliced almonds

2 tablespoons raisins or currants

½ cup fresh basil leaves

1 tablespoon dried oregano

Grilled or toasted bread, for serving

1.   In a large bowl, toss the eggplant with the 1 tablespoon of salt. Transfer to a colander and drain for 2 hours or up to overnight.

2.   Shake the eggplant to remove any excess water and drain the dark liquid. In a large saucepan, heat 1 tablespoon of the olive oil over medium-high heat. Add half of the eggplant and cook until it softens and begins to brown, 3 to 4 minutes. Transfer to a large bowl. Add 1 more tablespoon of oil to the pan and repeat with the remaining eggplant. Transfer to the bowl.

3.   Add another tablespoon of oil, then add the celery, onion, bell pepper, sun-dried tomatoes, olives, capers, and garlic. Cook until the onion is translucent and beginning to brown, about 4 minutes. Transfer to the bowl with the eggplant.

4.   Return the pan to the heat and add the remaining 1 tablespoon of oil. Add the canned tomatoes and simmer for 5 minutes. Reduce the heat to low and add the vinegar, sugar, and a few pinches of salt. Add the cooked veggies to the pan along with the pine nuts, almonds, and raisins. Cook for 5 minutes to meld and marry the flavors, allowing the vegetables to absorb the sweet and sour tomato flavors. Remove from the heat and add the basil and oregano. Double-check for seasoning, adding another pinch or two of salt if needed. Serve warm or chilled with bread. Eggplant caponata holds well in an airtight container in the refrigerator for up to 2 weeks.

With sweet and sour flavors from a mix of vinegar, soy sauce, and honey, this stir-fry has a bit of an agrodolce thing going on, which is exactly what eggplant wants. Cooking this in a wok is just a different way of thinking about agrodolce, which is a great way of changing up the flavor of everyday home cooking. The heat of the wok here sears the eggplant perfectly, then helps glaze it evenly with the honey-soy mixture. Jaime and I love eating this for a vegan dinner along with steamed rice. I love using long, slender eggplants like Japanese or Chinese ones because the skin is tender and softens nicely in the hot wok. Plus, their seeds are smaller and less bitter than those of other eggplants. You can also toss some cooked rice, egg noodles, or pasta into the wok.

Stir-Fried Eggplant

with Celery, Pine Nuts, and Calabrian Chiles

Serves 4

4 or 5 Japanese or Chinese eggplants (about 2 pounds), quartered lengthwise and cut into 3- to 4-inch pieces

Kosher salt

2 tablespoons young balsamic vinegar

2 tablespoons soy sauce

2 tablespoons honey

5 tablespoons canola oil or other neutral high-heat oil

1 tender celery heart, stalks sliced on a bias into 2-inch-long pieces, leaves reserved

½ medium red onion, cut into wedges and separated into petals

3 garlic cloves, thinly sliced

¼ cup jarred whole Calabrian chile peppers, drained, stemmed, and halved

1 cup loosely packed fresh basil leaves

¼ cup toasted pine nuts (peanuts or almonds are nice too)

1.   In a large bowl, toss the eggplant with 1 tablespoon of kosher salt and place in a colander to drain for 30 minutes. Meanwhile, in a small bowl, combine the vinegar, soy, and honey with ¼ cup of water.

2.   Working in two batches, in a large wok or wide skillet, heat 2 tablespoons of the oil over medium-high to high heat. Add half of the eggplant and stir-fry until slightly charred and softened, 3 to 4 minutes. Transfer the cooked eggplant back to the colander to drain any excess oil. Repeat with 2 more tablespoons of oil and the remaining eggplant, and transfer to the colander to drain.

3.   Place the wok back over medium-high or high heat. Add the remaining 1 tablespoon of oil along with the celery, onion, and a few pinches of kosher salt. Stir-fry until the vegetables are wilted, translucent, and beginning to brown, 3 to 4 minutes. Add the garlic and chiles and stir-fry for 30 seconds, then deglaze with the honey-soy mixture. Add the cooked eggplant back to the pan, reduce the heat to medium, and let it all simmer for a few minutes. Toss in the basil leaves, celery leaves, and pine nuts and serve.

Get It

You can buy celery hearts with tender stalks and leaves at most markets, but by all means you can use regular celery. I just recommend peeling the outer stalks so they're nice and tender.

I like to use whole chiles for this recipe, stemmed and halved, leaving the seeds in for flavor and spice. If you're not feeling the heat, you can seed the chiles, or use 2 tablespoons of Calabrian chile paste instead.

Get It

I've learned that the trick to the very best spiedini (skewers or kebabs) is tossing your main ingredients with your oil, salt, lemon, and herbs ahead of skewering so each piece on the skewer is packed with flavor. You can use any meaty seafood here, like swordfish or scallops, which work well when skewered and grilled. Having these skewers with this sweet-sour pickled eggplant agrodolce is like having Sicily on a plate! Match this dish with a crisp white wine from Mt. Etna, and you'll feel like you're in Italy and the healthiest person in the world.

Bay-Grilled Tuna Skewers

with Pickled Eggplant Agrodolce

Serves 6

3 tablespoons everyday olive oil

2 tablespoons finely grated lemon zest (from 2 lemons; use a Microplane)

2 garlic cloves, finely grated (use a Microplane)

2 tablespoons chopped fresh flat-leaf parsley or oregano

2 to 2½ pounds tuna steak, cut into 2-inch chunks

1 pint cherry tomatoes

16 fresh bay leaves (from a ½-ounce container)

Kosher salt

Pickled Eggplant Agrodolce (recipe follows)

½ cup fresh basil leaves, torn, for garnish

1.   In a large bowl, combine the olive oil, lemon zest, garlic, and parsley; add the tuna pieces and toss. Using six 12-inch metal or soaked bamboo skewers, alternate pieces of cherry tomato, tuna, and bay leaves. There should be 2 or 3 pieces of tuna per skewer and cherry tomatoes at both ends to hold everything tight. (I like to place the bay leaves next to the fish pieces on the skewer, which adds *awesome flavor*.) Season the skewers with a few pinches of salt.

2.   Preheat a grill to high (500° to 600°F). Grill the skewers for 2 minutes, then flip and grill for another minute. Check the sides of the tuna; I look for lightly seared sides and a red center. If a thermometer gives you ease, shoot for 115°F internally for rare tuna (add an additional 30 seconds or so for medium-rare, medium, etc.). Serve the tuna skewers with the pickled eggplant agrodolce and top with fresh basil. Be sure to drizzle some of the pickling marinade from the eggplant over the top.

Get It

If you aren't already, you will become obsessed with fresh bay leaves, just like me! I buy them anytime I see them, and if I could, I'd plant a bay laurel tree! They impart amazing flavor to any dish, but especially when they're side by side with an ingredient, like they are with the tuna here. They hold in the fridge for a few months in an airtight container.

If you don't have a grill, feel free to grill the tuna skewers on a cast-iron grill pan. Just be sure to preheat the grill pan over high heat.

Get It

Pickled Eggplant Agrodolce

I like using long, slender Japanese or Chinese eggplants for this pickle because the seeds are compact, so they're perfect for slicing and pickling. The slices are little flavor sponges that become meaty but tender. I start this recipe by purging the peeled eggplant with salt to remove the bitterness, then I quickly blanch the slices. This is so that the eggplant absorbs some water, preventing it from over-absorbing the pickle marinade and becoming too vinegary. You can play around with the ratio of sugar and vinegar to make your perfect pickle. Any leftover pickled eggplant agrodolce usually ends up on my next sandwich or antipasti platter.

Makes about 2 cups

3 large Japanese eggplants (about 1 pound), peeled and sliced about ¼ inch thick

Kosher salt

½ cup everyday olive oil

1 teaspoon fennel seeds

½ small red onion, thinly sliced

1 garlic clove, thinly sliced

¼ cup red or white wine vinegar

3 tablespoons sugar

1 tablespoon Calabrian chile paste or sambal oelek

1 tablespoon dried oregano (preferably wild Calabrian)

1 tablespoon chopped fresh flat-leaf parsley

1.	In a large bowl, toss the eggplant slices with 1 tablespoon of kosher salt. Transfer to a colander and let drain for 30 minutes.

2.	In a small skillet, heat the olive oil over medium heat. Add the fennel seeds and toast for 1 minute. Remove the pan from the heat and add the red onion and garlic, letting them sizzle and sweat. Set aside.

3.	Bring a medium saucepot of water to a boil and season with a few generous pinches of kosher salt. Meanwhile, in a medium bowl, combine the vinegar, sugar, chile paste, oregano, and a few pinches of salt. Stir to dissolve the sugar in the vinegar, then stir in the olive oil mixture.

4.	Add the sliced eggplant to the boiling water and blanch for 45 seconds to 1 minute; the eggplant will become barely tender and begin to puff slightly. (This happens so fast; please don't overcook as they will become mushy.) Quickly drain and transfer the eggplant to the bowl with the vinegar and oil marinade. Stir to combine. Let the slices absorb the agrodolce marinade at room temperature for 30 minutes.

5.	Stir in the chopped parsley and season with a few more pinches of salt. The eggplant agrodolce can be enjoyed right away, or it can be refrigerated in an airtight container for up to a month.

Involtini is the Italian word for "rolls"; you might see these called rollatini or rotolo too. I like to think of this involtini as a mock lasagna, with eggplant standing in for the pasta. You can make eggplant involtini with a myriad of things like cheese and breadcrumbs, plain mozzarella, or lamb and rice. The beauty is that the eggplant absorbs so much of the flavor of the other ingredients, while bringing its own earthy, slightly bitter personality to the dish. I love topping this with a mix of sweet roasted corn, cherry tomatoes, and mint, giving the dish an awesome blast of summer.

Mozzarella-Stuffed Eggplant Involtini

with Roasted Corn and Cherry Tomatoes

Serves 4 to 6

2 ears of corn in their husks

2 large eggplants (about 1 pound each), stemmed

Kosher salt

3 tablespoons everyday olive oil

1½ cups Homemade Lemon Ricotta (page 173) or whole milk ricotta (see page 8)

4 tablespoons chopped fresh flat-leaf parsley

1 garlic clove, finely grated (use a Microplane)

1 ball whole milk mozzarella, cut into ¼-inch-thick slices, slices halved into half-moons

2 cups Oven-Roasted Tomato Sauce (page 392) or your favorite tomato sauce

1 cup cherry tomatoes, quartered

1 tablespoon chopped fresh mint, plus leaves for garnish

1 tablespoon super-special extra-virgin olive oil

1. Preheat the oven to 400°F. Place the ears of corn, in their husks, directly on the oven rack. Roast for 30 minutes, until the husks have darkened and the corn kernels are tender (they steam inside their husks). Set aside to cool, leaving the oven on.

2. Meanwhile, on a cutting board, stand one of the eggplants stemmed end up. Using a sharp or serrated knife, cut long slices, about ¼ inch thick. You don't want a lot of peel on the slices, so I recommend shaving away some of it from your first and last slice; discard the peels. Repeat with the other eggplant. You should have 12 to 14 slices. Place a large colander inside a large bowl. Season the eggplant slices all over with 2 tablespoons of kosher salt and place in the colander. Let them purge for 30 minutes. Discard the liquid from the eggplant.

3. Line two large baking sheets with foil and lightly oil the foil with 1 tablespoon of the everyday olive oil. Lay the slices of eggplant on the baking sheets and drizzle with the remaining 2 tablespoons of everyday oil. Bake until softened and slightly browned, 20 to 25 minutes. Let cool.

4. In a medium bowl, mix the ricotta, 2 tablespoons of the parsley, and the garlic and season with a few pinches of salt. Using a spoon, dollop some ricotta on each slice of eggplant and schmear it over the eggplant. Place a half-moon of mozzarella on the narrow (tapered) end of each eggplant slice and roll the eggplant around the mozzarella, like a jellyroll.

5. In a 9 by 13-inch baking dish or large casserole, spread the tomato sauce. Arrange the eggplant rolls on top of the sauce, seam side down. Bake until the cheese begins to melt and gently ooze, about 15 minutes.

6.   While the eggplant bakes, husk the corn, then cut and scrape the kernels from the cobs (see page 118). Transfer to a medium bowl. Add the cherry tomatoes, chopped mint, and the remaining 2 tablespoons of parsley. Add the super-special extra-virgin olive oil and a few pinches of kosher salt and stir to combine.

7.   Turn the broiler to high and broil the eggplant 6 to 7 inches from the heat source for 5 minutes. Spoon the corn–cherry tomato salad over the eggplant, garnish with torn mint leaves, and enjoy!

During my first trip to Italy in 2009, I was taught this recipe by Chef Danilo Frisone at Ristorante Grano near the Pantheon. He taught me great technique that makes for the most delicious eggplant parm you'll ever have. It starts by salting the eggplant overnight, which creates a delicious creamy texture. Dipping the eggplant slices in ice water keeps the breading ultra light and crispy, and breading the eggplant slices right before you add them to the hot oil prevents them from getting soggy; it also helps the breading stay intact during frying.

Roman-Style Eggplant Parmigiana

Serves 4 as a main course or 8 as an appetizer

2 large firm eggplants, ends trimmed, sliced crosswise into 1-inch-thick slices

2 tablespoons kosher salt

3 quarts canola oil, for deep-frying

6 cups all-purpose flour

3 cups fine dry breadcrumbs (from Italian-style bread)

6 cups ice water

4 cups Oven-Roasted Tomato Sauce (page 392) or your favorite tomato sauce

½ cup freshly grated Parmigiano-Reggiano, plus some to garnish

8 ounces fresh mozzarella, thinly sliced

1 cup fresh basil leaves, for garnish

1.   Place the eggplant in a large mixing bowl and toss with the salt. Transfer it to a colander, then set the colander in the bowl. Cover with plastic wrap and refrigerate overnight or up to 2 days.

2.   Heat the oil in a large pot or deep-fryer to 350°F. While the oil is heating, place 3 cups of the flour in a medium bowl. In another bowl, combine the remaining 3 cups of flour with the breadcrumbs. Place the ice water in a third bowl.

3.   Shake any excess salt or liquid from the eggplant. Dip the eggplant slices in the flour, then dip in the ice water. Finish by coating the eggplant in the flour-breadcrumb mixture; be sure to pat and evenly coat each slice. Transfer the finished breaded eggplant to a rack set on a baking sheet while you bread the others.

4.   Line a large baking sheet with paper towels. Working in three batches, carefully place 1 eggplant slice at a time into the hot oil; there should be 5 or 6 slices per batch. Fry the eggplant for 8 to 10 minutes, flipping halfway through, until golden brown. Transfer to the baking sheet to cool.

5.   Preheat the oven to 350°F. In an 8 by 12-inch or 12-inch round baking dish, evenly pour 2 cups of the tomato sauce. You will be shingling the eggplants, so start by arranging the 3 largest eggplant slices in a row along one side of the dish. Over each slice, spoon 1 tablespoon of tomato sauce, sprinkle with parm, and shingle with a slice of mozzarella. Continue shingling the eggplant, sauce, parm, and mozzarella, filling out the rest of the dish. Spoon the remaining tomato sauce over the eggplant, and sprinkle with more parm. Top with the remaining sliced mozzarella. Cover with foil and bake for 30 minutes. See step-by-step photos on page 150.

6.   Remove the foil and bake for 30 minutes longer, until the cheese is melted and the top is golden brown. Let rest for 10 minutes. Garnish with more parm and basil leaves before serving.

Get It

You can season your flour-breadcrumb mixture if you want, but the eggplant gets nicely seasoned from the salting, plus the Parmigiano-Reggiano adds another layer of seasoning to the dish.

Get It

Roman-Style Eggplant Parmigiana

My friend Katia Amore tells me legend says this pasta gets its name from the character Norma in Vincenzo Bellini's opera *Norma*. As it's told, when Bellini's friends first saw the opera, they were so impressed that they started comparing anything great to their friend's opera. If something was excellent, it was said to be "*una vera Norma*" (a real Norma), and the epithet stuck when it was used to describe this pasta dish. I think this tastes like eggplant parm meets pasta, and I can totally understand why it has been compared to a phenomenal piece of music!

Rigatoni alla Norma

aka Eggplant-Parm Sauce

Serves 4 to 6

3 pounds Rosa Bianca eggplant (see Get It Get It), cut into large dice

Kosher salt

6 tablespoons everyday olive oil

4 garlic cloves, thinly sliced

2 cups tomato puree or tomato passata

12 ounces cherry tomatoes (use assorted colors or heirloom varieties), halved

1 pound dry rigatoni or mezzi rigatoni

1 cup fresh basil leaves, plus more for garnish

¼ cup freshly grated Parmigiano-Reggiano, plus more for finishing

Super-special extra-virgin olive oil, for garnish

3 ounces ricotta salata, finely grated

— Get It —

I love to use the Rosa Bianca eggplant, a beautiful Italian varietal that's globe-shaped with lavender skin. It has minimal seeds, and the flesh gets wonderfully creamy when cooked. If it's not available, American, Italian, or the thinner Asian varieties of eggplant will work well too.

— Get It —

1.   In a large bowl, toss the eggplant with 2 tablespoons of kosher salt. Transfer to a colander to purge for 30 minutes to an hour, until the eggplant releases some of its liquid.

2.   In a large skillet over medium heat, heat 2 tablespoons of everyday olive oil and add half the eggplant pieces. Cook, undisturbed, until golden, about 4 minutes. Stir and continue to sear the other sides for another 2 minutes or so. Transfer to a medium bowl. Repeat with 2 more tablespoons of olive oil and the remaining eggplant. Transfer to the bowl.

3.   Heat the remaining 2 tablespoons of olive oil in the skillet over medium heat. Add the garlic and toast until golden, about 30 seconds. Add the tomato puree and stir continuously as the tomato puree bubbles and fries, about 1 minute. Add the cooked eggplant and cherry tomatoes and simmer over low heat for 15 minutes, stirring occasionally.

4.   Meanwhile, bring a large pot of salted water to a boil. Cook the pasta for 2 minutes less than the package directions state. Reserve 1 cup of the pasta cooking water before draining the pasta. Add the cooked pasta to the eggplant sauce, along with ½ cup of the pasta cooking water. Cook to marry the pasta and sauce, allowing the pasta to absorb the eggplant-tomato goodness, about 2 minutes. Stir in the basil and parm; add the remaining ½ cup of pasta water if dry. Taste for seasoning.

5.   To serve, garnish the pasta with a few fresh basil leaves, a sprinkle of parm, and a nice drizzle of super-special extra-virgin olive oil. Cover the top of the pasta with grated ricotta salata and serve. (Don't skimp on the ricotta salata—it makes this dish so special!)

Fruit

I love using fruit in savory recipes. I think for some folks it can seem a little foreign, but the Italians have a way of highlighting fruit effortlessly. Different fruits add texture, acidity, sweetness, and juiciness to a dish. In Italy, fruit has a place at every meal. The Italian breakfast table, for instance, includes fruit, pastry, salumi, and cheeses, and one of my favorite Italian breakfast dishes is roasted figs with whipped ricotta. Ever think of making apples the center of your salad bowl or serving sliced oranges layered with fennel, olives, and toasted almonds? You will now. I often add fruit as a condiment or to enhance a dish I am making. It honestly happens naturally. I rarely cook fish without some sort of citrus, and I love the surprise crunch of raw apple or pear in a salad and the juiciness of melon or stone fruit in a salad as well. Roasting grapes in the oven takes regular table grapes to the next level, intensifying their flavor and acidity by dehydrating their natural water content. I like using a spoonful of store-bought marmalade, jam, or preserves instead of sugar in a dish, or adding a spoonful to roasted brassicas for a unique pop of sweetness. Fruit is a great enhancement to so many dishes, and I encourage you to experiment and use it to add some zest and acidity to your cooking.

The tricky thing is that finding good fruit can be hard! It is—more than just about any other item in this book—the one ingredient you really want to buy in season and ideally locally. Too often, fruit is picked while it's not yet ripe so it can be shipped and look attractive in the supermarket. But wow, that fruit can be pretty bad. When you buy seasonal fruit that has been grown locally, chances are it has had time to ripen on the tree or vine, and it's going to taste *so* much better for that.

If you're shopping for stone fruits like peaches, plums, or apricots, feel them like you would an avocado. They shouldn't be too firm, but if they have a little pushback, you're one or two days away from prime eating time. You should also pay attention to what you're doing with the fruit. Making pie? Go for the ripest fruit you can find. Salad? Go for semi-firm.

Always. Wash. Your. Fruit. It's dirty. Even citrus! I generally store summer fruits like peaches, nectarines, melons, figs, and cherries in a wooden bowl on the kitchen counter—it's a great place to slowly ripen the fruit. Once ripened, enjoy it or refrigerate it for 1 day or so. I store winter fruits like apples, pears, and citrus in the fridge, which helps extend their shelf life. I like to eat apples, pears, and citrus cold—it's so refreshing.

Every piece of fruit begins as a flower, one of the natural world's most beautiful wonders. The circle of life is so evident, as the seeds move and fall to create more trees, plants, and . . . more fruit. It wouldn't happen without the bees, and here's Andrea the bee, out to pollinate!

Clockwise from top left: Satsuma and Fennel Seed–Roasted Pork Loin (page 177), Rigatoni al Limone with Whipped Ricotta and Pecorino Romano (page 176), Apple-Kale Salad with Charred Shallot-Tahini Vinaigrette (page 167), Vermouth-Roasted Pear and Tallegio Crostini (page 166), Citrus and Fennel Salad with Super-Roasted Almonds (page 172)

Who doesn't love caprese? Do you really even need a recipe for it? It's just a delicious mix of ripe tomatoes, fresh basil, mozzarella, extra-virgin olive oil, and salt. I love using stone fruit and tomatoes interchangeably. Cooking peaches halfway so that they're half-raw and half-roasted is freakin' delicious and creates a texture that mimics a tomato. This method of quick searing or charring and then marinating, then searing and charring again and marinating further, is inspired by Japanese yakitori. You can make this for four as an appetizer, but dang, with some good bread this is dinner for me and Jaime.

Balsamic-Glazed Peach Caprese Salad

Serves 4

4 semi-soft, just ripening peaches, pits removed, cut in half horizontally

Coarse sea salt (like Maldon)

¼ cup aged balsamic vinegar (see Get It Get It)

2 tablespoons everyday olive oil

8 ounces fresh mozzarella di bufala, sliced (bocconcini are good too)

1 cup fresh basil leaves

2 to 3 tablespoons super-special extra-virgin olive oil, for drizzling

Fresh cracked black pepper

1. Season the cut sides of the peaches with a few pinches of sea salt. On a large plate, drizzle the aged balsamic. In a large nonstick pan, heat the everyday olive oil over medium-low heat. Add the peaches cut side down and sear for 2½ to 3 minutes, giving the pan a little shake every minute or so to prevent them from sticking. (This is a slow sear so watch the heat here—you don't want to burn the peaches.) Using tongs, check the cut side of the peaches to see if they have begun to brown. Once they have, remove the pan from the heat and transfer the peaches cut side down to the plate with the balsamic. Let the peaches rest for 1 minute to absorb the vinegar. Return the peaches to the hot pan cut side down, and cook over medium-low heat for another minute, then place back on the plate with the balsamic, allowing them to rest for 1 minute. Return to the hot pan for 1 more minute for the final sear. Transfer the peaches back to the plate cut side up and refrigerate for 15 minutes to chill.

2. Cut the chilled peaches in half and arrange them on a large platter with the mozzarella. Season with sea salt. Tuck the basil leaves in between the peaches and mozzarella. Top with a generous drizzle of that super-special extra-virgin olive oil and some balsamic from the plate, if you want! Finish with fresh black pepper.

Get It

Looking for aged balsamic? My favorite is Essenza balsamic from Acetaia San Giacomo, which is aged about eight years. Please, whatever you do, don't reduce balsamic in a pot (it can easily burn) or purchase a glaze that has caramel coloring and corn syrup in it. If need be, mix equal parts young balsamic and honey for these peaches. For more on balsamic, see page 165.

Real mozzarella di bufala is made from water buffalo milk, which happens to be 90 to 95 percent lactose-free!

Get It

Panzanella is the great bread salad from Tuscany. Made with bread and cheese soaked in yummy tomato juices, it's supremely craveable. Since I'm a big fan of stone fruit, I thought: Why not make a version of panzanella that way? Plums, apricots, cherries, nectarines—they all add a sweet-tart flavor that's not too far off from tomatoes. If you don't like stone fruit, you can replace them with 3 more cups of chopped heirloom and cherry tomatoes. While feta adds a salty, zippy tanginess, feel free to use goat cheese or mozzarella instead.

Stone Fruit Panzanella

Serves 6

5 cups cubed Italian-style bread (large cubes, 1 inch-ish)

1 tablespoon everyday olive oil

2 garlic cloves, smashed and roughly chopped

2 medium tomatoes (like heirloom, beefsteak, or vine-ripened), halved

3 cups fresh stone fruits (like peaches, plums, apricots, nectarines, or cherries), pitted and cut into large pieces

½ seedless English cucumber, peeled and diced (about 1½ cups)

6 ounces sheep's milk feta, crumbled

3 tablespoons super-special extra-virgin olive oil

1 cup loosely packed fresh basil leaves, roughly torn

½ cup fresh dill sprigs

Coarse sea salt (like Maldon)

Fresh cracked black pepper

1. Preheat the oven to 375°F. In a large gallon-sized plastic bag, combine the bread cubes with the everyday olive oil and the chopped garlic. Seal the bag and shake the bread cubes well to evenly coat with the oil and garlic. Transfer to a foil-lined baking sheet and toast in the oven until golden and super crunchy, 15 to 20 minutes.

2. Meanwhile, set a box grater in a large bowl. Grate each tomato half (starting with the cut sides) into the bowl. Discard the peels. Add the stone fruits, cucumber, feta, super-special extra-virgin olive oil, basil, and dill; season with sea salt and black pepper. Stir well to combine. Let the mixture marinate while the bread is toasting.

3. Add the warm toasted bread cubes to the stone fruit mixture and toss thoroughly. Spoon the salad into a nice shallow bowl. Serve family style and enjoy!

Get It

The salad can be refrigerated
without the bread for 6 to
8 hours; add the bread when
you are ready to serve. (The
completed salad is still delicious
after it sits; I just prefer the
bread slightly soaked and
slightly crunchy.)

Get It

This recipe has been handed down for four generations in Jaime's family. He grew up making the scones with his Grandpa George. I am lucky enough that Jaime's mom, Kathy, took the time to teach me the secret family recipe! These scones (pronounced "scons" by Jamie's family) are basically a griddled buttermilk biscuit and, dang, they're so good and easy that I couldn't leave them out of this book. We usually make these for breakfast and for a crowd, but feel free to halve the recipe if you don't need so many. I love to serve sliced prosciutto or crispy slices of bacon with the scones to build little sandwiches. At Jaime's family home, they're always served with sausage cream gravy. But my favorite way to eat them is with tangy goat cheese butter and saba-blueberry jam.

George's Scones

with Saba-Blueberry Jam and Goat Cheese Butter

Makes 18 to 20 scones

3 cups self-rising flour, plus more for dusting (see Get It Get It)

2 sticks cold salted butter, cut into small cubes

1½ cups buttermilk (preferably organic or whole milk buttermilk)

Saba-Blueberry Jam (page 164), for serving

Whipped Goat Cheese Butter (page 117), for serving

1.   Lightly dust your work surface with flour. In a large bowl, using a large fork or pastry cutter, cut the butter into the flour. Using a wooden spoon, slowly stir in the buttermilk until the mixture is just combined and sticky. Turn the dough out onto the work surface. Using your hands and a bench scraper, knead the dough, pulling it together. Don't overwork it; you want to keep the butter in little bits throughout. Using a rolling pin, roll the dough to about a ¾-inch thickness, then using a 3-inch round biscuit cutter, cut out about 20 rounds, rerolling scraps as necessary.

2.   Heat a griddle (see Get It Get It) to 375°F and place the scones directly on the griddle. Cook for 10 minutes, until deep-golden brown, then flip and cook for another 10 minutes, until golden and crispy on both sides. Serve the scones warm, with the blueberry jam and goat cheese butter.

— Get It —

If you don't have self-rising flour, you can make your own. Combine 3 cups of all-purpose flour with 1½ tablespoons of baking powder and ¾ teaspoon of fine sea or table salt.

I use a plug-in countertop pancake griddle, but you can also use a large nonstick pan or griddle pan. If using a pan, heat over medium heat and monitor the heat as the scones cook. You don't want them to sizzle too loudly—just a light sizzle is good.

— Get It —

The Perfect Pair

Melon and prosciutto is a match made in heaven, à la corn and butter, balsamic and tomatoes ... Romeo and Juliet. Using a knife or mandoline, I like to cut my sweet, ripe melon into thin slices that mimic the slices of prosciutto. I'm also very happy when this duo is combined with fresh mozzarella in a salad. Melon has a pretty short season, peaking in summer. You can tell if a melon is ripe and ready by smelling it or by looking at the stem end: If it's still green, chances are the melon needs more time on your counter to ripen. Once ripened, it will keep in the fridge for a few days if you're not ready to eat it quite yet. A farmer friend gave me another useful tip—look for the resting spot on a melon (the brown patch where it sat on the ground). This indicates that it has had time to ripen on the vine. Brown spots are a good thing!

Saba is grape juice that's cooked down so it's almost a syrup. It's also known as cooked grape must or *mosto cotto* and is the first step in making true balsamic vinegar. I love to use it in a jam or compote because it adds a deep, tart molasses-like layer of flavor to the fruit. This jam can also be made with mixed berries like raspberries, blackberries, and strawberries. Figs, grapes, plums, or peaches would be fantastic too. This is also great over vanilla ice cream for a blueberry sundae!

Saba-Blueberry Jam

Makes about 2 cups

¼ cup sugar

¼ cup saba (my favorite is from Acetaia San Giacomo)

1 teaspoon finely grated lemon zest (use a Microplane)

1 tablespoon fresh lemon juice

12 ounces blueberries (1 pint)

In a small pot, combine the sugar, saba, lemon zest and juice, and 1 tablespoon of water. Cook over low heat for 5 minutes, stirring occasionally, to dissolve the sugar. Bring the mixture to a bubbling simmer, slightly caramelizing around the edges of the pan. Add the blueberries and continue to simmer for 5 minutes, or until most of the blueberries have erupted and the juices coat the back of a spoon. Remove from the heat and transfer the jam to a bowl to cool. The jam can be refrigerated for 2 weeks.

This is such an easy way to make the *most* delicious strawberry sauce. The recipe works best using the gorgeous red berries you get in season from a local market. The beauty of this is that the berries cook in their own juices, using just a bit of sugar and heat to transform into a most delicious sauce. Eat this on any and all breakfast sweets like French toast, pancakes, and waffles, or try the sauce over ice cream! This is also stellar served alongside cheese. If possible, make these the day before you want to serve them, to let them chill and thicken.

Easy Macerated Strawberries

Makes 2 cups

1 quart strawberries (1½ pounds), stemmed and quartered or halved

2 tablespoons sugar (preferably Sugar in the Raw or cane sugar)

1.   Place the strawberries and sugar in a medium heatproof metal bowl and cover tightly with two sheets of plastic wrap. Fill a medium saucepot with a few inches of water. Set the bowl over the water and bring to a boil. Cook over (not in) the boiling water for 25 minutes. You will notice that the strawberries will look all juicy and softened when they're done.

2.   While the berries are cooking, prepare a medium bowl with ice water. Remove the plastic wrap and set the hot bowl of berries in the ice bath. Gently stir with a rubber spatula to cool them down. (The strawberries will firm up as they chill, absorbing some of their syrup. The syrup also thickens as it cools.) Once chilled, transfer the macerated strawberries and syrup to an airtight container. They can be refrigerated for up to a month.

What? Balsamic Vinegar Is Made from Grapes?

On my first trip to Italy in 2009, I met Andrea Bezzecchi of Acetaia San Giacomo. He was a friend of a friend and went out of his way to meet me in Parma. We embarked on a detour to his *acetaia* (vinegar workshop) to taste true balsamic and see the traditional production of it. From that moment, I didn't know I was gaining a lifelong friend, but I did learn that balsamic vinegar is Italy's most misunderstood product. I was then on a quest to preach the word of balsamic and get every possible chance to hang with Andrea.

It can be very confusing when shopping at the store for balsamic, as there can be as many as 20 bottles, all with varying labels with different key words on them. I'm here to shed a little light on balsamic.

Real balsamic is made from grapes, unlike industrial balsamic vinegar, which is an astringent mixture made with soured wine (aka vinegar) and often caramel coloring. True balsamic vinegar can only be produced in two provinces in the Emilia-Romagna region, Modena and Reggio Emilia. To make it, trebbiano and lambrusco grapes are juiced and cooked in a big copper pot over direct fire. This creates "must," a thickened grape syrup. The process reduces the water content in the liquid and intensifies its sweetness. The must is then placed in a series of wooden barrels, called a *batteria*, for aging. A batteria consists of barrels, usually anywhere from five to nine of them, that descend in size. These are commonly made of different types of wood. What you might also not know is that balsamic is made from a blend of grapes from different harvests over time. Every year the grapes from the new harvest are picked, juiced, and cooked. The new must is used to top off the largest barrel, and thus starts a process of shifting half of the contents from each barrel down

through the descending-sized barrels. At this time, half of the balsamic from the smallest barrel is removed and bottled. The rest of the balsamic then sleeps soundly in the barrels until the next harvest, aging in the acetaia (which is usually in the attic in most farmhouses).

How long the vinegar is aged determines its labeling: anywhere from twelve to twenty-five years (or even longer!) and the European Union calls it *tradizionale* (also marked as DOP, which means "protected designation of origin"). This aged vinegar is a rich, perfect balance of sweet and sour and is used sparingly—a drop or two over tomatoes, Parmigiano, steak, vegetables, or ice cream is all you need. I don't call for using this remarkable vinegar in the book, though by all means, you should feel free to get some!

A more accessible category of vinegar coming out of these provinces is called *condimento* grade, and it can vary in quality. Many trusted producers are bottling their younger balsamic vinegar as condimento balsamic; I like to use the youngest and least thick for vinaigrettes and sauces. For drizzling on a dish as a finishing touch, I look for a more aged or thicker condimento, such as Acetaia San Giacomo's Essenza vinegar (my favorite) from Reggio Emilia. The key is to stick to vinegar made with grapes or grape must and not with coloring.

When grape must is further reduced to a syrup, the result is called *saba*. Saba is supremely thick and sweet—I liken it to a grape molasses. My favorite thing to do with saba is mix it with club soda for a saba soda! Sometimes I mix in a shot of bourbon for a great cocktail.

Just remember, when shopping, to look at the ingredients. If the bottle says it's made with cooked grape juice or must and that's it—ideally just one ingredient on the label—then that's the real deal.

In Italy, the breakfast table often includes big bowls of whole fruit, and I'm always blown away by how juicy and amazing red pears are. I think Bosc pears are another good option, even though they're slightly more astringent than red pears. The truth is, roasting any pear in butter and vermouth will take it from pretty good to incredible! Pears are finicky and they need to ripen, so I recommend buying them several days before you plan on eating them and leaving them on the counter where you can monitor their ripening. Don't put them in the fridge. This is a great crostini for entertaining because you can make the pears ahead of time and assemble and broil the crostini when you're ready to serve. If you think you'd like a touch more sweetness, feel free to drizzle these with some aged balsamic or honey.

Vermouth-Roasted Pear and Taleggio Crostini

Serves 4 to 6

2 tablespoons unsalted butter

2 ripe red or Bosc pears, peeled, halved, and cored

Kosher salt

Leaves from 6 to 8 fresh thyme sprigs (about 2 tablespoons)

¼ cup sweet vermouth

1 teaspoon everyday olive oil

6 to 8 slices of rustic-style European bread (½ inch thick)

6 ounces Taleggio cheese or any other gooey, melty washed-rind cheese (see Get It Get It)

1 teaspoon poppy seeds

1. In a large nonstick skillet, melt the butter over medium heat. Place the pears cut side down in the skillet and season with a pinch of salt. Let the pears sear in the butter for 5 to 6 minutes, until caramelized. Turn the pears over, season with another pinch of salt, and cook until they begin to soften and caramelize on the other side, about 4 minutes. Add the thyme leaves and sweet vermouth. Turn the heat down to low, flip the pears again, and cook until glazed, 3 to 4 minutes. Transfer the pears to a platter and drizzle the glaze from the pan over them. Let cool. Once cool, cut each pear half lengthwise into about 4 slices.

2. While the pears are cooling, preheat the oven to 425°F. Line a baking sheet with foil and brush with the olive oil. Arrange the bread slices on the baking sheet and toast until golden brown, about 10 minutes.

3. Okay, now to top the crostini. Taleggio is a deliciously earthy, funky cheese with a washed rind, so it's up to you how much funk you are feeling. Feel free to either trim the rind or simply slice the cheese with the rind. Place the Taleggio on the toasted bread slices. Arrange the pear slices on top and drizzle with any remaining glaze.

4. Turn the broiler to high. Broil the crostini 3 to 4 inches from the heat source for 4 to 5 minutes, until the cheese begins to melt. Remove from the oven and garnish with the poppy seeds. Serve immediately.

Get It

I'm wild about Taleggio cheese on these crostini, because it adds a great earthy funk and it melts so beautifully. But if you're not so into that funk, feel free to trim off the rind before using it, or try raclette, Camembert, or Brie.

Get It

I love this hearty combination of kale and apples. Be sure not to slice the apples too thinly, as they will lose their crunch and texture. Both the kale and the apples hold up beautifully to the creamy dressing, making this a perfect salad to plant on the dinner table without worrying about it wilting!

Apple-Kale Salad

with Charred Shallot–Tahini Vinaigrette

Serves 4 to 6

1 large or 2 small bunches of Tuscan kale, washed, stemmed, leaves cut into 1-inch-wide ribbons

Kosher salt

Charred Shallot–Tahini Vinaigrette (recipe follows)

2 medium apples (like Honeycrisp or Gala), halved, cored, and sliced

4 or 5 red or French breakfast radishes, thinly sliced or quartered

4 ounces sheep's milk feta cheese, crumbled (1 cup)

¼ cup Spiced Seeds (page 366)

Small fresh dill sprigs, for garnish

Place the kale in a large mixing or salad bowl and season with salt. Add half of the dressing and, using a wooden spoon, gently toss until the leaves are fully dressed. Add the apples, radishes, feta, and the remaining dressing and gently fold the salad together. Sprinkle the spiced seeds and dill over the top and serve.

Charred Shallot–Tahini Vinaigrette

Not all tahini is equal, and I consider tahini quality somewhat like olive oil in how much it can vary. I'm a huge fan of Soom Foods, which is a female-owned company that sources single-origin sesame seeds from Ethiopia. They roast and press the sesame seeds into an incredible paste with flavor beyond compare.

Makes ¾ cup

2 tablespoons everyday olive oil

1 medium shallot, peeled and sliced into ¼-inch-thick rings (you can sub onion too)

3 tablespoons tahini paste, mixed well

2 tablespoons fresh lemon juice

2 tablespoons sherry vinegar or white wine vinegar

1 teaspoon honey

1 teaspoon ground sumac (optional)

1 teaspoon toasted sesame seeds (optional)

Kosher salt

1.　In a small skillet, heat 1 teaspoon of the oil over medium-high heat. Add the shallot rings and cook until lightly charred, about 3 minutes. Flip and continue to cook until dark brown on both sides. Remove from the heat and set aside to cool.

2.　In a food processor, combine the cooled shallot, remaining oil, tahini, lemon juice, vinegar, honey, and sumac and sesame seeds, if using. Pulse to combine, until just mixed and a bit chunky. Season with a few pinches of salt. The dressing can be refrigerated for up to 2 weeks.

I was taught how to make this apple mostarda on my first trip to Italy. I was staging at Dal Pescatore, helmed by Chef Nadia Santini and her mother-in-law, Nonna Bruna. Nonna Bruna taught me how to make this spicy condiment, which is enjoyed all over Italy as a counterpoint to rich dishes including cured meats and cheeses. It is also the secret ingredient in the delicious Tortelloni di Zucca (pumpkin-stuffed pasta) on page 372. I love to use the mostarda in a variety of ways. It's a perfect condiment on a cheese and charcuterie board, delicious added to the center of a grilled cheese sandwich, and wonderful finely chopped and added to roasted mushrooms or winter squash. Making apple mostarda is simple, but it takes several days. The process starts by tossing apples with sugar to draw out their moisture so the apples create a syrup from their own juices. Once that syrup is heated and poured back over the apples, more liquid is exuded. This process is repeated for several days, which might seem tedious but really only takes a few minutes. The apples will have retained an irresistible crunch, but they'll also be soft and wonderful, as well as fragrant and spicy.

Apple Mostarda

Makes about 2 cups

4 Granny Smith apples (about 2 pounds), peeled, halved lengthwise, cored, and sliced lengthwise ¼ inch thick

1½ cups granulated sugar

2 tablespoons apple cider vinegar

1 tablespoon hot mustard powder (like S&B Hot Mustard or Colman's) or mustard oil (typically found in Indian markets)

Kosher salt

1. In a large bowl or mason jar, toss the apples and sugar until evenly coated. Cover with plastic wrap and place in a cool place in your kitchen. On a piece of tape or on the plastic wrap, write the date and the numbers 1, 2, 3, 4, 5, and 6.

2. Each day, drain the sugar syrup that collects with the apples. Place the syrup in a small saucepot and bring to a boil over high heat. Pour the boiling syrup over the apples and re-cover the bowl immediately with the plastic wrap. Mark off each day as completed to keep track of the process. Repeat this step for the remaining days, draining, boiling, and reusing the syrup. You will notice the apples darkening and shrinking, and the amount of syrup will continue to increase.

3. Once the apples have cooled after the sixth day of cooking, drain the syrup into a large skillet over high heat. Bring to a boil, then add the apples and stir well. Continue to boil, stirring the apples often with a rubber spatula, for about 10 minutes. You might notice that the apples seem to inflate slightly. (This is a good sign.) Turn the heat down to low and cook, stirring often and folding gently, until the apples darken and deepen in color and begin to shrivel, about 20 minutes.

4. Transfer the apples to a medium bowl. In a small bowl, combine the vinegar and mustard powder; stir into the apples and season with a few pinches of salt. Store the apple mostarda in an airtight container in the fridge for up to 1 month.

─ Get It ─

If you want to speed up the process on this mostarda, you can double down and do it in 3 days. Just cook the apple syrup twice a day, allowing cooling time between each pass.

─ Get It ─

Get It

You can make mostarda with a variety of fruit. Plums, peaches, and pears are great and can be prepared just like the apples. I also like using rhubarb for a tart-sweet mostarda, or figs. For rhubarb, cut the stalks on a bias into 2-inch pieces. The figs just need to be cut in half. Given the tender nature of these two ingredients, I refrain from the final cooking process in the syrup. (This technique helps retain their texture.) After the sixth day, drain the syrup and transfer it to a saucepot. Simmer over low heat until reduced by 75 percent, then pour the hot syrup over the fruit.

Get It

Get It

I like using hot-smoked salmon or trout here instead of cold-smoked salmon, which has a totally different texture. If you can't find hot-smoked salmon, you can bake off a seasoned salmon fillet, then cool and flake it into the salad. Or if you're planning to grill some salmon, make an extra one to use in this salad the next day!

Get It

Fish and grapes might seem like a strange combo, but this dish is inspired by a classic French dish called flounder Veronique, which is roasted flounder and vermouth sauce studded with champagne grapes. I have seen renditions of that dish made with salmon, so here we are! Hot-smoked salmon flaked into a salad is nice with the crunch of celery, and the roasted grapes in the dressing add a bit of acidity. The roasted green grapes in the vinaigrette are also a nod to the vermouth in the original dish. I like buying a variety of grapes, since they provide different levels of sweetness and acidity. There are a lot of excellent grapes at the market in late summer and fall—some of my favorite varietals are Jupiter and Canadice. For the vinaigrette, the green globe grape has just the right flavor.

Grape, Celery, and Hot-Smoked Salmon Salad

Serves 4

4 celery stalks, quartered lengthwise and chopped

2 cups red, black, or green grapes, halved

Roasted Green Grape Vinaigrette (recipe follows)

Coarse sea salt (like Maldon)

1 large or 2 small heads of escarole or romaine, washed and dried

1 head of curly endive or radicchio, washed and dried

Handful of mixed herbs (like tarragon, parsley, and/or chives)

Fresh cracked black pepper

1 pound hot-smoked salmon, broken into large flakes

1 cup walnuts, toasted, lightly chopped

In a large wooden salad bowl, toss the celery and grapes with half of the vinaigrette, and season with a pinch or two of salt. Gently fold in the greens and herbs, along with a bit more vinaigrette. Season with salt and pepper. Fold in the flaked salmon and toasted walnuts. If you would like a bit more dressing, drizzle the remaining dressing over the top.

Roasted Green Grape Vinaigrette

The vinaigrette can be refrigerated in an airtight container for a few days.

Makes about 1 cup

1 cup seedless green grapes

1 teaspoon everyday olive oil

Kosher salt

2 tablespoons Dijon mustard

1 tablespoon finely grated lemon zest (use a Microplane)

2 tablespoons fresh lemon juice

1 tablespoon sour cream or plain Greek yogurt

1 tablespoon fresh tarragon, chopped

1 tablespoon minced fresh chives

2 tablespoons super-special extra-virgin olive oil

Fresh cracked black pepper

1. Position the oven rack 5 inches from the heat source and turn the broiler to high. On a foil-lined baking sheet, toss the grapes with the everyday olive oil and a pinch of salt. Broil for 6 to 8 minutes, until slightly charred and blistered. Let cool for 5 minutes.

2. In a food processor, combine the mustard, lemon zest and juice, yogurt, tarragon, chives, and a few generous pinches of salt; pulse to combine. Drizzle in the super-special olive oil, then add the grapes and pulse to gently combine. Taste and season with a bit more salt and pepper.

When people ask me what I'd take to a desert island, I always say lemon and olive oil. If you have those two things, you can make just about anything taste good! I really love lemon, and I feel like it—along with oranges—deserves to be the star of this salad. I know it's popular to shave fennel for salads, but I think it tends to get watery and sad pretty quickly that way. I prefer it sliced a little thicker, which keeps it nice and crunchy with all the citrus. You can actually use any citrus you like—even just oranges would be fine. The secret is draining off the citrus juice and using it to make the vinaigrette for the onions and olives, marinating them a bit. Another secret is giving the almonds a deep toast in the oven, which brings out the best flavor. (If you don't like toasting nuts, Trader Joe's actually sells them roasted.)

Citrus and Fennel Salad

with Super-Roasted Almonds

Serves 4

2 oranges (ideally a mix of Cara Cara, Valencia, blood, and/or navel)

1 small lemon or Meyer lemon

½ small red onion, thinly sliced

⅓ cup pitted green olives, chopped

2 tablespoons everyday olive oil, plus more for drizzling

¼ cup whole almonds (skin on or blanched, whichever you have)

3 mandarins or clementines

1 grapefruit (preferably Ruby Red)

1 large or 2 small fennel bulbs, trimmed (fronds reserved), cored, and sliced about ⅛ inch thick

1 cup loosely packed fresh basil leaves

Coarse sea salt

Fresh cracked black pepper

1. Preheat the oven to 350°F. Finely grate the zest of the 2 oranges and the lemon (not the grapefruit or mandarins, however) into a large bowl. Squeeze the lemon juice into the bowl with the zest. Stir in the red onion, olives, and olive oil.

2. Place the almonds on a small baking sheet and toast until fragrant and dark golden brown; the interior of the almonds should be a nice caramel brown color, about 15 minutes. Transfer to a work surface to cool, then roughly chop the almonds.

3. Fit a medium bowl with a strainer. Using a serrated knife, trim each end of the mandarin oranges and the grapefruit and set them flat on a work surface. Cut away the peel and white pith, following the shape of each piece of fruit. Working over the bowl, hold the cleaned citrus in your hand, and using a small paring knife, cut in between the membranes to release the sections into the strainer. Squeeze the juice from the membranes into the bowl. Transfer the juice to the red onion mixture.

4. In a salad bowl, toss the fennel and citrus sections with the onion mixture. Fold in the basil leaves and season with a pinch or two of sea salt and some cracked pepper. Top with the fennel fronds and chopped almonds and serve.

Get It

You can prep the salad through Step 3 and refrigerate everything separately for several hours before serving. Unlike a lot of salads, this one is also great for leftovers the next day!

Get It

Ricotta is the magic behind so many Italian dishes, lending an amazingly creamy and light texture that can't be beat. I like making my own because it's so simple, and the texture of homemade ricotta is way better than the kind you buy at the supermarket. High-end ricottas from gourmet markets can be delicious, but they're expensive. Try your hand at making your own. I think you'll get hooked!

Homemade Lemon Ricotta

Makes 10 to 12 ounces

1 quart whole milk, not ultra pasteurized

½ cup heavy cream

½ teaspoon kosher salt

2 tablespoons fresh lemon juice

1. In a large heavy-bottomed saucepot, bring the milk, cream, and salt to a simmer over medium-high heat, whisking occasionally. Once the milk mixture reaches a simmer, stir in the lemon juice. Let the mixture come back to a simmer; watch the curds and whey separate. Do not stir or break up the curds. Remove the pot from the heat and let sit for 15 minutes.

2. Place a colander inside a large bowl and line the colander with cheesecloth or a lint-free towel or sheet. Using a ladle, gently transfer the curds into the colander, allowing the excess whey to collect in the bowl beneath. Drain the ricotta for 10 minutes; the longer it drains, the drier it will become. Transfer the ricotta to an airtight container and keep refrigerated for up to a week. If you plan to use the whey, strain it again, then transfer to an airtight container and refrigerate for up to 1 week.

― Get It ―

If you're going to take a stab at making this ricotta, don't throw away the whey! This protein-rich liquid is milky and lemony and can add rich flavor to many things. You can use it in ragùs in place of stock, and as a braising liquid for meats and vegetables. I like using it to poach eggs too—so yummy!

― Get It ―

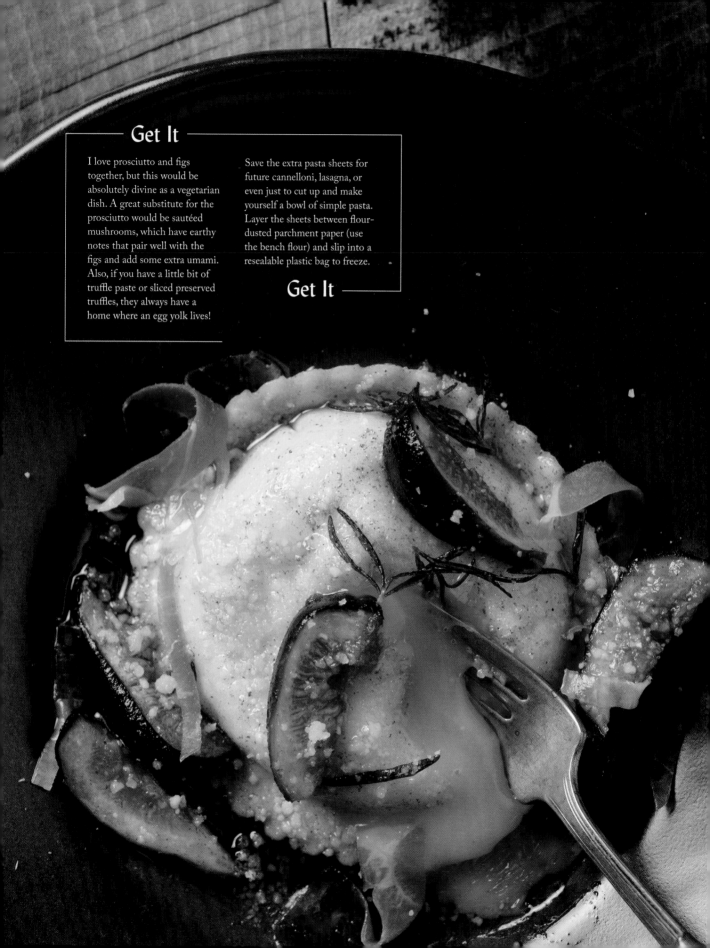

Get It

I love prosciutto and figs together, but this would be absolutely divine as a vegetarian dish. A great substitute for the prosciutto would be sautéed mushrooms, which have earthy notes that pair well with the figs and add some extra umami. Also, if you have a little bit of truffle paste or sliced preserved truffles, they always have a home where an egg yolk lives!

Save the extra pasta sheets for future cannelloni, lasagna, or even just to cut up and make yourself a bowl of simple pasta. Layer the sheets between flour-dusted parchment paper (use the bench flour) and slip into a resealable plastic bag to freeze.

Get It

If you can make ravioli, you can make raviolo, which is just a giant ravioli. This might not be the best pasta to tackle if you've never made fresh filled pasta before, but I've taken some of the anxiety out of the dish by plating the boiled raviolo right away, then topping with the browned butter, figs, parm, and prosciutto. You can play around with how you finish the dish, though I think browned butter and parm should always be included in the mix. If you have truffles, they would be outstanding here. This is not an everyday dish, but a real winner for a celebratory meal.

Egg Yolk–Filled Raviolo

with Fresh Figs and Prosciutto

Makes 6 raviolo

Raviolo Filling

2 cups Homemade Lemon Ricotta
(page 173) or whole milk ricotta
(see page 8)

2 ounces prosciutto (4 to 6 slices),
finely chopped

½ cup freshly grated Parmigiano-
Reggiano

Kosher salt

Fresh cracked black pepper

One recipe Raviolo (page 267)

Finishing

Kosher salt

1 stick unsalted butter

Leaves from 2 fresh rosemary
sprigs

8 fresh, ripe Black Mission or
Brown Turkey figs, quartered

½ cup freshly grated Parmigiano-
Reggiano

2 ounces prosciutto (4 to 6 slices),
cut into ¼- to ½-inch-wide
strips

2 tablespoons aged balsamic

Fresh cracked black pepper

1. **Make the raviolo filling.** (See page 266 for photos.) In a medium bowl, combine the ricotta, chopped prosciutto, and parm with a pinch or two of kosher salt and black pepper. Place the filling in a pastry bag or a sturdy resealable plastic bag. Snip off the corner of the bag before piping.

2. **Shape the raviolo.** Follow the directions on page 267 to shape and fill each raviolo. If you're cooking the ravioli immediately, keep finished ones covered with a clean lint-free towel as you roll and shape the remaining pasta. If you're not using them immediately, sprinkle a generous amount of bench flour on top of them, cover with a clean lint-free towel, and wrap tightly in plastic. The pasta can be refrigerated like this overnight.

3. **Finish the dish.** Bring a large pot of water to a boil and season generously with kosher salt. Meanwhile, in a medium skillet, melt the butter over medium heat until browned, about 2 minutes. Add the rosemary, letting it sizzle and fry for 30 seconds, then add the quartered figs and a few pinches of kosher salt. Cook for a minute, until the figs are slightly softened but still hold their shape. Keep warm over low heat while you cook the raviolo.

4. Before you cook these delicate raviolo, be sure to have plates or shallow bowls ready for serving. Carefully place the raviolo in the boiling water and stir to gently nudge or flip them; cook for 2½ to 3 minutes, until the raviolo are floating and the pasta feels tender around the edges. Using a slotted spoon or skimmer, gently remove each raviolo one at a time and transfer to a plate. Top with the grated parm, then spoon the hot butter and figs evenly over the top. Finish with the prosciutto strips, the balsamic, and some fresh cracked black pepper.

This pasta is insanely creamy and bright, balanced with the sharp, funky, salty flavor of pecorino cheese. Don't try to sub Parmigiano; it won't work because it has too much natural sweetness that would get lost here. I love making this with rigatoni, 'cause the ridges grab the sauce so perfectly. One thing to note: If you are so inclined, the whipped ricotta–pecorino made in Step 1 is fantastic dolloped over steamed asparagus, or any kind of simple pasta too!

Rigatoni al Limone

with Whipped Ricotta and Pecorino Romano

Serves 4 to 6

1¼ cups Homemade Lemon Ricotta (page 173) or whole milk ricotta (see page 8)

¾ cup freshly grated Pecorino Romano, plus more for garnish

3 tablespoons fresh lemon juice

Kosher salt

1 pound short or full-sized dry rigatoni

1 tablespoon unsalted butter

1 tablespoon finely grated lemon zest (use a Microplane), plus julienned zest from 1 lemon for garnish (see Get It Get It)

1 garlic clove, thinly sliced

¼ teaspoon chile flake

2 cups ricotta whey from Homemade Lemon Ricotta (see Get It Get It)

2 tablespoons minced fresh chives, for garnish

1.   In a food processor, combine the ricotta, pecorino, lemon juice, and a pinch of salt and blend until the mixture is super smooth and a soft whipped consistency has formed, about 3 minutes. You may want to stop halfway and push the mixture down the sides of bowl to ensure all of the ricotta gets whipped.

2.   Bring a large pot of water to a boil and season generously with salt. Cook the rigatoni for 2 minutes less than the directions for al dente pasta specified on the package.

3.   While the pasta cooks, heat another large pot or saucepan over medium-high heat. Add the butter and allow it to brown, about 3 minutes. Add the grated lemon zest, along with the garlic and chile flake, and cook until fragrant, about 1 minute; add the ricotta whey. Once the pasta is ready, reserve ½ cup of the pasta cooking water, then drain the pasta and add to the pot with the whey mixture; bring the pasta to a simmer and let it marry into the whey sauce. Once the whey has reduced by about half and the pasta is al dente, stir in the whipped ricotta. Cook, stirring continuously, until the pasta is coated in a creamy velvety sauce, 2 to 3 minutes. The sauce will thicken as it cools, so add a bit of pasta water to thin it if needed. Top with the chives, some grated pecorino, and the julienned lemon zest to serve.

— Get It —

For the lemon zest garnish, I opt for a thin julienne (thin strips). Using a peeler, peel the lemons and use a paring knife to shave off any of the bitter white pith from the peels. Stack the cleaned peels on top of each other, and carefully cut into thin strips. This adds a beautiful touch to the pasta, with a real pop of lemony brightness.

Because this recipe calls for using both the Homemade Lemon Ricotta and its whey, it takes some extra effort. However, if you'd like to bypass making the ricotta, you can substitute fresh whole milk ricotta from the store. In place of the whey, melt 2 tablespoons of unsalted butter in 1 cup of the warm pasta cooking liquid and add 1 cup of additional tap water to that.

Get It —

Listen to Your Vegetables

I grew up picking Satsuma mandarins with my grandpa. They're available during the winter and have a more complex flavor than other mandarins. I love their sweetness and juiciness, plus they're seedless and easy to peel. This recipe might seem like a pork dish, but don't be fooled—the orange is definitely the star here. You get the amazing citrus fragrance in the rub and tons of orange flavor from the juicy charred segments.

Satsuma and Fennel Seed–Roasted Pork Loin

Serves 6

2 tablespoons fennel seeds

One 4½- to 5-pound bone-in pork loin roast, tied with butcher's twine (ask for a 7-bone center-cut rack, tied; see Get It Get It)

Kosher salt

2 pounds Satsuma mandarins (or tangerines or clementines)

3 large garlic cloves

6 tablespoons everyday olive oil

2 tablespoons chopped fresh rosemary, plus leaves from 2 sprigs for garnish

1 tablespoon smoked paprika (preferably Spanish pimentón de la Vera)

2 fennel bulbs, trimmed with a bit of the stalks attached, quartered

4 large Yukon gold potatoes, peeled and cut into ½-inch slices

3 shallots, cut into ½-inch rings

½ cup pitted black olives (like kalamata, Taggiasca, or Leccino)

Fresh cracked black pepper

2 tablespoons honey

1. Heat a small skillet over medium heat. Add the fennel seeds and toast for 3 to 4 minutes, stirring often. (I like to give the pan a little shake!) Once the fennel seeds are fragrant and the color has deepened, remove from the heat. Transfer to a medium mixing bowl. Then, using a smaller metal mixing bowl, press down to crack the seeds.

2. Season the pork all over with salt and place on a small baking sheet. Into a medium bowl, using a Microplane, grate the Satsuma zest and the garlic. Peel and separate the Satsumas into segments and set aside for later. To the bowl, add 3 tablespoons of the olive oil, along with the cracked fennel seeds, chopped rosemary, and smoked paprika and mix well. Using your hands, schmear the Satsuma rub all over the pork rack. Cover with plastic wrap and refrigerate for 2 hours or overnight.

3. Preheat the oven to 450°F. In a large roasting pan or baking pan, toss the fennel, potatoes, shallots, and olives with the remaining 3 tablespoons of oil; season generously with kosher salt and cracked black pepper. Spread the veggies evenly in the bottom of the roasting pan. Place the marinated pork roast on top of the veggies, in the center of the pan. Roast for 15 minutes, then reduce the heat to 400°F. Continue to roast for another 45 minutes, until a thermometer inserted in the center of the roast registers 135°F. (The temperature will increase as the roast rests.)

4. Transfer the pork to a rack set over a baking sheet and cover loosely with foil. Let rest for 15 to 20 minutes. Using a spatula, mix the veggies. Add the Satsuma segments and drizzle with honey. Turn the broiler to high and carefully adjust the oven rack so it's 3 to 4 inches from the heat source. Broil the vegetables for 8 to 10 minutes, until they have a nice golden, roasted color, stirring once halfway through; watch the veggies carefully so they don't burn. Remove from the oven and toss with the fresh rosemary leaves. Slice the pork into chops (by cutting in between the bones) and serve alongside the roasted vegetables.

Get It

To tie your roast yourself, cut kitchen twine into six pieces, each about 12 inches long. Place each piece of twine under the pork roast, between the bones, and tie it tightly around the roast, knotting it by the bones.

Get It

Leaves
& Greens

Ah, greens. These seemingly simple leaves are jam-packed full of vitamins, minerals, and fiber and are a great source of iron, calcium, magnesium, and folate—there is a real powerhouse of nutrients hidden in these guys. And they also taste great! So it's no surprise that I try to incorporate greens into as many of my meals as possible.

There are a lot of different greens that range from tender and mild to hearty and bitter. I always stash three or four different kinds of greens in my fridge at home. I keep lettuce or salad greens like green leaf and Bibb lettuce in the crisper, and I always have some heartier greens like kale and Swiss chard around for wilting in olive oil with a thin shave of garlic and a pinch of chile flake. To mix things up, I usually try to have bitter greens (aka chicories) handy too, like radicchio, frisée, escarole, and endive. Chicories make for such good salads!

Let's talk about chicories, which are so popular in Europe but perhaps less so here in the US. They're truly adored in Italy, where bitter flavors are celebrated. Americans tend to like to rid foods of bitterness! But I want you to try and embrace that palate-wakening bite. If you take radicchio, dandelion greens, puntarelle, endive, or frisée and toss it in a high-acidity dressing, it's magical! Especially when that salad becomes a side dish alongside a great roast chicken or sizzling steak. It's not very different from pairing with a great wine.

My Italian friends often wonder why we sell so many of our greens precut and cleaned in plastic boxes or bags in the US. In Italy, greens are sold whole and not so well cleaned, and they're much cheaper this way—not to mention there is also no plastic waste. I am a big believer in buying greens whole, so I rarely buy the prewashed greens or bagged lettuces at the store. I get a much better shelf life on my greens if I wash and spin them myself.

I have strong feelings about the best ways to clean our leafy friends. Lettuces are fairly easy to clean, but you have to be vigilant with hearty greens like kale, spinach, collards, mustards, and turnip greens—they are masters at hiding sand and grit. To wash well, fill a bowl (or your sink!) with cold water and submerge the greens in the water. Let them soak for about 5 minutes. Then lift the greens from the water, dump out the dirty water, and clean out the bowl. I can't emphasize how important it is to clean the bowl before you refill it with fresh water. Repeat this process until the greens are fully clean and the water in the bowl is too. You can test this visually, but I suggest you also feel around the bowl for grit. Sometimes you can't see it.

Once you've cleaned and dried your greens (a salad spinner is the best for this), you can layer them in gallon-sized bags, between paper towels. They should store in the fridge like this for up to 2 weeks.

I encourage you to explore the world of greens and how far you can take them. Try using chopped greens to finish soups and stews or to fold into eggs or omelets. Or add some kale or spinach to your green juice or smoothie to kick-start your day! Eating greens just makes me feel good, so I try to have a few on my plate at every meal. Let's face it too: Sometimes you just need a salad!

Meet aerobics instructor Coach Kale, workin' out these head lettuces. These greens are the key to a fit and healthful life!

Egg White Frittata with Spinach, Tomatoes, and Feta (page 185); Pallotte Verdi (page 199); "Insalata di Campo" (page 184); Wilted Escarole with Chiles and Toasted Garlic (page 202); Swiss Chard Rolls Stuffed with Farro, Sundried Tomatoes, and Feta (page 195)

Don't be fooled looking at the ingredients below and saying, "Why is that even a recipe?" I am here to tell you that this is a fundamental part of understanding tender baby greens and salads. Early in my career, there were about five lettuces that ruled the salad plate, but then mesclun and spring mixes took the world by storm and really shook things up. Just to be clear, I'm talking about the tender baby lettuces available at farmstands and the like, and not the kinds that come in bags and boxes at the supermarket— those don't taste like anything. The best way to treat these delicate but flavor-packed greens is to toss them lightly with olive oil. Vinegar, lemon, or anything water- or acid-based weighs down the lettuce. By coating them with a thin layer of oil first, you preserve the integrity of the little baby greens.

Insalata di Campo

aka Tender Spring Greens Salad

Serves 2 to 4

5 to 6 ounces tender spring lettuce mix or arugula, washed and spun dry

2 teaspoons peppery super-special extra-virgin olive oil

Coarse sea salt (like Maldon)

2 teaspoons fresh lemon juice

Freshly grated Parmigiano-Reggiano, for serving

In a wooden salad bowl, gently toss the cleaned greens with the olive oil and a pinch of sea salt until the leaves are lightly coated with a shine of oil. Gently toss with the lemon juice. Top with grated parm and serve immediately.

Get It

This is such an easy salad that can be gussied up with lots of additions. Here are some to try:

✢ Fresh herbs like snipped chives, yellow celery leaves, tarragon, or parsley

✢ 1 ounce finely grated ricotta salata or Parmigiano-Reggiano (about ¼ cup; use a Microplane)

✢ 2 radishes, thinly shaved on a mandoline

✢ 1 small fennel bulb, thinly shaved on a mandoline

Get It

I always wonder what to do with all those leftover egg whites after making pasta dough. They can be scrambled, but honestly, they have no flavor and the texture is just bad. My solution is to make this quick and awesome frittata. You can add anything you like to it—think peppers, mushrooms, potatoes, bacon, sausage—but the recipe below is my go-to egg white frittata mix. This is a great "pantry" recipe, meaning that you don't need to go to the store to make it. I use frozen greens because they're heartier once thawed, but you can totally use fresh greens. Just be careful to fully wilt them down. When working with egg whites, I find that letting them cook without stirring creates the best texture.

Egg White Frittata

with Spinach, Tomatoes, and Feta

Serves 4

1 tablespoon plus 1 teaspoon everyday olive oil

½ small yellow or red onion, thinly sliced

8 ounces frozen spinach, slightly thawed

Kosher salt

1 cup egg whites

4 ounces crumbled feta

2 small ripe tomatoes, thinly sliced crosswise

¼ cup Peperonata with its oil (page 285; optional, but if you have it, use it!)

2 tablespoons torn fresh herb leaves (like parsley, basil, chives, and oregano)

1.   Set an oven rack about 3 inches from the heat source and turn the broiler to high. In an ovenproof 10-inch nonstick pan, heat 1 teaspoon of the oil over medium-high heat. Add the onion and cook until golden, about 5 minutes. Add the spinach and season with a pinch or two of salt. Cook, spreading the spinach evenly in the pan with a rubber spatula, until dry, 3 to 4 minutes.

2.   Drizzle the remaining 1 tablespoon of olive oil around the outside edge of the pan, then pour in the egg whites. Tip and swirl the pan, rotating the egg whites around the surface, filling the nooks and crannies of the spinach. With a rubber spatula, loosen the sides of the egg whites around the edge of the pan. At this point, the bottom of the egg whites will be cooked but the top still runny. Remove from the heat.

3.   Add the crumbled feta, sliced tomatoes, and peperonata to the top of the eggs. (If you aren't using the peperonata, I recommend drizzling another 1 tablespoon of olive oil on top.) Broil the frittata until the edges and the cheese are golden, about 5 minutes. Add the fresh herbs and let sit for a minute before serving. You can serve the frittata right from the pan, or remove it and slice into wedges to serve.

Get It

The sturdy nature of these greens means that they hold up well to the dressing and can be dressed up to 10 minutes before serving.

I tend to like making the mix of chicories for this salad in bulk. I wash and prep the greens, then layer them in a gallon-sized bag with paper towels. They hold in the fridge for about 5 days. It's so convenient to have them ready to go for a quick salad at any given time!

You can use whole or sliced almonds too, just adjust the cooking time and watch for the color and smell.

Get It

Italians love bitter foods, and the chicory family of lettuces is a perfect introduction to some of these flavors. In Rome, one of my favorite salads is puntarelle with an anchovy-garlic vinaigrette. Puntarelle is a crazy bitter green from the chicory family. In Roman markets, a special wire cutter is used to julienne or shred it. Puntarelle is super challenging to find here, so instead I opt for the chicories that are readily available in the market like escarole, frisée, and radicchio. Feel free to use a mix of the chicories, and if you can't find one, just bulk up with another. You can also sub in arugula, watercress, or dandelion greens. I like to think of this dressing as the OG dressing that inspired Caesar Cardini to create the Caesar salad in Mexico!

Roman Tricolore Chicory Salad

with Mandarin Orange and Toasted Almonds

Serves 4 to 6

½ cup slivered almonds

¼ teaspoon everyday olive oil

1 small head of escarole, large leaves cut into bite-sized pieces, smaller leaves left whole

1 small or ½ large head of frisée, leaves torn into bite-sized pieces

1 small head of radicchio, leaves torn into bite-sized pieces

2 heads of Belgian endive, cut crosswise into 1-inch pieces

3 or 4 Satsuma mandarins, peeled and segmented

Roman Anchovy-Garlic Vinaigrette (recipe follows)

1. Heat a small skillet over medium heat. Add the almonds and olive oil and toast, tossing or stirring continuously, until super fragrant and golden brown, 3 to 4 minutes. Remove from the heat and cool. (Don't be scared to take the almonds to a golden-brown color; the super-toasty flavor of the almonds accents the salad so well.)

2. To prepare the salad, combine the escarole, frisée, radicchio, and endive in a large salad bowl. Top with the mandarin orange segments and toasted almonds. Dress the salad with the vinaigrette and serve.

Roman Anchovy-Garlic Vinaigrette

Makes about 1 cup

2 tablespoons fresh lemon juice

2 tablespoons white or red wine vinegar

1 tablespoon colatura or Vietnamese-style fish sauce (optional, but good!)

1 small garlic clove, very finely grated (use a Microplane)

1 white or brown anchovy fillet, minced (about 1 teaspoon)

1 teaspoon Dijon mustard

½ teaspoon sugar

½ cup everyday olive oil

Coarse sea salt (like Maldon)

Fresh cracked black pepper

In a small mixing bowl, combine the lemon juice, vinegar, colatura (if using), garlic, anchovy, mustard, and sugar. Slowly whisk in the olive oil until combined. Season with a pinch of sea salt and fresh cracked black pepper to taste. This dressing will hold in your fridge in an airtight container for 2 weeks.

This is a recipe that my Oma, Gertie Grueneberg, made at every big family meal. We liked calling it "green mountain salad" because that is the German translation for Grueneberg. (In Italian, "green mountain" translates to *monteverde*, which is how I named the restaurant.) When opening Monteverde, I included my own version of this, and it has been on the menu ever since. Some guests come back just for this salad! Why? Well, there are two secrets to it. The first is that the vegetables are dressed and allowed to marinate for at least 15 minutes, developing lots of extra flavor. The other secret is my grandmother's favorite seasoning in the vinaigrette: Lawry's seasonings! Of course, I like to make my own seasoning, but feel free to use Lawry's like Oma did. If you don't have garlic salt or lemon pepper, you can use 1 minced garlic clove, 1 teaspoon ground black pepper, and 1 tablespoon kosher salt, and increase the lemon zest to 1 tablespoon instead.

My Oma's Green Salad

with Crunchy Vegetables and Avocado–Red Wine Vinaigrette

Serves 6

½ seedless cucumber, peeled and chopped

2 celery stalks, cut on a ¼-inch bias

2 small carrots, peeled, then thinly shaved with a Y-peeler

½ cup quartered radishes

8 to 10 cherry tomatoes, halved

1 ripe avocado, halved, pitted, peeled, and diced

1 tablespoon finely chopped fresh flat-leaf parsley

1 tablespoon finely chopped chives

1 tablespoon finely chopped fresh tarragon

Avocado–Red Wine Vinaigrette (recipe follows)

2 or 3 heads of Little Gem lettuce, washed, dried, leaves torn or chopped

½ head of radicchio, leaves separated and torn

Kosher salt (optional)

1.   In a large salad bowl (preferably wooden), combine the cucumber, celery, carrots, radishes, tomatoes, avocado, parsley, chives, and tarragon. Toss the vegetables with ¼ cup of the vinaigrette. Let marinate for at least 15 minutes and up to 1 hour at room temperature.

2.   When you're ready to serve, gently toss the Little Gem and radicchio with the vegetables. Drizzle with ⅓ to ½ cup more dressing to taste, then toss gently. Season with a few pinches of salt (if using) and serve immediately.

Avocado–Red Wine Vinaigrette

This dressing is full of zip and tang. I love it with the crunchy vegetables and Little Gem lettuce. It's also great to use as a marinade, so consider putting it on your favorite hearty veggies (like brassicas) before roasting in the oven. You can also use it to marinate chicken and shrimp before grilling.

Makes 2 cups

½ cup red wine vinegar

1 tablespoon garlic salt

2 teaspoons lemon pepper

1 teaspoon finely grated lemon zest (use a Microplane)

1 tablespoon fresh lemon juice

1 cup everyday olive oil

1 avocado, halved, pitted, peeled, and diced

In a blender or food processor, or in a bowl using a hand blender, combine the vinegar, garlic salt, lemon pepper, lemon zest, and lemon juice. With the motor running, drizzle in the olive oil. Add the avocado and pulse a few times to incorporate the avocado into the vinaigrette; it should be slightly chunky. Due to its high acidity, this dressing will last in your fridge in an airtight container for up to 4 months.

This is a decadent egg dish that would be a dream for brunch with friends and family. I prefer using full-grown spinach over baby spinach because it has much more texture and flavor. Instead of adding milk or cream, the mascarpone cheese creates a more creamy, luxurious texture and elevates the humble scrambled eggs. The most important technique is the swirl of the pan, which creates thin layers of egg "crepes" to make the dish even more unique.

Scrambled Eggs and Spinach Florentine

Serves 4

8 large eggs

½ teaspoon kosher salt

2 tablespoons unsalted butter

1 bunch of large-leaf spinach, washed, stems trimmed, leaves chopped (4 to 5 cups)

½ cup mascarpone cheese

¾ cup shredded Fontina cheese (about 3 ounces)

3 fresh chives, snipped

Fresh cracked black pepper

1 loaf of crusty Italian-style bread, sliced and toasted

1.   Put the eggs in a large bowl, season with ¼ teaspoon kosher salt, and whisk to break up the egg yolks slightly.

2.   In a large nonstick skillet, melt the butter over medium heat. Add the spinach, season with ¼ teaspoon kosher salt, and cook, stirring occasionally with a rubber spatula, until wilted, about 3 minutes. Add the eggs but do not stir. Holding the handle of the pan, gently swirl the pan to set the eggs on the outside edges. Use the spatula to push down the cooked eggs from the sides and again swirl the pan.

3.   Before the eggs are fully set, turn the heat to low and add the mascarpone and Fontina to the center of the pan. Gently fold the egg mixture into the center, incorporating the cheeses with the spatula, 3 to 4 minutes. Again, there is no stirring at this point, only gentle folding so as to not break up the sheets of egg. Transfer to a serving plate and garnish with chives and black pepper. Serve with freshly toasted bread or tomato bread (see Get It Get It).

— Get It —

To make these eggs even more special, serve them with tomato bread: Cut a ripe, juicy tomato in half and rub it cut side down on toasted bread slices while squeezing gently. Add a drizzle of super-special extra-virgin olive oil and a pinch of sea salt to finish.

— Get It —

This great classic Tuscan soup is packed with flavor and hearty enough to eat like a stew. Its name is a nod to Chicago: "A couple two, three" is a very Chicago way of saying a few, which works for this soup because I like to use many greens here! Feel free to change up or add more varieties of greens. Swiss chard, spinach, collards, green cabbage, and escarole are all great choices. The other part of the name of the soup, *ribollita*, means "reboiled." Its origins come from Tuscany and the Italian *cucina povera* (peasant kitchen), utilizing all the bits and pieces from the table to make a second meal or dish. In Italy, food waste is often turned into amazing, soulful dishes.

Couple Two, Three Greens Ribollita Soup

Serves 8

2 tablespoons everyday olive oil, plus extra for drizzling

3 celery stalks, diced

1 medium carrot, diced

1 small bulb fennel, cored and diced

1 large yellow onion, diced

Kosher salt

One 28-ounce can crushed tomatoes with their juice

2 dried bay leaves

1 pinch of chile flake (optional)

Best Dried Beans, with their cooking liquid (page 74; see Get It Get It)

8 cups vegetable stock, chicken stock, or Charred Onion Vegetable Stock (page 325)

One 2- to 3-inch piece Parmigiano rind

1 small bunch of turnip or mustard greens, stemmed, leaves chopped

2 bunches of Tuscan kale, stemmed, leaves chopped

1 small head of savoy cabbage, cored and chopped

2 cups cubed crusty Italian-style bread (like ciabatta)

1 tablespoon red wine vinegar

2 fresh rosemary sprigs

Fresh cracked black pepper

Freshly grated Parmigiano-Reggiano, for serving

Giardiniera-style pickled peppers in olive oil, for serving (optional; see Get It Get It)

1.   In a large heavy-bottomed pot, heat the oil over medium-high heat. Add the celery, carrot, fennel, and onion, and cook until softened and golden, about 3 minutes. Season with a few pinches of salt. Add the crushed tomatoes, bay leaves, and chile flake (if using), and simmer, stirring often, until the tomatoes reduce a bit, about 5 minutes. Add the cooked beans and their liquid, along with the stock and parm rind; bring to a boil. Add the greens, kale, and cabbage, stirring to allow them to soften in the broth; season with a few more generous pinches of salt. Reduce the heat to low, cover, and simmer the soup, stirring occasionally, until it has thickened slightly, 45 minutes to an hour.

2.   Stir in the bread and 1 cup of water and bring the soup back up to a boil. Stir in the vinegar, then add the rosemary. Cover, turn off the heat, and let sit for 5 minutes. Remove the parm rind and rosemary and discard them. Season with salt and fresh black pepper. To serve, ladle the ribollita soup into bowls and sprinkle with a spoonful of grated parm and some fresh black pepper. If you are up to it, add some giardiniera peppers with their oil, just like we do in Chicago. If you aren't using giardiniera, then a generous drizzle of olive oil (don't be shy with the oil) will do—it's just how the Tuscans do it.

Get It

I like this soup best with home-cooked beans, but you can sub two cans of cranberry, cannellini, or great Northern beans with their liquid if you prefer.

Spicy giardiniera peppers are a staple condiment in Chicago, as they are a key topping on deep-dish pizza and a main ingredient in sausage and peppers, but they're most commonly used on the famed Italian beef sandwich. I like adding them to this soup for some zip and spice.

Get It

Horta is a traditional Greek dish made with boiled dandelion greens, extra-virgin olive oil, and lemon juice. The Greeks believe that eating these greens is the secret to a long, healthful life. My chef friend Roel Alcudia taught me the secret of his horta, which is adding a bit of olive oil to the water when boiling the greens. By creating a thin barrier of oil on the leaves, the acid from the lemon juice isn't absorbed by them, so they're more marinated than pickled. You can certainly make this recipe using dandelion greens, if you want to go the more traditional route, but I love using colorful rainbow Swiss chard. Note that the miso is not a traditional ingredient, but I like the little element of surprise and umami in the mix.

Swiss Chard Horta

Serves 4 to 6

Kosher salt

4 tablespoons everyday olive oil, plus more for drizzling

2 large bunches of rainbow Swiss chard, washed

1 teaspoon white miso

2 teaspoons fresh lemon juice

Finely grated zest of 1 lemon

1. Line a baking sheet with paper towels. Bring a large pot of generously salted water (it should taste like the ocean) to a boil. Add 2 tablespoons of the oil. Cut each chard leaf lengthwise through the stem, splitting the leaves in half. Working in a few batches, group the leaves with the stems together. Place the chard in the boiling water stem first and boil for 30 seconds, then push the whole leaves into the water. Boil for 2 minutes, until the leaves are tender. Using a slotted spoon or skimmer, transfer to the lined baking sheet. Refrigerate to cool.

2. In a large mixing bowl, toss the chilled chard leaves with the remaining 2 tablespoons of olive oil. In a small bowl, dissolve the miso in the lemon juice and stir in the zest. Add to the chard and toss well. Serve chilled. The chard is best served the same day, but it can be refrigerated overnight. (It will just darken a bit.)

Get It

I like to spice it up a bit from time to time by adding a tablespoon of Calabrian chile paste or sambal oelek to the marinade.

Get It

I admit that I love anything stuffed: pasta, veggies, cabbage, eggplant, mushrooms . . . it all means extra deliciousness to me. Here I stuff Swiss chard with a filling that's a lot like a grain salad with Greek flavors. I also include the chard stems, which often get discarded. Don't throw them away! They're so full of natural sweetness that I think you'll love. My favorite thing is to eat these rolls hot, and then save some for the next day, when I eat them cold. If you're a lunchbox-type of person, they're excellent packed to go too.

Swiss Chard Rolls

Stuffed with Farro, Sun-Dried Tomatoes, and Feta

Serves 4 as a main or 8 as a side dish

Kosher salt

½ cup farro

2 tablespoons plus 2 teaspoons everyday olive oil

2 large or 3 small bunches of red, white, or rainbow Swiss chard (8 to 10 leaves total), washed

1 small red onion, diced

1 garlic clove, thinly sliced

½ cup pitted kalamata olives, sliced or chopped

½ cup oil-packed sun-dried tomatoes, drained and chopped

8 ounces feta (preferably a creamy style made with sheep's milk)

½ cup fresh mint leaves, roughly chopped, plus more for garnish

¼ cup pickled peppers (like Greek peperoncini), chopped

2 tablespoons unsalted butter, cut into pieces, plus more

Jaime's Radish Tzatziki (page 323) or 1 cup plain whole milk Greek yogurt or labneh

Get It

This recipe packs in a lot of fresh mint, but you can also use a combination of fresh herbs if you have them—try fresh dill, basil, and parsley.

Get It

1. In a large pot of boiling salted water, cook the farro until al dente yet tender, 10 to 12 minutes. (You cook farro like you would a dry pasta.) Using a slotted spoon, transfer the farro to a strainer to drain. Bring the water back up to a boil; add 2 teaspoons of the olive oil to the pot.

2. While the water is coming up to a boil, set your Swiss chard on a work surface. Cut away the stems at the base of each leaf; cut off the tough ends and discard, then finely dice the stems so all the pieces are roughly the same size. Trim any thick part of the stem remaining on the leaves, cutting a small V at the base if necessary to make sure the leaves are easy to roll.

3. Working in two batches, blanch the Swiss chard leaves in the boiling water until softened and pliable, 1 to 2 minutes. Be careful to not overcook them as the leaves will tear and fall apart when rolling. Using a slotted spoon or skimmer, transfer the blanched leaves to a baking sheet lined with paper towels to cool.

4. Pour out the water, wipe out the pot, and place it back on the stove over medium heat. Add the remaining 2 tablespoons of olive oil along with the onion, garlic, and chard stems. Cook until softened, 5 to 6 minutes. Add the olives, sun-dried tomatoes, and the cooked farro. Stir to combine. Remove from the heat and add the feta, mint, and pickled peppers and mix to combine.

5. Preheat the oven to 425°F. Lightly butter a 9 by 13-inch baking dish. On a large cutting board, lay out the blanched leaves and place about ¾ cup of filling in the center of each leaf. Working with one roll at a time, fold the sides of the leaf in, then begin rolling the leaf up around the filling, like a cigar. Place the Swiss chard rolls seam side down in the baking dish and top with small cubes of butter. Bake for 20 minutes. Let stand for 5 minutes. Garnish with fresh mint and serve with tzatziki. While these rolls are great eaten hot, they can also be served chilled, similar to Greek dolmades (stuffed grape leaves).

I have a love affair with both Tuscan kale and soffritto, so this dish really speaks to me. Soffritto is the building block of most great sauces and braises in the Italian kitchen. It typically consists of vegetables, aromatics, fat (bacon or olive oil), and tomatoes to help caramelize it. Tuscan kale is my kale of choice, because it holds its texture when cooked—its bumpy leaves are perfect for grabbing onto the soffritto and tomato sauce. But this can also be made with many different greens too, like cabbage, bok choy, or Swiss chard.

Braised Tuscan Kale

with Butternut Squash Soffritto

Serves 4

3 ounces pancetta or thick-cut bacon, diced (½ cup)

1 teaspoon everyday olive oil

1½ cups diced butternut squash (see Get It Get It)

1 small red onion, finely chopped

Kosher salt

1 tablespoon fresh thyme leaves

One 14½-ounce can crushed tomatoes

2 large or 3 small bunches of Tuscan kale, washed, stemmed, leaves torn into 3-inch pieces

1½ cups Charred Onion Vegetable Stock (page 325) or your favorite stock

Fresh cracked black pepper

1.   In a large saucepot, cook the pancetta in the olive oil over medium-high heat until the fat is rendered and the pancetta is golden and crispy, about 5 minutes. Transfer the pancetta to a paper towel–lined plate.

2.   Return the pot to medium heat. Add the squash and onion and season with a heavy pinch of salt. Cook until the vegetables are softened and beginning to caramelize, about 8 minutes.

3.   Add the thyme and stir with a wooden spoon to loosen the brown bits from the pancetta on the bottom of the pot. Add the crushed tomatoes and cook until thickened and reduced by more than half, 8 to 10 minutes.

4.   Add the kale and slowly wilt it into the vegetable mixture, stirring. Season with another pinch or two of salt. Add the stock and reduce the heat to medium-low. Cook until the kale is softened and the mixture has cooked down and formed a thick, stew-like consistency, 20 to 25 minutes. Check for seasoning. I like to finish the braised greens with lots of black pepper. Serve them with the crispy pancetta on top.

── Get It ──

I recommend using precut squash from the produce department of your grocery store. Otherwise, 1 small or ½ medium squash will do here.

You can easily make this dish vegetarian. Substitute 1 cup of stemmed, sliced shiitake mushrooms for the bacon and increase the olive oil to 2 tablespoons.

── Get It ──

Get It

For best results, I like to use a dense Italian-style loaf of bread here. Look for a filone or Tuscan-style loaf. Most Italian bakeries will have something that will work. Ciabatta will be too light and airy.

I think this is a winner for vegetarians. It's versatile enough to add any leafy green you like, even broccoli, but I suggest sticking with a green veg so it's a good match with the cheese.

Get It

I first learned about these meatless meatballs on a visit to an amazing agriturismo (working farm) in Abruzzo. I had one of my top 10 meals ever at La Porta dei Parchi in Anversa degli Abruzzi, though the food was super humble. When I tried their pallotte, made with just bread, milk, eggs, and cheese and lightly fried, I realized how truly special these "meatballs" are. They represent the best of *cucina povera*— simple peasant cooking born from using what is available. I like making mine with kale (it sneaks in some healthful deliciousness, as well as a nice color!) and fresh chile, and I like the crunch from deep-frying. Don't skip the fresh tomato sauce, which is bright and acidic and helps the pallotte sing.

Pallotte Verdi

aka Kale and Bread Meatless Meatballs with Fresh Tomato Sauce

Makes 18 pallotte; serves 6 to 8

Pallotte

2 tablespoons everyday olive oil

2 tablespoons minced fresh red chile (like finger or Fresno chiles), or 1 tablespoon Calabrian chile paste or sambal oelek

3 garlic cloves, minced

2 medium bunches of Tuscan kale, washed and stemmed

Kosher salt

1 pound Italian-style bread, diced into 1-inch pieces (8 cups)

2 cups whole milk

2 large eggs

4 ounces Manchego cheese, shredded with the large holes of a box grater (1 cup)

½ cup freshly grated Pecorino Romano

1 teaspoon dried oregano

1 teaspoon red wine vinegar

Finishing

2 quarts neutral oil, for frying

4 cups fine dry breadcrumbs

Fresh Tomato Sauce (page 391)

¼ cup freshly grated Pecorino Romano, for garnish

Finely grated zest of 1 lemon

2 fresh oregano sprigs, for garnish

1. **Make the palotte.** In a large sauté pan, heat the olive oil over medium-high heat. Add the chile and garlic and toast until golden, about 1 minute. Add the kale and cook, stirring often, until wilted and softened, 3 to 4 minutes. Season with a few pinches of kosher salt. Transfer the kale to a strainer or colander set in a bowl to let any excess liquid drip off for about 10 minutes. Transfer to a work surface and roughly chop the kale mixture.

2. Meanwhile, in a large mixing bowl, cover the bread with the milk. Using your hands (I like to wear gloves), combine the bread and milk; you can also pulse them in a food processor until the bread has softened and takes on an oatmeal-like texture. Add the chopped kale and mix to combine. Mix in the eggs, Manchego, pecorino, oregano, and vinegar. If you find the mixture is too wet and sticky, add a bit of dry breadcrumbs.

3. Line a baking sheet with parchment paper. Using a ¼-cup measuring cup, scoop the mixture (roughly 2 ounces) and roll into balls; place the balls on the baking sheet. Refrigerate for 30 minutes or until fully chilled; the pallotte should be firm to the touch. These can be covered and refrigerated for up to 3 days in advance before frying.

4. **Finish the pallotte.** When you are ready to serve, in a large pot, heat the oil to 350°F. Line a baking sheet with a rack or paper towels. Place the breadcrumbs in a shallow dish or bowl. Using your hands, roll the pallotte in the breadcrumbs to coat, then carefully lower 5 or 6 meatballs into the hot oil. Fry until golden brown and hot, 4 to 5 minutes; you can check with a thermometer to ensure the balls have reached 160°F. Using a slotted spoon or skimmer, transfer the cooked pallotte to the prepared baking sheet. Repeat with the remaining pallotte. If they cool too much, feel free to warm them in a 250°F oven before serving. Serve with fresh tomato sauce, topped with grated pecorino, lemon zest, and fresh oregano leaves. You can place the tomato sauce in a casserole dish and place the crispy pallotte on top, or just serve the sauce on the side.

I am obsessed with this green pesto and not just because it tastes crazy good—this dish is one of Jaime's favorite pastas, in fact. I love that it includes healthy kale and olive oil, as well as an irresistible crunch from (also healthy) walnuts! I serve the pasta hot most of the time, but it's also incredible served cold as a pasta salad.

Bucatini Verde

with Tuscan Kale Pesto and Walnuts

Serves 4 to 6

½ cup plus 1 teaspoon everyday olive oil

2 bunches of Tuscan kale, stemmed, leaves torn into 2-inch-ish pieces

1 cup tightly packed fresh basil leaves

½ cup fresh flat-leaf parsley leaves

1 cup walnut pieces

2 garlic cloves

Kosher salt

Finely grated zest of 1 lemon (use a Microplane), plus extra for garnish

2 tablespoons lemon juice

½ cup freshly grated Pecorino Romano, plus more for garnish

2 pinches of chile flake

1 pound dry bucatini, spaghetti, or other strand pasta

Super-special extra-virgin olive oil, for drizzling

Get It

To understand my method for making pesto this way, see page 241.

To freeze the pesto, transfer it to an airtight container and place a small piece of plastic wrap directly on the surface of the pesto, sealing it from the air in the top of the container. The pesto freezes beautifully for 1 to 2 months.

Get It

---

1. Place ½ cup of the olive oil in the freezer until chilled, at least 15 minutes. Fill a large bowl with ice water and add 2 packed cups of the torn kale along with the basil and parsley. Soak for 10 to 15 minutes. Reserve the remaining kale leaves.

2. Meanwhile, in a medium skillet, heat the remaining 1 teaspoon of oil and the walnuts over medium heat, tossing to coat the walnuts. Cook, tossing or stirring often, so the walnuts toast slowly and evenly, about 6 minutes. The walnuts should deepen in color and become fragrant. Remove from the heat and cool. If the nut pieces are big, coarsely chop them.

3. In a blender or food processor, combine the chilled olive oil with the garlic and a pinch of kosher salt. Using your hands, lift half of the greens from the ice water and gently shake. Place in the blender. Using a spoon or spatula, gently push the greens down into the oil. At high speed, blend until smooth. Add the remaining chilled greens, pushing them down and blending until smooth. Transfer the kale pesto to a bowl; set that bowl in the ice bath. Carefully stir in the lemon zest and juice along with ½ cup of the walnuts, the pecorino cheese, and the chile flake.

4. Bring a large pot of salted water to a boil. Cook the pasta until al dente, following the package directions. Add the remaining kale to the pot with the pasta during the last 2 minutes of cooking. Before draining, reserve ½ cup of the pasta water. Drain the pasta and return it to the pot. Off the heat, toss the pasta with the kale pesto, drizzling in the reserved pasta cooking water to create a creamy sauce. (I like to toss this pasta off the heat because we are conducting a lightning-fast—Vegas style!—pasta marriage ceremony.) Transfer the pasta to plates, top with the remaining walnuts, sprinkle with grated pecorino, and drizzle with super-special olive oil.

This might very well be the simplest dish in the book. I don't think most folks think about eating wilted lettuces like escarole and chicory, but they're so flavorful and they hold up well once they're cooked. The trick here is not adding all of the greens at once. If you cook them in two batches, you end up with a combination of textures—some of the greens will be softer and more wilted, and the rest will be a little bit more crunchy. This is a great alternative to sautéed spinach, so give it a try!

Wilted Escarole

with Chiles and Toasted Garlic

Serves 4

1 tablespoon everyday olive oil

1 large garlic clove, sliced

¼ teaspoon chile flake

2 medium-ish heads of escarole, washed, leaves roughly torn

Kosher salt

1 tablespoon fresh lemon juice

In a large skillet, heat the olive oil over medium-high heat. Add the garlic and cook for 1 minute, until toasted. Add the chile flake and half of the escarole. Toss well and season with salt. Add ¼ cup of water and cook, stirring, until the escarole is softened, about 2 minutes. Reduce the heat to medium-low and fold in the remaining escarole. Cook for 2 minutes, or until softened. Add the lemon juice, season with salt to taste, and serve.

What?? I Can Cook My Lettuce??

We tend to think mainly about cooking heartier greens, but I'm here to tell you that you can cook lettuces too! For starters, I love grilling romaine or radicchio—all I do is slice it lengthwise through the stem (keeping the stem attached), then give it a quick char on the grill so it stays nice and crispy on the inside. I finish it with a simple drizzle of olive oil and some sea salt and presto! It's ready for a great grilled lettuce salad. Another thing to try is using lettuce in soups: I often fold green leaves into wonton soup or chicken noodle soup—anything nice and brothy that will help it wilt. Or try a wilted lettuce salad with hot bacon dressing, like they do in the South. So good!

The thing about Italy is that you can eat pasta in one place, then drive ten miles down the road and eat the same pasta and it'll be called something else. This shape, for instance, is called tortelli in Reggio Emilia, but it's called ravioli in Bologna. Bailey and I were working on an inspired version of our own for Monteverde. Bonding over our love for miso soup, we landed on adding some white miso, which sneaks a little umami into the dish. That, combined with the craveable flavors of spinach, parm, mirin, and scallions, creates delicious harmony here. I can't stress enough the need to use adult spinach because all spinach is not created equal. Baby spinach is watery and bland and cooks down to nothing, while adult spinach is packed with flavor. Just buy the big bunches and clean the leaves well.

Spinach Tortelli

with Leeks, Miso, and Hazelnuts

Serves 4 to 6

Tortelli

2 tablespoons unsalted butter

2 green onions or scallions, white parts thinly sliced, green tops reserved for garnish

12 ounces fresh mature spinach, washed and stemmed

Kosher salt

2 cups grated Parmigiano-Reggiano

16 ounces whole milk ricotta (see page 8) or 2 cups Homemade Lemon Ricotta (page 173)

Fresh cracked black pepper

A few pinches of ground nutmeg

The Essential Egg Yolk Pasta Dough (page 256)

½ cup "00" flour mixed with ½ cup semolina (aka bench flour), for dusting

ingredients continue

1.   **Make the tortelli filling.** In a large nonstick skillet, melt the butter over high heat. Add the green onions and cook until translucent but not brown, 1 to 2 minutes. Add the spinach and cook, stirring often with a rubber spatula, until fully wilted and the pan is dry, about 5 minutes. Season with a pinch of kosher salt. (It is important that your pan is dry, but if not, you may want to drain the spinach in a colander if it seems wet.) Transfer the spinach to a small baking sheet or a plate and refrigerate for 10 minutes.

2.   In a food processor, combine the chilled spinach with the parm and blend until smooth, 10 to 15 seconds. Transfer to a bowl, fold in the ricotta, and season with a few pinches of salt, black pepper, and nutmeg. Wrap the bowl tightly with plastic wrap and refrigerate until you're ready to make the tortelli. The filling can be refrigerated overnight.

3.   **Shape the tortelli.** (See page 265 for photos.) Cut each ball of pasta dough in half so you have four pieces total. Work with one ball of dough at a time and keep the other pieces wrapped in plastic. Set your pasta machine to the thickest setting, which is usually 1. Flatten the dough slightly with a rolling pin, creating a rectangle shape; be mindful to match the width of your roller. (This will create consistent-sized pasta sheets.) Feed the dough through the roller. Continue to feed the dough through the roller on increasingly thinner settings; you might need to add a little bench flour to one side of the dough if it's feeling a little sticky or wet. Continue rolling the dough until you've reached setting 5; run the dough through twice. Transfer the dough to a work surface that's lightly dusted with bench flour. Use a pizza cutter or a sharp knife to cut the dough into two long sheets, each about 16 inches in length and about 6 inches in width. Cut each sheet in half lengthwise, creating four sheets total, each about 16 by 3 inches.

recipe continues

Finishing

1 tablespoon everyday olive oil

1 large or 2 small leeks, white parts only (save the greens for stock), split lengthwise, thinly sliced, and soaked in cold water to loosen any dirt

1 cup chicken or vegetable stock or low-sodium broth

¼ cup mirin

2 tablespoons white miso

6 tablespoons unsalted butter

¼ cup green onion tops (reserved from the tortelli), thinly sliced

⅓ cup toasted hazelnuts (see page 9), chopped

Finely grated zest of 1 orange (use a Microplane)

4. Scoop the filling into a pastry bag or sturdy resealable plastic bag; snip off the corner. Starting with one strip of dough and keeping the rest covered with a clean lint-free towel while you work, pipe about 1 tablespoon of filling across the lower half of the dough, leaving 1 inch between mounds; you should have about six mounds in all. Fold the dough over lengthwise and press to seal, using your hands to firmly press and seal each tortelli. Cut the tortelli and trim the excess dough. Use the tines of a fork to create indentations around the edges of each tortelli. Transfer the finished tortelli to the prepared baking sheet. If you're using the tortelli immediately, keep them covered with the towel while you roll and shape the remaining pasta. If you're not using the tortelli immediately, sprinkle a generous amount of bench flour on top of the pasta, cover with a clean lint-free towel, and wrap tightly in plastic. The tortelli can be refrigerated like this overnight.

5. **Finish the tortelli.** Bring a large pot of water to a boil and season generously with kosher salt. In a large nonstick or stainless-steel skillet, heat the olive oil. Add the leeks and cook over medium heat until translucent but not browned, 2 to 3 minutes. Add the chicken stock, mirin, and miso. Stir well to dissolve the miso into the sauce and bring to a simmer. Stir in the butter.

6. Meanwhile, add the tortelli to the boiling water and cook, stirring every minute or so to prevent the tortelli from sticking to each other. Cook until tender and floating, 3 to 4 minutes. Using a skimmer or a slotted spoon, transfer the cooked tortelli to the pan with the sauce. Jiggle the pan slightly to rotate the tortelli, allowing them to get coated with and absorb the sauce, for 4 to 5 minutes. To serve, garnish the tortelli with the green onion tops, chopped hazelnuts, and orange zest.

Get It

If you are having trouble finding adult spinach, I recommend using green Swiss chard leaves instead. They are sturdy enough to hold their own after cooking, with a sweet green flavor that's similar to spinach. Frozen spinach works well in a pinch too.

Get It

Mushrooms

Mushrooms. Are. Incredible. They capture the essence of the earth, adding a unique texture and savory flavor to recipes, with hints of umami. I think they are the most chillaxed vegetable in this book, like a yogi! They don't overpower other flavors, and they go well with just about everything—meat, fish, chicken, pasta, cheese . . . you name it.

Mushrooms are almost all water, so the key to eking out the most flavor is to roast or sauté them until they're crispy and browned. The golden rule of mushroom cooking is to give them enough time to develop that color, which means don't be tempted to stir them a lot! They're also excellent shaved raw into salads.

There are so many different types of mushrooms, so it helps to think of them in two main groups: cultivated (farmed) and wild. When I'm cooking at home, I usually stick to using cultivated mushrooms from local stores and farmers' markets (also Asian markets, where I often get the best bang for my buck) because they're pretty clean and ready to go right into recipes. Mushrooms are spectacularly flexible, so feel free to play around with different types of mushrooms if a recipe calls for them to be chopped or mixed into something. Except for stuffed mushrooms, you can pretty much swap any mushroom for another, though if you swap cultivated for wild, you might want to double the

quantity to maximize the flavor. And while mushrooms are delicious enough to stand on their own, they make a stellar stand-in for meat in many recipes (like my Porcini Bolognese with Tagliatelle on page 223).

Wild mushrooms are special, not just because they have such incredible, unique flavor, but they can cost up to three times more than cultivated mushrooms—or more. So I recommend making them the star in a dish. Chanterelles, porcini, black trumpets, and hedgehogs are some of my favorites, though porcini are harder and harder to come by, and the quality is hit-or-miss.

The important thing to keep in mind when buying wild mushrooms is that they are typically sandy or dirty and might even come with a little friend or two. Please don't be alarmed; they just need to be washed. As a young cook, I would spend hours meticulously cleaning wild mushrooms, as it's easy to become obsessive over them. You just don't want to wash a wild mushroom too far in advance (no more than a few hours), because as soon as they get wet, they get slimy.

To start, cut the mushrooms ahead of washing, as there can be pockets of hidden dirt. Dunk the mushrooms in a bowl filled with warm water, then pull them out by hand or with a strainer; the goal is to keep the dirt or sand in the bottom of the bowl. Repeat this process until the water is clear. A salad spinner is a wonderful tool for drying mushrooms. I give them a few spins to get all the water off, then place them on a clean kitchen towel and store them in the fridge covered with the towel.

Have fun with the wild world of mushrooms, and don't be scared if you find a worm now and then—it's natural!

The fun-guys are groovy, funky, and laid back. Mushrooms love to jam with any veg in any dish.

Clockwise from top: Shaved Mushroom and Celery Salad with Truffle Vinaigrette (page 212); Mushroom Tart with Robiola and Strawberries (page 220); Stuffed Cremini Mushrooms (page 221); Corzetti Pasta with Chanterelles, Brown-Buttered Pecans, and Wild Greens (page 225)

Back in 2016, after Monteverde had just opened, I wanted to plan a special New Year's Day dinner for all of my friends. I was planning a very opulent, celebratory meal with caviar, foie gras, steak, and stuffed cabbage—and a great salad. But in my planning, I had overlooked the salad, so I had to pull it together from what was in the cooler at the restaurant. I grabbed some mushrooms, radishes, and celery, along with some ripe avocados and a block of Parmigiano, and got to work. Everyone was blown away by it, and my friend Eric kept saying, "Everything was spectacular, but *that salad though!*" We all agreed that my cooler salad was the best thing on the table that night. Soon after, we put it on the restaurant's menu, and forever it will be known as #thatsaladtho. If you have access to fresh black truffles or fresh porcini mushrooms, this is a perfect dish for them. You can also add other seasonal vegetables if you prefer; I like asparagus, fennel, and mixed radishes.

Shaved Mushroom and Celery Salad

with Truffle Vinaigrette, aka #thatsaladtho

Serves 6

12 ounces trumpet royale (aka king oyster) or large white button mushrooms, very thinly sliced or shaved (preferably on a mandoline)

3 large radishes, very thinly sliced or shaved (preferably on a mandoline)

8 celery stalks, sliced ¼ inch on a bias, tender yellow leaves reserved (see Get It Get It)

1 avocado, halved, pitted, peeled, and sliced

1 teaspoon finely grated lemon zest (use a Microplane)

¼ cup fresh lemon juice

2 tablespoons Dijon mustard

Kosher salt

¼ cup plus 2 tablespoons everyday olive oil

1 teaspoon black truffle paste

Fresh cracked black pepper

1 loosely packed cup shaved Parmigiano-Reggiano

In a medium bowl, combine the mushrooms, radishes, celery, and avocado. In another medium bowl, whisk the lemon zest, lemon juice, and mustard, and season with a few pinches of salt. Slowly whisk in the olive oil until emulsified. Whisk in the truffle paste and season with black pepper to taste. Add the dressing to the vegetables, season with salt again, add the parm, and gently toss. Serve immediately.

Get It

I love peeled celery! Peeling eliminates that pesky stringy quality that can be unpleasant. It only takes a minute and it's well worth it, in my opinion.

Don't be intimidated by shaved cheese—all you need is a vegetable Y-peeler to shave it.

Get It

Cleaning Morels

Cleaning morel mushrooms is unlike cleaning other mushrooms, as their web-like texture is like a super sponge, holding on to grit and sand. Anyone who has prepared morels knows the frustration of the sand issue, but have no fear, I am here to help you! Here are a few tips for managing morels:

1. Cut the morels crosswise into ½- to 1-inch rings, depending on their size. Cutting them lengthwise will cause them to lose their unique shape when cooking. Never, ever leave them whole. It is impossible to remove all of the sand if they are left whole.

2. Veggie Washing Machine Move: Submerge them in slightly warm water—I find the warm water helps loosen the sand. Much like when you're cleaning greens, agitate the morels in the water and then lift them from the bowl. Place them in another bowl of clean warm water. When draining the dirty water, check to see how much sand is in the bottom of the bowl. Use your hands to check for sand and grit (not just your eyes) by feeling the inside of the empty bowl. Repeat until there is no more sand to the touch and the water is clear. Do a final rinse with cold water, then spin them in a salad spinner to dry.

3. Store the clean morels on a clean kitchen towel on a baking sheet or platter in the refrigerator until you are ready to use them. They will keep like this for 1 day.

4. Morels, like porcini, have been known to have a few creepy crawlies in them, but don't worry. The cleaning process removes them, and at least you'll know the mushrooms are organic!

Don't let the long recipe title scare you away from this easy and addictive dish! A little care with the common combo of mushrooms and eggs goes a long way—once you try these eggs cooked in browned butter, it's a game changer. Feel free to use any green you have on hand, as spinach, kale, and Swiss chard all would work well in this dish. And of course, if you can't find any of these fancy mushrooms, use what you can find. Cremini, button, portobello, and shiitake are most common. If you go this route, I recommend using a mix for maximum earthy flavor. Slice them about ¼ inch thick for the best sear.

Pan-Roasted Fancy Mushrooms

with Golden Fried Eggs, Bitter Greens, and Balsamic

Serves 2 as a main or 4 as part of a brunchy spread

2 tablespoons everyday olive oil

8 ounces assorted fancy mushrooms (like beech, maitake or hen of the woods, and oyster), torn into bite-sized pieces (see Get It Get It)

Kosher salt

3 tablespoons unsalted butter

4 large eggs

2 garlic cloves, sliced (I love to use spring garlic when it's in season)

Leaves from ½ fresh rosemary sprig

5 ounces bitter greens (like curly endive, radicchio, escarole, or dandelion greens), washed and torn into 2- to 3-inch pieces (4 cups)

1 tablespoon young balsamic vinegar

Coarse sea salt (like Maldon)

¼ cup freshly shaved Parmigiano-Reggiano (use a Y-peeler)

1.   Heat a 12-inch cast-iron skillet over medium-high heat and add the olive oil and mushrooms. Using a heatproof spatula, spread the mushrooms in an even layer. Cook undisturbed until golden on one side, 1 to 1½ minutes, then stir and repeat until the mushrooms are golden all over, about 5 minutes longer. Season with a few pinches of salt. Transfer to a bowl.

2.   Lower the heat to medium. Add the butter and let it brown slightly, then pour the eggs into the quadrants of the pan, one at a time. Let them fry and bubble until the egg whites become golden-crispy on the edges but the yolks are still runny, 3 to 4 minutes. Halfway through the cooking process, add the garlic slices and rosemary to the butter in the spaces between the eggs. (Be careful, as the eggs will pop and splatter during this process.) Remove the pan from the heat and, using a spatula, transfer the eggs to a platter or baking sheet.

3.   Return the pan to medium heat. Add the mushrooms, bitter greens, and balsamic vinegar. If you have an aged balsamic that is slightly thicker and sweeter, it's fine to use it here! Just drizzle it on top of the dish instead of adding it to the pan. Stir to combine, then cook until warmed and the greens are slightly wilted, 1 to 2 minutes. Season with a pinch of salt. Place the eggs back in the pan and remove from the heat. Sprinkle a pinch of sea salt on top of each egg yolk, garnish with shaved parm, and serve.

Get It

A lot of mushrooms are sold in clusters that are attached at the root. There is no need to cut these; rather, I like to separate them by tearing them into pieces. And make sure to give the mushrooms enough time to pan-roast and become crispy and golden, which creates the most robust and irresistible mushroom flavor.

Crack the eggs into small bowls so that you can easily place them into the pan without a shell sneaking in.

Get It

This is it. Such simplicity. Funghi trifolati is just a fancy name for sautéed mushrooms with garlic and parsley—perhaps the *most* delicious sautéed mushrooms ever! The key is to work in batches so as not to overcrowd the pan, and to cook the mushrooms over moderate heat for the best color. This recipe starts with everyday olive oil and finishes with golden butter, garlic, and fragrant herbs. Use this as the base for a simple mushroom pasta or as a starter for scrambled eggs, or serve the mushrooms with steak or on a pizza. Funghi trifolati is also great on bread with a drizzle of balsamic vinegar and shaved parm.

Funghi Trifolati

Makes 2 cups

12 ounces assorted cultivated and wild mushrooms (like trumpet, maitake or hen of the woods, beech, oyster, button, cremini, chanterelle, porcini, morel, black trumpet, and hedgehog)

2 tablespoons everyday olive oil

3 garlic cloves, smashed

1 to 2 tablespoons unsalted butter (up to you!)

2 fresh rosemary sprigs

2 fresh thyme sprigs

Coarse sea salt (like Maldon)

1.   To prepare the mushrooms, cut or tear them into similar sizes and shapes; if small, leave them whole. Heat a large skillet over medium-high heat. Add 1 tablespoon of the olive oil and let the oil heat up before adding the mushrooms. Add between one-third and one-half of the mushrooms— just enough to fill the bottom of the pan. Reduce the heat to medium, then let the mushrooms do their thing; they are there to sear and caramelize until golden brown, about 2 minutes. Then stir once and sear on the other side, about 1 minute. Move the mushrooms to one side of the pan.

2.   In the empty space in the pan, add ½ tablespoon of the oil, more mushrooms, and the garlic cloves. Repeat cooking until golden brown, about 2 minutes, then stir and cook for another minute or so. If you still have mushrooms to cook, then push those to the side with the others, and add the remaining oil and mushrooms.

3.   Once all the mushrooms are cooked, add the butter, rosemary, and thyme. Let the butter and herbs baste and perfume the mushrooms for about 1 minute, gently stirring, until the mushrooms and butter begin to turn golden. Season with a few pinches of salt. Remove from the heat and let the mushrooms sit in the warm pan for 2 minutes to allow them to soak up all the goodness in the butter baste. Serve hot.

— Get It —

What is important here is learning how the mushrooms cook, starting with releasing their natural water, then caramelizing. A little butter baste and some fresh herbs enhance the amazing flavor. Feel free to play around with the herbs—you can use parsley, chives, tarragon, even dill.

— Get It —

Sott'olio means "under oil," and it's a classic Italian way of preserving everything from tuna to vegetables. Once an ingredient is covered in fat, like a confit, it can be held safely for quite some time because no air can get to it. Porcini are the king of the mushroom world. If you have ever had a fresh porcini, you know just how special these mushrooms are. They have a magical combination of flavor and texture and are so deliciously meaty! Porcini are available sporadically in season, so if you can find them, I strongly recommend scooping them up. Fresh porcini are great shaved raw into salads, as well as sautéed and tossed with fresh pasta, but to enjoy them throughout the year, I preserve them in olive oil. If you can't find porcini but want to preserve some mushrooms, I recommend trying trumpet royale, king trumpet, or oyster mushrooms as their meaty texture is most like porcini. You can enjoy these porcini right out of the jar, but the possibilities for dishes are endless! I like them on pizza, pasta, and bruschetta, alongside a cheese and salumi plate, in eggs, and as an accompaniment to grilled or roasted meats and fish. Don't hesitate to use the preserving oil too!

Porcini Sott'Olio

aka "Under Oil"

Makes 3 cups

1 pound fresh porcini mushrooms

¾ cup everyday olive oil

6 dried bay leaves

Coarse sea salt (like Maldon)

2 garlic cloves, halved

¾ cup sherry vinegar or white wine vinegar

3 fresh mint sprigs

3 fresh oregano sprigs

Get It

When choosing porcini, feel for solid, heavy, dry mushrooms. They get stickier the older they are, so be on the lookout for that when buying. Porcini—morels too—aren't cultivated, so you never know what you're gonna get! If a mushroom feels hollow, it's possible it has some wiggly critters. Don't throw those mushrooms away—just try to work around a worm if you find one.

Get It

---

1. To prepare the mushrooms, brush off any dirt using a pastry brush, paring knife, or lint-free towel. Cut the porcini through the stem in half or quarters to keep their shape. (They are truly the iconic toadstool-shaped mushroom! Porcini are wild, so they sometimes come with a little dirt and even a wiggly critter.)

2. In a medium bowl, combine ½ cup of the olive oil with the bay leaves. In a large sauté pan over medium heat, heat the remaining ¼ cup of olive oil. Working in two batches, sear the mushrooms on their cut sides until golden, then flip and cook until golden on all sides, 3 to 4 minutes. Season with a few pinches of coarse sea salt. Using a spatula, transfer the mushrooms to a baking sheet. Repeat with the remaining porcini, searing until golden brown and transferring them to the baking sheet.

3. Add the garlic cloves to the pan and toast for 30 seconds, then add all of the mushrooms back. Add the vinegar and ¼ cup of water to deglaze the pan, scraping up any browned bits. Let simmer and reduce by half, about 3 minutes. Transfer the mushroom mixture to the bowl with the olive oil and bay leaves. Push the mushrooms under the oil and let cool on the counter for 3 hours.

4. Once cool, add the mint and oregano and transfer the sott'olio mushrooms to a jar or an airtight container. Try to keep the mushrooms covered with oil; if needed, add a bit more oil to cover. These will hold in your fridge for months in a jar as long as the oil covers them.

This special little appetizer can easily be served at breakfast, brunch, or as a pre-dinner treat. I really like the way fruit and mushrooms work together—the earthiness of mushrooms is so well complemented by sweet fruit. In the summer, you could switch out the strawberries for figs, peaches, apricots, or plums, and in the cooler months, pears and apples would be delicious. I don't use puff pastry often, but I like keeping it in the freezer to make something special now and then without having to make dough from scratch.

Mushroom Tart

with Robiola and Strawberries

Serves 8

One 14-ounce package puff pastry, thawed

All-purpose flour, for dusting

Funghi Trifolati (page 216)

8 ounces 3-milk soft, ripened cheese (like Robiola Tre Latte or a French triple crème; see Get It Get It), cut into roughly 1-inch pieces

½ cup hulled and quartered or halved ripe strawberries

Fresh cracked black pepper

Coarse sea salt (like Maldon)

1 large egg beaten with 1 tablespoon cold water, for the egg wash

1.   Line a large baking sheet with parchment paper. Lay the puff pastry on a lightly floured cutting board. Using a rolling pin, roll the dough out until it's about 12 by 15 inches. Using a paring knife, score the dough slightly, creating a 1-inch border around the perimeter of the rectangle. Using your rolling pin, roll the dough around the pin to help transfer it to the prepared baking sheet. Freeze for 20 minutes. (This is important when cooking puff pastry so that it bakes and puffs nicely. If it's totally thawed, I feel like it eats oily.)

2.   Preheat the oven to 425°F. Evenly spread the mushrooms over the inner rectangle of the dough, leaving the border clean. Feel free to place the herb sprigs from the funghi trifolati all over too. Top with the cheese, strawberries, some fresh cracked black pepper, and a few pinches of sea salt. Using a pastry brush, brush the egg wash all over the dough border.

3.   Bake in the middle of the oven for 25 to 30 minutes, until the tart is golden, puffed, and all caramelized business. Let cool for 10 minutes, then cut and serve slightly warm. You can also make the tart 2 to 4 hours ahead and rewarm it in the oven for 5 minutes before serving.

── Get It ──

You can use Taleggio, Brie, or any soft ripened cheese for the tart, as well as goat cheese or a fresh farmer's cheese. The level of funkiness is up to you!

── Get It ──

If you're getting served stuffed mushrooms, chances are you're at a party . . . and it's 1975! I think it's high time to bring back the stuffed mushroom. They're so much fun to eat and easy to prepare for a party ahead of time. You can keep them covered in the fridge overnight before searing and roasting. Figs and mushrooms might not seem like the most natural match, but figs and goat cheese play so well together, and mushrooms want to get in on that party! One note of caution: Don't serve these right out of the oven, as they are like molten lava and will surely burn the roof of your mouth!

Stuffed Cremini Mushrooms

Serves 6

1 pound cremini mushrooms

2 tablespoons plus 2 teaspoons unsalted butter

3 ounces sliced prosciutto (4 to 5 thin slices), cut into thin strips and chopped

1 scallion or green onion, white and green parts thinly sliced and separated (about 2 tablespoons each)

2 garlic cloves, minced

2 tablespoons chopped dried figs

1 teaspoon fresh thyme leaves, plus 2 sprigs

Fresh cracked black pepper

One 10½-ounce log fresh goat cheese, softened

¼ cup panko (Japanese breadcrumbs)

1 tablespoon minced fresh flat-leaf parsley

2 tablespoons everyday olive oil

1. Preheat the oven to 425°F. Stem the mushrooms and place the stems in a food processor; set the mushroom caps aside. Pulse the stems until finely chopped, about 30 seconds.

2. Line a plate with paper towels. In a medium skillet, heat 2 tablespoons of the butter over medium-low heat. Once melted and slightly golden, add the prosciutto and fry until deep red and crispy, about 5 minutes. With a slotted spoon, transfer the prosciutto to the paper towel–lined plate.

3. Return the skillet to the heat. Add the scallion whites and garlic and toast until fragrant and slightly golden, about 1 minute. Add the chopped mushroom stems and dried figs and cook until the mushrooms have sweated and the pan looks dry, about 3 minutes. Add the thyme leaves and a few cracks of black pepper. Remove from the heat and scrape into a medium bowl. Mix in the goat cheese and half of the crispy prosciutto. Using a spoon, fill the mushroom caps and smooth and shape the filling; gently apply pressure so that the filling is tightly packed into each mushroom.

4. Return the skillet to medium heat. Melt the remaining 2 teaspoons of butter and add the panko. Cook, stirring continuously, until deep golden brown, about 3 minutes. Add the parsley and the reserved prosciutto and toss to combine. Remove from the heat.

5. In a large cast-iron skillet, heat the olive oil over medium-high heat. Add the mushrooms and sear until they begin to sizzle heavily and splatter slightly, 2 to 3 minutes. Transfer the skillet to the oven and bake the mushrooms for 15 minutes.

6. Remove the skillet from the oven and add the thyme sprigs to the pan. Let the mushrooms rest for at least 10 minutes. Before serving, top the baked mushrooms with the prosciutto breadcrumbs and sliced scallion greens.

Get It

Searing and then roasting the mushrooms in a cast-iron pan is a game changer because they develop the best texture. It's so much better than baking the mushrooms on a baking sheet.

Get It

Get It

I love cooking the ingredients in layers, and it's so important in this recipe to spend time caramelizing and seasoning in every step. This is how you develop rich, robust flavor in a sauce.

Get It

I love traditional Bolognese and wanted to create a vegetarian version that was as satisfying as its meaty counterpart. This is good enough to fool any meat eater! I use three kinds of mushrooms for texture as well as flavor, and I think it's important to layer the flavors as you cook—this is why I season with kosher salt throughout the whole process. This is a fantastic sauce to use with any dry pasta, as well as for fresh tagliatelle. Leftover Porcini Bolognese is *so* great on a burger with Swiss cheese or in an omelet the next day.

Porcini Bolognese

with Tagliatelle

Serves 6 (Makes 8 cups)

Sauce

2 ounces dried porcini mushrooms

1 medium carrot, roughly chopped

1 small turnip, roughly chopped

1 celery stalk, roughly chopped

1 small yellow onion, roughly chopped

1 pound cremini (Baby Bella) or button mushrooms

8 tablespoons everyday olive oil

8 ounces trumpet royale or oyster mushrooms, sliced

4 ounces shiitake mushrooms, stemmed and sliced

Kosher salt

3 tablespoons tomato paste

One 15-ounce can crushed tomatoes or tomato passata (see page 396)

1 cup dry red wine

1 small piece Parmigiano-Reggiano cheese rind (optional)

Chile flake

½ cup heavy cream

1 tablespoon minced fresh rosemary leaves

Fresh cracked black pepper

ingredients continue

1. **Make the sauce.** In a large bowl, cover the dried porcini with 4 cups of warm water and let stand for 20 minutes.

2. Drain the mushrooms, reserving the water. Roughly chop the mushrooms.

3. Meanwhile, in a food processor, pulse the carrot, turnip, celery, and onion until finely minced. Set aside. Pulse the cremini mushrooms until finely minced. Set aside.

4. In a large heavy-bottomed pot, heat 3 tablespoons of the oil over medium heat. Add the trumpet royale and shiitake mushrooms and cook until they begin to exude their liquid. Season with a generous pinch of salt and continue to cook, stirring occasionally, until they begin to brown, about 8 minutes. (Try to keep them in an even layer on the bottom of the pan.) Transfer the mushrooms to a large bowl.

5. Add another 1 tablespoon of the oil to the pot and add the minced vegetables. Season with salt. Cook until lightly browned and caramelized, about 6 minutes. Add 2 more tablespoons of the oil to the pot, along with the minced cremini and chopped porcini; the mixture will look wet. Cook, stirring occasionally, until the moisture is gone, 6 to 7 minutes. Transfer to the bowl with the trumpet and shiitake mushrooms.

6. Increase the heat under the pot to medium-high. Add the remaining 2 tablespoons of oil and the tomato paste. Stir the tomato paste so it browns a bit on the bottom of the pan, about 1 minute. (Do not be afraid if you see dark bits forming; this is the flavor you want!) Add the crushed tomatoes, season with salt, and cook, stirring often, until reduced a bit, about 2 minutes. Add the red wine and cook, scraping up any browned bits from the bottom of the pot, until reduced by half, about 2 minutes. Stir in the mushroom-vegetable mixture along with the reserved mushroom water

recipe continues

Finishing

Kosher salt

Hand-Cut Ribbon Pasta
(page 263), cut for tagliatelle

2 tablespoons unsalted butter

1 tablespoon chopped fresh thyme

1 tablespoon chopped fresh
rosemary leaves

¼ cup freshly grated Parmigiano-
Reggiano cheese

Fresh cracked black pepper

(be careful not to add any grit from the bottom of the bowl). Add the parm rind (if using) and a pinch of chile flake and simmer on low heat for 45 minutes.

7.   Discard the parm rind. Stir in the heavy cream and rosemary and cook for another 10 to 15 minutes, until the sauce is reduced and melded. Season with salt and pepper to taste. Your Bolognese is ready to serve with your favorite pasta! The sauce can be refrigerated for 1 week or frozen for up to 3 months. Feel free to make ahead of time or freeze your leftovers.

8.   **Finish the dish.** Heat a large pot of water, season well with salt, and bring to a boil.

9.   Meanwhile, in a very large skillet or saucepan, heat 6 cups of the Bolognese over low heat. Add the fresh tagliatelle to the boiling water and boil until floating and al dente, about 2 minutes; reserve ¼ cup of the pasta cooking water. Using tongs, gently lift the tagliatelle from the boiling water and transfer it to the Bolognese. Add the reserved pasta cooking water, along with the butter, thyme, and rosemary. Gently fold the tagliatelle into the Bolognese. Remove from the heat once married, about 2 minutes. Serve immediately, topped with the grated parm and fresh cracked black pepper. The remaining 2 cups of Bolognese can keep in an airtight container in the refrigerator for up to a week.

The combination of chanterelles and nettles gives this dish a strong sense of place in the Italian mountains. Stinging nettles can't be touched by bare hands, as they have small spikes on the leaves that can inflame the skin, so they're best handled with gloves. Nettles are only edible when cooked, but please don't be scared—they have incredible health qualities and are quite delicious. If you don't have nettles, you can also use kale, spinach, or dandelion greens. I adore chanterelles for their foresty, woodsy-like flavor, as well as their buttery and velvety texture. Little baby button chanterelles may just be the cutest, but all chanterelles are something to behold—they are really the iconic shape of the mushroom family. This is not a recipe where you can substitute sour cream for the crème fraîche. Sour cream has more stabilizers, and as such, it won't melt nice and creamy!

Corzetti Pasta

with Chanterelle Mushrooms, Brown-Buttered Pecans, and Wild Greens

Serves 4

2 tablespoons unsalted butter

½ cup chopped pecans or walnuts

Kosher salt

1 tablespoon everyday olive oil

8 ounces chanterelle mushrooms, washed and spun (see page 209)

1 medium shallot, minced

¾ cup white wine

Corzetti Pasta Coins (page 260) or 1 pound dry corzetti, gemelli, cavatelli, or penne

2 ounces wild or hearty greens (like stinging nettles, dandelion greens, or Tuscan kale), washed, cut into wide ribbons (2 cups)

½ cup crème fraîche

½ cup freshly grated Pecorino Romano, plus more for garnish

1 tablespoon fresh marjoram or oregano leaves, lightly chopped, plus more for garnish

Fresh cracked black pepper

Super-special extra-virgin olive oil, for drizzling (optional)

1.   To prepare the brown-buttered pecans, in a small skillet, melt the butter over medium heat. Add the pecans and cook, stirring continuously, until golden brown, about 2 minutes. Transfer the nuts to a bowl or plate and reserve.

2.   Bring a large pot of water to a boil and season generously with kosher salt. In a large saucepan, heat the everyday olive oil over medium-high heat. Add the chanterelles and cook undisturbed. (These mushrooms will be wetter due to washing.) Once you see the mushrooms begin to sear and turn golden brown, about 2 minutes, stir, and season with a few pinches of kosher salt. Stir in the shallot and ¼ cup of the brown-buttered pecans and cook for 2 minutes. Add the wine, scraping up any browned bits on the bottom of the pan. Reduce the heat to a low simmer.

3.   Meanwhile, boil the corzetti for 2 minutes, or until the pasta is tender yet al dente. Add the greens to the pasta water and cook for 30 seconds. Add ½ cup of the pasta cooking water to the saucepan with the mushrooms. Drain the pasta and greens and add to the saucepan. Stir briefly, then let the pasta and sauce marry over low to medium-low heat, just enough heat to see a light simmer. Add the crème fraîche, pecorino, and marjoram and stir to combine, creating a light, creamy sauce. Taste for seasoning and add a bit more salt if desired.

4.   Transfer the corzetti to a shallow platter or place right into bowls. Garnish with the remaining pecans and fresh marjoram, and top with a little more pecorino and fresh cracked black pepper. If you're up to it, drizzle with a touch of extra-virgin olive oil. Enjoy!

When I was little, I had a great babysitter named Wilma, and wow, was she a great cook. My favorite dish she made was her chicken Dijon. When I was lucky enough to go out to an Italian restaurant, I would always order scallopine dishes like chicken marsala or picatta. This recipe is a nod to Wilma and to those memorable scallopine dishes of my youth. I really love showcasing morels here because they bring so much flavor to the dish, and they hold up exceptionally well to the vermouth, tomato, and Dijon, but you can also use trumpet, shiitake, cremini, or hen of the woods (maitake). I really like the tang of crème fraîche, but if you can't get it, heavy cream will do in a pinch. I don't recommend using sour cream, however, as the stabilizers have a negative effect on the sauce.

Chicken Scallopine with Morels

Serves 4 to 6

1 cup all-purpose flour

2 large eggs

2 pounds boneless skinless chicken breasts, butterflied and pounded thin (see Get It Get It)

Kosher salt

Fresh cracked black pepper

3 to 4 tablespoons everyday olive oil

8 ounces fresh morel mushrooms, washed well and sliced (see page 209)

1 tablespoon unsalted butter

1 medium shallot, thinly sliced (½ cup)

1 cup freshly grated tomato, from 2 ripe medium tomatoes, with skins discarded

2 tablespoons Dijon mustard

¼ cup dry vermouth or dry white wine

1½ cups Light Artichoke Stock (page 30) or your favorite chicken or veggie stock

2 tablespoons crème fraîche

2 tablespoons fresh tarragon leaves

1. Preheat the oven to 300°F. Place the flour in a wide, shallow bowl. In another wide, shallow bowl, beat the eggs with ¼ cup of cold water. Season the chicken breasts with salt and pepper. Dredge each breast in the flour, then in the egg wash, followed by the flour again. Transfer to a baking sheet while you bread the rest.

2. In a large nonstick skillet, heat 1 tablespoon of the oil over medium heat. Working in two or three batches, cook the chicken over medium-low heat until golden, 3 to 4 minutes per side. Transfer to a casserole or baking dish and keep warm in the oven. Repeat with 1 tablespoon of olive oil and the remaining chicken, wiping out the pan if the bits of flour in it are browned. There is no need to rush this step; if your heat is too high, your flour will be raw in places and burnt in others. Keep the chicken scallopine in the warm oven.

3. Return the skillet to medium heat. Add the remaining 1 tablespoon of olive oil and the morel mushrooms. Sear until soft, 4 to 5 minutes. Season with a few pinches of salt. Transfer to a bowl. Add the butter and shallot to the skillet and cook until just beginning to brown, about 1 minute, then add the tomato pulp and mustard. Cook, stirring, until combined and reduced, about 2 minutes. Add the morels back to the skillet, then add the vermouth and scrape up any browned bits. Add the stock and simmer until reduced and a sauce-like consistency forms, about 5 minutes. Off the heat, stir in the crème fraîche and tarragon. Spoon the sauce over the chicken and serve immediately. Garnish with black pepper.

Olives &
Olive Oil

I put olive oil on *everything*; it just makes everything taste better. If I had to pick only one ingredient to have on a desert island, it would be olive oil. Once you put olive oil and salt on anything—raw or cooked—you're good to go: vegetables, fish, cheese, meat! The Italians taught me that a splash of olive oil also magically melds the flavors of a dish. My love for olive oil took hold when I first saw a live olive tree in Italy. Did you know that in Puglia alone there are 60 million olive trees, one for every Italian? Olive trees are majestic, and they can produce fruit for hundreds of years. They grow wonderfully gnarled and tangled, deeply grounding themselves in the earth over time.

There are said to be over 400 varieties of olives grown in Italy, which is a lot to work with when it comes to picking which ones to eat! The color of an olive is determined by its level of ripeness: Green is unripe, black is fully ripe. Olives are also characterized by how they're processed. Fresh olives from the tree are sharp and bitter, and processing removes the bitter compound called oleuropein, which is found in the skin. Olives can be oil-cured, water-cured, brine-cured, and dry-cured.

When it comes to green olives, I adore buttery, crispy Castelvetrano olives from Sicily, which are as good in a martini as in salad or pasta. Cerignola olives from Puglia are also deliciously buttery, but don't be fooled into buying red or black ones, which are dyed. My favorite Italian black olives are Leccino (from Tuscany) and Taggiasca (from Liguria). They're amazing olives with a salty flavor. They're brined, pitted, and cured in olive oil, which makes that olive oil totally delicious and perfect for finishing dishes. If you can't find Leccino or Taggiasca, Greek kalamatas are probably the easiest olives to buy (well, aside from the canned kind that go on pizza), and I think they work in a variety of recipes. Moroccan cured olives are another delight, but they're super strong-tasting and best used sparingly as instant flavor bombs. I generally buy pitted olives for cooking and use the ones with the pits for marinating.

Now, on to olive oil. It is a complicated, mysterious world when it comes to olive oil. What is extra-virgin olive oil anyway? Why is it important? Why can it be so expensive? How do you know which one to buy? These are the questions I get asked a lot. For starters, there are many laws or guidelines for what can go on the label. "Made in Italy" or "Produced in Italy" doesn't mean much.

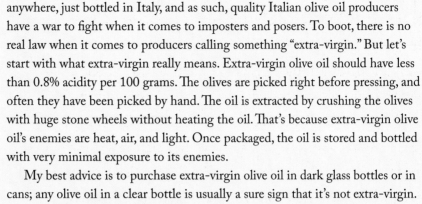

That basically means the olives could be from anywhere and the oil pressed anywhere, just bottled in Italy, and as such, quality Italian olive oil producers have a war to fight when it comes to imposters and posers. To boot, there is no real law when it comes to producers calling something "extra-virgin." But let's start with what extra-virgin really means. Extra-virgin olive oil should have less than 0.8% acidity per 100 grams. The olives are picked right before pressing, and often they have been picked by hand. The oil is extracted by crushing the olives with huge stone wheels without heating the oil. That's because extra-virgin olive oil's enemies are heat, air, and light. Once packaged, the oil is stored and bottled with very minimal exposure to its enemies.

My best advice is to purchase extra-virgin olive oil in dark glass bottles or in cans; any olive oil in a clear bottle is usually a sure sign that it's not extra-virgin. Quality producers will put a press date or expiration date on the label, so look out for that when making a purchase. Another thing to keep an eye out for is a place of origin; the chances are that bottles marked with a place of origin are of higher quality because they are not made from a blend of olives. These three things will steer you toward some super-delicious olive oil! Extra-virgin olive oil is good for roughly two years, and it's best kept far from the heat of the stove.

When it comes to cooking, I use relatively inexpensive extra-virgin olive oil, which I refer to in this book as "everyday olive oil." As with finer olive oil, I tend to look for bottles that are dark, as I mentioned, so I know that it's a quality oil. For finishing or drizzling on dishes, I use what I call "super-special extra-virgin olive oil" because just a drizzle adds incredible flavor to anything from salad, cheese, and seafood to pasta, meat, and even ice cream and chocolate desserts. If you're looking to buy some great olive oil for finishing dishes, Southern Italian olive oil from Sicily or Puglia will be light and fruity; Tuscan olive oil is super peppery; and Ligurian olive oil is fruity and a little spicy.

No matter what you use, extra-virgin olive oil is one of the healthiest foods out there, full of polyphenols and antioxidants. It is beyond good for your food, and your heart too!

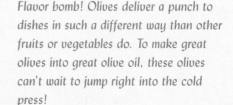

Flavor bomb! Olives deliver a punch to dishes in such a different way than other fruits or vegetables do. To make great olives into great olive oil, these olives can't wait to jump right into the cold press!

Clockwise from top left: Olive Oil–
Roasted Lamb with Potatoes and Olives
(page 250), Black Olive and Celery Gratin
(page 237), Charred Olives Marinated
in Orange and Fennel Seed (page 236),
María Nava's Lemon Olive Oil Risotto
(page 247), Genovese Pesto (page 240)

I am in love with snacks, especially those from Venice, which are called *cicchetti*. I think you will find these cicchetti completely irresistible. I use Castelvetrano olives, which I think have the best green olive flavor, but you can use any pitted green olive you like. For the stuffing, I use a soft goat cheese; sometimes I mix it up with a flavored goat cheese, like garlic and herb, or black pepper. The fried sage is optional, but it adds such a nice hit of color and herbiness. Try these crispy, creamy olives with your next Bloody Mary! If you haven't had these, you haven't really lived! For a little extra something special, try wrapping these stuffed olives with 1½ tablespoons of raw sausage, then bread and fry. Give it a try!

Fried Goat Cheese–Stuffed Olives

and Sage with Honey

Serves 6 to 8

4 ounces fresh goat cheese (plain or garlic and herb), softened at room temp for 30 minutes

Two 10-ounce jars pitted Castelvetrano olives, drained (about 1½ cups)

1 cup all-purpose flour

1 large egg, beaten with ½ cup buttermilk or whole milk

1 cup semolina

Kosher salt

3 cups frying oil, like peanut or canola

½ cup fresh sage leaves (optional)

2 tablespoons delicately flavored honey (like acacia, wildflower, or orange blossom)

A few pinches of fennel pollen or toasted fennel seeds (optional)

1. Place the softened goat cheese in a pastry bag or in a sturdy resealable plastic bag; snip off the corner. Stuff the olives with the goat cheese, filling them fully.

2. Line a baking sheet with parchment paper. Prepare three small bowls with the breading ingredients: one with the all-purpose flour, one with the beaten egg and buttermilk, and the final bowl with the semolina. Season the all-purpose flour and semolina each with a few pinches of kosher salt. Working in batches, first coat the olives evenly with all-purpose flour, then place in the egg wash, coating evenly. Using a slotted spoon, remove the olives from the egg wash and toss well with the semolina, coating them evenly. Place the breaded olives on the baking sheet and dust with a bit of the remaining semolina. They can be refrigerated, uncovered, for several hours until you are ready to fry.

3. In a small, deep-sided pot, heat at least 4 inches of oil over medium-high heat. Heat the oil to 350°F; do not exceed 375°F. Line a baking sheet with paper towels. Working in batches, fry the olives for 30 seconds, or until golden brown and crispy. Using a skimmer or slotted spoon, transfer them to the paper towels. Repeat with the remaining olives.

4. Add the sage leaves and fry for 30 to 45 seconds, or until crispy and dark green; transfer to the paper towels. Serve the fried olives and sage leaves drizzled with the honey and sprinkled with the fennel pollen (if using).

— Get It —

Italian wine bars and fried food stalls often serve their fritti misti in a paper cone, and I love to serve these just like they do in Italy. Take a square of parchment paper and fold it in half, creating a triangle. Then roll the far corners of the triangle toward the center to form a cone. Tape the overlapping pieces of paper or fold the corners over the top and presto! Get 'em while they're hot!

Get It —

I admit that the combination of olives and orange isn't making new waves, but charring the olives first is something special. I find that heating them up helps the olives absorb the flavor of the fennel seeds and oranges far more than just tossing them cold. The warming of the olives also helps meld all the flavors together. This is a really fun way to dress up those olives you pass by at the olive bar. Listen to your olives!

Charred Olives

Marinated in Orange and Fennel Seed

Serves 6 as a snack

2 small oranges (like Valencia, navel, Cara Cara, or blood oranges)

¼ cup everyday olive oil

2 cups mixed olives, pitted or with pits (it's up to you!)

2 teaspoons fennel seeds

¼ cup fresh mint, lightly chopped, plus a few leaves for garnish

1.   Using a Microplane, finely grate the orange zest into a medium bowl. Cut the stem ends of the oranges and using a serrated knife, cut away the white pith, following along with the shape of the orange. Working over the bowl, segment the oranges by cutting in between their membranes; let the segments fall into the bowl. Squeeze any juice left into the bowl. Add the olive oil.

2.   Heat a medium sauté pan or skillet over medium heat for 3 minutes. Add the olives and fennel seeds and cook, undisturbed, allowing them to sear and turn golden brown, about 3 minutes. Give the pan a little shake to rotate the olives and continue to cook for another 3 to 4 minutes until seared on both sides. (You might even hear the olives start to squeal!) Transfer the olives to the bowl with the orange mixture and toss to coat. Let them cool for 5 minutes, allowing them to absorb the orange juice mixture.

3.   Fold in the fresh mint and transfer to a serving bowl. Garnish with additional mint leaves. The olives can be served immediately (they are *awesome* when they are warm) or at room temperature or chilled. They can be refrigerated for a week.

Get It

I love to serve these with toasted or warmed bread, which is perfect for dipping in the yummy olive marinade. Another great idea is to use pitted olives here, then pour the whole mix over grilled tuna for a stellar dinner.

Get It

Celery is such a divisive vegetable that people seem to love or hate. I love it. It's a staple as a building block for many recipes, but rarely do you see it as the star of a dish. I'm here to change that! Celery wants to be a key player, just like broccoli or asparagus. For this gratin, I was inspired by a Southern Italian dish in which celery is boiled, sautéed, and baked, and I thought it would be fun to play around with that and add some breadcrumbs for a little crunch. Celery is one of those fridge warriors that can be kept for a few weeks, making this a great last-minute side dish.

Black Olive and Celery Gratin

Serves 4 to 6

Kosher salt

1 large bunch of celery (about 1½ pounds), stalks cut on a bias into 2-inch-long pieces

1 large leek (white part only), cut into ½-inch rounds (I save the green tops for stock)

½ cup pitted black olives, chopped (I like to use oil-cured olives here, like Taggiasca or Leccino)

2 tablespoons chopped fresh oregano, plus a few sprigs for garnish

2 pinches of chile flake

3 tablespoons everyday olive oil

½ cup plain dry breadcrumbs (from Italian-style bread)

½ cup freshly grated Pecorino Romano

Finely grated zest (use a Microplane) and juice from 1 small lemon, for garnish

1.   Preheat the oven to 400°F. Bring a large pot of water to a boil with ¼ cup of salt. This is blanching water (see page 10), and I like mine to be salty like the ocean, about 1 tablespoon of salt per quart of water. Blanch the celery for 5 minutes, then add the leek and blanch for 1 additional minute. While the vegetables are blanching, in a large bowl, combine the olives, chopped oregano, chile flake, and 1 tablespoon of the olive oil.

2.   Using a skimmer or slotted spoon, remove the celery and leeks from the boiling water and toss in the bowl with the olive mixture.

3.   In a small bowl, combine the breadcrumbs, cheese, and 1 tablespoon of olive oil. In a medium baking or casserole dish (I use a 7 by 10-inch casserole dish, but you can use an 8 by 8-inch dish), spoon one-third of the celery mixture, followed by one-third of the breadcrumb mixture. Repeat with two more layers, then drizzle with the remaining 1 tablespoon of olive oil. Bake until the breadcrumbs are toasty and golden brown, 35 to 40 minutes. To serve, top with finely grated lemon zest and a squeeze of fresh lemon juice, along with the oregano sprigs.

In Italy, the olive oil harvest is celebrated with bread and oil, and this dish embodies that celebration. The name derives from *fetta*, which means "slice," and *unta*, which means "oily." Let me tell you, this is just about the most delicious oily slice you'll ever eat, especially when it's topped with sweet cherry tomatoes and creamy burrata cheese! Because the olive oil is the star ingredient, you really need a great one. I suggest looking for a finishing oil from Tuscany or Puglia. Try to buy one in a dark bottle labeled with a date of production so you know it's fresh and high quality for finishing.

Olive Oil–Soaked Bread Fett'unta

with Cherry Tomatoes and Basil

Serves 8

8 thick (about 1 inch) slices of rustic European-style bread (like sourdough or ciabatta)

8 ounces cherry tomatoes, halved (about 1½ cups)

¼ cup plus 1 tablespoon peppery super-special extra-virgin olive oil (like one from Tuscany or Puglia)

Coarse sea salt (like Maldon)

¼ cup fresh basil leaves, torn, plus a few leaves for garnish

1 ball fresh burrata or mozzarella (about 4 ounces)

1.　Preheat the oven to 425°F. Place the sliced bread on a rack set in a baking sheet, or just set the bread directly on the oven rack. Toast until golden and the exterior is beginning to crisp, yet the inside of the bread is still soft, about 10 minutes. Transfer the toasts to a platter.

2.　Meanwhile, in a small bowl, dress the cherry tomatoes with the 1 tablespoon of olive oil, a pinch of sea salt, and the basil; let marinate while the bread toasts.

3.　Drizzle the remaining ¼ cup of olive oil over the toasts. (Yes, this is a lot of olive oil, but *dang*, it's so good and good for you!) Tear the burrata and mix the firm and creamy parts all together with a spoon. Place the burrata on the toasts and spoon the marinated cherry tomatoes over the top. Garnish with a few basil leaves and sprinkle with another pinch of sea salt. Enjoy immediately.

This is the OG of pestos, hailing from Genoa in Liguria. It's traditionally made by hand using a marble mortar and wooden pestle, but it's hard to find that amazingly tender Genovese basil in the US, so I opt to use a blender instead. I realize that it's contradictory to talk about the great Genovese pesto and how much I love mortars and pestles and then make mine in a blender. The main reason is the basil. Genovese basil is a DOP basil grown in Liguria. Its leaves are small, thin, compact, and so tender. The basil has no option but to become a smooth sauce in the mortar. Our American basil is a bit heartier, so I think it works best in the blender, which aerates the pesto, creating an uber-light spread. Of course, if you find Genovese basil, try it in the mortar and pestle! My favorite part of this recipe is the technique for soaking the basil and parsley in ice water, which helps the herbs plump up a bit and absorb some of the water. This aids in emulsifying the pesto, and it also prevents the leaves from bruising and turning black from the friction of the blender, locking in the best green color and fresh flavor.

Genovese Pesto

Makes 2 cups

2 tablespoons pine nuts

¾ cup everyday olive oil

3 cups packed fresh basil leaves (from about 4 ounces fresh basil)

1 cup fresh flat-leaf parsley leaves (from ½ bunch)

1 small garlic clove

½ cup freshly grated Parmigiano-Reggiano

½ cup freshly grated Pecorino Romano

Kosher salt

1. In a small nonstick skillet, toast the pine nuts over medium heat, tossing or stirring continuously, until golden brown, 3 to 4 minutes. Transfer to a plate to cool.

2. Place the olive oil in the freezer until chilled, at lest 15 minutes. Meanwhile, fill a large bowl with ice water. Submerge the basil and parsley in it. Let soak for 5 minutes.

3. Remove the oil from the freezer and transfer to a blender along with the garlic. Working in two batches, lift the herbs from the ice water, shaking most of the excess water from the leaves (not all; a bit of water will make a smooth pesto) and add to the blender. Blend on high speed until combined, then repeat with the remaining herbs. Set the bowl of ice water aside. Finally, add the cheeses, pine nuts, and a pinch or two of salt and blend on high until the pesto is smooth.

4. Transfer the pesto to a small bowl and place the bowl in the ice bath. Stir the pesto and chill until cold. Transfer the pesto to an airtight container and keep refrigerated for up to 2 weeks. To store the pesto in the freezer, apply a small piece of plastic wrap directly on its surface, sealing it from the air in the top of the container. The pesto freezes beautifully for up to 3 months. I like to freeze it in 1-cup servings, as I often use 1 cup at a time.

Get It

I always toast pine nuts in a skillet. I like this technique better than toasting in the oven because the nuts toast more evenly (see page 9).

Now that you have mad pesto skills, have fun with the herb and nut combinations. I love to add mint to this pesto in the summer—you can sub mint for all the basil for a mint pesto, or for half the basil for a summer herb pesto.

Get It

Pesto Perfection

Pesto is *the best*. It's the most delicious sauce you can make ahead of time, staying awesome and bright-tasting for several days in your fridge. Score! It's full of fresh flavors and textures and has so many different uses. Pasta is the most common use for pesto, but you can also spread it on toast in the morning with a fried or poached egg on top, or mix it into grilled veggies for a surprising tasty side dish. I also love putting a dollop into soup. These are just a few of the many things you can do!

Pesto gets its name from the piece of equipment that it is made with: the humble mortar and pestle. The mortar is the bowl, typically made from wood, ceramic, metal, or stone, and the pestle is the tool used to crush and grind the ingredients in the mortar. The mortar and pestle is perhaps one of the most ancient culinary tools in use today, dating back as far as the Stone Age. Remarkably, it hasn't changed much from its original form.

Many cultures have their own version of a mortar and pestle. In Mexico, the stone *molcajete* is used for a variety of dishes including guacamole and salsa. In Thailand, the Thai clay mortar and pestle is shaped like a deep cone and used to prepare curries and classic *som tam* (green papaya salad). In Japan, a *suribachi* is a ceramic mortar with a wooden pestle that's used to grind sesame seeds and other spices. No matter how you like to cook, every household should have a mortar and pestle.

In Italy, the great mortar and pestles are typically made of marble, and the bowl can be either shallow or deep. There are wooden pestles out there, but I prefer the weight of a marble pestle when making a pesto. The motion of the pestle against the mortar, pulverizing the nuts, garlic, and herbs, and then emulsifying the oil and cheese, is almost godly. Making a pesto by hand with a mortar and pestle is a technique that teaches the feel of the pesto and how to understand the delicate balance of ingredients in a good one.

Even though I believe that making pesto by hand with a mortar and pestle is best (especially when making small amounts), I know that we all don't have time to make pesto this way. I love the chunkiness and texture of a handmade pesto, but sometimes the smooth, silky texture of one made in a blender is great too!

Pesto Genovese (classic basil pesto) is the first pesto you need to conquer. As the OG of all pestos, it's made from a delicate balance of basil, Parmigiano-Reggiano, Pecorino Romano, pine nuts, garlic, and olive oil. While this pesto is the most well known, unfortunately it's not always delicious and fresh-tasting because many store-bought pestos lose that fresh herbiness and zip while sitting on the shelf.

I think my pesto is truly the most delicious pesto you can make. Why? Because I learned easy, foolproof tricks in Italy that inform almost every batch of pesto I make, especially in a blender. All too often, pesto made in a blender or food processor results in a watery, chunky, oily concoction with dark, bruised herbs, as opposed to the beautifully emulsified sauce it is meant to be. Here are a few tips to help you make it great:

1. Heat is the number one enemy when making pesto. By chilling down your olive oil, you minimize the effects of the heat and friction from the blender. Keeping things cold preserves those precious herbs, locking in the freshest taste with no bitterness.

2. Soaking the herbs in ice water helps them absorb some water and plumps them up, which helps create a creamy, cohesive pesto texture. Hydrating and chilling the leaves also prevents the herbs from bruising and discoloring during the pesto-making process.

3. Layering is key. Instead of starting by blending the herbs dry—and beating them to death to get them chopped!—I first blend the chilled olive oil and garlic. Then, when the herbs go in, there is some liquid to help get those blades turning.

Growing up in Texas meant I ate a lot of locally caught shrimp; there was always some stashed in the freezer, ready for a meal. I love shrimp cocktail, and this is a really fun twist on that. When I first started as a line cook at Spiaggia, my then sous chef Gray McNally (who is now a longtime friend, as well as a farmer for Monteverde) taught me a foolproof technique for cooking shrimp that prevents it from becoming rubbery and overcooked. A combination of boiling water and cold shrimp creates the ideal temperature for poaching, and the result is the most tender shrimp imaginable. Feel free to add whatever you like to the boiling water—even just crab boil seasoning and lemon juice tastes great. This shrimp cocktail recipe takes some inspiration from a Sicilian agrodolce, marinating the shrimp in a sweet-sour mix of honey and lemon. Then, for a hint of a Southern-style pickled shrimp, I like adding celery, capers, and bay leaves.

Sicilian Summer Shrimp "Cocktail"

Serves 4 to 6

8 dried bay leaves

2 teaspoons fennel seeds

2 teaspoons coriander seeds

1 teaspoon mustard seeds

Kosher salt

2 pounds large wild-caught shrimp, peeled and deveined

3 celery stalks, sliced diagonally ¼ inch thick (about 2 cups)

½ cup pitted Castelvetrano olives, sliced

2 tablespoons drained capers

½ teaspoon chile flake

1½ teaspoons celery salt

½ cup super-special extra-virgin olive oil

Freshly grated zest and juice of 1 lemon (about ⅓ cup of juice)

1 lemon, thinly sliced

1 tablespoon wildflower honey

1 loaf crusty bread, cut into chunks for dipping (see Get It Get It)

1. In a medium pot, bring 6 cups of water, 2 of the bay leaves, the fennel seeds, coriander seeds, and mustard seeds to a boil; add 2 tablespoons of salt. Place the shrimp in a large, heatproof mixing bowl. Strain the poaching liquid over the shrimp through a fine-mesh sieve and discard the spices. Let the shrimp cool in the liquid, about 30 minutes; the shrimp should be opaque throughout.

2. In a large bowl, combine the remaining 6 bay leaves, the sliced celery, olives, capers, chile flake, celery salt, olive oil, lemon zest, juice, and slices, and the honey. Drain the shrimp, add to the large bowl, and toss well to combine. You can serve the shrimp right away, or cover and refrigerate overnight. When you're ready to serve, arrange the shrimp on a large serving platter and pour the vegetable mixture over the top. Remove the bay leaves and discard. Serve with a delicious crusty bread, toasted if you prefer.

Get It

Scarpetta is *essential* with this dish! That means to dip the bread in the delicious olive oil marinade—it's a must.

Get It

This tuna salad, made with supremely silky and flaky homemade tuna conserva, is the bomb diggity! Don't be intimidated by the tuna conserva—it's just tuna poached in olive oil with some lemon, garlic, and herbs. Serve this as you wish: with crackers, sliced tomato salad, or as a traditional sandwich, tuna tartine, or tuna melt! I like to top my tartine-style tuna with arugula and shaved radishes.

The Best Tuna Salad

Makes about 5 cups (I tasted it so many times I'm not sure! Ha ☺)

Olive Oil–Poached Tuna Conserva (page 246), drained and flaked

¼ cup pitted kalamata olives, chopped

¼ cup peperoncini peppers, chopped, plus 1 tablespoon peperoncini juice

2 celery stalks, finely chopped

2 tablespoons chopped yellow celery leaves

2 tablespoons chopped green onion or scallion (about 1)

2 tablespoons chopped fresh flat-leaf parsley

2 tablespoons drained capers

1½ to 2 cups Tuna Oil Aioli (recipe follows)

Kosher salt

Fresh cracked black pepper

In a large bowl, combine the flaked tuna with the olives, peperoncini and its liquid, celery, celery leaves, green onion, parsley, and capers. Fold in the aioli to your desired consistency. (I recommend starting with 1½ cups, then adding more if you want it a bit saucier.) Season with salt and lots of fresh black pepper.

Tuna Oil Aioli

This aioli has subtle grassy bitter notes from the extra-virgin olive oil, but it balances really nicely with the other ingredients like poached tuna, peperoncini, olives, capers, and celery. I use 1½ cups of aioli for the tuna salad, but you can use all 2 cups, depending on how soft and creamy you like yours. The aioli is great on other sandwiches like fried egg, club, or hearty roast beef!

Makes 2 cups

3 tablespoons fresh lemon juice

2 tablespoons capers, drained

1 tablespoon Dijon mustard

1 tablespoon fresh thyme leaves

1 tablespoon chopped fresh flat-leaf parsley

1 large egg yolk

½ teaspoon kosher salt

1 pinch of sugar

Olive oil from the Olive Oil–Poached Tuna Conserva (page 246)

Fresh cracked black pepper

In a food processor, combine the lemon juice, capers, mustard, thyme, parsley, egg yolk, salt, and sugar. With the machine on, slowly drizzle the cooled oil from the tuna. I like to start with barely a dribble of oil to get the emulsification going. Then once the aioli begins to thicken, I pour a steady stream of oil into the food processor. Taste the aioli and if needed, adjust the seasoning with a bit more olive oil and fresh cracked black pepper. Transfer to a bowl or an airtight container and chill for 10 minutes before mixing into the tuna. The aioli can be refrigerated for up to 5 days.

Get It

There are so many ways to jazz up this tuna salad. Some ideas from me: diced tart apple, sweet or dill pickles, fresh tarragon, chopped hard-boiled egg, Calabrian chiles, artichoke hearts, or roasted zucchini. If you don't want to make the aioli, you can use mayo instead.

Get It

Big in Southern Italy, preserving and canning tuna in olive oil dates way back 'cause it's such a perfect way to preserve the fish. I think it's tricky to find great-quality canned or jarred tuna, but some brands from Italy and Spain are incredible. Making your own is so cool and delicious. Poaching tuna is relatively simple, as long as the tuna doesn't get too hot. First you marinate the fish for an hour at room temp, then bake it low and slow. As a rule, poaching is great for tougher cuts of tuna. The best thing is using the poaching oil in an aioli so nothing goes to waste here! I love to mix this tuna into pasta dishes like puttanesca, tuna casserole, or tuna sandwiches (see page 245). It's tasty folded into all different salads, from green and leafy ones to a hearty grain salad, and it's perfect in a classic Niçoise.

Olive Oil–Poached Tuna Conserva

Makes 2 steaks

3 large garlic cloves, finely grated (use a Microplane)

Finely grated zest of 1 lemon (use a Microplane)

½ teaspoon granulated sugar

Kosher salt

1 pound tuna (ahi, big-eye, or albacore), cut into 4 pieces

4 fresh or 2 dried bay leaves

2 cups everyday olive oil

Handful of fresh thyme, rosemary, and/or oregano sprigs

1. In a small bowl, combine the garlic, lemon zest, sugar, and 1 teaspoon of kosher salt and mix into a paste. Set the tuna steaks in a small casserole dish; they should have about an inch of space around them. Schmear the tuna steaks with the garlic mixture, then place the bay leaves on top. Let the tuna sit at room temperature for 1 hour, flipping halfway through.

2. Preheat the oven to 225°F. Add the olive oil and the herb sprigs to the fish. Cover with a piece of parchment paper that touches the oil to keep the tuna submerged. Bake for 30 minutes, or until the tuna is opaque and firm. Insert an instant-read thermometer into the meaty part of the fish—you are shooting for 100° to 105°F.

3. Remove from the oven and let the tuna rest, covered, for 30 minutes. To use right away, drain the oil and discard the bay leaves and herb sprigs; keep the oil to store the tuna. Using your hands or two forks, gently flake the tuna. You can store the poached tuna in the refrigerator for up to 2 weeks. Make sure it's submerged in oil; air is the enemy here. When ready to use, remove the tuna from the oil and flake it into bite-sized pieces.

Years ago, on a trip to Piedmont, I visited my friend Maria Nava at Acquerello, and she made me an amazing lunch of the lightest and most delicious lemon risotto, along with salad and grissini. She offered to show me how to make the risotto, starting with boiling the rice. I was like, "What??" I had been taught to stand tirelessly over the pot, stirring and slowly adding the stock or water. But no. Maria explained that the movement from the boiling creates the starch, so there is no need to stand and stir. Mind blown! In 17 minutes—which is exactly the same every time I make it—the risotto is done. Maria also taught me to use water instead of stock, which allows the rice to taste like rice. And instead of butter, which can make risotto a rich, heavy gut bomb, she uses extra-virgin olive oil, which adds beautiful flavor and creaminess. Once you try this method and taste the risotto, you will never go back to standing over a pot of risotto again.

Maria Nava's Lemon Olive Oil Risotto

Serves 6

Kosher salt

1½ cups Acquerello Carnaroli rice (see Get It Get It)

¾ cup freshly grated Parmigiano-Reggiano, plus more for finishing

2 tablespoons freshly grated lemon zest

¼ cup fresh lemon juice

¼ cup lemon extra-virgin olive oil (see Get It Get It), plus more for drizzling

1. In a medium or 5-quart saucepot, bring 6 cups of water to a boil over medium-high heat. Once the water is boiling, add a few pinches of salt and the rice. Cook at a strong, bubbling simmer over medium heat for 17 to 20 minutes; stir occasionally. (This method lets the boiling of the water agitate the rice, creating the creamy, starchy texture you want.)

2. Once the rice is cooked, the water is absorbed, and the rice is creamy, delicious, and al dente, reduce the heat to low. Stir in the grated parm, 1 tablespoon of the lemon zest, and the lemon juice, allowing the cheese to melt. Remove from the heat and slowly drizzle in the lemon extra-virgin olive oil; season with a bit of salt if needed. Serve immediately or keep the rice warm on low heat; the risotto will thicken as it sits and cools. Top the risotto with grated parm, a drizzle of lemon extra-virgin olive oil, and the remaining lemon zest.

Get It

I don't usually specify brands, but this is one of those times where the brand can make *all* of the difference in the dish. Acquerello, in Piedmont, makes extraordinary white rice from brown rice through a slow and methodical process of tumbling, aging, and reintroducing the germ that contains so much of the nutrients in the rice. I got to visit Acquerello and I was truly blown away. The rice is available online and at many gourmet markets. If you are in a pinch and can't get Acquerello, I suggest using another Carnaroli rice (not Arborio).

For the ultimate lemon flavor, I use lemon extra-virgin olive oil, which is made by processing lemon rinds with olives—one of my favorites is made by De Carlo. If you don't have it, you can substitute super-special extra-virgin olive oil.

Get It

Get It

To make the pesto in a food processor, pulse the pistachios, garlic, and herbs a few times to break them down. Add the olives and capers and drizzle 4 tablespoons of the oil into the mixture. Add the cheese, lemon zest and juice, and chile flake. With the motor running, drizzle in the remaining olive oil and pulse until a sauce forms.

Get It

Redolent with nutty pistachios, briny olives, capers, parsley, and tarragon, this pesto is just so fresh and green. It's the perfect match for seafood and also a fun Southern Italian take on a traditional Genovese pesto. You can use the pesto as a dip or schmear with crostini for an appetizer, or as a condiment alongside grilled seafood. It would also be great in a sandwich instead of mustard or mayo, or used as a base for salad dressing—just add vinegar and olive oil. I also suggest adding grilled or sautéed shrimp or pulled rotisserie chicken to the mix—either mixed in with the pesto and pasta at the end or simply placed on top for a great presentation.

Paccheri Pasta

with Green Olive–Pistachio Pesto

Make 2 cups pesto; serves 4 to 6 with pasta

¾ cup shelled unsalted pistachios

1 large garlic clove

1 cup packed fresh flat-leaf parsley leaves and stems, coarsely chopped

½ cup packed fresh tarragon leaves, coarsely chopped

8 tablespoons everyday olive oil

1½ cups pitted green Castelvetrano olives

¼ cup drained capers

¼ cup freshly grated Pecorino Romano, plus more for garnish

1 tablespoon finely grated lemon zest (from 1 lemon; use a Microplane)

2 tablespoons fresh lemon juice

⅛ teaspoon chile flake

Kosher salt

1 pound dry paccheri, rigatoni, or penne

Super-special extra-virgin olive oil, for drizzling

1. Heat a small skillet over medium-low heat. Add the pistachios to the dry skillet and toast, shaking the skillet every so often, until lightly browned all over, about 3 minutes. Transfer to a plate and let cool completely.

2. In a large, heavy granite or marble mortar, combine ½ cup of the cooled pistachios and the garlic. Firmly smash the ingredients in the bottom of the mortar using the pestle, twisting the pestle around the bottom in a circular motion every 15 to 20 seconds. Add the parsley and tarragon and continue smashing and twisting until everything is softened. Once the ingredients are softened, continue to work them in a circular motion for about 1 minute, until the nuts are crushed and a coarse paste has formed. Add 2 tablespoons of the everyday olive oil, along with the olives and capers, and continue to combine the ingredients using both the smashing and the circular motions with the pestle. (Please note that you may want to loosen the mixture from the sides every now and then with a small spoon.)

3. Add the remaining 6 tablespoons of everyday olive oil along with the cheese, lemon zest and juice, and chile flake. Continue to press down and stir with the pestle until the mixture resembles a chunky pesto. From start to finish the pesto should take about 4 minutes of work in the mortar. At this point, the pesto can be refrigerated in an airtight container for up to 3 days.

4. When you're ready to eat, bring a large pot of salted water to a boil. Add the pasta and cook according to the package directions until al dente. Drain, reserving ½ cup of the pasta cooking water. Add all of the pesto to the large pot, pour the hot pasta over the top, and stir to combine. Drizzle in the remaining pasta water as needed to help the pesto coat the pasta. Serve immediately with a healthy drizzle of super-special extra-virgin olive oil, a sprinkle of pecorino, and the remaining ¼ cup of pistachios.

This recipe is inspired by whole roasted lamb dishes served in Rome in the springtime. I love how the olive oil, white wine, and lamb juices come together to form an unctuous sauce. For a fresh finish, I love to garnish the lamb with more herbs on top; parsley and dill would be delicious. The potatoes cooked in the olive lamb juices turn out to be the big sleeper hit. Isn't it just like the veggies to steal the show?!?

Olive Oil–Roasted Lamb

with Potatoes and Olives

Serves 6

6 thick-cut (1 to 1½ inches) lamb
   shoulder chops (about 4 pounds)

Kosher salt

Fresh cracked black pepper

1½ pounds small Yukon gold
   potatoes, pierced with a fork

5 tablespoons everyday olive oil

½ cup peeled garlic cloves

6 oil-packed anchovy fillets
   (I love brown anchovies from
   Cantabria, Spain)

2 cups dry white wine
   (like pinot grigio)

1 cup pitted black olives (like
   Leccino, Taggiasca, Gaeta,
   Alfonso, or kalamata)

10 fresh thyme sprigs

3 fresh rosemary sprigs, cut into
   3-inch pieces

1 lemon, thinly sliced

2 tablespoons aged balsamic
   vinegar

2 tablespoons super-special extra-
   virgin olive oil

1½ teaspoons fennel pollen or
   ground toasted fennel seeds
   (optional)

1.   On a baking sheet, season the lamb chops with salt and pepper. Let sit at room temperature for 1 hour or so.

2.   Place the potatoes in a medium saucepot and cover with cold water. Bring to a boil and season well with salt. Once boiling, par-cook the potatoes for 10 minutes, until the outsides are just becoming tender but the centers are still firm. Drain.

3.   Preheat the oven to 375°F. Heat an extra-large (12- to 14-inch) cast-iron or enameled cast-iron skillet over medium heat for 3 minutes. Add 3 tablespoons of the everyday olive oil. Add the lamb chops and sear, turning after 4 minutes or so, until golden brown all over. (You might have to brown the shoulder chops in batches.) Transfer the lamb to a clean baking sheet and set aside.

4.   Discard half of the oil in the pan. Reduce the heat to low. Add the garlic and anchovies and cook, stirring often, until toasted, about 3 minutes. Add the white wine and over medium heat, using a wooden spoon or spatula, scrape up the fond (those browned bits on the bottom of the pan) and mix it into the sauce. Once the wine comes to a boil and is reduced by half, remove the pan from the heat. Nestle the lamb and potatoes into the pan. Carefully spoon the pan sauce over the potatoes and lamb, basting them well. Transfer to the oven and roast for 20 minutes, until the lamb is caramelized and the sauce sticks to the chops.

5.   Remove from the oven and add the olives, thyme, rosemary, and lemon slices, and drizzle the remaining 2 tablespoons of everyday olive oil over the top. Nestle everything into the pan and sauce; baste one more time. Increase the oven temperature to 425°F and roast for another 25 minutes, or until the lamb, potatoes, and lemon slices begin to turn golden brown. Remove from the oven and let rest for 15 minutes. To serve, lightly smash the potatoes in the pan. Drizzle with the balsamic vinegar and super-special extra-virgin olive oil and sprinkle with fennel pollen, if using.

This super-toasty and rich garlic-chile oil was inspired by the Japanese condiment called *mayu*, a scorched black garlic oil that's typically served with ramen. I love the bitterness and depth of flavor that it adds to dishes. My version of that oil uses cherry tomatoes, as well as chile flake for heat. When the tomatoes get added to the oil, they not only stop the cooking of the garlic and chile flake, but they blister and steam and intensify the overall flavor here. This oil is perfect on eggs, roasted veggies, pizza, pasta, noodles, soups, seafood, rice bowls, or just about anything you want to spice up!

Super-Toasted Chile-Garlic Oil

Makes about 1 cup

¾ cup everyday olive oil
8 garlic cloves, thinly sliced
2 tablespoons chile flake
6 whole cherry tomatoes
1 teaspoon kosher salt

1.   In a small saucepan, heat the olive oil over medium-low heat. Add the garlic and cook until toasted, about 5 minutes. Add the chile flake and continue to cook until the garlic and chile flake begin to turn a deep, dark golden brown (see Get It Get It), about 5 minutes. Remove from the heat, then add the cherry tomatoes and salt. Let sit for 5 minutes to meld.

2.   Transfer to a blender and blend on high speed for a few seconds, until the garlic begins to break down. Transfer the chile-garlic oil to a bowl if you're using it right away, or keep stored in an airtight container in the refrigerator for up to a month.

— Get It —

Don't be too worried about how dark the garlic gets. The goal is to take the garlic and chile flake pretty far, so they develop a dark roasted color and flavor. I love to make this in double batches and keep it in the fridge.

— Get It —

Pasta

I am obsessed with pasta—both dry and fresh. Dry pasta is my go-to for a quick and relatively easy meal; fresh pasta is special 'cause you actually get to make it yourself by hand. People have been making fresh pasta for over 2,000 years, and I think it's essential for all of us to make it at least once. There is definitely a place for both dry and fresh pasta in the kitchen, depending on your pasta game plan.

Let me start by explaining the key difference between the two. Dry pasta is typically made from semolina (durum) wheat and water, which creates a strong, toothsome dough—perfect for extruding into hollow or round shapes. Fresh pasta is made with "00" flour (a soft, fine wheat flour) and lots of eggs. The dough is ideal for sheeting, and it's strong and pliable (and also silky and tender) enough to stretch and shape around fillings.

When making fresh pasta, there are a few things that are great to have handy. For starters, I always use a combo of half coarsely ground semolina and half "00" flour for dusting, sheeting, and storing. I call this "bench flour." When working with your dough, it's best to use a lightly oiled wooden board to prevent the pasta from drying out too quickly, or just use a plastic cutting board. I use a spray bottle of water for misting if my pasta dries out a bit, but a damp pastry brush works well too. Good stainless-steel pastry wheel cutters are easy to buy nowadays, but if you're super serious about pasta making, seek out bronze cutters from Italy. I suggest investing in a small set of ring mold cutters (not biscuit cutters); inverting the cutter and using the soft edge to help seal and shape your filled pasta is a great trick. Linen towels permit the perfect balance of humidity and dryness when it is time to hold fresh pasta, but to freeze it, I put it on parchment paper–lined baking sheets. Once frozen, I transfer it to resealable plastic bags. (Always cook your frozen pasta straight from the freezer.) Finally, I love a good, old hand-cranked pasta machine, but in reality, I use the pasta sheeter attachment on my stand mixer to make beautiful sheets of silky fresh pasta dough.

The most important ingredient for fresh pasta dough is eggs. Eggs in Italy have bright, beautiful yolks that are almost a dark reddish-orange. This is due to the diet and living conditions of the chickens. Chickens naturally peck around for worms, bugs, and seeds, and the rich color of the egg yolks can be attributed to that, plus the ability to roam. I recommend buying pasture-raised eggs versus "cage-free" eggs. Better yet, look for local eggs at farmers' markets or sign up for a CSA share to get access to happy chickens and their super-delicious eggs.

As a rule, fresh pasta tends to go best with creamy, buttery sauces (especially combined with vegetables), light tomato sauces, tender ragù sauces, and smooth pestos. Dry pasta is perfect to stand up to richer tomato sauces, chunky pestos, and hearty meat ragù-style sauces. I like to assess the sauce and ask myself, "What kind of noodle does this dish need?" Simply put, fresh pasta likes more delicate sauces, and dry pasta likes the heartier ones. For pairing vegetables, it's more about how the vegetable is processed or cut. It's good to match the shapes—for example, if the pasta is a twirling shape, then try slicing the veggies thinly. For a fork pasta (I call these "stabbing pastas"), the veggies can be chunkier.

One of my all-time favorite fresh pasta dishes is tagliatelle with Bolognese ragù; I think it is *the* dish. It's composed of layers of flavor and tradition, perfectly bound with thin delicate egg pasta ribbons. It's pure joy. On page 223, you can find my vegetarian version made with four types of mushrooms and layered in the same way as the traditional meat version.

In every chapter of this book, you'll find recipes using both dry and fresh pasta. I have tried to share a wide range of shapes and sauces, and I encourage you to experiment using both fresh and dry pasta. Some of my favorites—though there are so many—include the Double Artichoke Spaghetti Aglio e Olio (page 35), Asparagus Cannelloni (page 56), Rigatoni with Pea Pesto (page 81), Ricotta Ravioli (page 399), and Pumpkin Pesto Gnocchi (page 368). As I see it, just about every vegetable lines up to be stuffed into or paired or twirled with fresh or dry pasta. This is why pasta is such a great way to showcase veggies in a whole new light! ————————————

Welcome to Monte Farina! These egg explorers are on a quest to become pasta as they seek to crack into the flour volcano.

This pasta dough is perfect for all filled pasta shapes. Its high egg content gives the dough a tender texture and rich flavor. I use this dough for ribbon pastas too—it makes such a special meal!

The Essential Egg Yolk Pasta Dough

Makes 1 pound fresh pasta dough

2 cups (300g) "00" pasta flour, plus more for dusting

2 Grade A large eggs

6 Grade A large egg yolks

1.   Place the flour, eggs, and egg yolks in the bowl of a stand mixer fitted with the dough hook attachment. Mix on medium-low speed for 6 to 7 minutes, until the dough begins to come together in a ball with minimal flour left in the bowl. Increase the speed a notch and mix for 2 to 3 minutes longer, until a homogenous dough has formed. Turn the dough out onto a work surface and wrap in plastic wrap. Let rest for 20 minutes.

2.   Gently knead the dough into a ball for about 1 minute. Cut the dough in half. Knead one piece (cover the remaining half with plastic wrap) on the work surface. Using one hand, rock the dough back and forth in a rotating motion, gently pushing it into the work surface. Knead for 1 to 2 minutes, until the ball is very smooth. Wrap tightly in plastic wrap. Repeat with the second piece of dough. Refrigerate for at least 1 hour or overnight, letting the balls of dough rest at room temperature for an hour before rolling.

3.   Alternatively, make the dough by hand. On a clean work surface, build a mound with the flour. Create a well in the center and add the eggs and yolks. Using a fork, incorporate the flour into the eggs in a circular motion, mixing until the dough becomes stiff. Begin kneading the dough, adding a little flour as necessary to prevent sticking. Continue kneading with both hands until the dough is smooth, about 10 minutes. Divide the dough into two equal balls. Wrap them tightly in plastic wrap and refrigerate for at least 1 hour or overnight. Sometimes you'll notice small dark speckles in the dough after it has rested overnight. Don't be alarmed—this is just the flour oxidizing, and it won't affect the taste at all.

Troubleshooting Potential Pasta Dough Problems

1. For starters, eggs! They are not all the same size. You should have a little over ¾ cup of cracked egg mixture.

2. How fresh or dry your flour is can have an impact on the dough. Sometimes you will need to adjust the ratio of flour to egg. Here are a few pointers:

   ✽ If your dough is crumbly after the first 6 to 7 minutes of mixing, it needs a bit more hydration. Add in a small amount of cold water (1 teaspoon to 1 tablespoon), then continue to mix for another minute or two, until the dough just starts to come together.

   ✽ If your dough is still crumbly, add a touch more water, but refrain from adding liquid too soon after that first addition. The dough will continue to hydrate and soften as it rests.

   ✽ On the other side, if your dough comes together quickly within the first 6 to 7 minutes of mixing, this could be a sign that it will be overhydrated after it rests. Add in a tablespoon or two of flour to balance the hydration, making it a bit dryer.

3. If you live in an area with high humidity (or are making this recipe in the thick of the summer), you may want to reduce the egg yolks by 1. Alternatively, in drier climates, you may want to increase by 1 egg yolk.

A *sfoglia* is literally a "sheet" in Italian, and the women who roll them out by hand are known as *sfogline* (just one is a *sfoglina*). In Bologna, these fresh, egg yolk–rich sheets of pasta are rolled by hand with a *matturello* (a super-long rolling pin). Learning to make pasta sheets rolled by hand or machine is the first step before moving on to make other shapes. The simple sheets are quite useful in the kitchen, whether layered and baked in lasagna or cannelloni or cut small into the handkerchiefs known as *fazzoletti*.

Fresh Pasta Sheets

Makes sixteen 5 by 6-inch pasta sheets

½ cup "00" flour mixed with ½ cup semolina (aka bench flour), for dusting

The Essential Egg Yolk Pasta Dough (page 256)

Kosher salt

Everyday olive oil or olive oil spray

1.   Line a large baking sheet with a clean linen towel and dust it lightly with bench flour. Work with one ball of dough at a time and keep the other half wrapped in plastic. Lightly dust a work surface with bench flour.

2.   Set your pasta machine to the thickest setting, which is usually 1. Flatten the dough slightly with a rolling pin, creating a rectangle shape; be mindful to match the width of your roller. (This will create consistent-sized pasta sheets.) Feed the dough through the roller. Continue to feed the dough through the roller on increasingly thinner settings; you might need to add a little bench flour to one side of the dough if it's feeling a little sticky or wet. Continue rolling the dough until you've reached setting 5, and then transfer it to the dusted work surface.

3.   Cut the sheets into 5 by 6-inch sections. Place the first layer on the towel-lined baking sheet. Dust with a bit more of the bench flour and top with a sheet of parchment paper. Repeat with the remaining dough; use parchment between the sheets of pasta. When you are finished with all of the pasta, cover with another towel. If you are planning to refrigerate the sheets to blanch later, wrap the whole baking sheet tightly with plastic wrap so the pasta doesn't dry at the edges. This can be refrigerated overnight. The pasta sheets can also layered between sheets of parchment and frozen on a baking sheet, then transferred to a resealable plastic bag and frozen for up to 1 month.

4.   Line a baking sheet with parchment paper. Bring a large pot of water to a boil and season with a few pinches of kosher salt. Prepare a large bowl with ice water. Working in four batches, quickly blanch the sheets in boiling water for 1½ to 2 minutes. Using tongs or a skimmer, carefully remove the sheets from the pot and plunge them in the ice water to chill. Transfer the cooked pasta sheets to the parchment-lined baking sheet. Using your hands or a pastry brush, lightly oil the sheets. Repeat with the remaining pasta. Your pasta is now ready to use.

Corzetti pasta coins hail from Liguria, also famous for pesto, Taggiasca olives, and the beautiful Cinque Terre! Any pesto goes well with corzetti because they form little cups that hold the sauce nicely. These are really fun and simple to make; all you do is roll out your dough and cut the coins, then stamp them. It's easy to do all at once too. It's okay to let the coins dry out on your counter for up to 30 minutes because the drying helps set the imprint of the stamp. You'll notice that I only roll the dough to the number 4 setting—this is because the pasta gets pretty thin when it's stamped. If you have any scraps left after stamping, gather and wrap them with plastic wrap and let them rest for 15 minutes. Then go right ahead and reroll them to make more coins.

Corzetti Pasta Coins

Makes about 12 ounces

½ cup "00" flour mixed with ½ cup semolina (aka bench flour), for dusting

The Essential Egg Yolk Pasta Dough (page 256)

Get It

There are several artisans making corzetti stamps and selling them on Etsy. Some of my favorite are Romagnoli Pasta Tools (romagnolipastatools.com/corzetti/) and the Wood Grain Gallery (etsy.com/shop/TheWoodGrainGallery). They can also be found at kitchen stores like Williams-Sonoma and online at Amazon. If you don't have a corzetti stamp, try using a circular cookie cutter to cut the coins, and then use the textured end of a meat mallet to create a design.

Get It

1. Line a large baking sheet with a clean linen towel and dust it lightly with bench flour. Work with one ball of dough at a time and keep the other piece wrapped in plastic. Lightly dust a work surface with bench flour.

2. Set your pasta machine to the thickest setting, which is usually 1. Flatten the dough slightly with a rolling pin, creating a rectangle shape; be mindful to match the width of your roller. (This will create consistent-sized pasta sheets.) Feed the dough through the roller. Continue to feed the dough through the roller on increasingly thinner settings; you might need to add a little bench flour to one side of the dough if it's feeling a little sticky or wet. Continue rolling the dough until you've reached setting 4, and then transfer it to the dusted work surface.

3. Each corzetti stamp comes with two pieces. The bottom part of the stamp has a circular cutter on one end. You will use that to cut the coins out of the dough. Try to keep the cuts close to each other to get as many coins as possible. Then place each coin on the designed end of the bottom stamp and, using the top stamp, press down firmly to imprint the design onto the coin. It's best to do this quickly—if your pasta begins to dry, it could make it challenging to imprint the stamp. If your coins dry out, try spritzing them with a light spray of water and let them sit for 1 minute before stamping. Dust with bench flour and let rest on the counter. Repeat with the remaining dough.

4. When you are finished with all of the pasta dough, place the coins on the prepared baking sheet. Cover with another towel and refrigerate until you are ready to use. You can also wrap the whole baking sheet tightly in plastic and refrigerate the pasta overnight. The corzetti can also be frozen on a baking sheet, then transferred to a resealable plastic bag and frozen for up to 1 month. Cook in a pot of boiling salted water for about 2 minutes, or just until the corzetti are floating and al dente. When cooking from frozen, add 1 minute to the cooking time.

It's fun to choose the right sauce for the right pasta ribbon. The widest ribbon, pappardelle, is perfect for the heartiest of sauces, from meat and vegetable ragùs to chunky tomato sauce, or tossed with all types of vegetables. Tagliatelle is the perfect middle-ground pasta ribbon that works with traditional Bolognese ragù, lighter vegetable sauces, or chunkier pestos. Tagliolini is the thinnest, most delicate ribbon, and is great with seafood or tender young vegetables like thinly sliced summer squash, cherry tomatoes, artichokes, and asparagus, and great with a smooth pesto like the Genovese Pesto on page 240.

Hand-Cut Ribbon Pasta

Pappardelle, Tagliatelle, and Tagliolini

Makes about 1 pound fresh pasta ribbons

½ cup "00" flour mixed with ½ cup semolina (aka bench flour), for dusting

The Essential Egg Yolk Pasta Dough (page 256)

1. Line two large baking sheets with clean linen towels and dust lightly with the bench flour. Work with one ball of dough at a time and keep the other half wrapped in plastic. Lightly dust a work surface with bench flour. Set your pasta machine to the thickest setting, which is usually 1. Flatten the dough slightly with a rolling pin, creating a rectangle shape; be mindful to match the width of your roller. (This will create consistent-sized pasta sheets.) Feed the dough through the roller. Continue to feed the dough through the roller on increasingly thinner settings; you might need to add a little bench flour to one side of the dough if it's feeling a little sticky or wet. Continue rolling the dough until you've reached setting 5, and then transfer it to the dusted work surface.

2. Sprinkle the pasta sheet with bench flour, and then cut the pasta into 10- to 12-inch-long sheets. Transfer each sheet to one of the prepared baking sheets. Repeat the process with the remaining dough, adding a sheet of bench flour–dusted parchment paper between each layer of dough.

3. To cut the pasta sheets into ribbons: Stack two sheets of pasta on top of each other, making sure to dust liberally with the flour between sheets. Tightly roll the sheet of pasta from the short side to form a tube or cylinder, like a cinnamon roll. Using a sharp knife, trim any dry edges from the pasta, then cut the cylinder into ¼- to ½-inch-wide ribbons for tagliatelle or ¾- to 1-inch-wide ribbons for pappardelle. For tagliolini, cut the pasta into ⅛-inch-wide ribbons. Unroll the pasta ribbons and toss again with a little of the flour; spread on a prepared baking sheet and reserve until you are ready to cook. You can keep the fresh ribbon pasta in the refrigerator for up to 2 days. To do so, return it to the linen towel–lined baking sheets and dust with bench flour. Drape with another clean towel and cover with plastic wrap. The pasta can also be frozen on the baking sheet, then transferred to a resealable plastic bag and frozen for up to 1 month. Cook in a pot of boiling salted water for 30 seconds to 1 minute, or just until the pasta is floating and tender. When cooking from frozen, add 1 minute to the cooking time.

Ravioli is the most common shape of filled pasta. Ravioli can be large or small, round, square, or even rectangular. Any filling in the book will work well in ravioli too!

Ravioli

Serves 4 to 6

½ cup "00" flour mixed with ½ cup semolina (aka bench flour), for dusting

The Essential Egg Yolk Pasta Dough (page 256)

4 cups pasta filling (see page 175 and 399 for recipe ideas)

Get It

This pasta shape relies on the dough being freshly rolled and still damp so it seals shut. If the dough's surface has dried a bit and you notice a skin forming, I recommend having a small spray bottle of water handy to dampen the pasta sheet, or even a slightly wet pastry brush will do the trick. Just be careful to not wet the dough too much, as it will become too sticky to handle.

Get It

1. Line a large baking sheet with a clean linen towel and dust it lightly with bench flour. Work with one ball of dough at a time and keep the other half wrapped in plastic. Lightly dust a work surface with bench flour.

2. Set your pasta machine to the thickest setting, which is usually 1. Flatten the dough slightly with a rolling pin, creating a rectangle shape; be mindful to match the width of your roller. (This will create consistent-sized pasta sheets.) Feed the dough through the roller. Continue to feed the dough through the roller on increasingly thinner settings; you might need to add a little bench flour to one side of the dough if it's feeling a little sticky or wet. Continue rolling the dough until you've reached setting 5, and then repeat one more time on setting 5. Transfer the pasta to the dusted work surface and cut it in half. Cover one half with a sheet of parchment paper, then with a clean linen towel.

3. On the uncovered pasta sheet, evenly pipe or spoon dollops of filling (1 to 1½ tablespoons) in two rows on the dough, 1½ to 2 inches apart. Uncover the second sheet of dough and lay it top side down (so the floured side is facing up) over the mounds of filling; use your hands to gently stretch the dough so it covers the filling. Using the top, dull side (not the cutting side) of a 2¼-inch ring mold, gently press around each mound of filling to start shaping the ravioli and seal the dough. (You don't need to push down too hard.) Then, using the flip side of the ring mold, press around the mounds again, this time a little more firmly, to seal and shape the ravioli in advance of cutting it out.

4. Use a 2¾-inch ring mold cutter to cut out each ravioli and transfer them to the prepared baking sheet. Cover the ravioli with another towel until you are ready to cook them. Repeat with the remaining dough and filling. If you're not using the pasta immediately, sprinkle a generous amount of bench flour on top of the pasta, cover with a clean lint-free towel, and wrap tightly in plastic. You can refrigerate the ravioli for a few hours or up to overnight. They can also be frozen on a baking sheet, then transferred to a resealable plastic bag and frozen for up to 1 month. Cook in a pot of boiling salted water for 2 to 3 minutes, or just until the ravioli are floating and the sealed part (where it's thickest) is tender. When cooking from frozen, add 1 minute to the cooking time.

Raviolo is the same shape as ravioli, but the main difference is that they are very large and are double stuffed. The classic (and my favorite) filling for a raviolo is creamy ricotta nestled with an egg yolk (page 266). That pasta first became popular at Ristorante San Domenico outside of Bologna and is a real showstopper. There is no need to fuss with a sauce—a little melted or browned butter over the top is all a raviolo needs. This is decadence wrapped up in dough!

Raviolo

Serves 6

¼ cup "00" flour mixed with ¼ cup semolina (aka bench flour), for dusting

The Essential Egg Yolk Pasta Dough (page 256)

2 heaping cups raviolo filling (see page 175)

6 large egg yolks

Coarse sea salt (like Maldon)

Get It

This pasta shape relies on the dough being freshly rolled and still damp so it seals shut. If the dough's surface has dried a bit and you notice a skin forming, I recommend having a small spray bottle of water handy to dampen the squares, or even a slightly wet pastry brush will do the trick. Just be careful to not wet the dough too much, as it will become too sticky to handle. For a veggie-forward twist, the polenta (page 130), potato (page 311), and winter squash (page 372) fillings could be used in the place of the ricotta filling.

Get It

1. Line a large baking sheet with a clean linen towel and dust it lightly with bench flour. Work with one ball of dough at a time and keep the other half wrapped in plastic. Lightly dust a work surface with bench flour.

2. Set your pasta machine to the thickest setting, which is usually 1. Flatten the dough slightly with a rolling pin, creating a rectangle shape; be mindful to match the width of your roller. (This will create consistent-sized pasta sheets.) Feed the dough through the roller. Continue to feed the dough through the roller on increasingly thinner settings; you might need to add a little bench flour to one side of the dough if it's feeling a little sticky or wet. Continue rolling the dough until you've reached setting 5, and then repeat one more time on setting 5. Transfer the pasta to the dusted work surface and cut into 5 by 6-inch sheets. Cover the sheets with a towel as you work. Repeat with the remaining dough.

3. Scoop the filling into a pastry bag or a sturdy resealable plastic bag; snip off the corner. Working with one pasta sheet at a time, pipe a 2½- to 2¾-inch-wide donut-shaped circle of filling, about 2 inches high; leave a crater in the center for the egg yolk. Pipe or fill in the bottom of the crater with about 1 inch of filling. Gently nestle 1 egg yolk into the ricotta ring and season with a pinch of coarse sea salt. Gently stretch another pasta sheet over the top of the raviolo. Cup your hand into a C shape and press and seal the top sheet around the filling. Use the dull side (not the cutting side) of a 3½-inch fluted or straight ring mold to gently press around the mound of filling to start shaping the raviolo and to seal the dough. Rotate the ring mold around the filling to remove any air and seal. Then, using the next size up ring mold (4 inches), press the cut side around the raviolo, pressing firmly to cut through the dough. Carefully transfer the assembled raviolo to the prepared baking sheet and cover with a clean lint-free linen towel. Repeat with the remaining dough and filling. Sprinkle the tops of the raviolo with a bit of bench flour, then cover with the towel and refrigerate until you are ready to cook. (You can refrigerate the egg yolk raviolo for a few hours.) Cook in a pot of boiling salted water for 2½ to 3 minutes, or just until the pasta is floating and the sealed part (where it's thickest) is tender.

In Emilia-Romagna, tortelli are the other answer to ravioli. To make the tortelli shape, the pasta sheet gets folded over so the tortelli are sealed on only three sides. This way, you use all of the dough with no waste. I like to think of tortelli as the big cousin to agnolotti, which are similarly folded and shaped, but bite-sized. With this shape, it's key to roll your sheet of pasta to the full width of the roller.

Tortelli

Serves 4 to 6

½ cup "00" flour mixed with ½ cup semolina (aka bench flour), for dusting

The Essential Egg Yolk Pasta Dough (page 256)

4 cups pasta filling (see page 203 and 311 for recipe ideas)

1. Line a large baking sheet with a clean linen towel and dust it lightly with bench flour. Cut each ball of pasta dough in half so you have four pieces total. Work with one ball of dough at a time and keep the other pieces wrapped in plastic wrap. Lightly dust a work surface with bench flour.

2. Set your pasta machine to the thickest setting, which is usually 1. Flatten the dough slightly with a rolling pin, creating a rectangle shape; be mindful to match the width of your roller. (This will create consistent-sized pasta sheets.) Feed the dough through the roller. Continue to feed the dough through the roller on increasingly thinner settings; you might need to add a little bench flour to one side of the dough if it's feeling a little sticky or wet. Continue rolling the dough until you've reached setting 5, run the pasta through twice, and then transfer it to a work surface that's lightly dusted with bench flour. Use a pizza cutter or sharp knife to cut the pasta into two long sheets, each about 16 inches in length and about 6 inches in width. Cut each sheet in half lengthwise, creating four sheets total, each about 16 by 3 inches.

3. Scoop the filling into a pastry bag or a sturdy resealable plastic bag; snip off the corner. Starting with one strip of dough and keeping the rest covered with a clean linen towel while you work, pipe about 1 tablespoon of filling in mounds across the lower half of the dough, leaving 1 inch between mounds; you should have five to six mounds in all. Alternatively, use two spoons to place or dollop the filling onto the dough. Fold the dough over lengthwise and, using your hands, firmly press and seal each tortelli. Cut between each tortelli and trim the excess dough; I recommend using a pastry wheel cutter. Use the tines of a fork to create indentations around the edges of the tortelli (or, if your pastry wheel cutter is fluted, feel free to use it for cutting). Transfer the finished tortelli to the prepared baking sheet. Repeat with the remaining dough and filling. If you're using the pasta immediately, keep it covered with a clean lint-free towel while you roll and shape the remaining pasta. If you're not using the pasta immediately, sprinkle a generous amount of bench flour on top of the pasta, cover with a clean lint-free towel, and wrap tightly in plastic. The pasta can be

Get It

This pasta shape relies on the dough being freshly rolled and still damp so it seals shut. If the dough's surface has dried a bit and you notice a skin forming, I recommend having a small spray bottle of water handy to dampen the squares, or even a slightly wet pastry brush will do the trick. Just be careful to not wet the dough too much, as it will become too sticky to handle.

Get It

refrigerated like this overnight. The tortelli can also be frozen on a baking sheet, then transferred to a resealable plastic bag and frozen for up to 1 month. Cook in a pot of boiling salted water for 2 to 3 minutes, or just until the pasta is floating and the sealed part (where it's thickest) is tender. When cooking from frozen, add 1 minute to the cooking time.

Tortelloni are the classic filled pasta shape from Emilia-Romagna. They can be shaped a few different ways, but here I chose the fold that I think is the best one to start with. The tiny little sister to the tortelloni is the tortellini, which, legend has it, is modeled after Venus's belly button. Tortellini are also very similar to cappelletti, which are shaped after the pope's hat. I love to use the winter squash and polenta filling for these, as it is slightly firmer and denser and easy to stretch the dough around.

Tortelloni

Serves 4 to 6

½ cup "00" flour mixed with ½ cup semolina (aka bench flour), for dusting

The Essential Egg Yolk Pasta Dough (page 256)

4 cups pasta filling (see page 130 and 372 for recipe ideas)

Get It

This pasta shape relies on the dough being freshly rolled and still damp so it seals shut. If the dough's surface has dried a bit and you notice a skin forming, I recommend having a small spray bottle of water handy to dampen the squares, or even a slightly wet pastry brush will do the trick. Just be careful to not wet the dough too much, as it will become too sticky to handle.

If the tortelloni shape is too complicated, you can just form the filled dough into triangles and call them triangoli!

Get It

1. Line a large baking sheet with a lint-free towel and dust lightly with bench flour. Cut each ball of pasta dough in half so you have four pieces total. Work with one ball of dough at a time and keep the other pieces wrapped in plastic. Set your pasta machine to the thickest setting, which is usually 1. Flatten the dough slightly with a rolling pin, creating a rectangle shape; be mindful to match the width of your roller. (This will create consistent-sized pasta sheets.) Feed the dough through the roller. Continue to feed the dough through the roller on increasingly thinner settings; you might need to add a little bench flour to one side of the dough if it's feeling a little sticky or wet. If the pasta starts getting too long, you can cut the piece in half. You want this pasta thin and manageable. I recommend once you've reached setting 5, run the pasta through twice and then transfer it to a work surface that's lightly dusted with bench flour.

2. Scoop the filling into a pastry bag or a sturdy resealable plastic bag; snip off the corner. Cut the long strips of pasta dough into 12-inch lengths. Trim the strips to straighten the edges, then cut the pasta sheet into 2½- to 3-inch squares. (You can discard the scraps or reroll and use for another shape, like tagliatelle.) Place 1 scant tablespoon of filling into the center of each square. Fold the square into a triangle, gently pressing the edges to seal. Using your thumb, gently press the pocket of filling up toward the peak of the triangle, then pull the two corners downward and press to seal. Transfer the finished tortelloni to the prepared baking sheet. Repeat with the remaining dough and filling. If you're using the pasta immediately, keep it covered with a clean lint-free towel while you roll and shape the remaining pasta. If you're not using the pasta immediately, sprinkle a generous amount of bench flour on top, cover with a clean lint-free towel, and wrap tightly in plastic. The pasta can be refrigerated like this overnight. The tortelloni can also be frozen on a baking sheet, then transferred to a resealable plastic bag and frozen for up to 1 month. Cook in a pot of boiling salted water for 2 to 3 minutes, or just until the pasta is floating and the sealed part (where it's thickest) is tender. When cooking from frozen, add 1 minute to the cooking time.

Making gnocchi is kind of terrifying. The dough is temperamental, and ultimately you just have to learn the feel of making it, which is why I believe it's best made by hand. You can't be scared to add too much flour, but you also can't be scared to add too little. I learned to make gnocchi from Chef Tony Mantuano of Spiaggia in Chicago, who makes the best. He recommends using older potatoes (those with the eyes sprouting are the most ideal) and not overworking the dough. You will need some special tools to make these, including a ricer, a bench scraper, and a gnocchi board (although a fork will work too). Most important: It's essential to have a glass of wine, hot tea, or another soothing beverage nearby while you work! Many sauces go well with gnocchi, but my favorites are ones that are thick enough to dress them. There isn't time for a marriage ceremony (see page 401) with gnocchi as they are so tender. I love gnocchi with all pestos, any tomato sauce, and with the rich salumi sauce on page 315. We want to enrobe the gnocchi with glorious goodness.

Potato Gnocchi

Serves 4 to 6

4 medium-to-large russet potatoes (2¼ to 2½ pounds), rinsed

Kosher salt

1¼ cups (250g) "00" flour, plus a little more for dusting

½ cup freshly grated Parmigiano Reggiano (use the fine holes of a box grater, not a Microplane)

3 large egg yolks, lightly beaten

1.   Preheat the oven to 350°F. Place the potatoes directly on the middle oven rack and bake for about 45 minutes, or until the potatoes are soft and the peels begin to wrinkle. While the potatoes are baking, set up your work space, as you want to start mixing the dough soon after you rice the potatoes.

2.   Carefully cut the hot potatoes in half and let cool for a minute. Using a clean kitchen towel, scoop out the soft potato from the peel. Using a ricer, mash the potatoes in a bowl. Check the weight of the riced potatoes; you want a yield of 1 pound (455g).

3.   Transfer the riced potatoes to a large cutting board or work surface. Season with a few pinches of salt. Using a sifter or a fine-mesh sieve, sprinkle ¼ cup of flour onto the potatoes. Using a bench scraper, cut the flour into the potatoes, creating hash marks. Fold the potato mixture onto itself using the bench scraper. Sprinkle with the cheese and drizzle the egg yolks over the potato mixture.

4.   Sift on another ½ cup of flour, then use your hands to fold the dough together. Pat it into a rectangle. Sprinkle the remaining ½ cup of flour on top. Fold the dough and knead it gently by hand, adding more flour if needed, until the dough loses its stickiness and it begins to firm up, about 2 minutes. Wrap the dough in plastic wrap and let sit at room temperature for 15 minutes.

5.   I recommend testing the dough for texture before forming all the gnocchi. If you find the dough is too soft, try sifting in a bit more flour. When shaping, if you find the gnocchi a little sticky, dust the ropes of

dough with a little additional flour. Line a baking sheet with parchment paper and lightly dust with flour. Pat the dough into a rectangle about 1 inch thick. Using the bench scraper, cut the dough into 9 or 10 pieces. Roll each slice into even-sized ropes, ¾ to 1 inch thick. Cut each rope into 1-inch pieces. Using a gnocchi board, set a piece cut side down against the board and push it down, rolling with your finger to create the characteristic ridges on the gnocchi. You can use a fork if you do not have a gnocchi board. Repeat to make the remaining gnocchi. Allow the gnocchi to gently roll off the board. Using the bench scraper, transfer the gnocchi to the baking sheet. Allow the gnocchi to rest in the refrigerator for 20 to 30 minutes before cooking (they do not need to be covered).

6.   Bring a large pot of water to a boil and salt it generously. Fill a large bowl with ice water. Pick up the parchment to dump all the gnocchi at once into the boiling water (I find the less you handle these, the better). Blanch the gnocchi until they begin to float, about 2 minutes. Using a skimmer or slotted spoon, gently lift the gnocchi from the pot into the ice bath. Allow the gnocchi to chill in the ice bath for 2 minutes (see Get It Get It). Gently remove the gnocchi from the ice bath and transfer to a bowl. Toss them with 1 teaspoon of olive oil to prevent sticking. Refrigerate until you are ready to use them. Once chilled, you can warm up the gnocchi in a sauce or brown them in oil or butter without any fear of them overcooking.

─── Get It ───

I like to blanch the gnocchi and then shock them in ice water as it sets the texture, preventing them from turning to mush. The gnocchi can be blanched one day in advance.

─── Get It ───

Nope, this isn't a recipe for pasta! "Then why is it in this chapter?" you ask. Because these cookies are a great way to use the extra egg whites remaining when you are making fresh pasta. My Grandma Lillian always made these cookies, usually with chocolate and pecans, though I prefer them with chocolate chips and shredded coconut. The takeaway? Have fun with the mix-ins and use all kinds of dried fruits, nuts, and chips! And if you were wondering, the name of this recipe comes from the "forgotten" treat left in the oven overnight. They're also called Forget-Me-Nots in the South. Just don't turn your oven on the next morning without taking the cookies out first!

Coconut-Chocolate Forgotten Cookies

Makes 16 cookies

2 large egg whites

½ teaspoon cream of tartar

¾ cup sugar

½ teaspoon pure vanilla bean paste (optional)

¾ cup bittersweet chocolate chips

1 cup unsweetened shredded coconut

1.   Preheat the oven to 350°F. Line a baking or cookie sheet with foil or parchment paper. Using a stand mixer with the whisk attachment or an electric hand mixer, whip the egg whites and cream of tartar at high speed until soft peaks form, about 2 minutes. Gradually add the sugar and whip on high until stiff peaks form, about 3 minutes. Turn off the mixer and scrape down the bowl with a rubber spatula to ensure that all of the sugar is incorporated. Add the vanilla paste (if using) and whip on high speed for 2 minutes, until stiff peaks form. Turn off the mixer. Using the rubber spatula, gently fold in the chocolate chips and coconut.

2.   Using two spoons, drop golf ball–sized mounds of the meringue onto the prepared baking sheet. (I like to shape them to look like mountain peaks versus smooth scoops.) Transfer to the preheated oven, then turn the oven off. Let the cookies sit in the oven overnight, or for at least 8 hours. Enjoy with your favorite sorbet or sherbet. The cookies can be kept at room temperature in an airtight container for up to a week or frozen for 2 months.

Peppers

The world of peppers encapsulates both sweet and spicy (they're all technically part of the genus *Capsicum*) and, wow, there are a lot of great peppers to be had. Sweet bell peppers can be found all over Italy, and they're plentiful in American grocery stores year-round. In addition to bell peppers, you'll find fantastic heirloom peppers in farmers' markets in season. These are the elongated, sometimes funky-shaped peppers that come in a range of colors. They can be sweet or hot and they're incredible. A favorite among chefs is the Jimmy Nardello (sometimes these are also called Italian frying peppers), which is thin-skinned, mild, and sweet. Peppers are so versatile that I always keep a bag of baby ones in my fridge to add color and sweetness to recipes. During the summer, I stock up on locally grown sweet and spicy peppers from farmers' markets.

In Italy, sweet peppers are roasted, fried, stuffed, and eaten raw in salads and crudités. Italians also serve a lot of marinated peppers, often as a condiment alongside meats and cheese. As a rule, Italians tend to eat less spicy food than Americans, so you don't see a lot of spicy chile peppers in Italian cuisine. However, there is one region in Italy known for spicy foods and that is Calabria. Its cuisine is centered on the prized Calabrian chile. I love adding dried, crushed Calabrian chiles to dishes for zip and heat. (Chile flake is one of the easiest things to reach in my spice cabinet 'cause I love adding a pinch here and there.) You can also buy whole or crushed Calabrian chile peppers packed in olive oil. The whole cherry peppers might be elongated or shaped like a cherry bomb, and the good news is that they can be used interchangeably.

The tricky thing about peppers is that unless you're using straight-up bell peppers, it can be hard to know if a pepper is sweet or spicy. Take shishito peppers, for example. Some are totally mild, while others can set your mouth on fire! Here's my advice: If you're not sure how spicy your pepper might be, use your nose. I often slice a pepper and give it a good sniff; I can tell how spicy it is by the mild to aggressive sting in my nostrils, which I much prefer to hurting my hands or tongue.

When shopping, look for peppers that are firm and glossy, and try to avoid any that are wrinkled or soft. Once you get peppers home, they can be refrigerated for about a week. ————————————————

Peppers love to dance all around
the kitchen! Lively, energetic,
sometimes sweet, sometimes
spicy. They jazz up any plate!

Clockwise from top left: Calabrian Pimento Cheese (page 283), Peperonata (page 285), Orecchiette with Italian Sausage and Calabrese Red Pepper Pesto (page 290), Grilled Shishito Peppers with Crunchy Garlic and Lime Vinaigrette (page 284), Roasted Garlic and Herb Chicken with So Many Peppers (page 292)

The texture of this Spanish romesco sauce, made with charred tomatoes and peppers, resembles a thick pesto. In Spain, this sauce is traditionally eaten with char-grilled baby onions and leeks; diners use their hands to peel the onion and dip it into the romesco. It's a messy delicacy that's so good! The sauce is so great with roasted potatoes and any grilled veggies like asparagus, zucchini, and eggplant. It is also delicious schmeared on bread or dolloped on top of grilled or roasted seafood and meats.

Roasted Red Pepper Romesco Sauce

Makes about 2 cups

¼ cup everyday olive oil

1 small yellow onion, sliced

4 garlic cloves, smashed and roughly chopped

Kosher salt

4 medium char-roasted red bell peppers, peeled and roughly chopped (see page 285)

¼ cup peanuts or almonds

¼ cup green pumpkin seeds (pepitas)

2 tablespoons drained capers

1 medium tomato, roughly chopped

2 teaspoons pimentón de la Vera (Spanish smoked paprika)

2 tablespoons sherry vinegar

2 tablespoons fresh lemon juice

1 tablespoon roughly chopped fresh rosemary leaves

2 tablespoons super-special extra-virgin olive oil

1.   In a medium saucepot, heat the everyday olive oil over medium-high heat. Add the onion and garlic and season with a few pinches of kosher salt. Cook, stirring often, until the onion becomes translucent and begins to brown lightly, about 3 minutes. Stir in the roasted peppers, peanuts, pumpkin seeds, and capers and let toast until the mixture begins to darken and caramelize, about 3 minutes. Add the tomato and pimentón, scraping up the bottom of the pot, and cook for about 3 minutes; the juices from the tomatoes should deglaze the browned bits.

2.   Remove from the heat. Add the sherry vinegar, lemon juice, rosemary, and a few more pinches of salt. Stir to combine, then let sit for 5 minutes. Transfer the mixture to a food processor, being sure to scrape in any bits from the pot. Process the mixture, drizzling in the super-special olive oil, until smooth. The romesco sauce can be refrigerated in an airtight container for up to 2 weeks.

Pimento cheese from our local farmers' market in Texas was something I always loved growing up, though I hated the grocery store version made with cottage cheese. A year or two after moving to Chicago, I was homesick and decided to make my own version, using Calabrian chiles in place of pimentos. Smoky, spicy, and complex in flavor, Calabrian chiles are my favorite. Now my friends request this appetizer more than any other for all of our fun outdoor events—at the lake house, Fourth of July BBQ, you name it. If you have any leftover, this also makes the best-ever grilled cheese sandwich and a delicious burger topping.

Calabrian Pimento Cheese

Makes 3 cups

1 small red bell pepper or ½ cup roasted piquillo peppers (jarred is okay)

1 teaspoon finely grated lemon zest (use a Microplane)

1 tablespoon fresh lemon juice

2 tablespoons chopped oil-packed Calabrian chiles

2 tablespoons finely chopped scallions

2 tablespoons finely chopped fresh dill

½ cup mayonnaise (see Get It Get It)

¼ cup sour cream

6 ounces Manchego cheese (preferably aged 3 to 6 months), grated on the large holes of a box grater (about 1½ cups)

6 ounces sharp white cheddar cheese (see Get It Get It), grated on the large holes of a box grater (about 1½ cups)

1 tablespoon freshly grated Pecorino Romano

Fresh cracked black pepper

Kosher salt (optional)

1.   If using a fresh bell pepper, light a gas burner or a grill to high heat. Place the bell pepper over the flame and char, rotating occasionally, until the skin is completely blackened. (Alternatively, you can char the pepper under the broiler; see page 285.) Transfer the pepper to a bowl, cover tightly with plastic wrap, and let steam until cool, about 10 minutes. Using a paper towel, remove the charred skin from the outside of the pepper. Remove and discard the core and seeds.

2.   Finely chop the roasted pepper and place in a medium bowl. Add the lemon zest and juice, Calabrian chiles, scallions, dill, mayonnaise, and sour cream and stir until combined.

3.   In a separate bowl, toss the Manchego, cheddar, and pecorino until combined. Add to the roasted pepper mixture, folding with a rubber spatula until combined. Season with black pepper to taste. I usually don't add extra salt, but this will depend on the saltiness of the cheeses used.

4.   Cover and refrigerate the pimento cheese for at least 2 hours or overnight. Serve well chilled with toasted bread, sturdy crackers, potato chips, and/or raw vegetables.

Get It

If you prefer more heat in the dip, add ¼ teaspoon ground cayenne pepper or more Calabrian chiles to taste.

I prefer using Duke's (Southern superstar) or Hellman's (aka Best Foods; classic and always accessible) mayo here.

The sharp white cheddar cheeses from Cabot or Kerrygold are my favorites because they're the sharpest of sharp cheddars and they're available in most grocery stores.

Get It

Shishito peppers are a Japanese varietal that came on hot in the early aughts. They're usually grilled or fried and eaten as an appetizer, sprinkled with coarse salt and maybe served with a soy dipping sauce. Their size makes them excellent for snacking. I love the bold green chile flavor they have, but watch out! Eating shishitos is like playing spicy pepper roulette: One out of every ten or so can be crazy hot! I am obsessed with the crispy, crunchy, garlicky chile oil action here, which I like to drizzle on everything. It's extra delicious, so feel free to double the recipe and use it on all sorts of things like grilled seafood, sliced tomatoes, steamed rice, and all the veggies, especially summer and winter squash. Store any leftovers in an airtight container in the fridge for up to a month.

Grilled Shishito Peppers

with Crunchy Garlic and Lime Vinaigrette

Serves 4

1 pound shishito peppers

2 tablespoons everyday oil

2 large garlic cloves, minced

1 teaspoon chile flake

Coarse sea salt (like Maldon)

1 tablespoon toasted sesame seeds

Finely grated zest of 1 lime
(use a Microplane)

2 tablespoons fresh lime juice

1 teaspoon tamari or ½ teaspoon
soy sauce

1. Using four 12-inch metal or soaked bamboo skewers, skewer the shishito peppers through their sides near the stem (this is the strongest part of the pepper). Preheat a gas grill to high, 500° to 600°F.

2. Meanwhile, in a small skillet, heat the olive oil over medium-low heat. Add the garlic, chile flake, and a few pinches of sea salt. Let the garlic sizzle and turn golden brown, about 2 minutes. (I like to swirl the pan to move the garlic around so that it toasts evenly.) Once the garlic begins to turn color, remove from the heat; it will darken as it cools. Add the toasted sesame seeds to the mixture in the skillet. In a small bowl, combine the lime zest and juice with the tamari.

3. Grill the peppers for 2 minutes on each side, or until charred. Transfer to a platter. Drizzle the soy-lime vinaigrette over the peppers, followed by the crunchy garlic–oil mixture. Serve immediately. Alternatively, you can remove the peppers from the skewers onto a platter and dress with the lime vinaigrette, then top with the crunchy garlic oil.

Get It

Be on the lookout for red shishito peppers too! When shishitos are allowed to ripen on the vine, they turn red like other peppers do.

For optimal flavor absorption, dress these peppers with the vinaigrette as soon as they come off the grill.

Another great thing to do with grilled shishitos is to toss them with the tasty prosciutto butter on page 322.

Get It

These marinated peppers add such a good zesty tang to everything! Try them over pasta, in an omelet, or on a sandwich. I also love to use peperonata and their marinade as a quick salad dressing. In the summer, mix it up and use a variety of freshly harvested peppers from the market.

Peperonata

Makes 3 cups

1 pound baby sweet peppers, sliced into ¼-inch rings and seeded

4 ounces spicy red peppers (like red finger chiles or Fresnos), sliced into ¼-inch rings and seeded

Kosher salt

1 cup everyday olive oil

1 garlic clove, crushed and minced

2 teaspoons fennel seeds

¼ cup white or red wine vinegar

⅓ cup chopped fresh flat-leaf parsley

2 tablespoons chopped fresh oregano

1 tablespoon drained capers

1.   Place the sliced peppers in a medium bowl and toss with two generous pinches of salt. Let sit for 10 to 15 minutes before charring the peppers. In a large bowl, stir the olive oil with the garlic.

2.   Set a cast-iron skillet over medium-high heat. Working in batches, add the peppers and cook, stirring occasionally, until lightly charred, about 5 minutes. Season with a pinch of salt. Add to the bowl with the olive oil and garlic. Repeat with the remaining peppers. Toast the fennel seeds with the last batch of peppers.

3.   Let the peppers marinate in the oil for about 10 minutes. Add the vinegar, parsley, oregano, and capers and stir to combine. Serve right away or refrigerate in an airtight container for up to a month.

How to Char-Roast Peppers

Place your peppers directly on the gas burner or grill grates over high heat. As you see the peels begin to char and turn black, use fire-safe tongs to rotate the peppers; char all the skin on the pepper, if possible. The timing for charring depends on the size and shape of the pepper. A medium bell pepper usually takes 4 to 5 minutes to char all around. You can also use the broiler. Place the peppers on the oven rack directly under the broiler. I recommend placing a foil-lined tray on the lower rack to catch any juices. Use fire-safe tongs to rotate the peppers to ensure they char all over. If you use an electric broiler, rub the peppers with a bit of oil before charring. If using a charcoal grill, you can nestle the peppers right in the hot coals to char.

Transfer the charred peppers to a bowl, cover with plastic wrap, and let sit for 5 to 10 minutes to loosen the charred skin and soften the pepper as it cools. When the peppers are cool enough to handle, use a paper towel to wipe away the burnt skin. Don't stress over how much char you remove; little black char flakes are good! Remove and discard the stem and seeds. Whatever you do, don't—under any circumstances—rinse the peppers under water, or you'll end up with watery, flavorless roasted peppers.

Don't forget that you can char spicy peppers too! I suggest using gloves when handling them.

— Get It —

Here's a fun fact: There's no oil in the pan so the peppers won't smoke up the kitchen while they're charring. I would still keep the exhaust fan running though as the spicy peppers char.

— Get It —

This simple dish is known in Italy as *peperoni friarello*, which are fried peppers. To make my version of the dish, I love using Italian frying peppers, which have a mild flavor and thin skin. When the peppers are dressed with olive oil, they essentially fry from the intense heat of the broiler. After I peel them, I hit those vulnerable peppers with a hot, garlicky herb oil and some balsamic vinegar so they can marinate and take on the best flavor. I love the tang of goat cheese with the sweet peppers, but you can use mozzarella or feta too. Just don't forget plenty of bread so you can pile the peppers and cheese on and dig in.

Baked Goat Cheese

with Roasted Summer Peppers

Serves 6 to 8

2 pounds assorted sweet peppers (use a mix of varieties: long and short, different colors, etc.)

5 tablespoons everyday olive oil

Kosher salt

1 large garlic clove, thinly sliced

Leaves from 3 or 4 fresh oregano sprigs

Leaves from 1 fresh rosemary sprig

1 tablespoon balsamic vinegar

One 10½-ounce log fresh goat cheese, cut into ½-inch pieces

Toasted or grilled bread, for serving

— Get It —

When I make this dish, I like using different varieties of frying peppers, including Melrose, Jimmy Nardello, Cubanelle, and Oranos, and baby bell peppers for their colors and shape. It's also fun to include pimiento or cherry peppers (which have a moderate spice level) in the mix too.

— Get It —

1. Set the top oven rack about 5 inches from the heat source and turn the broiler to high. Line a baking sheet with foil and set a rack in it. In a large bowl, toss the peppers with 1 tablespoon of the olive oil and a generous pinch of salt. Place the peppers on the rack. Broil until the skins begin to char, 3 to 4 minutes (some peppers may split). Remove from the oven and turn each pepper over. Broil another 3 to 4 minutes, until charred on that side too. Remove from the oven and cover with a sheet of foil to cool slightly, about 10 minutes. Turn the oven temperature to 425°F.

2. When cooled down, peel the peppers; it's okay if some skin remains on them. Remove the stems. Cut the peppers lengthwise; any longer peppers can be halved crosswise as well. (I like to keep the shape of the peppers intact as much as possible.) Remove the seeds; it's also okay if some seeds remain. Transfer to a medium bowl.

3. In a small skillet over medium heat, heat the remaining 4 tablespoons of olive oil. Add the garlic and toast until it begins to turn golden brown, about 30 seconds. Add the oregano and rosemary; be careful, as the herbs can splatter a bit when they hit the hot oil. Remove from the heat. Pour the hot garlic-herb oil over the roasted peppers. Drizzle the balsamic on top and season with a few pinches of salt.

4. In a shallow, medium-sized flameproof casserole or baking dish, spread two-thirds of the peppers, followed by all the goat cheese. Top with the remaining peppers. Bake in the middle of the oven until the goat cheese is warmed and softened and the peppers have a slight bubble, about 15 minutes.

5. Turn the broiler to high and broil the peppers 5 to 6 inches from the heat source to caramelize the top of the peppers and goat cheese, about 3 minutes. Serve with the grilled or toasted bread.

We like to make stuffed peppers at Monteverde for staff meal because we can fill them with all sorts of odds and ends. For this recipe, I love using Maria Nava's Lemon Olive Oil Risotto (page 247) as the creamy binder for the pepper filling. It's quick and easy to make—almost as easy as steaming rice—so don't let that deter you from making these. Feel free to use almost any veggie you like for the filling, from chopped peppers, artichokes, or broccoli, to cabbage, Swiss chard, or spinach. I just suggest when you roast the vegetables to make sure they get nicely golden and crispy—you don't want them adding any extra water to the filling. The filling here is plenty delicious, so these peppers don't really need a sauce. However, I love to serve them with the Calabrian Chile Hot Sauce on page 333 for some real heat and zip. It's easy to whip up while the peppers bake.

Lemony Rice–Stuffed Peppers

with Roasted Cauliflower, Fennel, Feta, and Dill

Serves 6

1 small head of cauliflower, cored and cut into small florets (I love to use orange or purple cauliflower)

1 small fennel bulb, cored and chopped (about 2 cups)

¼ cup chopped fennel fronds (optional)

½ medium onion, chopped (I love a red onion here)

A few pinches of chile flake

3 tablespoons everyday olive oil

Kosher salt and fresh cracked black pepper

4 medium red, orange, or yellow bell peppers or long sweet peppers

2 cups of Maria Nava's Lemon Olive Oil Risotto (page 247) or your favorite rice or risotto, cooled

¼ cup plus 2 tablespoons toasted slivered almonds

One 7-ounce block sheep's milk feta cheese, crumbled by hand

¼ cup chopped fresh dill

A few pinches of pimentón de la Vera (Spanish smoked paprika)

Calabrian Chile Hot Sauce (page 333), for serving (optional)

1. Preheat the oven to 425°F. Line a baking sheet with foil. In a large bowl, combine the cauliflower, fennel, fennel fronds, onion, and chile flake. Toss with 2 tablespoons of the olive oil and season with a few generous pinches of kosher salt. Arrange the veggies on the baking sheet. Bake for 45 minutes, stirring halfway through, until golden brown.

2. At the same time as the veggies are baking, line another baking sheet with foil. Cut the peppers in half lengthwise through the stems. Using a paring knife, cut the seeds out but leave the stems attached, creating little pepper boats. Arrange the peppers cut side up on the baking sheet. Drizzle with the remaining 1 tablespoon of olive oil and season with a few pinches of salt. Bake the peppers for 10 minutes. (This helps softens the peppers slightly and seasons them.) Drain any water that collects in the pepper boats.

3. In a medium bowl, combine the chilled risotto with the roasted veggies, ¼ cup of the almonds, half the feta, and 2 tablespoons of the dill. Taste for seasoning and add a bit more salt and black pepper if needed. Stuff the peppers with the rice mixture and be sure to fill in their nooks and crannies. (Hands are the best for this, and I like to wear gloves.) Top the peppers with the remaining feta, pushing the cheese into the rice mixture so that it won't dry out and burn as the peppers bake.

4. Increase the oven temperature to 450°F. Bake the stuffed peppers for 30 minutes, or until they look roasted and browned on the bottoms and the tops are toasty and golden. In a small bowl, combine the remaining 2 tablespoons of almonds and the remaining dill. Sprinkle over the peppers and dust with the smoked paprika. Serve with the Calabrian Chile Hot Sauce alongside, if desired.

Listen to Your Vegetables

There is some major pepperpalooza action going on in this recipe. Sausage and peppers
are a huge part of Chicago's Italian identity, and I wanted to be sure to include a dish as an
homage to that! Orecchiette is served in many ways in Puglia, where it hails from, but the
most classic is with sausage and rapini (broccoli rabe). I channeled that vibe here, but chose
to highlight peppers as the star. I think you'll love the little chunks of sausage throughout
the pasta and the luscious red pepper pesto that brings the whole dish together.

Orecchiette

with Italian Sausage and Calabrese Red Pepper Pesto

Serves 6 to 8

Kosher salt

3 tablespoons everyday olive oil

1 pound spicy Italian sausage,
    casings removed

About 8 Italian frying peppers (like
    Melrose or Jimmy Nardello) or
    baby sweet bell peppers, sliced in
    ½-inch rounds (4 cups)

3 garlic cloves, thinly sliced

1 pound dry orecchiette (preferably
    handmade, from Puglia or
    Abruzzo; see Get It Get It)

Calabrese Red Pepper Pesto
    (recipe follows)

2 cups loosely packed fresh basil
    leaves (set aside a few leaves for
    garnish)

1 tablespoon finely grated lemon
    zest (from 1 large lemon; use a
    Microplane)

2 tablespoons fresh lemon juice

¼ cup freshly grated Pecorino
    Romano

1.   Bring a large pot of water to a boil and season generously with kosher
salt. Meanwhile, in a large saucepot over medium heat, heat 1 tablespoon
of the olive oil. Add half of the sausage to the pot in bite-sized nuggets and
cook, stirring occasionally, until golden brown, about 6 minutes. Transfer to
a colander and set in a bowl to drain. Add another 1 tablespoon of oil and
repeat to cook the remaining sausage; transfer to the colander to drain.

2.   Return the saucepot to medium heat. Add the remaining 1 tablespoon
of olive oil. Add the peppers and cook, stirring occasionally, until slightly
browned, 5 to 6 minutes. Halfway through cooking the peppers, add the
garlic and season with a few pinches of kosher salt. Return the sausage to
the pot and remove from the heat.

3.   Add the orecchiette to the boiling water and cook for the shortest
recommended time, until just al dente. Reserve ½ cup of the pasta cooking
water and drain the pasta. Add the pasta to the sausage and peppers and
place over medium-low heat. Add the reserved ½ cup of pasta water and
stir in half of the red pepper pesto, creating a creamy sauce. Add the basil,
lemon zest, and lemon juice, and season with a few pinches of salt, if
needed. To serve, dollop with the remaining pesto and top with a few basil
leaves, then sprinkle with the pecorino.

Get It

Not all dry orecchiette, aka little ears,
are the same. My favorite brands are
handmade Sabatelli from Puglia and
Rustichella d'Abruzzo. The dough is
denser and made with "00" flour and
semolina, creating a chewier, thicker,
more traditional orecchiette. You will
see actual grooves on the pasta ear
where they were hand-stretched. In
Puglia, this is the most iconic pasta
shape, made by women on the Bari
streets. Extruded orecchiette from
brands such as DeCecco or Barilla
are thinner and uniform in thickness
and size, and ultimately not super
different from other shapes like
rigatoni and penne. If you can find
handmade orecchiette, it's worth
getting!

Get It

Calabrese Red Pepper Pesto

The style of this pesto is Calabrian, but the spice is not. There is a great balance here of roasted sweet pepper flavor with creaminess and a hint of heat. If you love spice, then feel free to add more chiles. This pesto would be great with bread, spread on a bagel or sandwich, or topped on roasted or grilled veggies. If you want a little more tang, swap the ricotta for fresh goat cheese.

Makes a little over 3 cups

1 tablespoon everyday olive oil

½ small red onion, thinly sliced

2 garlic cloves, thinly sliced

2 tablespoons Calabrian chile paste or sambal oelek

2 large red bell peppers, roasted, peeled, and chopped (see page 285; about 2 cups)

½ cup oil-packed sun-dried tomatoes, drained and chopped

Kosher salt

½ cup whole milk ricotta

½ cup freshly grated pecorino (from Calabria, Sardinia, or Romano)

¼ cup freshly grated Parmigiano-Reggiano

½ cup fresh basil leaves, lightly chopped

1.   In a medium saucepot, heat the olive oil over medium heat. Add the onion, garlic, and chile paste and cook, stirring occasionally, until the onion starts to sweat and begins to brown, about 2 minutes. Add the peppers and sun-dried tomatoes and cook until the peppers and tomatoes begin to soften, 2 to 3 minutes. Remove from the heat and season with a few generous pinches of salt. Set aside for 10 minutes to cool slightly.

2.   Scrape the pepper mixture into a food processor. Add the ricotta, pecorino, parm, and basil, and a few more pinches of kosher salt. Blend for 20 seconds, or until smooth. Store the pesto in an airtight container in the refrigerator for up to 1 week.

Everyone needs a simple back-pocket roast chicken recipe. I think spatchcocking is the best way to cook chicken at home because the chicken cooks so evenly, and fairly quickly too. I like roasting the chicken on a rack, but this method of cooking the bird over the peppers is insanely delicious. The peppers totally steal the show! They start with a hard sear and roast to eke out their flavor, then they stew in a mix of the chicken drippings and their own juices. The chicken and peppers get finished with a very yummy mix of roasted garlic, fresh herbs, and lemon, making the whole dish just pop!

When it comes to the peppers in this dish, I like using a fun and colorful mix of sweet and spicy—it's a great time to go crazy at the farmers' market in the summer! Look beyond just bell peppers—try Cubanelle, banana peppers, Hungarian wax, Melrose, Hatch green chiles, just to name a few. If you do opt to use spicy peppers, I recommend wearing gloves when you're seeding and chopping them.

Roasted Garlic and Herb Chicken

with So Many Peppers

Serves 4

One 3½- to 4-pound whole chicken, spatchcocked (see Get It Get It)

Kosher salt

2 heads of garlic

3 tablespoons everyday olive oil

2 pounds mixed sweet peppers, seeded and cut into quarters or slices about 2 inches thick

1 cup whole pickled peperoncini peppers

1 pound vine-ripened tomatoes, quartered

1 tablespoon dried oregano

1 teaspoon fennel seeds

2 tablespoons lightly chopped fresh rosemary leaves

2 tablespoons lightly chopped fresh flat-leaf parsley

1 tablespoon finely grated lemon zest (use a Microplane)

¼ cup fresh lemon juice

1 loaf crusty bread, warmed

1. Set the chicken on a large baking sheet and season all over with salt (I use 1½ to 2 teaspoons). Let the chicken sit, uncovered, at room temperature for 1 hour or refrigerate for up to 6 hours.

2. Preheat the oven to 350°F. Using a sharp knife, slice off the tapered end from each head of garlic, exposing the little cloves. Set both heads of garlic on a sheet of foil, drizzle with 1 teaspoon of the olive oil, and season with salt. Wrap in the foil. Roast for 1 hour (perfect timing for the chicken to marinate). Remove the garlic from the oven and let cool.

3. Increase the oven temperature to 450°F. Place a large cast-iron skillet in the oven for 10 minutes to heat. In a large bowl, combine the peppers, peperoncini, tomatoes, oregano, fennel seeds, and 2 tablespoons of the olive oil. Season with a few generous pinches of salt and toss well. Carefully add the pepper mixture to the hot skillet in the oven. Cook for 15 minutes to let the peppers and tomatoes begin searing and roasting. (The smells coming out of your oven will make your stomach surely growl, and you will hear a steady sizzle, which is a song of the flavor gods.)

4. Meanwhile, rub the remaining 2 teaspoons of olive oil into the chicken skin. Carefully remove the hot skillet from the oven and place the chicken skin side up on top of the roasting peppers. Place back in the oven and roast for 30 minutes. (You are forcing the peppers to break down while the drippings and juices from the chicken stew them.)

5. While the chicken roasts, squeeze the roasted garlic from the heads into a small bowl. Add the rosemary, parsley, and lemon zest and juice. Remove the chicken from the oven. Carefully tilt the pan and, using a small ladle or spoon, collect ¼ cup or so of the pan juices. Mix the pan juices with the roasted garlic–herb mixture, then carefully schmear it all over the chicken and around the pan. Place the skillet back in the oven for 15 minutes longer to allow the herb mixture to melt into the chicken skin. Remove from the oven and let the chicken rest in the skillet for 10 minutes.

6. To serve, carefully transfer the chicken to a cutting board. Using a sharp knife, separate the leg quarters from the bird and split the thighs and legs. Carefully remove the chicken breast and wings from the bones and slice. Nestle the sliced chicken breast into the pan with the peppers and place the bone-in thighs, legs, and wing pieces alongside the breast. Serve with warm crusty bread to soak up all the yumminess.

Get It

A spatchcocked chicken has had its backbone removed so it can lie flat; it makes for more even cooking than a whole bird. You can often buy spatchcocked chicken at markets, or you can ask you butcher to do it for you. The other option is doing it yourself, which is pretty easy if you have a set of sturdy poultry shears and a sharp knife. To do so, place a few paper towels on a large cutting board to help steady the bird and absorb excess liquid. Set the chicken on the board breast side down, with the legs facing toward you. Using a pair of kitchen or poultry shears, cut alongside the backbone, between the backbone and the thighs. Repeat on the other side of the backbone to remove it; freeze the backbone for making stock. Then, using a heavy, sharp knife, split or crack the breastbone slightly from inside the cavity, being careful to not cut through to the breast meat. Flip the chicken over and gently push down on the breast with your hands, flattening the bird. Tuck the wing tips back behind the breast. Your chicken is now ready to roast beautifully!

If you are just not keen on a spatchcocked bird, you can also use any combination of chicken parts you like or a split chicken. My only tip is to get pieces that are relatively the same size so the chicken cooks evenly.

Get It

I wanted to come up with a way to make steak and peppers—which is a very classic combination all over the world—unique and craveable. I love a good kebab, and I had the idea of skewering sweet baby peppers and skirt steak, which are about the same thickness and grill together beautifully. This isn't like a traditional meat and veg kebab, where there are big hunks of each thing to cook through. Bonus: Baby sweet peppers have a nice long shelf life, so they're perfect to keep on hand for all sorts of things! To make this a complete meal, I love to serve these skewers with the Roasted Red Pepper Romesco Sauce on page 282. You can grill bruschetta (thick slices of bread) for each skewer, then place the hot skewers right on top of the bruschetta to rest, allowing the bread to soak up all of the yummy juices. Double yum with romesco schmeared on the bruschetta. Serve with a simple green salad, and you're good and happy.

Baby Sweet Pepper and Skirt Steak Skewers

Serves 4

2 teaspoons fennel seeds

1 teaspoon cumin seeds

2 pinches of chile flake

2 tablespoons everyday olive oil, plus more for drizzling

2 garlic cloves, finely grated (use a Microplane)

Leaves from 1 fresh rosemary sprig

1 teaspoon kosher salt, plus more for additional seasoning

1½ pounds skirt steak, trimmed and cut into 1½-inch pieces (see Get It Get It)

1 pound baby sweet peppers, halved lengthwise and seeded

Lemon wedges, for garnish

Roasted Red Pepper Romesco Sauce (page 282), for serving (optional)

1.   In a small sauté pan, toast the fennel and cumin seeds over medium-high heat for 2 minutes. Transfer to a mortar and pestle or spice grinder and grind the seeds with the chile flake. Transfer to a medium bowl and add the olive oil, garlic, rosemary, and salt and stir to a paste. Add the steak and pepper petals and toss well.

2.   Using four 12-inch metal or soaked bamboo skewers, skewer alternate pieces of pepper and steak. (Sometimes I double up on pepper slices if the steak pieces are thicker or to keep the steak and pepper components even on the skewers.)

3.   Preheat a gas grill to high, 500° to 600°F (a charcoal grill is great too). Using a grill brush or a ball of crumpled foil, clean the grates once hot. Lightly season the skewers with a pinch of kosher salt, then drizzle with olive oil. Place on the grill, cover, and cook, rotating the skewers every 2 to 3 minutes, until seared and charred all over, about 10 minutes total. Serve with lemon wedges and romesco, if desired.

Get It

If you're using bamboo skewers, I soak them in water for a few hours or overnight, as they tend to burn on the grill. I have metal skewers, and they are a big part of my home cooking. It's so nice to have them in my kitchen arsenal, offering a fun opportunity for preparing veggies, meat, and seafood. You can skewer anything (well, almost)!

These skewers are just as much about the peppers as the steak, so be sure to alternate between pepper and steak. Skirt steak isn't super uniform, as it tapers and becomes thinner in parts.

This is okay; just try to cut it into roughly 1½-inch pieces. Once they are skewered, the peppers and steak have a similar thickness. Baste each on the skewer as they are grilled. *Yum.*

Get It

Potatoes

Potatoes have an important place in human history. As long as 1,800 years ago, potatoes were being grown in South America. They were introduced to Europe in the sixteenth century, and are now one of the largest crops grown around the globe. Who doesn't love a potato? Potatoes are like eggs—there are a thousand ways to cook them. This is why potatoes are my pantry warriors. They're easy to keep on hand for so many things! And as humble as the potato is, I think it often steals the show from everyone else on the plate. There are just so many ways to use a potato that I feel like they deserve their very own chapter in this book.

When I was growing up, there was only one type of potato in our house: the russet (Idaho) potato. What an incredible workhorse potato the russet is—it's in your French fries, hash browns, and mashed potatoes, to name a few, but for me the ultimate use of the russet is a perfect baked potato. I grew up on baked potatoes; I think they were the simplest dinner my mom or I could throw together. I have since upped my baked potato game, and I now find russets are the perfect potato for mashing, making a filling, and for creating the best gnocchi. That's because they have a lot of starch, which acts as a glue of sorts.

Waxy potatoes are another category of potato that have a place on the table. These are your new potatoes, baby, creamers, Red Bliss, and fingerlings. I like these for steaming, boiling, and roasting because of their thin skin and buttery sweet interior. Yukon golds and white and purple potatoes fall somewhere between waxy and starchy, and I use them for just about everything! As for sweet potatoes, I find orange sweets (aka Garnets) to be a little watery, so I prefer white, yellow, and purple sweet potatoes for their amazing texture.

Keep your potatoes stored in a cool dark place, not in the fridge. Give them a good scrub before cooking, and try to leave the peels on whenever you can. Those peels have excellent built-in texture, flavor, and nutrients! ————

The pantry sleeper, potatoes can stay tucked
away, ready whenever the craving strikes—no
menu planning required. These guys are beyond
versatile and the most reliable veg in the
kitchen. We all love these humble tubers.

Clockwise from top left: Grilled Japanese
Sweet Potatoes with Honey Butter and
Pimentón (page 310); Cheesy Potato Frico
(page 313); Purple Potato–Filled Tortelli
with Black Truffle, Red Onion, and Honey
(page 311); Broccoli and Cheese Twice-Baked
Potatoes (page 306)

This was one of the most memorable dishes I had in Pantelleria, an island southwest of Sicily. Pantelleria is well known for capers and passito wine, a sweet wine made from dried grapes. Pantellerian capers are legendary, and Italians take them quite seriously—if you can get your hands on some salted capers from Pantelleria, don't hesitate! Pantelleria is also famous for this delicious potato salad, known on the island as Pantesca salad, which is unlike anything I grew up eating. The base is olive oil (no mayo here!), and there's no cheese to be found. It's a bright and punchy vegan potato salad that I think is a game changer. This salad is perfect with grilled seafood—anything from fish and shrimp to calamari and octopus. It's also great for entertaining because it can be assembled ahead of time.

Pantesca Potato Salad

with Caper-Almond Pesto

Serves 6 to 8

1½ pounds fingerling potatoes

Kosher salt or coarse sea salt (like Maldon)

2 pints cherry tomatoes, halved

½ small red onion, cut into ¼-inch slices (you want them thin, but with a little heft for crunch)

½ cup mixed pitted olives, sliced or roughly chopped

Caper-Almond Pesto (recipe follows)

Fresh cracked black pepper

1 cup fresh basil leaves

¼ cup toasted slivered or sliced almonds, for garnish

1 tablespoon capers, either salted or brined (if using salted, rinse in cold water for 5 to 10 minutes)

Super-special extra-virgin olive oil, for drizzling

1. In a large saucepot, cover the potatoes with cold water and season with 1 tablespoon of salt. Bring to a simmer over medium heat and cook until the potatoes are just tender, about 30 minutes. Do not overcook the potatoes; they should have a bit of resistance when pierced with a fork or knife. Drain, transfer to a cutting board, and let cool.

2. Slice the cooled potatoes into 1-inch-thick rounds. Transfer to a wooden salad bowl or mixing bowl. Add the cherry tomatoes, red onion, and olives. Toss with the pesto and add a pinch or two of salt and fresh cracked black pepper. Toss gently with the fresh basil. Top with the almonds and capers and a generous drizzle of super-special olive oil. The salad can be served immediately or refrigerated for a few hours. It gets better as it marinates and is awesome the next day; I just suggest adding the tomatoes and basil right before serving.

Caper-Almond Pesto

Makes about 1½ cups

½ cup everyday olive oil

Freshly grated zest and juice of 2 lemons (¼ cup juice)

½ cup toasted slivered almonds

½ cup fresh flat-leaf parsley, roughly chopped

½ cup fresh oregano

¼ cup capers, either salted or brined (if using salted, rinse in cold water for 5 to 10 minutes)

1 garlic clove, peeled

Kosher salt

In a food processor, combine the olive oil with the lemon zest, lemon juice, almonds, parsley, oregano, capers, and garlic. Season with a pinch or two of salt. Pulse until chunky but well combined. You can refrigerate this pesto in an airtight container for up to 3 days before using.

— Get It —

If you didn't know, capers are the young bud of the caper plant. If left on the plant, they flower. They're typically preserved in salt or brine to make them edible.

— Get It —

Traditionally, Genovese pesto is served with potatoes, green beans, and little hand-twisted pastas called trofie. I love that pasta so much, but it takes a long time to make. So instead of doing the trofie, I made this amazing potato salad. Who doesn't love a potato salad?!? There are myriad styles, many of which are heavy with mayo and hard-boiled eggs and such. I can promise you that the freshness and bright flavors in this one will make it your new favorite.

Genovese Pesto Potato Salad

with Green Beans

Serves 6 to 8

2 tablespoons pine nuts

3 pounds baby or fingerling potatoes (rainbow color, if available), halved

Coarse sea salt (like Maldon)

8 ounces French green beans (haricots verts), trimmed

8 ounces sugar snap peas, trimmed

Genovese Pesto (page 240)

2 tablespoons freshly grated pecorino or Parmigiano-Reggiano

1 cup fresh basil leaves

1.   In a small skillet, toast the pine nuts over medium heat until golden brown, 3 to 4 minutes. Transfer to a plate to cool.

2.   In a medium saucepan, cover the potatoes with cold water and place over high heat. Season generously with salt. Bring to a boil, then reduce the heat to a simmer and cook until the potatoes are tender, about 20 minutes. Drain and cool.

3.   Meanwhile, bring a large pot of heavily salted water to a boil. This is blanching water (see page 10), and I like mine to be salty like the ocean, about 1 tablespoon of salt per quart of water. Prepare a large bowl with ice water. Add the green beans to the boiling water and blanch for 2 minutes, or until bright green and crunchy. Using a slotted spoon, transfer the beans to the ice water to stop them from cooking further. Add the snap peas to the pot and blanch for 1 minute, or until bright green and crunchy. Transfer to the ice water to cool. Drain the beans and peas.

4.   In a large salad bowl, toss the potatoes, green beans, and sugar snap peas with 1 cup of the pesto and season with a pinch or two of salt. Garnish with the pine nuts, cheese, and basil leaves. Dollop the remaining pesto on top of the salad. You can serve the salad immediately, but it gets even more delicious as it marinates! Feel free to make it a few hours ahead of time and keep it in the fridge; serve chilled.

Get It

This is a great picnic or party salad because it can be made ahead of time and it tastes so good. You can even make it over a few days. Prepare the pesto a couple of days ahead, then make the salad the day before or morning of, and garnish with the pine nuts, cheese, and basil to serve.

Get It

Listen to Your Vegetables

Baked potatoes were an easy meal for me and my mom to make when I was little, though those were usually microwaved in plastic wrap! Yikes. The potato is one of the humblest foods, but it has the ability to be a superstar. Adding cheese and broccoli to potatoes is pretty traditional, and why mess with something that works so well? Every Christmas, Jaime's Grandma Nina makes twice-baked potatoes that I've always loved. Her secret is adding cream cheese, which guarantees creaminess. If you have leftover filling (I always do), you can bake it off in a small dish, or try folding it into scrambled eggs for breakfast the next day.

Broccoli and Cheese Twice-Baked Potatoes

Serves 6

6 medium russet potatoes
  (about 3 pounds)

Kosher salt

6 tablespoons unsalted butter

1 pound broccoli (about 2 large
  crowns), trimmed, tender stalks
  roughly chopped, florets cut into
  small pieces

1 medium leek, trimmed, halved
  lengthwise, washed, white and
  light green parts thinly sliced

1 garlic clove, thinly sliced

2 cups shredded sharp white
  cheddar cheese

4 ounces cream cheese

4 ounces fresh goat cheese

Fresh cracked black pepper

— Get It —

You can stuff the potatoes and
refrigerate them overnight.
Bring to room temperature for
an hour or so before baking.

The best way to salt these
potatoes before baking is to do
it after they've been washed
and they're still a little damp,
so the salt sticks. Also, try to
incorporate the cheeses into the
potatoes while they're still hot
so it all mixes together nicely.

— Get It —

1. Preheat the oven to 425°F. Wash the potatoes and sprinkle with kosher salt (about 1 teaspoon total). Bake directly on the oven rack for 1 hour, or until tender.

2. Meanwhile, in a medium skillet, melt 2 tablespoons of the butter over medium heat. Add the broccoli, leek, and garlic and sweat for 1 minute. Season with a few generous pinches of salt and add ½ cup of water. Stir, then cover and reduce the heat to low. Steam for 5 minutes. The broccoli is done when it's tender yet still a little firm. Remove from the heat.

3. Set aside 1 cup of the cooked broccoli mixture. Transfer the remaining broccoli mixture to a food processor. Pulse until chopped but not pureed. Transfer the chopped broccoli to a large mixing bowl and add 1 cup of the shredded cheddar along with the cream cheese, goat cheese, and the remaining 4 tablespoons of butter. Stir well and season with black pepper.

4. Once the potatoes have finished baking, carefully transfer to a platter to cool slightly, 5 to 10 minutes. Using a serrated knife, split the tops of the potatoes to expose the insides. Hold a potato half in a towel in one hand, and using a spoon, scoop out the insides and transfer them to the bowl with the broccoli mixture. Be careful not to tear the potato skin. Continue with the remaining potatoes. Arrange the empty skins on the platter. Mix the hot potato-broccoli mixture and check for seasoning with salt and pepper.

5. Using a spoon, fill the potato skins with the broccoli mixture. I like to overfill them slightly, as I love a fully stuffed potato! Top the potatoes with the remaining 1 cup of cheddar and the reserved broccoli mixture. You can hold the potatoes like this for up to 2 hours before baking.

6. Transfer the stuffed potatoes to a baking sheet lined with foil. Bake until the cheese is melted, the skin of the potatoes has slightly crisped, and the potatoes are hot, 20 to 25 minutes. Serve immediately.

You can't really go wrong smashing potatoes with butter and parsley, but I wanted
to come up with a way to make the dish even better. The answer is grilling!
While boiling makes potatoes nice and tender on the inside, grilling makes the
skins crunchy and flavorful, resulting in a very happy potato—and eater too!
This is super simple, and I think you'll be hooked once you try it this way.

Grilled Parsley Potato Smashers

Serves 4

8 to 10 medium-ish red potatoes
   (about 2 pounds)

Kosher salt

1 stick unsalted butter

¼ cup crème fraîche

¼ cup roughly chopped fresh dill

¼ cup roughly chopped fresh flat-
   leaf parsley

2 to 3 scallions, sliced
   (about ½ cup)

Fresh cracked black pepper

1.   In a medium pot, cover the potatoes with cold water. Bring to a boil
and season with a few pinches of kosher salt. Cook over medium-high heat
until just tender but al dente, 20 to 25 minutes. Drain. Keep the pot handy.

2.   Preheat your grill to high heat, so it's about 500°F. Grill the potatoes,
turning every 3 to 4 minutes, until the skins are charred all over, about
15 minutes total. Return the potatoes to the pot and add the butter. Using a
potato masher, wooden spoon, or spatula, smash the potatoes to break them
apart, but still leave them very chunky. Add the crème fraîche, dill, parsley,
and scallions and season with salt and pepper; mix to combine. Serve hot.

Get It

These can also be made in the
oven by charring your potatoes
under the broiler after boiling.
Set the top oven rack to 4 to
5 inches below the heat source
and broil until the skins begin
to crackle and char.

Get It

I make this at home when I'm craving a hearty steakhouse-style side dish. It's based on a classic combo of potatoes, onions, and cheese, though it definitely veers away from ordinary! I am a big fan of Japanese sweet potatoes because they have such great texture and flavor, but you could sub another sweet potato. Part of the magic here is how nicely the potatoes meld with the pungent blue cheese and soft, sweet leeks. The other highlight is the salt-roasted skins on the potatoes, which get all crispy and delicious.

Baked Sweet Potatoes

with Melted Leeks and Blue Cheese

Serves 6

2 to 2½ pounds Japanese or Garnet sweet potatoes (choose similar-sized potatoes if possible)

Kosher salt

2 tablespoons everyday olive oil, plus more for oiling

4 tablespoons unsalted butter

2 large leeks (white parts only), halved lengthwise, washed, then sliced into thin half-moons (about 2½ cups)

5 fresh thyme sprigs, plus leaves from 6 sprigs for garnish

4 ounces creamy blue cheese (like Saint Agur or Gorgonzola dolce), broken into bite-sized pieces (any dark rind should be discarded)

1. Preheat the oven to 400°F. Line a baking sheet with foil and set a rack in the baking sheet. Rinse the potatoes. While the skins are still wet, place the potatoes in a large mixing bowl and toss with 1 teaspoon of salt. Set the potatoes on the rack. Bake until just tender to the touch yet slightly firm inside, about 1 hour. Remove from the oven and let cool for 15 minutes. Increase the oven temperature to 450°F and set an oven rack near the heat source. (If you have a convection oven, set the heat to 425°F.)

2. Remove the rack from the baking sheet and lightly oil the foil. Cut the potatoes into ¼-inch-thick rounds, leaving the skin on. Arrange the potato slices in a single layer on the baking sheet and drizzle with the olive oil. Bake the potatoes near the heat source until crispy, about 20 minutes.

3. Meanwhile, in a medium saucepot, melt the butter over medium-low heat. Add the leeks, stir well, and season with a pinch of salt. Add the thyme sprigs and cook, stirring occasionally, until the leeks are softened and translucent but not browned, 6 to 7 minutes. Remove from the heat and discard the thyme sprigs.

4. In a large casserole dish, spread half of the leeks. Arrange the potatoes evenly over the leeks, then top with the remaining leeks. Top with pieces of the cheese. Place the casserole in the oven to warm the leeks and melt the cheese, 8 to 10 minutes. Serve hot, garnished with fresh thyme leaves.

— Get It —

A convection oven circulates hot air, helping foods cook faster and brown more nicely. It's not necessary to have a convection oven, but if you do, I think there are some dishes that benefit from it, like these crispy potatoes. If you have an air fryer, you can try the crisping stage of the potatoes in there too!

— Get It —

Not all sweet potatoes are created equal. I wish I could say I love Garnets since they're so ubiquitous, but I'm not a huge fan. I love Japanese sweet potatoes because their texture is so different from that of Garnets. They come in different varieties and colors: Okinawan has white skin with a deep purple center, Satsumaimo has red skin and a white center, and Murasaki has purple skin with a white center. The beauty is that they're all interchangeable! All of these Japanese sweets are a little starchy and dry, but they become richer and creamier than Garnets when they're cooked. The good news is that there are many different kinds of sweet potatoes available nowadays, so be on the lookout—baby sweet potatoes are really special too, and great on the grill. When you par-bake and grill these potatoes, they develop a crispy, charred skin, and they love to soak up the honey butter. I finish these with pimentón de la Vera, which adds an earthy, smoky jazziness to the dish, but without any heat.

Grilled Japanese Sweet Potatoes

with Honey Butter and Pimentón

Serves 4 to 6

2 to 2½ pounds Japanese sweet potatoes, washed

2 tablespoons everyday olive oil

Kosher salt

4 tablespoons unsalted butter, softened

2 tablespoons honey

Coarse sea salt (like Maldon)

1 tablespoon pimentón de la Vera (Spanish smoked paprika)

2 tablespoons thinly sliced fresh chives or green onions

— Get It —

Choose similar-sized potatoes, so that they cook at the same rate. How long you bake them in the oven really depends on the size of the potato you choose. Check them after the first 30 minutes to see where they are at; you are just looking to begin the cooking process. Think of the potatoes as being like rare steak: slightly cooked on the outside yet still pretty raw in the center.

— Get It —

1. Preheat the oven to 350°F. In a large bowl, toss the sweet potatoes with 1 tablespoon of the olive oil and season with kosher salt. Place in a baking dish and cover with foil. Bake the potatoes until they begin to feel soft to the touch but they're still firm in the centers, about 1 hour; check halfway through for doneness. Transfer the potatoes to a cutting board and cut lengthwise in half or in quarters, depending on their size. If you are able to find super-baby sweet potatoes, then leave them whole.

2. Put the sliced potatoes on a foil-lined baking sheet and drizzle with the remaining 1 tablespoon of olive oil. Toss gently, ensuring the cut sides of the potatoes get slightly oiled. Season with another pinch or two of kosher salt.

3. In a small bowl, stir together the softened butter and honey and season with a pinch of coarse sea salt. Set aside.

4. Preheat a grill to high heat (500° to 600°F) for 5 minutes. Place the sweet potatoes on the grill, skin side down, and grill for 5 minutes, allowing them to char. Flip the sweet potatoes and grill for another 5 minutes or so. Flip again to evenly char on all sides, about another 5 minutes. To finish, flip the potatoes back on their skin side and char for another 5 minutes to crisp the skin. If you don't have a grill, bake the potatoes in a 425°F oven on a baking sheet for 20 minutes, until golden brown. You can also char the slices 3 to 4 inches under the broiler for 2 to 3 minutes per side, until the edges are lightly charred and crisped. Transfer the potatoes to a platter or bowl and gently dollop the honey butter on them, allowing the honey butter to melt and letting the potatoes absorb some of that yumminess. Gently toss the potatoes, then dust with the pimentón and chives, and another pinch of coarse sea salt, if you want. Serve immediately.

These tortelli are like amazing black truffle–baked potato pierogis. This atypical pasta celebrates all things grown underground: potatoes, onions, and truffles. It's a tuberpalooza! The filling here might remind you a bit of the ultimate baked potato, with sour cream, cheese, and onion. The truffle and honey make this seriously next-level, but if you don't have access to actual truffles, you can get the same flavor from truffle oil or paste!

Purple Potato–Filled Tortelli

with Black Truffle, Red Onion, and Honey

Serves 4 to 6

Tortelli

1½ pounds purple potatoes or Yukon gold, Butterball, or yellow waxy potatoes (5 or 6 medium potatoes)

Kosher salt

1½ cups freshly grated aged Northern Italian cheese (like Montasio, Piave, or Asiago)

4 ounces fresh goat cheese

4 tablespoons unsalted butter

¼ cup minced red onion

3 tablespoons sour cream

Fresh cracked black pepper

The Essential Egg Yolk Pasta Dough (page 256)

½ cup "00" flour mixed with ½ cup semolina (aka bench flour), for dusting

Finishing

Kosher salt

5 tablespoons unsalted butter

1 small red onion, cut into wedges and separated into petals

2 tablespoons fresh thyme or rosemary leaves

1 tablespoon truffle paste, or a drop or two of truffle oil

ingredients continue

1. **Make the tortelli filling.** Preheat the oven to 400°F. Line a baking sheet with foil and set a rack in it. Rinse the potatoes; in a large bowl, season them with a teaspoon of kosher salt. (The salt will help draw out the moisture from the potatoes as they cook.) Place the salted potatoes on the rack. Bake for about 45 minutes, until the potatoes are soft and tender. Let cool for 10 minutes, or until the potatoes are cool enough to handle but still warm. Peel the potatoes. Rice or mash them into a medium bowl. Add the grated cheese and goat cheese and stir to melt them.

2. In a small skillet, melt the butter over medium heat. Add the onion and a few pinches of kosher salt. Cook the onion until translucent, about 2 minutes. Add the hot buttered onion to the potatoes and mix well. Add the sour cream and a few generous pinches of salt and fresh cracked black pepper. Scrape the filling into an airtight container and refrigerate for a few hours before using. The filling can be stored overnight.

3. **Shape the tortelli.** (See page 269 for photos.) Cut each ball of pasta dough in half so you have four pieces total. Work with one ball of dough at a time and keep the other pieces wrapped in plastic. Set your pasta machine to the thickest setting, which is usually 1. Flatten the dough slightly with a rolling pin, creating a rectangle shape; be mindful to match the width of your roller. (This will create consistent-sized pasta sheets.) Feed the dough through the roller. Continue to feed the dough through the roller on increasingly thinner settings; you might need to add a little bench flour to one side of the dough if it's feeling a little sticky or wet. Continue rolling the dough until you've reached setting 5, run the pasta through twice, and then transfer it to a work surface that's lightly dusted with bench flour. Use a pizza cutter or sharp knife to cut the pasta into two long sheets, each about 16 by 6 inches. Cut each sheet in half lengthwise, creating four sheets total, each about 16 by 3 inches.

recipe continues

2 tablespoons delicately flavored honey (like acacia or wildflower; I *love* Mieli Thun brand)

¼ cup freshly grated aged Northern Italian cheese (like Montasio, Piave, or Asiago)

1 small black truffle, thinly shaved, or preserved truffle slices in oil (optional, of course!)

Get It

If you aren't into buying truffles, opt for a truffle-studded aged pecorino cheese, which would add great truffle flavor without the commitment of buying a few products. My favorite truffle bang-for-the-buck is summer truffles, which are great around June to late September. They have awesome aroma and flavor without breaking the bank. To buy, try my friends at Regalis Foods (regalisfoods.com) or Rare Tea Cellar (rareteacellar.com). If you don't have a truffle shaver, not to worry! Use your Microplane!

Get It

4. Scoop the filling into a pastry bag or a sturdy resealable plastic bag; snip off the corner. Starting with one strip of dough and keeping the rest covered with a clean linen towel while you work, pipe about 1 tablespoon of filling in mounds across the lower half of the dough, leaving 1 inch between mounds; you should have about six mounds in all. Fold the dough over lengthwise and press to seal, using your hands to firmly press and seal each tortelli. Cut in between the tortelli and trim the excess dough. Use the tines of a fork to create indentations around the edges of the tortelli. Transfer the finished tortelli to the prepared baking sheet. Repeat with the remaining dough and filling. If you're not using the pasta immediately, sprinkle a generous amount of bench flour on top of the pasta, cover with a clean lint-free towel, and wrap tightly in plastic. The pasta can be refrigerated like this overnight.

5. **Finish the tortelli.** Bring a large pot to a boil and season generously with kosher salt. Meanwhile, in a large saucepan or a very large skillet, cook the butter over medium heat until browned, about 2 minutes. Add the red onion petals, season with a few pinches of kosher salt, and allow them to soften and gently caramelize, about 3 minutes. Add the thyme and reduce the heat to low.

6. Add the potato tortelli to the boiling water and cook until they begin to float and the edges of the pasta are tender to the touch, about 2 minutes. Using a slotted spoon or skimmer, transfer the tortelli to the pan with the brown butter and gently toss, coating each tortelli with the butter. Add the truffle sauce and season with another pinch or two of salt. To serve, drizzle the tortelli with honey and top with the grated cheese and fresh shaved truffle (if using).

This *frico di patate* (cheese frico with potatoes) hails from Friuli, where potatoes are grown in abundance. The key to authentic frico is using a Northern Italian cow's milk cheese like aged Montasio, Asiago, or Piave. These cheeses have a mild, buttery, aged cow's milk flavor and unlike Parmigiano-Reggiano, they're not too dry, so they melt nicely into the potatoes. In Italy, frico are enjoyed as a snack for aperitivo, often alongside cured hams, cheese, and even a little honey. But once you try this, you'll agree that they're awesome every time of day! These are so great with just the cheese and potato, but get crazy with it! Mix in a little grated onion, finely chopped prosciutto, or chopped fresh herbs like thyme, chives, or rosemary . . . yum!

Cheesy Potato Frico

Serves 6 to 8 (but let's be real— once you taste this, it's hard to stop eating!)

2 pounds small russet potatoes

Kosher salt

4 ounces aged Northern Italian cow's milk cheese, like Montasio, Piave, or Asiago, shredded on the large holes of a box grater (1½ cups)

Fresh cracked black pepper

6 tablespoons everyday olive oil

— Get It —

If you have two similar-sized pans, feel free to make two frico at the same time. If you want to keep the frico warm, you can hold it in a 250°F oven for up to 30 minutes.

It's important here to cool the potatoes down fully (for at least 4 hours) after boiling, for the best texture. I like using my hands and a good paring knife to cut the potatoes into chunks, kind of like my grandma always cut her potatoes—and most vegetables!

— Get It —

1. In a medium pot, cover the potatoes with cold water and season with a few pinches of kosher salt. Bring to a boil, then reduce the heat to a rolling simmer. Cook until the potatoes are tender when pierced with a fork, 25 to 35 minutes. Drain and cool. Using a paring knife, peel the potatoes, then place on a plate and refrigerate, uncovered, overnight.

2. The next day, using a paring knife, cut the potatoes into chunks and place in a medium bowl. Add the shredded cheese, a few pinches of kosher salt, and some black pepper. Mix well, incorporating the cheese and potatoes but being careful not to mash the potatoes. You want chunks of potato and cheese; as the cheese melts, it becomes the glue that holds it all together.

3. Heat an 8-inch nonstick skillet over medium-low heat. Add 1 tablespoon of the olive oil. Spoon half of the potato mixture into the pan, using a spatula or spoon to press the potato mixture together to create a single cake or patty. Drizzle 1 more tablespoon of the oil around the edges of the pan, allowing it to drip down under the sizzling cake. Let cook for 8 to 10 minutes; you will notice that the edge of the frico will begin to brown. Occasionally, run a rubber spatula around the edge of the frico and the pan. Give the pan a little wiggle to see if the cheese is crisping, and use your spatula to push the mixture down into the pan to keep it compact. I also like to rotate the pan 180 degrees, as the burner can have hot spots. The frico is ready to flip once you see the edges have turned a darker brown and the cheese on top has begun to melt.

4. To flip, using oven mitts, place a plate or rack on top of the pan and flip it, inverting the frico onto the plate or rack. Then slide the frico back into the pan to let the other side cook and crisp. Drizzle 1 more tablespoon of the oil around the edges of the pan. Cook for another 8 to 10 minutes, rotating the pan occasionally. Transfer the frico to a rack or a parchment paper–lined plate. Repeat with the remaining potato mixture and olive oil. To serve, cut it into wedges.

Get It

If you don't have time to chop
by hand or just don't want to,
you can pulse the carrot and
onion in a food processor and
separately pulse the prosciutto
and salumi as well.

Get It

This amazing sauce was born from an excess of scraps of cured meats that I wanted to use up. It's a great sauce that packs a ton of flavor. I love it so much over pillowy gnocchi, but it can be eaten with other pasta too, like rigatoni, penne, spaghetti, or bucatini. Just take note: Since the sauce is made with salumi, you won't need to add any salt. Not craving the hearty meat sauce? These gnocchi would be absolutely divine tossed with the Porcini Bolognese (page 223) or any of the pestos in the book.

Potato Gnocchi

with Salumi Sauce

Serves 4 to 6

Sauce

3 teaspoons everyday olive oil

1 pound mild Italian sausage, removed from the casings

3 ounces sliced prosciutto or country ham, chopped

3 ounces mixed sliced salumi (like salami, soppressata, and pepperoni), chopped

1 yellow onion, finely chopped

1 medium carrot, finely chopped

¼ cup tomato paste

One 28-ounce can whole peeled tomatoes with their juice, crushed by hand

1 cup dry red wine

1 fresh rosemary sprig

Finishing

Potato Gnocchi (page 272), blanched

1 tablespoon unsalted butter

1 tablespoon chopped fresh flat-leaf parsley

½ teaspoon dried oregano

1 or 2 pinches of chile flake

¼ cup freshly grated Parmigiano-Reggiano

1. **Make the sauce.** In a large pot, heat 1 teaspoon of the olive oil over medium-high heat. Add the sausage and cook, stirring occasionally and breaking up the pieces with a wooden spoon, until the sausage is golden, about 8 minutes. Add the prosciutto and salumi, stirring to break up any clumps. Cook until the salumi has rendered some of its fat and the mixture is combined, 2 to 3 minutes. Transfer to a colander set in a bowl to drain the excess fat.

2. Place the pot back over medium-high heat and add the remaining 2 teaspoons of olive oil. Add the onion and carrot and cook until slightly golden, 5 to 6 minutes. Stir in the tomato paste, then add the crushed tomatoes. Cook until the tomatoes are slightly reduced, 2 to 3 minutes. Add the red wine and drained sausage mixture (discard the fat) and stir to combine. Bring the sauce up to a boil, then reduce the heat to low and cover. Simmer for 30 minutes, stirring halfway through, until thickened and the flavors have melded.

3. Remove the sauce from the heat and add the rosemary. Let sit for 5 minutes, then remove the rosemary and discard. The salumi sauce can be refrigerated in an airtight container for up to 1 week or frozen beautifully for 3 to 4 months.

4. **Finish the dish.** When you're ready to serve, bring the salumi sauce up to a simmer over medium heat, adding ¼ cup of water to loosen the sauce slightly. Using a rubber spatula or wooden spoon, gently fold in the blanched gnocchi and add the butter. Cook for 5 minutes; you want to warm the gnocchi in the sauce. Finish the gnocchi and sauce with the parsley, oregano, and chile flake. Serve immediately, sprinkled with the parm.

Roots & Bulbs

These ugly, sometimes gnarly vegetables are simply the underground roots and bulbs of plants. There are so many kinds of root vegetables that I've had to narrow down my favorites to highlight for this book. Grown underground, root veggies absorb a lot of nutrients from the soil, so they're packed with vitamins, antioxidants, fiber, and healthy carbohydrates. These complex, nutritious vegetables deserve respect in our kitchens. Do you really want to know what your root veggies are saying? They don't want to be forgotten! Pick them up and use them. If you walk into just about any produce area, you might notice that those rutabagas and turnips and beets are always there, looking for someone to take them home. I think this is because people just don't know what to do with them.

Roots can be sweet, spicy, or earthy. They're very versatile and can be eaten in myriad ways, from raw, steamed, and boiled to sautéed or grilled. My favorite method is slow-roasting, which concentrates flavor while enhancing natural sweetness. Some of these veggies, like turnips, radishes, beets, carrots, and celery root, are truly excellent shaved and eaten raw in salads and slaws. Turnips and parsnips love being pureed too!

Garlic and onions are also part of this vast root family, and honestly, I can't live without these kitchen staples. They're pungent when raw, but cooking can coax out the sweetest flavor. Just remember: What is the end result you're aiming for? Is it pungent? Keep them raw. Is it sweet? Slow-roast or sauté.

Keep a mix of onions in a wooden bowl on your counter for different uses too. I like yellow onions for cooking, red onions for salads, and white onions in salads and salsas.

Most root vegetables can be stored in cool cellars for several months, making them readily available year-round; in Chicago, you can get them from some local farmers even deep in winter. (Many of these vegetables get sweeter as they age, like carrots.) That said, peak season is fall through spring, except for beets, which are best in summer and fall. There is a common misperception that some root vegetables are bitter and tough and not worth the effort. That is not true! Once you get past their tough exteriors, what waits inside is a treat.

A simple rule when shopping for root vegetables is that the firmer they are, the better. When you get them home, they're best stored in a dark, cool spot. If you're planning to refrigerate them, put them in a paper or plastic bag unwashed; leaving root veggies uncovered causes them to soften quickly.

Because they're grown in dirt, root veggies can be dirty. To clean your root vegetables, use a scrub brush and gently scrub off any dirt—and hair-like roots, if your vegetable has them—under cool running water. You will need a strong peeler to get the tough skins off, so I recommend purchasing a sturdy Y-shaped peeler. Another root vegetable–friendly tool is a mandoline, which shaves the vegetables into perfect slices for salads and casseroles.

Keep in mind that some root veggies, like beets and radishes, also have delicious edible green tops. If you're out shopping and can buy the roots with their tops, don't miss out. Give those greens a good wash and then wilt or braise them with other greens.

You can pretty easily swap root veggies within recipes. Or mix them up: If a recipe calls for carrots, for example, blend in some parsnips and turnips too. Just remember that roots like their other root friends!

We dig the dirt! Roots and bulbs are earthy and sweet from their home below grade. Who knows what goes on down there, but maybe there's a disco ball beet partying with DJ Digg.

Jaime makes sure this tzatziki is on the table at every single summer event we do, from grill-outs and BBQs to picnics and low-key dinners. We love it with just about *everything*—especially grilled meats, fish, and veggies, as well as with pita chips and crudités, and spooned on a lamb burger. I also love to serve it with the Swiss Chard Rolls on page 195. What makes it really special is the spicy black radish, which adds a perfect pop to the cool yogurt and cucumber. If you can't find black radish, feel free to use peeled red or green radishes instead. It's actually not super radish-y—your guests won't likely know there's even radish in there—but trust me when I tell you this is the best tzatziki you'll ever have. The spiciness of the radish makes the tzatziki complex and delicious; your guests are going to ask why it is so good and different.

Jaime's Radish Tzatziki

Makes 3 cups

1 smallish black radish, peeled, grated on the large holes of a box grater (¼ cup; see Get It Get It)

½ cup grated seedless cucumber (grated on the large holes of a box grater)

½ small garlic clove, finely grated

2 cups plain whole milk Greek yogurt

2 tablespoons everyday olive oil

1 tablespoon red wine vinegar

1 tablespoon fresh lemon juice

Small handful each of fresh mint leaves and dill, chopped (about 2 tablespoons each)

Kosher salt

In a medium bowl, using a rubber spatula, combine the radish, cucumber, garlic, and yogurt. Stir in the olive oil, vinegar, lemon juice, mint, and dill and season with a few heavy pinches of salt. Cover and refrigerate for at least 3 to 4 hours before serving. The tzatziki can be refrigerated for 3 to 4 days.

Get It

Black radishes are from Spain and have a spicy peppery flavor. If you can't find black radishes, you can substitute any radish; just be sure to peel them.

Don't be afraid to mess around with the amounts of olive oil, lemon, and vinegar—they're in there to season the tzatziki, and you should feel totally comfortable adjusting the amounts to your liking.

Get It

Lillian's Pickled Beets 1:1:1

My grandparents grew lots of beets, and back then, you pickled those beets. Beet salads were definitely not a thing with my grandparents! My grandma's technique is so simple that I want you to try it, and I promise you won't be disappointed. It's really all about the ratios for the pickling liquid. Grandma starts by boiling whole beets, leaving some of the stem attached to avoid the beet color from leaching out into the water. Once they're tender, she uses a paring knife to peel them by hand, then the beets are sliced and placed into a large jar. She combines equal parts of the beet boiling water, distilled white vinegar, and sugar, plus a dash of pickling spice (her pickling spice includes coriander seeds, fennel seeds, and bay leaves; I like adding some chile flake and salt too), then brings that to a boil. She pours the boiling liquid over the beets, covering them. That jar goes into the fridge and the beets are ready to eat in about 2 days. You can keep them in the fridge like that for a few months, but they get softer as they pickle. If you can the beets in the jar, they will be good for a year or two; Grandma suggests keeping them in the fridge so they retain their pretty color. You can eat the beets simply sliced on a plate, or use them in a salad to add some extra zip. My grandpa enjoyed eating them as a side dish to most meals, but he really liked them best with roast beef and fried chicken!

Pinzimonio

Pinzimonio is one of the most delightful and simple raw dishes you can find in Italy. When I was in Tuscany, I went to Dario Cecchini's famous Antica Macelleria Cecchini in Panzano, and after tasting and eating so many beef dishes, these amazing crudités showed up at the table and wowed me! The key thing about pinzimonio is that the raw vegetables are served over a bed of crushed ice, like oysters, which creates a very special experience. The pinzimonio I've had in Italy is usually a combination of peeled carrots and celery, cherry tomatoes, fresh fennel slices, and tiny red pearl onions. It's traditional to serve it alongside a small bowl of excellent extra-virgin olive oil, another bowl of red wine vinegar, and sea salt—all for dipping however you like. That said, my dear friend and beekeeper Andrea Paternoster from Mieli Thun in Alto-Adige (see page 5) made the most incredible dip that I think is the ultimate with pinzimonio. He taught me to use an electric mixer or a whisk to beat honey with red wine vinegar, then gradually beat in extra-virgin olive oil, creating a light, airy, fluffy dip. If you're looking for an inspired way to serve crudités, you should give this pinzimonio a try.

Andrea's Honey Dip

Makes about ¾ cup

½ cup super-special extra-virgin olive oil

⅓ cup Mieli Thun honey

1½ tablespoons red or white wine vinegar

Kosher salt

Vigorously whisk the olive oil, honey, and vinegar together with a few pinches of salt and ½ tablespoon of water until smooth. Serve with lots of veggies like carrots, celery, fennel, endive, cauliflower, cherry tomatoes, and sweet onion on ice!

Vegetable stocks tend to be kind of boring, missing the body and soul of a meat stock. But my technique of charring the onions in the broiler adds a wonderful smoky char, which couples so well with the natural sweetness of the onions. This is a relatively quick stock to make, but it's essential to cook it at a bare simmer and not to boil it, for a slow extraction of clean flavor. I like to think of the cooking technique as more of a steep than a simmer, almost like making tea. This vegetable broth is full of deep, dark-roasted umami flavors. It is a perfect all-purpose stock for making stews, soups, and braises. If you'd like to make it even richer-tasting, you can char the onions longer; for a lighter vegetable stock, cut the broiling time for the onions by half.

Charred Onion Vegetable Stock

Makes about 2 quarts

Canola oil or another high-
    smoke-point oil (like safflower
    or grapeseed)

2 unpeeled yellow onions,
    quartered through the stem

Kosher salt

1 tablespoon everyday olive oil

3 celery stalks, roughly chopped

2 carrots or parsnips, roughly
    chopped

2 tablespoons tomato paste

½ teaspoon organic cane sugar
    (optional)

One 2- to 3-inch piece Parmigiano
    rind

4 dried bay leaves

2 whole cloves (optional)

1. Set an oven rack 4 to 5 inches from the heat source and turn the broiler to high. Line a baking sheet with foil and lightly grease the foil with canola oil. Arrange the quartered onions cut side down on the sheet. Drizzle and rub the skins of the onions with a teaspoon or so of the canola oil, then season with a pinch of salt.

2. Broil for 10 minutes, until the thin onion peel is nicely charred but not burnt. Then, using tongs, flip the onions cut side up and continue to broil until charred, about 10 minutes.

3. Meanwhile, in a large (6- to 8-quart) saucepot, heat the olive oil over medium-high heat. Add the celery and carrots and cook, stirring often, until they start to brown, about 10 minutes. Reduce the heat to low and stir in the tomato paste and sugar (if using) to coat and caramelize, about 1 minute. Add 8 cups of cold water along with the parm rind, bay leaves, and cloves, if using. Stir in the charred onions and cook for 20 minutes. Do not boil the stock; keep the heat low so it's barely a simmer.

4. Strain, discarding the solids. Keep the stock stored in the fridge for up to a week or frozen for up to 4 months.

Get It

Feel free to save your veggie scraps in the freezer for your future stock-making needs. I like saving parsnip and carrot peels, mushroom stems, and tomato scraps, which can be added to the pot with the water. You can never have too many veggies in your stock!

Get It

Clams can hide lots of little specks of sand and grit in their shells. The best way to purge them of that grit is to place them in a bowl, cover with cold water, and let them sit for 5 minutes or so, then change the water and continue this process until the water is clear. If you notice lots of sand and grit in the bowl, add a pinch or two of sea salt or cornstarch, which I find helps the clams release their grit. To store clams overnight in your fridge, cover them with a wet towel. Never store them in water. Don't force a clam open, as usually an unopened clam is a sign that it is dead and should not be consumed.

Get It

If you have a wok, you need to pull that baby out and get it on the stove! The heat of the wok intensifies the flavor of everything that is cooked in it. The intense rapid cooking style sears the clams and onions, forcing their natural water content to evaporate and concentrating the flavor. I love using a wok because it gets so hot, but you can also use a sauté pan here. To maximize the spring onions, I like to separate them into white and green parts, 'cause the white part handles the heat of the wok so well, getting nicely charred, while the green part adds a fantastic fresh onion flavor to finish the dish. I also love a simple linguine with white clam sauce, and I always use leeks or onions in it; I find the sweetness of onion goes so well with clams, versus the pungency of garlic.

Wok-Fried Spring Onions and Clams

with Orzo

Serves 4

Kosher salt or coarse sea salt (like Maldon)

8 ounces dry orzo

4 tablespoons everyday olive oil

2 large bunches of spring onions, leeks, or ramps (about 1 pound total), white parts thinly sliced, green parts cut into 1-inch pieces

2 cups cherry tomatoes, halved

2 tablespoons Calabrian chile paste or sambal oelek

1 tablespoon colatura or Vietnamese fish sauce

One 2-inch piece fresh ginger, peeled and grated

2 garlic cloves, thinly sliced or grated

Finely grated zest (use a Microplane) and juice of ½ lemon

2 pounds littleneck or Manila clams, cleaned (see Get It Get It)

1 cup white wine

2 tablespoons unsalted butter

1. Bring a large pot of water to a boil and season well with salt. Cook the orzo for 2 minutes less than the package states. Reserve ½ cup of the pasta cooking water and drain the pasta in a colander. Toss with 1 teaspoon of the olive oil.

2. In a medium bowl, combine the sliced spring onion white parts with the cherry tomatoes, chile paste, colatura, ginger, garlic, lemon zest and juice, 1 tablespoon of the olive oil, and a generous pinch of salt; toss well.

3. Heat a large wok or sauté pan over high heat. Add the remaining 2 tablespoons and 2 teaspoons of olive oil along with the clams and a pinch of salt and let the clams toast in the oil for 1 minute; be careful, as the clams will release a little bit of water, which can splatter. Add the marinated onions and toss well. Cook until the onions begin to soften and the mixture begins to sweat, 3 to 4 minutes. Add the white wine and the reserved pasta cooking water and deglaze the pan, scraping up any bits on the bottom. Cover, lower the heat to medium, and steam for 5 to 6 minutes, until the clams begin to open. Stir the clams a few times to prevent sticking and to help them to open.

4. Once the clams have started opening, reduce the heat to low. Cooked clams can open up at different times, so to ensure even cooking, I like to remove the first round of opened clams to a small mixing bowl. Once all of the clams have opened, you can add the opened ones back to the wok.

5. Add the cooked orzo, green onion pieces, and butter. Stir to combine. Season with another pinch of salt if needed, then serve.

There are so many beets salads out there that I thought, "Who needs another one?" So this is kind of a catch-all beet dish that works as an appetizer, a side dish, or even as a bruschetta topping, set out with crostini. The dish is inspired by a classic Northern Italian pasta dish that combines beets with ricotta and poppy seeds. Beets have such a nice earthy sweetness to them, but they need some acidity too, which is why I like marinating them in a bag with a little vinegar, honey, and olive oil.

Salt-Roasted Beets

with a Double Ricotta Schmear and Poppy Seeds

Serves 4

2 pounds assorted beets, trimmed, peeled, small beets left whole, medium and large beets halved or quartered

2 tablespoons everyday olive oil

Coarse sea salt (like Maldon) or kosher salt

1 tablespoon white wine vinegar or champagne vinegar

1 tablespoon wildflower honey

1 cup Homemade Lemon Ricotta (page 173) or whole milk ricotta (see page 8)

2 ounces pressed ricotta salata or smoked pressed ricotta, finely grated (use a Microplane; about ½ cup)

Poppy seeds, for garnish

Fresh dill sprigs, for garnish

Fresh cracked black pepper, for serving

1.   Preheat the oven to 400°F. Set a rack in a large baking sheet. In a large bowl, toss the beets with 1 tablespoon of the olive oil and liberally season with about 1 teaspoon salt. Arrange the beets in an even layer on a sheet of foil, then place another sheet of foil on top; crimp the edges together to create a sealed packet. Carefully transfer the packet to the prepared baking sheet. Bake for 1 to 1½ hours, until tender. To check for doneness, insert a paring knife into one of the larger beets.

2.   Let the beets cool slightly, about 5 minutes, then transfer to a large resealable plastic bag. Add the vinegar, honey, and the remaining 1 tablespoon of olive oil. Seal the bag and shake, then set aside and allow the beets to cool for 15 minutes or so. (The beets are like little sponges, and most vulnerable when they come out of the oven; placing them in the bag forces them to absorb the marinade.) At this point, they are ready to serve but can be refrigerated for up to 3 days.

3.   Meanwhile, place both ricottas in a food processor and whip for 30 seconds, until lightened and airy. Scrape the double ricotta schmear into a bowl and reserve. This can be made a few days in advance and stores well in an airtight container in the fridge.

4.   To serve, spread the double ricotta schmear evenly on a platter or onto four plates. Put the beets and any marinade juices in a mixing bowl, season with a generous pinch of salt, and toss. Nestle the beets into the ricotta and spoon the marinade over the top. Garnish with poppy seeds, lots of fresh dill, and fresh cracked pepper.

Celery root, also known as celeriac, is a root veggie that's great eaten raw (just be sure to peel it) or cooked. It has a delicate, sweet celery flavor. It's kind of overlooked in salads, and that's unfortunate because it can add great texture and crunch. You see it a lot in remoulades in New Orleans, and I've had great pickled celery root plates in Alsace. When I first got to thinking about putting this salad together, I tried shaving it into slices, but it was kind of hard to chew. I reflected on my experiences eating it in NOLA and Alsace, and figured I needed to try it shredded. Bingo! You can use a mandoline, but I find the grating attachment of my food processor even better—it is very quick and safe.

Shredded Celery Root Salad

with Blood Orange, Avocado, and Pistachio

Serves 4 to 6

Kosher salt

1 medium-to-large celery root (about 12 ounces), trimmed, peeled, and quartered

Finely grated zest of 1 blood orange, Navel orange, or Ruby Red grapefruit (use a Microplane)

⅓ cup black olives (like Leccino, Niçoise, or Taggiasca) or your favorite black olive, pitted and roughly chopped

2 tablespoons everyday olive oil

¼ cup freshly grated Pecorino Romano

Juice of ½ lemon

1 firm but ripe avocado, halved, pitted, peeled, and sliced

1 cup loosely packed arugula leaves

2 tablespoons shelled roasted pistachios, chopped

Super-special extra-virgin olive oil, for drizzling (optional)

1. Fill the bowl of a salad spinner or any large bowl with ice water and add ¼ cup of kosher salt. Shred the celery root either by using a mandoline or a food processor with the shredding/grating attachment. (If using the mandoline, please use the cutting guard as a precaution.) Add the shaved celery root to the ice water and let stand for 10 minutes; agitate with your hands to separate the threads of celery root.

2. To segment the orange, using a very sharp paring knife, trim the top and bottom of the orange. Remove the peel and pith, cutting along with the curve of the orange. Working over your salad bowl, carefully cut along the membranes to slice out each segment (aka supreming). Squeeze the remaining orange membrane to get the extra juice in the bowl.

3. To the salad bowl, add the orange zest along with the olives, olive oil, pecorino, lemon juice, and a big pinch of salt; mix well to combine. Drain the celery root well, then spin until dry. Stir into the salad bowl and let sit for 10 minutes, stirring a few times, to get it nicely marinated.

4. Top the salad with sliced avocado, arugula, pistachios, and a drizzle of super-special olive oil (totally optional, but I recommend it!). The salad will hold nicely for up to 30 minutes or so. Gently toss when you are ready to enjoy.

Get It

I like soaking the shredded celery root in ice-cold salted water not just because it helps make it extra crispy, but the salt seasons the celery root before it's dressed. This nifty trick makes the salad taste that much better!

You can shred the celery root ahead of time if it makes things easier. Drain and dry it, roll it up in some paper towels, pop it into a plastic bag, and store in the fridge for a few hours.

Get It

I find this soup simultaneously simple and deeply complex. The rich sweetness of caramelized celery root combined with the vermouth gives the soup a certain je ne sais quoi. I recommend using a strong blender for the silkiest results, but if the soup has a little texture, it's still delicious.

Caramelized Celery Root and Onion Soup

with Crème Fraîche and Hazelnuts

Serves 4

1 tablespoon everyday olive oil

1 large celery root, peeled and roughly chopped (about 4 cups)

Kosher salt

1 large yellow onion, halved lengthwise and very thinly sliced crosswise

1 garlic clove, thinly sliced

1 tablespoon unsalted butter

½ cup dry vermouth or 1 tablespoon rice vinegar

5 cups Charred Onion Vegetable Stock (page 325) or chicken or vegetable stock

½ cup crème fraîche or sour cream

¼ cup hazelnuts, toasted and roughly chopped (see Get It Get It)

About 2 tablespoons snipped fresh chives, for serving

Super-special extra-virgin olive oil, for drizzling

1.   In a large pot, heat the olive oil over medium heat. Add the celery root, season with a heavy pinch or two of salt, and cook, stirring often, until the celery root slowly turns golden brown, about 15 minutes.

2.   Add the onion, garlic, and butter, and cook for another 10 minutes, stirring often. Add the vermouth and deglaze, scraping up any browned bits on the bottom of the pot with a wooden spoon. Add the onion stock and bring to a boil, then reduce the heat to low and simmer for 25 to 30 minutes, until the celery root is tender. Season with salt.

3.   Working in batches, transfer the soup to a blender (fill it less than halfway) and carefully blend on high until smooth and airy; it's best to leave the lid slightly open and to cover the top with a kitchen towel while blending. You can also use an immersion blender. Return the soup to the pot once blended and rewarm if necessary. If the soup seems too thick, add a little more stock. Transfer the soup to bowls and serve with a dollop of crème fraîche, the chopped hazelnuts and snipped chives, and a drizzle of super-special olive oil. The soup can also be returned to the pot and kept warm over low heat until you're ready to serve.

Get It

If you can find toasted hazelnuts, get them! There are amazing hazelnuts coming out of Piedmont that are pretoasted. If you cannot find those, just simply toast raw hazelnuts in the oven at 350°F for about 10 minutes, until the nuts are fragrant and golden. Rub them in a clean kitchen towel to remove the skins before proceeding.

This soup can be made vegan. Substitute 1 tablespoon olive oil for the butter in Step 2 and use a vegetarian vegetable stock in place of the onion stock. Omit the crème fraîche in the garnish.

Get It

The key to these amazingly crispy sunchokes is smashing them so they're nice and thin, but not so thin that they fall apart. To help ensure that they come out just right, I suggest cooling the boiled sunchokes before smashing them, which helps them stay intact and also creates a crispier end product. I like to serve these for breakfast or brunch in place of hash browns or other potatoes. They have a latke-like flavor, so they would be awesome served with smoked salmon, sour cream, and everything bagel spice.

Smashed Crispy Sunchokes

with Calabrian Chile Hot Sauce

Serves 4

1 pound sunchokes (use smaller sunchokes, if possible)

Kosher salt

Canola oil, for pan-frying

Thinly sliced fresh chives or scallions, for garnish

Calabrian Chile Hot Sauce

3 tablespoons apple cider vinegar

3 tablespoons Calabrian chile paste or sambal oelek

3 tablespoons everyday olive oil

½ teaspoon sugar (preferably organic cane sugar)

5 cherry tomatoes

1. Using a paring knife, trim any dark spots or hair-like roots from the sunchokes. If the sunchokes are large, cut them in half so they are all similarly sized. Put the sunchokes in a bowl of cold water to soak for a few minutes to loosen up any dirt. Rinse well.

2. Place the sunchokes in a pot of cold water and season with a few pinches of salt. Bring to a rapid simmer over medium-high heat. Cook until the sunchokes are tender when pierced with a knife, 30 to 35 minutes. Remove from the pot and transfer to a paper towel–lined plate. Refrigerate for at least 30 minutes to cool slightly (they'll be easier to handle) and up to overnight.

3. Preheat the oven to 450°F and set a rack in the bottom third of the oven or the lowest possible setting. Set a chilled sunchoke on a cutting board and, using a small plate, press down on it, smashing it into a patty ½ to ¾ inch thick. Repeat with the other sunchokes.

4. Heat a large cast-iron skillet or heavy ovenproof sauté pan over medium heat. Add a thin layer of canola oil (about 2 tablespoons) to evenly coat the pan. Carefully add the smashed sunchokes to the pan and season with salt. Cook the sunchokes until golden brown on the bottoms, 6 to 7 minutes, depending on the size of your sunchokes. Carefully flip them so they stay intact; sprinkle with another few pinches of salt. Transfer the skillet to the lowest rack in the oven and roast the sunchokes for 10 to 15 minutes, until golden and crunchy.

5. **Meanwhile, make the Calabrian chile hot sauce:** Place the cider vinegar, chile paste, olive oil, sugar, and cherry tomatoes in the blender; add a few pinches of salt. Blend on high until smooth and combined.

6. Remove the sunchokes from the oven and serve right from the pan, or arrange on a plate with the hot sauce on the side. Garnish with chives.

Get It

Don't want to mess with the blender? You can use your favorite hot sauce for an easy swap. However, I do love this Calabrian hot sauce. Try it on the Lemony Rice–Stuffed Peppers with Roasted Cauliflower, Fennel, Feta, and Dill on page 288. It's so good on anything where hot sauce is a must!

Get It

Carrots are often overlooked as a main ingredient, as they function as such a workhorse ingredient in the kitchen. They're a key player in French mirepoix and Italian soffritto, for sure. This dish celebrates the unique sweetness and flavor of the carrot and utilizes not just the root but those delicious green tops too.

Cast-Iron Roasted Carrots

with Carrot Top Salsa Verde

Serves 4

1½ pounds rainbow carrots with tops (8 to 10 medium carrots, about 2 bunches; see Get It Get It)

¼ cup plus 1 tablespoon everyday olive oil

Kosher salt

1 tablespoon coarsely chopped fresh tarragon

1 tablespoon coarsely chopped fresh dill

1 tablespoon drained capers, chopped

1½ teaspoons minced shallot

Finely grated zest (use a Microplane) and juice of ½ lemon

1.   Preheat the oven to 450°F. Set a 12-inch cast-iron skillet in the oven to heat for 10 to 15 minutes.

2.   To prepare the carrots, remove the tops, leaving 1 inch or so of the green stem attached. Reserve the tender carrot tops for the salsa verde. Using a sharp knife, cut the carrots in half crosswise, separating the tapered end from the thicker top. Cut the thick pieces of carrots in half lengthwise. (This will allow the carrot pieces to cook at a similar rate.)

3.   In a large bowl, toss the carrots with 1 tablespoon of the olive oil and season with a generous pinch or two of salt. Carefully add the carrots to the hot pan in the oven and spread evenly. Place the pan back in the oven. You should hear the carrots sizzling as they roast. This is a very good thing! After 10 minutes, give the carrots a good stir, then cook for another 10 minutes. Remove from the oven and check to see if they are tender but a little toothsome; if not, give them a few more minutes.

4.   Meanwhile, chop the carrot tops; there should be about 1 cup of chopped leaves. In a small bowl, mix the chopped carrot tops with the tarragon, dill, capers, and shallot. Drizzle in the remaining ¼ cup of olive oil and stir to combine; season with salt. Stir in the lemon zest and juice to combine. The salsa verde is best used as soon as possible, but it can be refrigerated overnight. Drizzle it over the roasted carrots in the cast-iron pan and serve.

— Get It —

Feel free to use baby carrots with their tops attached, if you can find them at the market. There is no need to cut them down, as they are usually pretty evenly sized.

Look for carrot tops that feel tender to the touch, not rough and tough. If you can't find good carrot tops, or any carrots with the tops attached at all, feel free to sub 1 cup of fresh flat-leaf parsley leaves and stems in the salsa verde.

— Get It —

Get It

Try all different kinds of turnips for this recipe. I love Scarlet Queen and baby turnips like Hakurei. If you can find turnips with their greens attached, that's a win. If you're using baby turnips, you can leave them whole or cut them in half.

Get It

My grandmother grew turnips in her garden, and she liked cooking them in a "white sauce," which I am guessing was a béchamel sauce. Vegetables served this way have fallen out of style, but they're actually so delicious. Instead of messing with a béchamel here, I opted to use just cream, and then I treat the whole dish like a gratin, finishing it under the broiler until the Parmigiano gets all melty. On another note, turnips often get the cold shoulder at the grocery store. I love balancing their (sometimes) spicy-bitter flavor with the sweetness of onions and cream. This is so good as a side dish. Move over creamed spinach, there is a new creamy green in town!

Tender Turnips and Their Greens

with Cream, Parm, and Caramelized Onions

Serves 4

2 tablespoons everyday olive oil

1 large onion, thinly sliced

6 medium turnips
(1 to 1¼ pounds), trimmed, peeled, and cut into ⅛-inch wedges

½ teaspoon sugar (preferably Sugar in the Raw)

Kosher salt

1 bunch of turnip or mustard greens, washed, stemmed, leaves torn into bite-sized pieces

½ cup heavy cream

¼ cup freshly grated Parmigiano-Reggiano

1. In a 10- to 12–inch ovenproof skillet, heat 1 tablespoon of the olive oil over medium-low heat and add the onion. Slowly cook the onion slices, stirring occasionally, allowing them to caramelize, 10 to 15 minutes. Transfer the onions to a plate.

2. Raise the heat under the skillet to medium-high. Add the remaining 1 tablespoon of oil, then the turnips, sugar, and a pinch of salt. Cook for 10 minutes, until the turnips are golden brown. Add the greens and wilt, about 5 minutes. Add the cream and ½ cup of water and simmer for 5 minutes, or until thickened.

3. While the sauce is thickening, set an oven rack right under the broiler and turn the broiler to high. Stir the caramelized onions into the skillet and top with the grated parm. Place the skillet under the broiler for 2 to 3 minutes, until the parm is melted and golden. Serve hot!

To Peel or Not to Peel

This is a tough question because you don't really have to peel most root vegetables, except for ones with tough peels like salsify and celery root. As a rule, when I'm preparing to eat raw vegetables, I prefer peeling them, but if they're small or baby veggies, I leave them unpeeled and just give them a good scrub.

Now, if I'm cooking the vegetables, I like to pause and think about what I'm trying to achieve. Do I want the vegetable to absorb some of the flavor of what its being cooked in or with, or do I want it to develop its own flavor while it cooks? For instance, if I'm roasting vegetables, I don't need to peel them because leaving the veggies unpeeled locks in the most flavor while roasting. But if I'm braising, peeling makes a vegetable more open to absorbing the flavor of what it's being cooked in, and that's good! Pickled beets make an excellent example. When you're first boiling them, leave the peel on to prevent the beet from losing flavor while it cooks, but *after* it's cooked, you want to peel it so it can absorb the flavors from the pickling liquid.

This is a great example of how sometimes veggies like being treated like meat—in this case, I treat them like I would beef for a beef stew. As such, I sear the veggies in pancetta renderings, creating the first layer of flavor in this hearty stew, which gets so many additional layers from tomato paste, reduced wine, and charred onion stock. With so many delicious roots (even the horseradish root in the yogurt!), I think this recipe celebrates root vegetables more than any other. This is stellar served with soft and creamy polenta, but it also would be great with Maria Nava's Lemon Olive Oil Risotto (page 247) or with buttered pappardelle or egg noodles for root vegetable stroganoff vibes.

Braised Root Vegetable and Mushroom Stew

with Horseradish Yogurt and Herb Gremolata

Serves 4 as a main course or 6 to 8 as a side dish

3 tablespoons everyday olive oil, plus more as needed

2 ounces sliced pancetta (optional; see Get It Get It on page 340)

4 or 5 medium parsnips, trimmed, peeled, and sliced lengthwise

4 or 5 small turnips, trimmed, peeled, and quartered

1 medium rutabaga, trimmed, peeled, and cut into eighths

One 1-pound butternut squash, peeled, seeded, and cut into large chunks

Kosher salt

4 ounces trumpet royale mushrooms with stems, sliced into rounds

1 medium red onion, diced

3 garlic cloves, minced

2 tablespoons tomato paste

2 tablespoons brandy or whiskey

1 cup dry, fruity red wine, like cabernet sauvignon

1 cup canned crushed tomatoes (preferably Italian passata or strained tomatoes)

2 cups Charred Onion Vegetable Stock (page 325), or your favorite vegetable or chicken stock

ingredients continue

1.   Heat a large, heavy Dutch oven or cast-iron casserole over medium heat. Add 2 tablespoons of the olive oil and the pancetta and cook until crispy and the fat is rendered, about 2 minutes. Remove the pan from the heat and transfer the pancetta to a paper towel–lined plate.

2.   Return the Dutch oven to the stove over medium heat. Working in batches, sear the parsnips, turnips, rutabaga, and squash, allowing each piece to caramelize. (This should take 5 to 7 minutes per vegetable, about 25 minutes in total.) If the pan looks dry, add a little bit more olive oil. As they're browned, transfer the vegetables to a baking sheet. Season the seared vegetables with a few generous pinches of salt.

3.   Preheat the oven to 450°F. Add the remaining 1 tablespoon of olive oil and the mushrooms to the pot and cook, stirring occasionally, until they begin to release their liquid, about 5 minutes; season with a few pinches of salt. Add the onion and garlic and cook until golden, about 5 minutes; season with another pinch of salt. Stir in the tomato paste.

4.   Remove from the heat and add the brandy. Using a long match, carefully light the brandy and cook until the flames die down; you can also return the pot to the heat and just allow the brandy to cook and evaporate. Using a wooden spoon, scrape up any browned bits on the bottom of the pot. Add the red wine and simmer until reduced by about half, about 5 minutes. Add the crushed tomatoes and charred onion stock and bring to a rapid simmer. Taste the sauce for seasoning and adjust with a bit more salt to taste. (This is all about layering seasoning as you build the sauce.)

5.   Stir the butter into the sauce and nestle the seared veggies in an even layer in the pot. Carefully transfer the pot to the middle rack of the oven, and bake, uncovered, for 15 minutes. Using a paring knife, check the

recipe continues

2 tablespoons unsalted butter

2 tablespoons chopped fresh flat-leaf parsley

2 tablespoons chopped fresh dill

Finely grated zest of 1 lemon (use a Microplane)

Fresh Horseradish Yogurt (recipe follows)

Soft Polenta with Crème Fraîche and Parm (page 128), for serving (optional)

veggies for tenderness. The sauce should be reduced, yet still a little bit saucy. Let the stew rest for 5 to 10 minutes.

6. Meanwhile, in a small bowl, mix the parsley, dill, and lemon zest. To serve, sprinkle the gremolata over the stew and top with the crispy pancetta and generous dollops of horseradish yogurt. I love to serve this with soft polenta. Enjoy!

Fresh Horseradish Yogurt

If you want to use prepared horseradish in the yogurt, reduce the amount to 2 tablespoons. I love the spicy kick of horseradish, but feel free to tailor the spice level to your liking. Fresh horseradish has a beautiful aroma, but it needs acidity from lemon juice to activate its spiciness.

Makes 2 cups

One 3- to 4-inch piece fresh horseradish root, peeled and finely grated (use a Microplane; about ¼ cup)

2 tablespoons fresh lemon juice

2 cups plain whole milk or 2% Greek yogurt

Kosher salt

In a medium bowl, stir the grated horseradish with the lemon juice and yogurt. Add a few heavy pinches of kosher salt. The yogurt can be kept in an airtight container in the fridge for up to 4 days. Serve it cold.

Get It

If you want to keep this vegetarian, go for it! Just skip the first step and sear your veggies in extra-virgin olive oil. In place of the pancetta, I would recommend garnishing with a touch of pimentón (smoked paprika). This book is all about listening to what your vegetables want. Ultimately, these root vegetables are excited to be the star of the dish, and enjoy the thoughtful time spent searing and braising (and my veggies want to be seared in pancetta renderings ☺).

Change up the veggies each time you make this. Shoot for 2 to 2½ pounds of assorted root vegetables per batch. Just make sure you have a mix of roots that are sweet (like beets, carrots, parsnips, and sunchokes) and spicy (like rutabaga and turnips) for the best flavor.

Get It

This is the decadent side of root vegetables—a recipe that's simple but sophisticated enough to make a root vegetable lover out of anyone. *Fonduta* is just the Italian word for "fondue," and this delicious cheese sauce is good on just about everything. Putting it over veggies was partially inspired by my grandmother, who used to give us kids our vegetables with cheese sauce so we would eat them! How you position your oven racks will achieve different outcomes. Assuming the heat source in your oven comes from the bottom, I like placing the baking sheet with the veggies on the bottom rack so they get really nicely seared and caramelized from the heat. If the heat source comes from the top of your oven, then place the rack up toward the top instead.

Brown Butter–Roasted Root Vegetables

with Shallots and Fonduta

Serves 4 to 6

2 to 2½ pounds root vegetables (I like to use a mix of all the roots: radishes, sunchokes, turnips, beets, rutabaga, carrots), washed and cut into halves or quarters of a similar size

1 cup peeled and halved shallots (5 or 6 small shallots)

1½ tablespoons everyday olive oil

Kosher salt

1½ cups heavy cream

½ cup shredded Fontina or Gruyère cheese, shredded (use the large holes of a box grater; about 2 ounces)

2 tablespoons unsalted butter, cut into small cubes

Leaves from 2 fresh rosemary sprigs

Fresh cracked black pepper

Good-quality aged balsamic vinegar, for drizzling

1. Set an oven rack near the heat source of the oven and preheat the oven to 425°F. Place a foil-lined baking sheet on the rack to preheat.

2. In a large bowl, toss the vegetables and shallots with the olive oil and season generously with about 1½ teaspoons of salt. Carefully spread the vegetables on the heated baking sheet in an even layer. Roast the vegetables until caramelized and tender, about 30 minutes, stirring and rotating the baking sheet halfway through.

3. Meanwhile, in a small pot, heat the heavy cream over medium heat and simmer, whisking often, until reduced by half, about 10 minutes. I suggest dipping a spoon in the reducing cream to see how thick it is on the back of the spoon. It should be thick enough to coat the spoon but not run off. Reduce the heat to low and slowly whisk in the cheese, allowing it to melt and combine. Cover and hold the fonduta in a warm place on the stovetop; stir before serving. (This should stay nice and melty for about 30 minutes. You may need to rewarm it slightly over low heat.)

4. Carefully take the veggies out of the oven. Add the butter, rosemary, and a few generous cracks of black pepper, then place back in the oven and roast for 5 more minutes to allow the butter to brown. Remove from the oven and gently toss the vegetables to combine. Transfer to a bowl or a platter and drizzle with balsamic and the fonduta. Enjoy!

—— Get It ——

I often find bundled soup vegetables in the grocery store, which is a very convenient way to get a good mix of root vegetables for this dish.

—— Get It ——

This is a showstopper—the kind of dish you put in the center of the table and it's like, *BAM*. It's not a weeknight dish, but totally worth the weekend effort. I had an *aha* moment with the double use of carrots in here; there are shredded carrots in the filling, and the sauce is made primarily with carrot juice! It creates a sweet, earthy sauce that's reminiscent of tomatoes but totally unique—who ever saw a lasagna made with a carrot juice–based sauce? I also love the pinwheel-style of this lasagna. Rolling the pinwheels is a bit of extra work, but it ends up looking so pretty, plus there's a little crunch in every bite. One last plus: This is great to serve at a party, as it doesn't need to be cut—each person can take their own pinwheel—if they can eat just one!

Carrot and Lamb Merguez Sausage Lasagna

Serves 8

Carrot and Sausage Filling

2 teaspoons everyday olive oil

1 pound bulk lamb merguez sausage (see Get It Get It on page 344)

2 pounds carrots, trimmed, peeled, and shredded

Kosher salt

½ cup Castelvetrano or other pitted green olives, chopped

2 tablespoons golden raisins, chopped

¼ cup shelled unsalted pistachios, chopped (optional)

2 cups freshly grated Pecorino Romano

Two 10-ounce logs fresh goat cheese

⅓ cup chopped fresh flat-leaf parsley

Carrot-Tomato Sauce

1 tablespoon everyday olive oil

1 cup minced onion

One 6-ounce can tomato paste

4 cups fresh carrot juice

Assembling and Finishing

Kosher salt

1 pound dry lasagna sheets

5 or 6 slices of deli-style whole milk mozzarella (6 ounces)

1. **Make the filling.** In a large pot, heat the olive oil over medium heat. Add the sausage and cook until golden brown, 6 to 7 minutes, breaking it up with a wooden spoon as it cooks. Add the shredded carrots, season with salt, and cook for 5 minutes, until softened. Add the olives, raisins, and pistachios, if using, and cook for another minute. Transfer the filling to a large bowl and stir in the pecorino, goat cheese, and parsley to combine. Place the pot back on the stove to make the sauce.

2. **Make the sauce.** In the pot, heat the olive oil over medium-high heat. Add the onion and cook until softened, about 1 minute. Add the tomato paste and cook, stirring, to caramelize, about 30 seconds. Add the carrot juice, deglazing the pan. Bring up to a boil, about 5 minutes. Remove from the heat. (The sauce should be almost soup-like in consistency.)

3. **Assemble the lasagna.** Bring a large pot of water to a boil and add 2 tablespoons of salt. Working in two batches, cook the lasagna sheets for 1 minute less than the directions state. (If the suggested cooking time is 9 to 11 minutes, I recommend cooking for 8 minutes.) Lightly spray a large baking sheet, cutting board, or work surface with oil. Carefully remove the lasagna sheets from the boiling water and lay them on the sprayed surface, aligning them in vertical rows in front of you.

4. Preheat the oven to 375°F. Using a half-cup measure, spoon ½ cup of filling onto each lasagna sheet. Spread the filling along the sheets. Using your hands, tightly roll the lasagna sheets away from you, as you would a pinwheel or jelly roll.

5. Set aside 2 cups of the carrot-tomato sauce, then pour the remaining sauce into a large (12-inch) round enameled casserole or cast-iron pot. Starting in the center (so you can see the pinwheel effect), place the rolled

recipe continues

lasagna pinwheels in the pan with the sauce, nestling each pinwheel snugly against the next. Work your way toward the outside of the pan until you fill the whole pot. Pour the remaining sauce on top of the pinwheels. Place the mozzarella slices around the top of the lasagna, overlapping if needed.

6.   Spray a sheet of foil with nonstick spray to prevent the lasagna from sticking, then gently tent the lasagna with the foil. Place a foil-lined baking sheet one rack below where the lasagna will be in case of any bubbling overflow. Bake for 45 minutes. Uncover and bake for 20 to 25 minutes longer, until golden and bubbling. Serve hot.

Get It

You don't want big chunks of meat in here, so look to buy merguez in bulk (without casings). If you can't find it, you can buy links and remove the casings yourself with a sharp knife. You can also substitute 1 pound spicy Italian pork sausage mixed with 1 teaspoon ground cumin.

If you want to make your own merguez, mix 1 pound ground lamb with 1 tablespoon Calabrian chile

paste or sambal oelek; 1 minced garlic clove; 1 teaspoon each of ground cumin, ground coriander, and ground fennel seeds; and 1½ teaspoons of kosher salt. (I recommend toasting and grinding the spices fresh.)

If you want to omit the meat altogether, you can substitute 2 cups of cooked lentils seasoned with

1 tablespoon of Calabrian chile paste or sambal oelek; 1 minced garlic clove; 1 teaspoon each of ground cumin, ground coriander, and ground fennel seeds; and 1½ teaspoons of kosher salt. (I recommend toasting and grinding the spices fresh.)

Get It

Listen to Your Vegetables

On my first trip to Italy, I visited my friend Andrea Bezzecchi, who makes extraordinary vinegar at his Acetaia San Giacomo in Novellara (Reggio Emilia). I learned that traditional balsamic vinegar begins with grape must, made from whole pressed grapes complete with juice, skin, seeds, and stems. The must is cooked down and then fermented to make authentic balsamic vinegar. Saba, which is the essence of this delicious recipe, is reduced grape must that hasn't been fermented. It has a delicious concentrated grape flavor and lovely sweetness. The sweetness of saba balances beautifully with the bitterness from turnips and the acidity of the red wine vinegar in this dish. If you don't have saba, you can substitute 2 tablespoons of balsamic vinegar mixed with 2 tablespoons of honey. This easy-to-make sweet-sour chicken dish only requires one pot; it's delicious served with creamy polenta or the Grilled Parsley Potato Smashers on page 307.

Saba-Braised Chicken

with Turnips

Serves 2 to 4

4 bone-in, skin-on chicken thighs

Kosher salt

2 slices of bacon, cut into large squares

1 cup red pearl onions, peeled

3 medium turnips, peeled and cut into wedges

½ cup quartered dried figs

Fresh cracked black pepper

½ cup dry white wine (like sauvignon blanc)

½ cup chicken stock

¼ cup saba

2 tablespoons red wine vinegar

1 tablespoon fresh thyme leaves

1 tablespoon unsalted butter

1.   Preheat the oven to 375°F. Season the chicken on both sides with salt. Heat a large ovenproof saucepan over medium-low heat. Add the bacon and cook, turning once halfway through, until crispy and brown, 1 to 2 minutes per side. Transfer the bacon to a plate.

2.   Increase the heat to medium. Add the chicken skin side down and cook until the skin is crispy and deeply golden, about 7 minutes. Transfer to a plate.

3.   Reduce the heat to medium-low. Add the pearl onions and turnips, season with a few pinches of salt, and cook, turning occasionally with tongs, until browned all over, about 8 minutes. (Be patient here, because color is important.) Add the figs to soften slightly, about 2 minutes, then season with salt and fresh black pepper. Add the white wine and deglaze the pan, scraping up any bits from the bottom. Stir in the chicken stock, saba, red wine vinegar, and thyme, and add a bit more salt and black pepper as needed. Nestle the chicken thighs into the pan, skin side up. Transfer the pan to the oven and bake for 15 minutes, or until the chicken is cooked through.

4.   Carefully remove the saucepan from the oven and transfer the chicken to a deep serving platter. Return the saucepan to medium-low heat on the stovetop and bring the sauce to a simmer. Add the butter and stir to slightly thicken the sauce, about 1 minute. Spoon the sauce and vegetables over the chicken, and sprinkle with the crispy bacon pieces. Serve immediately.

Get It

I'm a fan of pearl onions and turnips here, but you can use any type of savory root vegetable—rutabaga is a great option. I also love using dried prunes or apricots in place of the dried figs. Fresh figs would also be stellar, if available.

Get It

Summer
Squash

& Winter Squash

Both summer and winter squash are part of the gourd family and grow on vines. Summer squash is harvested in warm months and is delightful eaten both raw and cooked. In the summer, I love exploring the market's bounty: green and gold zucchini, yellow crookneck, multicolored pattypan, and the round Eight Ball zucchini are some of my favorites.

Summer squash is easy to cook and wildly versatile—it's like a sponge and can absorb and take on many different flavors, making it a perfect side dish to meats and seafood. But perhaps the best part of zucchini season is when the beautiful, delicate flowers are available for stuffing and frying, or for folding into scrambled eggs or a cheese quesadilla.

Try to avoid buying summer squash that's bruised or has any dark markings on the skin. This is one vegetable, like a cucumber, where the flavor changes once it gets too old, and it can't be saved. Squash stays well in the fridge for a while, but it's best stored in a paper bag or another breathable material, just not plastic, which makes it slimy.

Winter squash is harvested in the fall, and because of its hard, thick skin, it can be easily stored through the winter (thus its name). Winter squash is far more hearty and robust than summer squash, with sweet and nutty characteristics. Winter squash is eaten cooked, and since most of the skin is tough (aside from delicata squash), it's best peeled and cut, or roasted whole and scooped. There are so many delicious fun winter squashes to eat to keep the winter from feeling too long. Some of my favorite varieties are delicata, butternut, spaghetti, kabocha, and acorn squash.

As a rule, larger squash have big seeds that I like to scoop out before cooking. Smaller squash have nice, compact seeds that can be left in for cooking. I love to use green pumpkin seeds (pepitas) to add crunch and more complex squash-y flavor to a dish. You can buy shelled green pepitas at the store. For a homemade snack, you can save the seeds from the inside of winter squash. Rinse them in a colander under cold water to remove the strings, then let dry on a towel-lined baking sheet for an hour. Toss them with olive oil and salt; you can add chile or curry powder too! Bake in the oven at 350°F for 20 to 25 minutes until golden brown, tossing every 10 minutes or so. Let cool and eat as a snack. Store in an airtight container in the pantry for up to a month.

If you're grilling squash, I suggest cutting it into rounds or, even better, long wedges, which char very nicely on the grill and intensify in flavor. Cutting into wedges also creates a backbone of sorts with the skin, so the zucchini doesn't fall apart on the grill.

Sometimes I salt and drain zucchini and sometimes I don't. If I'm using it for a filling, I drain it so it doesn't make the dish too watery. If I want to soften it ahead of cooking, I salt and drain it then too. This treatment also works before putting squash into salads to make it crunchy and delicious.

As I like to do with other veggies, I tend to grill squash dry (with no oil) so it gets charred, then finish it with super-special extra-virgin olive oil, lemon juice, and sea salt. It's dumb-easy but freakin' great. No need for fancy clothes here . . . this is like the perfect jeans and white tee of cooking!

Most often, it's best to cut winter squash in half, discard the seeds, and roast it, skin and all. Then all you have to do is scoop out the sweet flesh. When a recipe calls for diced winter squash, see if you can buy it peeled and cut at your market. If not, I highly suggest buying a strong Y-peeler for peeling that tough skin. See page 371 for a tip on cutting squash.

The Squash Squad is available year-round, always coming through. This dynamic duo of fire and ice are the superheroes of the kitchen. In a summer BBQ rut? Have no fear, Zucca Zucchini is here!

Clockwise from top left: Rob's Butternut
Squash Soup (page 364); Stuffed Delicata
Squash with Swiss Chard, Coconut Milk,
and Feta (page 365); Pumpkin Pesto
Gnocchi with Pancetta and Brussels Sprouts
(page 368); Butternut Squash Panzanella
(page 369)

This is an example of why Italians are such good cooks—they are masters at great ingredients done well. The key to this dish is making sure the zucchini is cooked enough, as al dente zucchini won't smash well. You want it soft and tender, and for those delicious zucchini juices to meld with the pecorino cheese. I like serving this for brunch with scrambled eggs or a frittata, but it's beyond tasty just spooned over toasted bread. One of my favorite ways to do lunch is to make a bunch of bruschetta and crostini and toppings like this zucchini, and serve them alongside a variety of meats and cheese and pickles so people can make their own crostini any way they like!

Smashed Baby Zucchini Bruschetta

Makes 8 bruschetta

Kosher salt

1 pound baby zucchini, cut into ¼-inch-thick coins

2 tablespoons super-special extra-virgin olive oil

1 tablespoon roughly chopped fresh mint, plus more leaves for garnish

Coarse sea salt (like Maldon)

¼ cup freshly grated Pecorino Romano, plus a little more for garnish

8 slices of ciabatta or rustic bread, grilled or toasted

1.   Bring a medium pot of water to a boil over high heat and season generously with kosher salt. This is blanching water (see page 10), and I like mine to be salty like the ocean, about 1 tablespoon of salt per quart of water. Prepare a medium bowl with ice water for shocking. Blanch the zucchini coins for 4 minutes, until soft and tender but still retaining their shape. Drain the zucchini and plunge into the ice water. Use your hands to agitate the coins in the ice water to chill the zucchini quickly. Drain in a colander for 10 minutes.

2.   In a medium bowl, toss the zucchini coins with the olive oil, mint, and a few pinches of coarse sea salt. Use an old-school potato masher to smash them until the zucchini is a spoonable consistency yet there are still visible chunks. Stir in the pecorino. Spoon the smashed zucchini over grilled or toasted bread and garnish with a few leaves of mint and more grated pecorino.

— Get It —

Baby zucchini work well here, as they are dense and their seeds are tiny. As squashes grow larger, their seeds do too, giving them a watery texture. If you can't find baby zucchini, just remove most of the seeds from a medium one.

— Get It —

The trio of zucchini, tomatoes, and onion is a winning combo, creating the perfect blend of flavor and texture. I find it much easier to grill a bunch of veggies on skewers rather than try to cook them individually on the grill. If possible, cut your veggies so the pieces are all roughly the same size. Plus, I like the way they all cook a little differently. I could eat these sesame za'atar skewers with a pile of fresh dill and a bowl of buttered steamed rice every day—yes, please!

Grilled Zucchini, Onion, and Cherry Tomato Spiedini

(Italian-Style Kebabs)

Serves 6

6 medium zucchini (about 2 pounds), cut into roughly 1- to 1¼-inch-thick coins

1 medium red onion, cut into 1- to 1¼-inch-wide petals (see Get It Get It)

12 ounces cherry tomatoes

Kosher salt

2 tablespoons everyday olive oil, plus more for drizzling

3 tablespoons Sesame Za'atar (page 395) or store-bought green za'atar

3 tablespoons super-special extra-virgin olive oil

1 tablespoon finely grated lemon zest (use a Microplane)

2 tablespoons fresh lemon juice

2 tablespoons lightly chopped fresh dill, plus more sprigs for garnish (I like to go heavy with the dill for garnishing)

1.   In a large bowl, toss the zucchini, onion, and tomatoes with a few generous pinches of kosher salt and the everyday olive oil. Using six 12-inch metal or soaked bamboo skewers (see page 295), alternate the veggies on the skewers. I find it easiest to skewer the zucchini right through the seeds, but if you have used big zucchini, try to skewer through the skin so the zucchini holds together on the grill.

2.   In a small bowl, combine the za'atar with the super-special extra-virgin olive oil, lemon zest and juice, chopped dill, and a few pinches of salt.

3.   Preheat a grill to high (500° to 600°F). Drizzle the skewers of vegetables with a bit more everyday olive oil and season generously with salt. Grill until seared and charred on the bottom, 7 to 8 minutes. (Resist the urge to flip them!) Flip and turn the skewers and cook for another 6 to 7 minutes, until everything is blistered and charred. Transfer to a serving platter. Drizzle with the sesame za'atar dressing and top with fresh dill sprigs. If you're serving family style, remove the charred veggies from the skewers and toss in a serving bowl with the sesame za'atar dressing.

Get It

I love grilled onions, which get deliciously charred on the outside with a crispy, delicate crunch of sweet onion in the interior. I find cutting them into ½-inch-thick rings works well for grilling most of the time, but if I am skewering them, petals are the only way to go. To cut onion petals, I first remove the larger outer layers of the onion and cut them into my desired size. Then I attack the center smaller heart of the onion, cutting it in half or thirds.

Get It

There are so many different ways that I can think of to eat squash blossoms! For those who are unfamiliar, squash blossoms are the edible flowers from squash plants, and are ideal for stuffing and cooking. At Monteverde I tempura-fry them, but at home I just bake them with breadcrumbs for that same crunch but with much less effort and cleanup. What many people don't know is that the blossoms come from both summer and winter squash, so they're available more often than you might realize. I still tend to think of them as the ultimate summer treat though. I like using larger blossoms for stuffing, but if you can only find the small ones, buy twice as many! Any leftover petals can be used in salads or scrambled eggs.

Baked Ricotta-Stuffed Squash Blossoms

Serves 4 to 6 as an appetizer

1 cup Homemade Lemon Ricotta (page 173) or whole milk ricotta (see page 8)

½ cup freshly grated Pecorino Romano

1 teaspoon dried oregano (preferably wild Calabrian)

1 teaspoon finely grated lemon zest

½ garlic clove, finely grated

Kosher salt

1 dozen large squash blossoms or 2 dozen smaller blossoms (See Get It Get It)

½ cup panko (Japanese breadcrumbs)

2 tablespoons everyday olive oil, plus a bit for oiling the pan

1 tablespoon chopped fresh flat-leaf parsley

Lemon wedges, for serving

1. In a medium bowl, fold the ricotta and pecorino with the oregano, lemon zest, garlic, and a pinch or two of salt. Place the filling in a pastry bag and cut the small end of the bag to pipe. Gently open a squash blossom enough to fit the tip of the pastry bag into the blossom. Squeeze the pastry bag, filling the blossom with the ricotta mixture. Be careful not to overfill the blossom. Once filled, twist the tops of the blossom to seal. Repeat with the remaining filling and blossoms.

2. Preheat the oven to 425°F and position the top oven rack 7 to 8 inches from the broiler. In a small bowl, combine the panko with the olive oil, chopped parsley, and a few pinches of salt. Lightly oil a small cast-iron skillet or flameproof casserole dish. Sprinkle half of the breadcrumbs in the pan and arrange the filled blossoms on top. Top with the remaining breadcrumbs. Bake for 10 minutes on the middle rack in the oven. The blossoms should begin to soften, a bit of the cheese should become slightly oozy, and the breadcrumbs will begin to turn golden brown.

3. Turn the broiler to high. Carefully move the pan to the top rack and broil for 1 minute to gratinée the breadcrumbs and blossoms. Serve with the lemon wedges.

Get It

This is a pretty simple filling, but it is just the beginning of what it can be. You can substitute Parmigiano, feta, fresh goat cheese, Fontina, or smoked mozzarella for the pecorino, and burrata for the ricotta. Minced anchovy (which is very traditional) or fresh herbs are great additions, and a real treat too! The key is to choose something that will pair well with the delicate squash flavor.

Look for blossoms with baby squash attached or just the blossom, either way works. If you can't find blossoms with the squash still attached, you can cut a baby zucchini into thin wedges and add it to the pan before you arrange the blossoms in it.

Don't own a pastry bag? You can place the filling in a large resealable plastic bag and snip off one corner of the bag with scissors. Voilà!

Get It

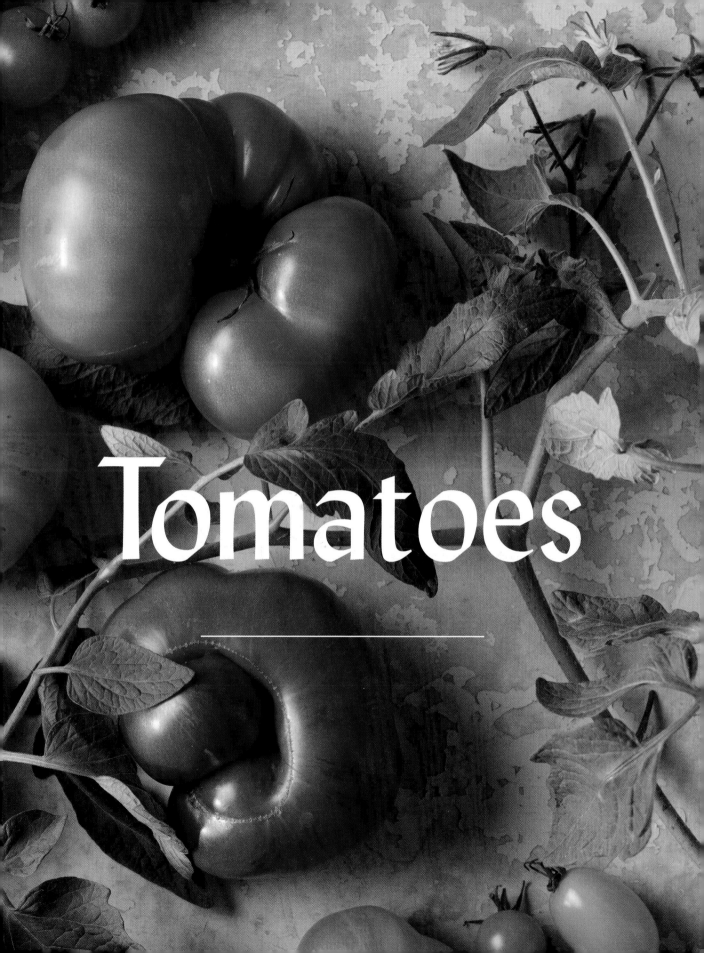

Tomatoes

Tomatoes might be my favorite thing to cook with, though they're the one thing I despised eating as a child. Even now, I can't stand an underripe slice of tomato on my burger or sandwich. My family liked eating tomatoes sprinkled with sugar, which I think is an old Southern thing, and probably took a mediocre tomato to a far better place, but I still didn't like them. But as an adult, I have seen the light. Nothing beats a perfectly ripe, juicy, sweet-tart, bursting-with-flavor tomato. I think if you wanted to taste the sun, a tomato is the way to do it. Have you ever tried a perfect Sungold cherry tomato? Now that's what I'm talking about!

Tomatoes could be the most important vegetable in Italian cooking. (Because they have seeds, tomatoes are actually a fruit, but they're most often utilized like a vegetable.) If tomatoes aren't the star of the dish, then they are playing key supporting roles that elevate the ensemble around them. What would Italian food look like if there were no tomatoes? The answer: Totally different from what it is today. Southern Italy's climate and volcanic soil are prime for growing tomatoes, and it has become quite an industry. Southern Italian cuisine is based on the mighty tomato! Think about some of the most iconic Italian dishes—Caprese salad, margherita pizza, spaghetti al pomodoro, marinara sauce—that are centered on the tomato.

We are blessed with the technology of greenhouse and hydroponic year-round tomato farming, providing us with decent fresh tomatoes most of the year. Those cherry, teardrop, grape, cocktail, and Kumato tomatoes that you see in clamshell boxes at the market are usually pretty good. I like keeping them around for sautés, scrambled eggs, salads, and pasta. But please, don't confuse them with the perfect summer tomato that ripens on the vine in the hot sun. *Those* tomatoes are hard to beat; they're best eaten sliced, drizzled with extra-virgin olive oil and sprinkled with sea salt.

When you are grating tomatoes for a sauce, look to beefsteak, roma, or vine-ripened tomatoes, where it's not so much about the sweetness but about the acidity. And no matter what, heirloom tomatoes can be used anytime a recipe calls for a fresh tomato.

Canned tomato land is a little more confusing. I'm not a fan of some canned tomato products. Canned diced tomatoes are full of flavorless water, and tomato puree often tastes like watery tomato paste. The best quality canned tomato product you can buy is whole peeled tomatoes, which have a thick sauce. I also like tomato passata (pulpy crushed uncooked tomatoes that have been strained of seeds and skin), an Italian product sold in glass jars. If you can't find tomato passata, you can use tomato puree or make your own: Pulse a can of whole peeled tomatoes in the food processor or food mill until crushed. One note about most canned tomatoes is that they want to be fried. This gets the canned flavor out and morphs the tomatoes into something robust and rich, creating a terrific layer of flavor.

Not to be forgotten are delicious sun-dried or oven-dried tomatoes, which add a punch of sweet, bright acidity without any water.

One final thing that must be said: Never, ever refrigerate your fresh tomatoes, which ruins the texture and flavor. They're very happy hanging out right on your kitchen counter!

Tomatoes are the garden loungers, loving to bask in the sun all day long. Ripen on the vine? Yes, please. Wanna taste the sun? Eat a tomato.

Clockwise from top left: Grecian Tomato Salad with Tomato-Oregano Vinaigrette (page 383), Soppressata Meatballs Stewed in Oven-Roasted Tomato Sauce (page 407), Hand-Grated Tomato Bruschetta (page 390), Sauce-Simmered Spaghetti al Pomodoro with Sesame Za'atar (page 395), Tomato-Almond Pesto (page 394)

I love a good Bloody Mary, but I often find prepared Bloody Mary mixes so unrefreshing. They're too thick, and they taste heavy and salty. Now, on the other hand, I love the fresh grilled tomato flavor in these Bloody Marys, and I end up feeling a little bit more virtuous after drinking them. I know the garnish game can get out of control, but I'm a bit of a purist and I like sticking with celery, olives, citrus, and a little sprig of fresh dill. But man, go to town if you want! Add chilled shrimp, mozzarella, salumi, pepperoncino—whatever you are feeling works with your Bloody Mary. I think it's easiest to make this in a pitcher and give it a good stir before pouring into glasses. You can add a vodka topper too . . . I won't be mad about it.

Grilled Tomato Bloody Mary

Serves 6

2 pounds ripe tomatoes

Kosher salt

6 ounces vodka

1 ounce Averna or Nardini Amaro

¼ cup Worcestershire sauce

¼ cup dill pickle juice

2 tablespoons olive juice

2 tablespoons fresh lemon juice

1 tablespoon hot sauce (preferably Crystal Hot Sauce)

1 teaspoon colatura or Vietnamese fish sauce (optional)

6 dashes Tabasco sauce

Fresh cracked black pepper

1 cup ice, plus more for filling the glasses

1 lemon wedge, for the rims

Celery salt or steak salt for the rim (optional)

Garnish Action

6 celery stalks (from the heart)

1 lemon, cut into wedges

1 lime, cut into wedges

12 Castelvetrano or other green olives

6 fresh dill sprigs

1. Preheat a grill to high. Grill the tomatoes directly on the hot grill grates until the skins are charred and the juices begin to pop out, 10 to 12 minutes. Don't have a grill? No problem, you can easily char the tomatoes under your broiler. Place the tomatoes on a foil-lined baking sheet 3 to 4 inches from the heat source. Broil for 4 to 5 minutes, rotating every minute or so, until blistered and softened.

2. Transfer the tomatoes to a blender with a few pinches of kosher salt. Blend on high until smooth. (You should have a little more than 4 cups of blended tomato juice.) Transfer to an airtight container and refrigerate until chilled.

3. In a large pitcher or mixing glass or jar, combine the grilled tomato juice, vodka, Averna, Worcestershire, pickle juice, olive juice, lemon juice, hot sauce, colatura (if using), Tabasco, and a few cracks of black pepper. Add 1 cup of ice and stir well to combine.

4. Rub a lemon wedge around the rim of 6 tall drink glasses and sprinkle the rims with your preferred seasoning or kosher salt. Fill the glasses with ice and pour the Bloody Mary over the top. Garnish each with a celery stalk, lemon wedge, lime wedge, 2 olives, and a dill sprig.

Get It

I recommend grilling the tomatoes a day ahead so the tomato juice has time to chill down fully. If you are planning to grill for dinner the night before, just put the tomatoes on to char while you prepare dinner. Voilà! Brunch is in the works.

If you want extra spice or kick, feel free to add a bit of prepared horseradish.

Get It

Listen to Your Vegetables

A few years back I went on a cruise through the Adriatic with the James Beard Foundation, which included a stop in Corfu, Greece. I had the most delicious Greek salads there, and I was enlightened by the fact that they're made with only the crunchy veggies—no lettuce at all! I also loved the inclusion of green bell pepper—a veggie I don't typically love, but in the salad, it added an amazing green, grassy flavor. This is just the most perfect salad on a summer day. After you've devoured every bite, there will be lots of tangy tomato vinaigrette in the bottom of the bowl. Do not throw that away! Take shots of this delicious tonic, or serve it with crusty bread to soak up all of the yumminess.

Grecian Tomato Salad

with Tomato-Oregano Vinaigrette

Serves 4 to 6

1 pound heirloom tomatoes, cut into thick wedges

1 pint cherry tomatoes, halved

1 seedless cucumber, peeled, sliced lengthwise, then sliced into ½-inch half-moons

1 small green bell pepper, cored, seeded, and cut into ¼-inch pieces

½ small red onion, thinly sliced

One 7-ounce block sheep's milk feta, cut into ½-inch pieces

½ cup pitted kalamata olives

2 tablespoons drained capers

Coarse sea salt (like Maldon)

Tomato-Oregano Vinaigrette (recipe follows)

Several handfuls of fresh herbs, for garnish (I love dill and parsley, as well as basil, oregano, and mint)

2 tablespoons super-special extra-virgin olive oil, for drizzling

Fresh cracked black pepper

1.　In a large salad bowl, combine the tomatoes, cucumbers, bell pepper, onion, feta, olives, and capers. Toss with a few pinches of coarse sea salt, then let sit for 5 minutes or for up to 30 minutes.

2.　Add the vinaigrette and gently toss, being careful to not mash up the veggies. Top with fresh herbs and drizzle with the olive oil. Finish with fresh cracked black pepper. If you want to make this salad in advance, layer the veggies in a bowl, then toss with the vinaigrette to serve.

Tomato-Oregano Vinaigrette

Makes about 1 cup

1 medium vine-ripened or heirloom tomato, halved and grated on the large holes of a box grater (½ cup)

2 tablespoons red wine vinegar

2 tablespoons fresh lemon juice

2 teaspoons dried oregano (preferably wild Calabrian, Greek, or Mexican)

¼ cup everyday olive oil

Coarse sea salt (like Maldon)

In a large measuring cup or a medium bowl, whisk the grated tomato with the vinegar, lemon juice, oregano, and olive oil. Season with a few generous pinches of sea salt. Stir well. You can use the vinaigrette right away or keep it in the fridge for a few hours.

── Get It ──

Feeling frisky? Add some *boquerones* (delicious marinated white anchovies from Spain) to this salad for an extra umami bite.

When buying feta cheese, look for one made with sheep's or goat's milk. I like French or Bulgarian feta, if I can find it!

Get It ──

Like ribollita, this is a great Tuscan soup that uses leftover or stale bread from the kitchen to create a soulful bowl of love. This is my go-to recipe for tomato soup, which I think is just perfect as is. The bread adds an entirely different texture and heartiness than you'll find in ordinary tomato soup, and I especially like toasting it first for an additional level of flavor. I bet this beats the pants off of any tomato soup you've ever had!

Pappa al Pomodoro

aka Tomato-Bread Soup

Makes about 8 cups; serves 6 to 8

4 tablespoons everyday olive oil, plus more for drizzling

1 large yellow onion, diced

6 garlic cloves, halved

2 dried bay leaves

¼ teaspoon chile flake

Kosher salt

Three 28-ounce cans whole peeled tomatoes

2 Parmigiano-Reggiano rinds (2- to 3-inch squares)

8 ounces Italian- or French-style bread, roughly cut into 1-inch cubes

½ cup freshly grated Parmigiano-Reggiano

Fresh basil leaves, for garnish

Fresh cracked black pepper

1. Heat a heavy-bottomed stainless-steel or enameled cast-iron pot over medium-high heat. Add 3 tablespoons of the olive oil along with the onion and garlic. Stir and cook until the onions are translucent and beginning to brown around the edges, about 5 minutes. Add the bay leaves and chile flake and season with a pinch of salt. Stir in the tomatoes and bring to a boil. Season with two generous pinches of salt and nestle the parm rinds into the tomatoes. Reduce the heat to low, cover, and cook for 1 hour, stirring halfway through. Make sure the soup is at a simmer and that the rinds are not sticking to the bottom of the pot.

2. Uncover the soup and stir in 2 cups of water. Stir well and remove from the heat. Let stand for 15 minutes to cool slightly. Discard the bay leaves and parm rinds, taste, and season with a few more generous pinches of salt.

3. Meanwhile, preheat the oven to 350°F. On a large rimmed baking sheet, toss the bread with the remaining 1 tablespoon of olive oil. Bake until golden and toasted, 30 to 40 minutes.

4. Working in two batches (do not fill the blender more than halfway), carefully blend the soup on high speed until smooth. (It's best to leave the lid slightly open and to cover the top with a kitchen towel while blending.) Transfer the pureed soup to a clean pot, then bring to a simmer over medium heat. Fold the toasted bread into the soup and cook, stirring occasionally, until the bread has softened and is beginning to break up, about 20 minutes. The soup will thicken as the bread softens and absorbs the soup. Adjust the texture to your liking by adding water to loosen the soup further. Serve topped with a healthy drizzle of olive oil, the grated parm, and some fresh basil and cracked black pepper.

— Get It —

Feel free to use chicken or vegetable stock in place of the water.

— Get It —

There's something so rewarding about great heirloom tomatoes in season. When they're thickly cut, they so nicely handle the coarse salt, crunchy bacon, and creamy blue cheese here. All of these flavors remind me of a steakhouse-style wedge salad, and in fact, this would be super delicious alongside a grilled steak. If you don't like blue cheese, feel free to sub fresh goat cheese or another creamy cheese to balance the bacon and fresh herbs. You can also add some bitter greens like endive, arugula, or dandelion to make this even more of a main-course salad.

Thick-Cut Tomato Salad

with Blue Cheese, Bacon, and Balsamic Onion Vinaigrette

Serves 6 to 8

Balsamic Onion Vinaigrette
  (page 369)

1½ to 2 pounds heirloom
  tomatoes, cut into 1- to 1½-inch
  slices

Coarse sea salt (like Maldon)

4 to 6 slices of crisply cooked
  bacon (6 ounces uncooked)

3 ounces blue cheese (preferably
  buttermilk blue)

½ cup fresh basil leaves

¼ cup fresh dill sprigs

1 tablespoon toasted sesame seeds

Fresh cracked black pepper

On a large platter, spoon half of the balsamic onions. Top with the tomatoes and season with a few pinches of coarse salt. Top with the bacon, blue cheese, basil, and dill. Spoon the remaining vinaigrette on top. Finish the salad with sesame seeds and fresh cracked pepper.

— Get It

I like to buy pretoasted sesame seeds, but if you can't find them, just toast a thin layer in a 225°F oven for about 5 minutes—watch them, as they brown quickly.

I'm a huge fan of sesame grinders, which you often see when you go to ramen shops. If you can get one, it's a great tool to have on hand, filled with toasted sesame seeds. Freshly ground sesame adds a terrific nutty layer of flavor to all kinds of dishes.

The balsamic onion vinaigrette is great here. If you are feeling a bit naughty, use some of the bacon drippings from the cooked bacon in place of the olive oil when making the onions.

Get It —

This is the *ultimate* pasta salad that can be used for picnics, parties, dinners at home . . . you name it. I first tried a version of this when my friend's mom, Peggy McNally, made it, and I was instantly obsessed. Peggy makes hers with spaghetti, but I prefer a short noodle. The beauty of this dish is that the cheese melts slowly when you add the hot pasta to the bowl, and the slow marinating allows the pasta to absorb all of the delicious tomato flavor.

Tomato-Basil Pasta Fredda

Serves 8 as a side dish

Fresh Tomato Sauce (page 391)

1 pint cherry or grape tomatoes, halved

2 tablespoons everyday olive oil

4 ounces Brie, Camembert, or triple crème cheese, cut into large chunks (rind is okay, but totally up to you!)

4 ounces sheep's milk feta, crumbled

1 tablespoon finely grated lemon zest (use a Microplane)

2 tablespoons fresh lemon juice

Coarse sea salt (like Maldon)

Kosher salt

1 pound dry small-shape pasta (gnocchetti, malloreddus, shells, or orecchiette)

1 cup tightly packed fresh basil leaves, torn, plus a few leaves for garnish

¼ cup toasted pine nuts, for garnish

1. In a large bowl, combine the tomato sauce, cherry tomatoes, olive oil, Brie, feta, lemon zest, and lemon juice with 2 pinches of sea salt. Toss gently to mix, then check for seasoning.

2. Bring a large pot of water to a boil and season well with kosher salt. Boil the pasta for 3 minutes less than the package directions specify for al dente. Drain the pasta in a colander and shake well to rid it of any excess water. Immediately add the hot pasta to the bowl with the tomato mixture. Stir to combine, then cover well with plastic wrap. Let marinate for at least 1 hour or overnight. Come by and shake the bowl a few times to mix while marinating.

3. When you are ready to serve, add the fresh basil and toss. Top the pasta with pine nuts and a few additional basil leaves before serving.

Get It

This pasta salad can be chilled for several hours and then served at room temperature. It's excellent to make it in the afternoon so it's ready for dinner.

To dress it up even more, I have been known to serve it with dollops of Genovese Pesto (page 240) and/or toasted breadcrumbs.

Get It

In Italy, this raw tomato dish is known as *salsa cruda*. Making it is so simple—you combine grated fresh tomatoes with extra-virgin olive oil and sea salt, spoon that over grilled bread and top it with fresh herbs. It sings! Sometimes I'll grill up a whole lot of bread and set the slices out with a bunch of different toppings for people to make their own crostini and bruschetta, and I always make sure that this is on the table. Lindsay Autry, my good friend and fellow contestant on *Top Chef*, taught me the technique of grating tomatoes while we were on the show together—she made a simple dinner for us at home one night using rice and grated tomato. This technique is common in Spain, especially when making *pan con tomate* (tomato bread), and it inspired me to make the most delicious fresh tomato sauce during the heart of tomato season. Grating the tomatoes creates a perfect texture, and their flavor really shines.

Hand-Grated Tomato Bruschetta

Makes 8 to 10 bruschetta

1 pound fresh ripe tomatoes (heirloom and vine-ripened are great options!), halved crosswise

Coarse sea salt (like Maldon)

1 tablespoon everyday olive oil, plus more for drizzling

8 to 10 slices of ciabatta bread (1 inch thick)

1 garlic clove

Fresh basil leaves, for garnish

1. On the large holes of a box grater or using a large-holed hand grater, working over a bowl, grate the tomatoes down to the peel. (Discard the tomato peels or save for a future stock.) Season the grated tomatoes with 2 to 3 generous pinches of salt. Stir in the olive oil.

2. When you are ready to serve, turn the broiler to high. Place the bread slices about 3 inches from the heat source and toast until the edges are slightly charred, 2 to 3 minutes per side. (If you have a grill pan or a grill, grill the bread without oil, so that you can get a good char without any burnt oil flavor.) Rub the bread with the garlic and spoon the grated tomato on top. Tear the basil leaves and place on top of the bruschetta. Drizzle with a little olive oil, sprinkle with a pinch of sea salt, and serve.

Pickled Green Tomatoes

While I love green tomatoes, they're not so easy to find. If you see some, grab them while you can! Green tomatoes are just red tomatoes that have been picked off the vine before they've had time to ripen. One of my favorite ways to treat green tomatoes is to make a giardiniera with them, like in the Pickled Cauliflower Giardiniera on page 98. The only difference is in the pickling part, where I omit the fennel seeds and add 1 tablespoon of ground turmeric and 1 teaspoon of celery seeds. When tomatoes are pickled like this, they're super delicious on seafood, in a chutney or a salad, or in a sandwich (especially a po' boy or the cornmeal fried fish on page 129). I also love them breaded and fried—the traditional way to eat a green tomato in the American South. The rule with green tomatoes is that they either need a little heat, or they need salt and sugar—and then, well, the sky is the limit!

— Get It —

This makes an incredible base for other toast toppings like burrata, mozzarella, or Manchego cheese, grilled or marinated vegetables, and cured meats and prosciutto.

— Get It —

This tomato sauce captures the true flavor of tomato season, yielding a sauce that's as bright as the sun. It's a perfect balance of sweetness and tang, and I like using it wherever I crave a light tomato sauce. The fresh tomato flavor makes it ideal for vegetables and light pastas, as well as in dishes like my Whole Bird Chicken Parm (page 402), Pallotte Verdi (page 199), and Tomato-Basil Pasta Fredda (page 388). I use it on crostini too, and wherever I like using diced tomatoes because it has a similar fresh flavor.

Fresh Tomato Sauce

Makes about 3½ cups

2 tablespoons everyday olive oil

1 garlic clove, thinly sliced

3 pounds fresh, ripe tomatoes, quartered

Kosher salt

2 heaping tablespoons roughly torn fresh basil leaves

1.   Heat a medium saucepan over high heat. Add the olive oil and allow to heat for 30 seconds, then add the garlic. Let cook until lightly golden, about 30 seconds. Add the tomatoes and bring to a medium boil over high heat, stirring often. Season with a few generous pinches of salt. Simmer until the tomatoes begin to soften and break down, 3 to 4 minutes. Reduce the heat to medium and simmer for 20 minutes, stirring occasionally and watching as the color turns from red to orange.

2.   Remove from the heat. Stir in the basil and taste for seasoning, adding another pinch or two of salt. Let cool for 10 to 15 minutes, then transfer the tomato sauce to a food processor and process until slightly smooth and combined, about 15 seconds. Refrigerate or freeze until you're ready to use it.

Get It

I love to save any tomatoes that may be bruised or are becoming too soft, as well as the trimmings and leftovers I have from slicing tomatoes for a sandwich or salad. I just plop them (whole or sliced) in the fridge for up to 3 days or so until I'm ready to make sauce. I also put them in the freezer so they're ready for when I want that fresh tomato flavor, then I thaw them and make sauce. I've used a mixture of cherry tomatoes and heirloom tomatoes in this sauce—whatever mix you use, just make sure the tomatoes are ripe. The key is to toast the garlic and cook down the fresh tomatoes, caramelizing their flavor.

Get It

I created this recipe to replace tomato sauce that cooks all day on the stovetop, which is often the way traditional Italian households do it. An all-day sauce is amazing, but it (obviously) takes a long time and can create a big mess. This version saves time in both cooking and cleaning—something everyone can use to make cooking more fun. The key to achieving the rich flavor comes from the cooking method. By drizzling the olive oil over the tomatoes and not stirring it in, the top layer of tomatoes gets some nice caramelization in the oven—it's kind of like a cheater way of frying them. I also use a Microplane zester to grate the garlic, imparting just the right amount of garlic flavor. I like to use this sauce in hearty meat dishes, like my Soppressata Meatballs Stewed in Oven-Roasted Tomato Sauce (page 392), and in less-meat-centric dishes too, like my Roman-Style Eggplant Parmigiana (page 149) and Sauce-Simmered Spaghetti al Pomodoro with Sesame Za'atar (page 395).

Oven-Roasted Tomato Sauce

Makes 8 cups

3 tablespoons everyday olive oil

Three 28-ounce cans whole peeled tomatoes (preferably San Marzano; see Get It Get It)

2 garlic cloves

2 dried bay leaves

2 teaspoons kosher salt

1 teaspoon dried oregano (preferably wild Calabrian)

1 teaspoon fennel seeds

2 handfuls of torn fresh basil leaves

— Get It —

I like using imported whole peeled Italian tomatoes for this recipe, specifically San Marzano, which are grown in volcanic soil and have more flavor because of it. I find canned San Marzano tomatoes are less watery and more flavorful than other canned tomato products.

This sauce is rich and robust and chock-full of chunky crushed tomatoes. If you are wanting a smoother sauce, feel free to sub 3 cans of crushed tomatoes or blend the sauce in a blender or food processor until smooth.

— Get It —

1.   Preheat the oven to 425°F. Pour 1 tablespoon of the oil into the bottom of a 9 by 13-inch flameproof baking dish; rub it all over the bottom and sides of the dish. Pour in the canned tomatoes. Using your hands, crush them; remove any skin that may be stuck to them. Using a Microplane, grate the garlic cloves over the top of the tomatoes. Stir in the bay leaves, salt, oregano, fennel seeds, and basil. Add the remaining 2 tablespoons of olive oil and let it sit on top of the mixture; do not mix it in. Bake for 1 hour.

2.   Turn the broiler to high and place the tomatoes about 2 inches from the heat source. Allow them to char slightly on top, for about 5 minutes. Let cool, then discard the bay leaves. Transfer the sauce to an airtight container and keep for up to 1 week in the refrigerator or up to 2 months in the freezer.

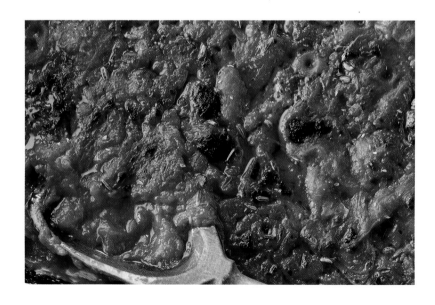

At Monteverde, we fondly call these little sweet-tart bursts of summer "ODTs." They bring a sweet burst of brightness and acidity to any number of dishes, from pasta, pizza, and toasts to salads, egg dishes, roasted veggies, seafood, and meats. Anyone who has ever grown cherry tomatoes knows just how abundant they can be at certain times of year, and this is an excellent way to make use of that abundance. Just remember: Low and slow is the best way to go when cooking these.

Oven-Dried Cherry Tomatoes

Makes about 1 cup

1 tablespoon plus ½ teaspoon everyday olive oil

1 pint cherry tomatoes, halved crosswise (we call that hamburger-style!)

Kosher salt

Preheat the oven to 275°F. Line a baking sheet with parchment paper or a silicone baking mat (like a Silpat). Using your hands, rub the ½ teaspoon of oil all over the prepared baking sheet. Arrange the tomatoes cut side up on the sheet. Drizzle with the remaining olive oil and season each tomato lightly with salt. Bake for 2½ to 3 hours, until the tomatoes are dried and shriveled. I check on them every hour for the first two, and then more often in the last stage of drying. Some tomatoes will dry faster due to their size or water content. Remove those to a plate while the rest are roasting. Once all the tomatoes are dried and shriveled, remove from the oven and allow to cool. If not using immediately, refrigerate the tomatoes in an airtight container for up to 3 days.

Get It

To preserve the tomatoes, transfer the cooled tomatoes to a jar or airtight container. Mix ½ cup of everyday olive oil with 1 teaspoon of dried oregano. Pour the oil over the tomatoes to cover. Keep refrigerated for up to 1 month.

These are perfect on the Hand-Grated Tomato Bruschetta (page 390). The tomatoes and their oil are also killer on the Olive Oil–Soaked Bread Fett'unta with Cherry Tomatoes and Basil (page 239).

Get It

I LOVE THIS PESTO. It is unlike the other pestos in this book, as it is vegan. This is known as pesto alla Trapanese, which comes from Sicily, where the best almonds are grown. Traditionally, it's tossed with a Sicilian strand pasta called busiate, but you can also sub bucatini or spaghetti. It brings a beautiful burst of texture, acidity, and brightness to so many things, from grilled bread and mozzarella to fish and shellfish.

Tomato-Almond Pesto

Makes 1½ cups

1 cup cherry tomatoes, halved

½ cup slivered almonds, toasted

½ cup sun-dried tomatoes packed in oil, drained (you can also use the Oven-Dried Cherry Tomatoes on page 393)

1 teaspoon finely grated lemon zest (use a Microplane)

1 tablespoon fresh lemon juice

¼ cup roughly chopped fresh flat-leaf parsley

¼ cup torn fresh basil leaves

Kosher salt

¼ cup everyday olive oil (feel free to use the oil from the sun-dried tomatoes)

In a food processor, pulse the cherry tomatoes, almonds, sun-dried tomatoes, lemon zest, lemon juice, parsley, basil, and a few pinches of salt until coarsely chopped. While the machine is running, drizzle in the olive oil and blend until combined. Alternatively, in a large, heavy granite or marble mortar, using a pestle, firmly smash the almonds and tomatoes with the lemon zest and lemon juice, twisting the pestle around the bottom in a circular motion every 15 to 20 seconds. Add the herbs and a few pinches of salt and continue smashing and twisting until softened. Once the ingredients are softened, continue to work them in a circular motion for about 1 minute, until the nuts are crushed and a coarse paste has formed. Drizzle in the everyday olive oil and combine the ingredients using both the smashing and circular motions with the pestle. Please note that you may want to loosen the mixture from the sides every now and then with a small spoon. The pesto can be refrigerated in an airtight container for up to 1 week.

This pasta is really special. I learned to make it at Nadia Santini's three-star restaurant, Dal Pescatore, in Lombardy. It is the perfect version of five ingredients done well. To me it embodies the beauty of the pasta marriage ceremony because the pasta cooks in the pomodoro sauce and pasta water, absorbing all of that incredible flavor. It's like an extended wedding, if you will. To read my full *aha* moment behind the pasta marriage ceremony, see page 401.

Sauce-Simmered Spaghetti al Pomodoro

with Sesame Za'atar

Serves 4 to 6

Kosher salt

1 pound dry spaghetti

1 tablespoon everyday olive oil

1 large garlic clove, thinly sliced

6 cups Oven-Roasted Tomato Sauce (page 392)

1 cup fresh basil leaves

Super-special extra-virgin olive oil, for drizzling

Sesame Za'atar, for finishing (recipe follows; optional)

1. Bring a large pot of water to a boil and season it delicately with kosher salt, as you will use a good amount of the pasta water in the sauce. Add the spaghetti and cook the pasta only halfway in the water; if the package says 10 minutes for al dente, then cook the spaghetti for 5 minutes. Do not drain.

2. Meanwhile, in a large saucepan, heat the olive oil over medium heat. Add the garlic and toast for 1 minute, or until golden brown. Add the tomato sauce and warm through. Add ½ cup of the pasta cooking water and, using tongs, transfer the pasta to the saucepan. Using a rubber spatula, stir the pasta with the sauce often to prevent sticking. Continue to cook over medium heat for 10 minutes, or until the pasta is al dente and has absorbed most of the sauce. Finish with fresh basil leaves. Serve with a drizzle of super-special olive oil, and sprinkle some za'atar over the top, if you like.

Sesame Za'atar

Inspired by the za'atars (spice blends made with sesame seeds) of the Middle East, this za'atar seasoning is full of yummy deliciousness. It's balanced with nuttiness from the sesame and bright acidity from the sumac and citrus zest, then rounded out by the fresh green herbs. Of course the chef in me likes to use it to jazz up the spaghetti, but it's truly optional.

Makes a little more than ½ cup

¼ cup toasted sesame seeds

1 tablespoon dried oregano

1 tablespoon fresh thyme leaves

1 tablespoon fresh sage leaves, lightly chopped

1 tablespoon fresh rosemary leaves, lightly chopped

1 tablespoon ground sumac

Finely grated zest of ½ orange

Place all the ingredients in a mortar and use a pestle to press and crush until well combined. You can also finely chop the herbs and mix everything in a bowl. The za'atar will keep in an airtight container in the fridge for up to 1 month.

Get It

I like to have toasted
breadcrumbs in my pantry
to garnish salads and pasta.
I love the extra crunch the
breadcrumbs add to this
pasta too. In a nonstick skillet
over medium heat, toast
1 cup of panko or coarse dry
breadcrumbs (from Italian-style
bread) with 1 tablespoon of
olive oil, stirring, until golden
brown, 3 to 4 minutes. Season
with a pinch or two of salt. Let
cool, then store in an airtight
container for up to 2 months.

Tomato passata is simply
uncooked tomato puree or pulp
that has been strained of seeds
and skins. It's available in jars in
most grocery stores, but if you
can't find it, you can substitute
tomato puree.

Get It

I like this sauce with seafood, and you can use it to spice up your chicken parm sandwich. Angel hair is tender, so it doesn't want to be tossed a lot in the wok. This is just so delicious that I crave it constantly. If you want, you can omit the shrimp here with no negative effect. This arrabbiata can be made vegetarian by omitting Step 2 and reducing the canola to 2 tablespoons.

Wok-Fried Arrabbiata

with Angel Hair Pasta and Shrimp

Serves 4

One 28-ounce can crushed tomatoes (preferably Italian passata or strained tomatoes)

½ cup tomato paste

1 cup cherry tomatoes, halved

1 cup fresh basil leaves

½ cup fresh flat-leaf parsley leaves, plus 2 tablespoons chopped fresh flat-leaf parsley

2 tablespoons Super-Toasted Chile-Garlic Oil (page 251), plus more for drizzling

Finely grated zest of 1 lemon (use a Microplane)

2 tablespoons fresh lemon juice

Kosher salt

3 tablespoons canola or other neutral oil

1 pound medium Gulf or wild-caught shrimp, peeled and deveined

1 small red onion, minced

1 pound dry angel hair pasta

½ cup toasted breadcrumbs (see Get It Get It)

1.   In a large bowl, stir together the crushed tomatoes, tomato paste, cherry tomatoes, basil, parsley leaves, chile-garlic oil, lemon zest, and lemon juice, and season with a generous pinch or two of salt. Set aside.

2.   Bring a large pot of water to a boil and season heavily with salt. Meanwhile, heat a wok over high heat. Add 1 tablespoon of the canola oil and the shrimp, season with salt, and stir-fry for 1 minute, or until partially cooked. Transfer to a bowl or plate.

3.   If necessary, reheat the wok until it starts to smoke, about 1 minute (and turn your exhaust fan to high ☺). Add the remaining 2 tablespoons of canola oil in a swirling motion to coat the sides of the wok. Add the onion and using a spoon or spatula, stir-fry until slightly golden, about 1 minute. Add half of the tomato mixture and stir-fry, pushing the tomato mixture up the sides of the wok. Let it fry and sizzle for about 3 minutes, until the color turns brick red and the sauce is caramelized. It's important to keep stirring to prevent burning. Add the remaining tomato mixture and stir-fry until thickened and the whole mixture is deepened in color and flavor, 3 to 4 minutes. Remove from the heat. Taste and season with another pinch or two of salt, if desired.

4.   Add the angel hair pasta to the boiling water and cook until al dente, following the package instructions. Before draining, reserve ½ cup of the pasta cooking water. Drain and add the pasta and the reserved pasta water back to the large pot. Set the pot over medium-high heat. Add the cooked arrabbiata sauce and shrimp. Toss well to coat.

5.   Divide the pasta into four bowls, spooning any remaining sauce and shrimp over the pasta. Top with the breadcrumbs and chopped parsley. Serve additional chile-garlic oil on the side, so guests can spice it up even more.

Baking sweet cherry tomatoes with olives, olive oil, and herbs is a great way to showcase tomatoes. Baking releases the juices into the olive oil, creating a tasty sauce, then broiling the tomatoes chars the skins for even more flavor. I think they are a perfect match for these luscious ricotta ravioli, which I learned to make in Sicily. I like sprinkling toasted pistachios over this for crunch and flavor, but you can totally opt out. If you can't find marjoram, mint, basil, or oregano are all equally good here.

Ricotta Ravioli

with Confit Cherry Tomatoes and Marjoram

Serves 4 to 6

Ravioli

1½ cups Homemade Lemon Ricotta (page 173) or whole milk ricotta (see page 8)

½ cup freshly grated Parmigiano-Reggiano

2 packed tablespoons fresh marjoram or oregano leaves, chopped, plus extra leaves for garnish

1 teaspoon finely grated lemon zest (use a Microplane)

½ garlic clove, finely grated (use a Microplane)

Kosher salt

Fresh cracked black pepper

½ cup "00" flour mixed with ½ cup semolina (aka bench flour), for dusting

The Essential Egg Yolk Pasta Dough (page 256)

Finishing

Confit Cherry Tomatoes (recipe follows)

¼ cup shelled roasted pistachios, finely chopped

1. **Make the ravioli filling.** In a medium bowl, combine the ricotta, parm, chopped marjoram, lemon zest, and garlic and season with a few pinches of kosher salt and black pepper. Transfer the ricotta filling to a pastry bag or a large resealable plastic bag and refrigerate until you're ready to use it. Snip off the corner of the bag before piping.

2. **Shape the ravioli.** Line a large baking sheet with a clean linen towel and dust it lightly with the bench flour. Work with one ball of dough at a time and keep the other half wrapped in plastic. Lightly dust a work surface with bench flour.

3. Set your pasta machine to the thickest setting, which is usually 1. Flatten the dough slightly with a rolling pin, creating a rectangle shape; be mindful to match the width of your roller. This will create consistent-sized pasta sheets. Feed the dough through the roller. Continue to feed the dough through the roller on increasingly thinner settings; you might need to add a little bench flour to one side of the dough if it's feeling a little sticky or wet. Continue rolling the dough until you've reached setting 5, and then repeat one more time on setting 5. Transfer the pasta to the dusted work surface and cut it in half. Cover one half with a sheet of parchment paper and then with a clean linen towel.

4. (For assembly photos, see page 265). On the uncovered pasta sheet, evenly pipe or spoon dollops of filling (1 to 1½ tablespoons) in two rows on the dough, about 1½ to 2 inches apart. Uncover the second sheet of dough and lay it top side down (so the floured side is facing up) over the mounds of filling; use your hands to gently stretch the dough so it covers the filling. Using the top, dull side (not the cutting side) of a 2¼-inch ring mold, gently press around each mound of filling to start shaping the ravioli and seal the dough. You don't need to push down too hard. Then, using the flip side of the ring mold, press around the mounds again, this time a little more firmly, to seal and shape the ravioli in advance of cutting it out. If the dough seems to have dried a bit when you're working with it, spritz it with a small spray of water.

recipe continues

5. Use a 2¾-inch ring mold cutter to cut out each ravioli; transfer to the prepared baking sheet. Cover the ravioli with another towel until you are ready to cook them. Repeat with the remaining dough and filling. You can refrigerate the ravioli for a few hours. If you're not using them immediately, sprinkle a generous amount of bench flour on top of them, cover with a clean lint-free towel, and wrap tightly in plastic. They can be refrigerated like this overnight. The ravioli can also be frozen on a baking sheet, then transferred to a resealable plastic bag and kept in the freezer for up to 1 month.

6. **Finish the ravioli.** To cook the ravioli, bring a large pot of water to a boil and season well with kosher salt. Place the ravioli in the boiling water and cook until the edges are slightly tender, about 3 minutes. Using a skimmer or slotted spoon, transfer the ravioli to a large serving platter or shallow bowl and gently spoon the confit tomatoes and juices over the top. Top with the pistachios and some fresh marjoram leaves.

Confit Cherry Tomatoes

These juicy confit tomatoes have many uses. They are great with fish, excellent served with cheese, and they can be folded into any grilled vegetable or grain salad that you fancy.

Makes about 3 cups

1 pound cherry tomatoes (assorted shapes, sizes, and colors are great)

½ cup everyday olive oil

¼ cup pitted black olives (like kalamata, Taggiasca, or Gaeta)

2 tablespoons fresh marjoram or oregano leaves

Coarse sea salt

1. Preheat the oven to 300°F. Combine the tomatoes, oil, olives, and marjoram in a 7 by 10-inch or other small flameproof baking dish and season with salt. Cover with foil and bake for 45 minutes, or until the tomatoes are blistered and have released some of their juices. The confit cherry tomatoes should be fragrant and intensified.

2. Position the top oven rack 3 inches from the heat source and turn the broiler to high. Remove the foil from the baking dish. Broil the tomatoes for 4 to 5 minutes, until their skins begin to char and toast. Turn off the oven and hold in the warm oven for up to an hour or so, or until the ravioli is ready. The tomatoes can be refrigerated in an airtight container for up to 1 week; rewarm in a 300°F oven before serving.

Get It

To make square ravioli, use your fingers (instead of a round ring mold) to cup and shape the mounds of filling. Press to seal. Use a pastry cutter with a straight or fluted edge to cut the ravioli squares, leaving a nice border of dough. As a rule, square ravioli have more pasta dough, and round ravioli have more filling.

Get It

The Pasta Marriage Ceremony

There's an old Italian cooking tradition called the pasta marriage ceremony, and it's one of the most important lessons I learned as a cook. Essentially, it's the act of cooking pasta in its sauce. I learned this on my first trip to Italy. I was staging at Dal Pescatore under the great chef Nadia Santini. She asked me to assist her in preparing family meal for the team. She asked if I had ever made spaghetti al pomodoro. I thought to myself, "Of course!" But on second thought, I had no idea, and I had to see how she made it. Nadia smiled and said she would show me. She grabbed a box of DeCecco spaghetti, a jar of tomatoes she had put up from the summer, 1 clove of garlic, olive oil, and a handful of basil. She dropped the pasta into a pot of boiling water, and, meanwhile, we heated some olive oil in a large saucepan and added the whole clove of garlic to the pan to toast it. She removed the garlic clove and added the jar of tomatoes. She then removed the pasta from the pot; it had only been 2 minutes or so. The pasta was still hard and straight. She put it in the saucepan with a few ladles of pasta water. We then shook the pan gently so the pasta could soften and nestle into the tomatoes. My mind was fully blown. What had just happened? The most simple and generic pasta dish had been elevated right in front of my eyes.

What I learned is that the secret is not only in the ingredients but in the technique. This idea of cooking the pasta in the tomato sauce gave this dish new meaning and importance to me. The pasta marriage ceremony is the technique of making perfect pasta. It's really easy, and you seriously won't ever want to cook pasta any other way.

The way I grew up making pasta was to cook the pasta fully in boiling water, then drain it and top it or mix it with sauce. But in Italy, the pasta is par-cooked in water until it's not even al dente, really, then it finishes cooking in its sauce. This adds *so much* flavor to the pasta. The pasta and the sauce, therefore, are not separate but one. The magic to the marriage of the two comes from the starchy pasta cooking water, which helps loosen the sauce and let it be absorbed into the pasta. Beautifully.

I use this technique with every sauced pasta I make, fresh or dry, except for pesto, which I don't like to cook because of its fresh herb flavor. At the restaurant, I use tongs to transfer the par-cooked noodles (which still have a good bit of cooking water clinging to them) to the skillet with the sauce, but at home, I suggest scooping out some of the pasta water and adding it to the sauce along with the par-cooked noodles to finish cooking.

Timing varies from pasta shape to shape, but as a rule, I cook dry pasta in its sauce for its final 3 minutes or so, and fresh pasta for only about 1 minute. I promise you'll *love* this technique. It's a real game changer.

This dish was born when I competed on *Beat Bobby Flay* and I was given chicken parm as my signature dish. Ironically, chicken parm is something I just don't normally make. After thinking about it, I got inspired to use the whole bird for an abundance of flavor, and to give some extra thought to the tomato sauce, which is often kind of overlooked. Using a fresh tomato sauce brings a bright, acidic hit to the crispy, umami-stuffed chicken! I also love adding fresh sliced tomatoes topped with grated parm, which get super juicy and delicious under the broiler. Who doesn't love a broiled tomato?? I know this recipe seems like a doozy, but it's so worth the effort—and if you want some shortcuts, be sure to look at Get It Get It.

Whole Bird Chicken Parm

with Broiled Tomatoes

Serves 4 to 6

Chicken Cutlets

8 garlic cloves (about ¼ cup)

1 tablespoon everyday olive oil

1 whole chicken (about 4 pounds)

½ cup fresh basil leaves, chopped

¼ cup freshly grated Parmigiano-Reggiano

2 tablespoons panko (Japanese breadcrumbs)

1 tablespoon finely grated lemon zest (from 1 large lemon; use a Microplane)

1 large egg

1 teaspoon dried oregano

1 teaspoon kosher salt, plus more for seasoning

½ teaspoon fresh cracked black pepper

2 slices of deli-style whole milk mozzarella

Breading

2 cups all-purpose flour

2 teaspoons kosher salt

2 whole eggs

1 cup whole milk

Toasted Breadcrumb Saltine Action (page 406)

ingredients continue

1. **Prep the chicken cutlets.** Preheat the oven to 350°F. Lay two 10-inch-square sheets of foil on top of one another. In the center of the foil, combine the garlic cloves with the olive oil. Bring the edges of the foil together to form a little pouch. Bake directly on the oven rack for 20 minutes, or until the garlic is tender. Set aside to cool.

2. Place the bird on your cutting board, legs facing toward you, breast side up. Using a sharp knife, free the thighs from the bird. Using your hand, bend the leg back and pop the thigh bone from the main carcass. Cut through the joint and skin to detach the leg completely. With the chicken still breast side up, use your knife to slice the breast meat away from the bone to remove each breast. Continue by removing the wing by the wishbone. Remove the wings and skin from the breasts (see Get It Get It on page 406 for uses). Place the leg quarters on the board, bone side up. Using your knife, cut around the tapered end of the leg so that you can remove the meat from the bone. Begin cutting around the leg and thigh bone; be sure to cut underneath the bone to free the meat (alternatively, you can just cut the meat away from the bone, since it will be diced anyway). Cut the skin-on thigh and leg meat into a 1-inch dice. Place the dark meat in a food processor and add the roasted garlic, basil, parm, panko, lemon zest, egg, oregano, salt, and pepper. Pulse about 15 times, until combined.

3. Place the breasts flat on the cutting board, leaving the tenderloins attached. To butterfly the breasts, place your hand flat on top of a breast and use a sharp knife to slice into one side, starting at the thicker end and ending at the thin point. Be careful not to cut all the way through to the other side. (If the breast splits, it's okay; you will just have 4 smaller cutlets.) Place a butterflied breast between two sheets of plastic wrap and pound gently until flattened and an even thickness (about ¼ inch thick is ideal). Repeat with the other breast. Refrigerate between the sheets of plastic until you are ready to stuff the cutlets.

recipe continues

Finishing

Olive oil spray

3 cups Fresh Tomato Sauce
(page 391)

3 or 4 slices of deli-style whole
milk mozzarella

2 or 3 small heirloom or vine-
ripened tomatoes, sliced about
¼ inch thick

1 cup freshly grated Parmigiano-
Reggiano

Fresh basil, for garnish

Super-special extra-virgin olive oil,
for drizzling

4.   Transfer the breasts, bone side up, to a small baking sheet. Lightly season with a few pinches of salt. Place 1 slice of mozzarella on top of each chicken breast. Divide the ground chicken mixture evenly on top of the mozzarella on each breast. Pat down the ground chicken, spreading it evenly. Cover the baking sheet with plastic wrap and freeze the stuffed chicken breasts for an hour, or until they are firm. (This will help enormously with the breading.) If you haven't already, make your toasted breadcrumbs while the stuffed chicken cutlets are deep-chilling.

5.   **Bread the breasts.** In a wide, shallow bowl, toss the flour with 1 teaspoon of salt. In another wide, shallow bowl lightly beat the eggs with the whole milk and 1 teaspoon of salt. Finally, place the toasted breadcrumbs in a third bowl.

6.   Gently pat the stuffed chicken cutlets in the flour, ensuring that all the nooks and crannies are well floured. Try to keep the breasts with the stuffing side up. Gently lift and place in the egg wash, tilting the dish so that the egg wash can roll over the chicken. (You can also spoon the egg wash over the top.) Using a fork, gently lift the chicken, allowing any extra egg wash to drip off. Transfer to the breadcrumb mixture. Shake the bowl and, using your hands, pat the breadcrumbs over the top, evenly coating the chicken. Transfer to a baking sheet. You can refrigerate the breaded chicken, covered, for up to 4 hours before cooking.

7.   **Finish the chicken.** Preheat the oven to 425°F. (If you have a convection oven, feel free to use it, as the extra hot air here is good; set the oven at 400°F.) Line a baking sheet with foil or parchment paper and set a rack in the baking sheet; spray the rack with oil. Place the chilled cutlets on the rack stuffing side up and bake for 25 to 30 minutes, until a breast registers 155°F when checked with a thermometer. Remove from the oven. Carefully position the oven rack so it's 6 to 7 inches from the heat source and turn the broiler to high.

8.   In an extra-large roasting pan, flameproof casserole dish, or a 12- to 14-inch cast-iron skillet, pour 2 cups of the tomato sauce. Nestle the chicken in the sauce, still stuffing side up. Dollop the remaining 1 cup of tomato sauce over the chicken. Top with the mozzarella and sliced tomatoes. Sprinkle the grated parm all over the tomatoes and chicken. Broil for 8 to 10 minutes, until the tomatoes and cheese begin to turn golden brown and bubbling. Remove from the oven and let cool for 5 minutes before serving. To serve, cut each cutlet into four slices, then garnish with fresh basil leaves and a drizzle of super-special olive oil.

Toasted Breadcrumb Saltine Action

I grew up with Shake 'n Bake and I *love* a saltine cracker, so
I created this mock Shake 'n Bake mixture that I think you'll
love. This can be stored in an airtight container in the freezer
to keep its freshness and used on anything that you would
want to shake and bake. Try it on zucchini, pork chops, or
cheese or as a topping for baked tomatoes. All delicious!

Makes 4 cups

6 tablespoons everyday olive oil

1 sleeve saltine crackers, pulsed in the
food processor for 15 seconds

2½ cups panko (Japanese
breadcrumbs)

2 tablespoons dried oregano

1 teaspoon kosher salt

½ teaspoon granulated garlic or
garlic salt

In a nonstick skillet over medium
heat, heat the olive oil. Add the
saltine crumbs and panko and toast,
stirring continuously with a rubber
spatula, until golden brown, 10 to
12 minutes. Add the oregano, salt,
and granulated garlic, remove from
the heat, and let cool.

Get It

Want to take this dish a step
further? Heck, you're tackling
the whole bird, so you might
as well go for it. Make crispy
chicken cracklings by placing
the chicken skin from the
breast on a baking sheet lined
with foil or parchment paper.
Season with a pinch or two of
salt. Bake at 375°F until golden,
rendered, and crispy, about
25 minutes. Remove with a
spatula to a platter lined with
paper towels to cool, then chop
the cracklings and sprinkle on
top of the chicken parm right
before serving. Plus, homemade
chicken stock is in your future!
Save the wings, excess chicken,
and carcass bones in the freezer
for your next batch of chicken
stock.

When breading, try to keep one
hand for the dry ingredients
and one hand for the wet
ingredients. I also like to use a
fork to coat the chicken in the
egg wash mixture.

Get It

This is a humble dish inspired by Southern Italian cooking, in which the meat is stretched out by adding bread, eggs, and seasonings, like an Italian meatloaf. In Italy, meatballs are served as an entrée—you don't see meatballs served with pasta. Rather, they're served as a *secondo* (second plate), typically in a bowl of rich tomato sauce like the one here. But don't worry, I won't judge if you choose to eat these with a big bowl of spaghetti! I also like to serve these meatballs as is with a crusty piece of bread, or on a sub roll for a meatball sandwich. Aside from the delicious results of slow-cooking in the rich tomato sauce, these meatballs get next-level flavor from ground soppressata, which adds umami and spice. You can also use mortadella, pepperoni, or prosciutto—the sky is the limit!

Soppressata Meatballs

Stewed in Oven-Roasted Tomato Sauce

Makes 12 large meatballs

8 ounces Italian country-style bread, cut into cubes (5 cups)

3 cups whole or 2% milk

5 ounces spicy soppressata or pepperoni, roughly chopped

2 garlic cloves

2 tablespoons pimentón de la Vera (Spanish smoked paprika)

2 tablespoons dried oregano

1 tablespoon fennel seeds

1 teaspoon fresh cracked black pepper

½ teaspoon kosher salt

½ teaspoon chile flake

2 pounds ground pork

2 large eggs

1 cup freshly grated Pecorino Romano, plus more for garnish

¼ cup chopped fresh basil or parsley, plus more for garnish

1 cup canola oil, if frying the meatballs

Oven-Roasted Tomato Sauce (page 392), blended smooth (see Get It Get It on page 408)

1. In a medium bowl, combine the bread cubes and milk, pushing the bread cubes down so that they're submerged in the milk. Let soak for 30 minutes. The bread will absorb about half of the milk.

2. Meanwhile, combine the soppressata, garlic, pimentón, oregano, fennel seeds, black pepper, salt, and chile flake in a food processor. Process for 1 minute, or until finely chopped. Place the ground pork in a large mixing bowl and add the soppressata mixture. (You don't have to clean out the food processor bowl.)

3. In a medium bowl fitted with a colander, drain the soaked bread. Squeeze the bread, draining about 1½ cups of the milk. Discard the milk. Transfer the soaked bread to the food processor and process for 30 seconds, until it reaches an oatmeal-like texture. Add the bread to the pork mixture, followed by the eggs, pecorino, and fresh basil. Using your hands, mix well to combine.

4. Line a baking sheet with foil. Form the mixture into 12 large meatballs, about the size of a tennis ball (¾ cup each) and place on the baking sheet. Refrigerate for at least 30 minutes before cooking. At this point the meatballs can be covered and refrigerated overnight. Be sure to reroll the chilled meatballs with your hands before cooking to get the perfect round shape.

5. If you are baking your meatballs, preheat the oven to 425°F and bake for 20 minutes, until firm and set. Remove from the oven and lower the oven temperature to 350°F.

recipe continues

6.   To fry the meatballs, heat 1 cup of canola oil in a large (12- to 14-inch) skillet on high heat for about 3 minutes, until the oil reaches at least 300°F. Working in two batches, add the meatballs to the oil; they should sizzle immediately. Fry until they are completely browned a very dark color (don't be scared!) on one side, about 7 minutes. Use tongs to turn each meatball and brown completely on all sides. Once fully browned, drain the meatballs on a paper towel–lined baking sheet or platter. (The advantage to this method is that you achieve a super-golden delicious sear on the meatballs.) Preheat the oven to 350°F.

7.   In a large ovenproof pot, heat the tomato sauce. When the sauce begins to bubble, add the par-cooked meatballs. Cover and bake in the oven for 1 hour. Serve piping hot, topped with grated pecorino and fresh basil.

Get It

When it comes to serving meatballs, I think a smooth sauce is beautiful—it dresses the meatballs in a more velvety way than a chunky sauce. You can blend the sauce in a blender or food processor, or use a hand blender before adding it to the meatballs to bake.

We shallow-fry our meatballs at the restaurant, but when I'm home, I don't love getting my kitchen super dirty, and I prefer to cook with less fat. The good news is that baking meatballs works really well. The downside is that you end up with flat-bottomed meatballs versus perfectly round ones. The closest you can get to round perfection is to make sure the meatballs are super chilled, then give them a final quick roll before putting them in the oven.

Get It

I am a big fan of the American South's tomato pies, and I wanted to make one for this book, but instead of going the Southern route with cheddar and mayo and the like, I ended on this version with a decidedly Italian spin. I love a creamy blend of Fontina, ricotta, and whole milk cottage cheese (yup, cottage cheese—you won't believe how well it works here) with silky fresh pasta sheets. The most brilliant part is baking the lasagna in a springform pan! This way, every piece has that ideal mix of crispy edges and soft, tender interior. I also love that this pays homage to heirloom tomatoes. They have a lot of water, so it's key to blanch and peel them, then use a mix of salt and sugar to cure and intensify their flavor. When you bite into this lasagna pie, you'll feel like you're eating the juicy inside of a whole tomato— no canned flavor here. I'm so pumped for this dish! I think you'll go bananas for it.

Heirloom Tomato Lasagna Pie

Serves 8

Kosher salt

2½ to 3 pounds ripe yet firm heirloom tomatoes (5 or 6, in assorted sizes and colors)

2 tablespoons coarse sea salt (like Maldon), plus more for seasoning

2 teaspoons granulated sugar

Fresh cracked black pepper

2 cups whole milk (4%) cottage cheese (not part skim! This is important!)

1 cup whole milk ricotta

12 ounces Fontina, shredded (3 cups)

2 tablespoons fresh thyme leaves

1½ teaspoons cornstarch

1 tablespoon unsalted butter

Fresh Pasta Sheets (page 259), blanched

8 ounces thin-sliced deli-style mozzarella

1 cup Oven-Roasted Tomato Sauce (page 392) or your favorite hearty marinara-style tomato sauce

½ cup freshly grated Pecorino Romano

1 cup fresh basil leaves

1. Bring a large pot of water to a boil. Generously season the water with kosher salt. Prepare a large bowl with ice water. Using a paring knife, core the heirloom tomatoes, removing the stem ends. Quickly blanch the tomatoes for 15 to 25 seconds, depending on their size; you may see the skins begin to split or pull away from the tomatoes near the core. Be careful not to overcook them; this will result in mealy tomatoes. Also, don't be alarmed if the skins don't begin to pull away—they will once they're in the ice water. Dunk the tomatoes in the ice water, allowing them to chill and stop the cooking process. Once chilled, peel them, revealing a beautiful silky-smooth tomato. Transfer the tomatoes to the strainer of a salad spinner or to a colander, then sandwich them between paper towels and gently press; return to the strainer.

2. In a small bowl, combine the coarse sea salt and sugar. Use this to season the tomatoes. Let the tomatoes drain for 30 minutes, then discard the liquid. Cut the tomatoes vertically into ½-inch-thick slices (I find that they hold their shape better when cut from top to bottom versus sideways, aka hamburger style) and place back in the strainer; spin the tomatoes a few times to remove any excess liquid hanging out! You can also pat them dry with paper towels. Gently transfer the tomato slices to a baking sheet or large platter. Season with coarse sea salt (again, I know, but yes, the tomatoes want it . . .) and black pepper.

3. While the tomatoes are draining, in a medium mixing bowl, combine the cottage cheese, ricotta, Fontina, thyme, cornstarch, and a pinch or two of sea salt. Preheat the oven to 400°F.

4. Set aside half of your prettiest tomato slices for the top layer of lasagna. Liberally butter a 10-inch springform pan. To create the pasta "crust" for the lasagna, first lay 2 sheets of pasta in the bottom of the springform pan.

ingredients continue

recipe continues

2 tablespoons everyday olive oil, plus more for the parchment paper

Super special extra-virgin olive oil, for drizzling

Dried oregano (preferably wild Calabrian, Greek, or Mexican), for sprinkling

— Get It —

When it comes time to bake the lasagna pie, please use parchment paper and not foil. The parchment allows the lasagna to breath and bake perfectly, and gives the tomatoes a chance to caramelize.

If you're using a convection oven, first cook the lasagna pie covered for 45 minutes, then uncovered for another 20 minutes or so.

If you choose to let the lasagna pie rest for a couple of hours, you can rewarm or recrisp it in the oven before you cut it. Heat the lasagna 6 inches under the broiler on high for 3 to 4 minutes.

I like to keep the pie on the bottom of the springform pan for transporting. If you want to move it to a platter, I recommend using two thin spatulas, like a fish or cake spatula, a bit of courage, and maybe a friend to help!

— Get It —

Then carefully drape a sheet of pasta along the inside of the pan, so that some of the pasta hangs over the rim and a bit lies in the bottom. Repeat with 6 more sheets of pasta, shingling them around the springform pan. Be sure that the pasta covers the bottom and sides of the pan to seal in the pie. (You are building a crust-like lining with the pasta sheets.)

5. Lay 3 mozzarella slices in the bottom of the pie, and top with 2 more sheets of pasta. Feel free to cut or tear the sheets in half to evenly fill the bottom of the pan as you layer. Top with half of the cottage cheese mixture and another 3 slices of mozzarella. Place 2 to 2½ pasta sheets on top of the cheese. Evenly spoon ½ cup of tomato sauce on top of the pasta layer, then top with the not-as-pretty sliced tomatoes, filling the pan evenly around. Sprinkle with ¼ cup of pecorino and top with the basil leaves. Top with 2 to 2½ pasta sheets, followed by the remaining cottage cheese mixture, the remaining mozzarella, and the remaining ½ cup of tomato sauce. Flip the overhanging pasta from the sides of the pan over to cover the top of the pie. They won't cover the whole top, which is okay—they will naturally leave the center of the pie exposed. Arrange the pretty sliced tomatoes on the top of the pie, overlapping a bit if needed. Drizzle the top and around the sides of the pan with the everyday olive oil.

6. Line a baking sheet with foil and set a rack in it. Cut a 10-inch round of parchment paper and lightly oil or spray the paper. Place the parchment oil side down on top of the pie. Using your hands, gently press down on the pie to compact the layers a bit. Set the pan on the prepared baking sheet. Bake for 1 hour, rotating the pan halfway through baking.

7. Remove the parchment and continue to bake for another 30 minutes. You will notice the sides of the pasta beginning to turn golden brown and the edges of the tomatoes beginning to char. Remove from the oven and insert a paring knife into the center of the pie; hold the knife in place for 10 seconds, then gently feel the tip with the inside of your wrist or lip to make sure the pie is hot. If not, place the lasagna back in the oven for 10 to 15 minutes longer.

8. Let the lasagna rest for at least 30 minutes, or even longer—I like to let it rest for up to an hour to allow the juices to settle. To serve, open the springform and remove the sides. Drizzle the pie with super-special extra-virgin olive oil and sprinkle with a few generous pinches of dried oregano. Cut into wedges and serve. YUM.

I've come to really love my broiler, which is the easiest way to mimic the way we cook at the restaurant, using super-high heat to char and sear foods for the best flavor. This simple broiled salmon is perfect for a weeknight dinner. The blistered cherry tomatoes release their sweet juices, combining with the garlicky oregano-scented oil for a perfect light sauce on the salmon. I like to serve this dish with steamed rice pilaf or toasted bread cubes, which soak up the sauce. When Jaime and I eat this, we flake the leftover salmon and toss it with greens and the blistered tomatoes for a quick and easy lunch the next day. This dish would be great with many other types of fish too, like halibut, snapper, or sea bass.

Broiled Salmon and Cherry Tomato Oreganata

Serves 4

Four 6-ounce center-cut salmon fillets (preferably from wild-caught salmon), skin removed

Kosher salt

Fresh cracked black pepper

1 pound multicolored cherry tomatoes, halved

½ lemon, thinly sliced

3 tablespoons everyday olive oil

2 tablespoons fresh lemon juice

2 garlic cloves, finely grated (use a Microplane)

2 tablespoons dried oregano (preferably wild Calabrian; see Get It Get It)

½ cup fresh flat-leaf parsley leaves, for garnish (optional)

1. Season the salmon fillets with salt and black pepper and arrange them in a flameproof casserole dish or a 9 by 13-inch baking dish. Place the cherry tomatoes around the salmon. Lay the lemon slices on the salmon fillets. In a small bowl, combine the olive oil, lemon juice, garlic, oregano, and a pinch of salt. Spoon the oreganata oil over the salmon and tomatoes. Let marinate on the counter for 30 minutes.

2. Turn the broiler to high. Broil the salmon 3 to 4 inches from the heat source for 6 to 8 minutes, allowing the tomatoes to blister and the lemons to char slightly on the edges. Remove from the oven, garnish with fresh parsley leaves, if using, and serve.

Get It

Not all dried oreganos are alike. I absolutely *love* the wild Calabrian oregano that is dried on the stem—its flavor and aroma are unparalleled. Try looking online and in your favorite Italian specialty market for it. I like the Tutto Calabria brand. If you have trouble finding wild oregano, opt for Greek or Mexican dried oregano. (See page 85 for more on this.)

Get It

ACKNOWLEDGMENTS

This book would not be possible without an incredible team.

Meg Sahs, we have come a long way since late drinks at Mondelli's! Thank you for always always supporting me and helping to achieve my dreams.

Kate Heddings, oh how we are forever bonded. Thank you for taking this journey with me and helping share the voices of the vegetables around us.

David Black, you are a force. Thank you for being more than an agent. You stand up for your authors in a way that makes us better. Thank you for pushing me to step up and out, to not give up, and to really dig deep and find my voice.

Stephen Hamilton, I consider myself beyond lucky and blessed that our paths would cross so many years ago (thank you, CeCe!) You are a true artist, seeing food through a totally unique lens, and you taught me so much. And to the crew at the studio, especially Diedre, Amy, Tom, Ben, Lynn, and John.

Andrew Jesernig and Sean Grady, your illustrations are pure joy. It was a real highlight every week to see where you had a taken each veggie's story.

Lorrie Jay, thank you for your thoughtful procurement of the amazing props used in every shot. Your styling shows us all the vegetables' inner selves.

Abby Schroder, thank you for saying yes to working on your days off, testing and prepping recipe after recipe. Thank you for the late nights and early mornings and putting Mr. Parms in his place. I am so thrilled that we can work together again. You are beyond talented, full of energy, and a joy of a human.

My editor at Harvest, Sarah Kwak, thank you for taking a chance on a first-time author and the possibility that the produce around us have lots to say. And to the rest of the team, Melissa Lotfy, Rachel Meyers, Jill Lazer, Lucy Albanese, Anwesha Basu, Katie Tull, Lisa McAuliffe, and April Roberts, thank you for making this book a reality!

Mia Johnson, thank you for designing a beautiful book; your design has captured the essence of listening to our veggies.

To my family and friends, you have always been my biggest support and have been excited to taste the wins and challenges, the ups and downs of my career. My earliest food memories are because of my family.

Jaime Canete, thank you for being you. I don't even know where to start. You are my rock, my light, my love and best friend.

Mom, thank you for all you sacrificed for me to have all I ever needed and for being awesome. Ralph and Lillian, you have made an impact on my life since I was little. This book would not be here without the many stories and recipes you've shared with me. To my aunt B, who always taught me to just add more butter and a crunchy topping to life. To my aunt Nancy, for getting me my first gig teaching cooking classes at the propane shop in Cuero, Texas. To my late uncle Randal, who first got me to start cooking at the age of eight and who made the best barbecue chicken I have ever had.

My best big sister, Kathryne Castellanos, who not only tested recipes for this book but also nudged me into uncharted waters in search of something great. Thank you for sending me to Chicago armed with a scrapbook résumé and a dream.

Rob Mosher, my brother and best friend. You have shown me a side of the world, through food, wine, dining, and service, that I never thought possible. You have the biggest heart of anyone I know, and I am so lucky to be in your clan.

And to the rest of the clan who has supported me along the way, David and Catrina Grueneberg, Kathy Simko, Janet "Nina" Morrison, Heather Early, Nick Bland, Steve Paluck, Cindee Black, Lisa Vera, Kathy Avinger, Wilma Leach, Sherri Harshman, Lindsey Brown, Ashley Christensen, Kait Goalen, Adam and Martha Derbyshire, Mindy Segal, Joe Kwon, Kelly Fields, Sarah Abell, Vanessa Vega and David Semanoff—y'all rock!

Thank you to the team at Monteverde past, present, and future. There are too many of you to name, but I hope you know how grateful I am for your commitment to our food, service, guests, and fellow team members. A big shout-out to the leaders at the time of the creation of this book: Bailey Sullivan, Francisco Jaimes, Amanda Adams, Kim Reyes, Justin Kaderabek, and Justin Spitz, you all know how to get it get it. And to those who have been in the Monteverde kitchen since the beginning, Besa Xhemo, Maria Perez, Flor Ortega, and Silvia Olascoaga. I am forever grateful.

To Chris Shepherd, I would not be here today without you having walked into my classroom at the Art Institute and taken me under your wing at Brennan's. The best part of all is my once-in-a-lifetime mentor is now one of my best friends.

To Tony and Cathy Mantuano, I need a whole book to thank you for everything you have taught and shared with me. Your love and care for Italian cuisine is contagious and has inspired me beyond my wildest beliefs.

To Bill Kim, you are why I love cooking with a wok. Thank you for teaching me. It's that fast, hard heat that's intoxicating.

Thank you to the farmers who work tirelessly growing delicious fruits and veggies while caring for our earth: Nichols Farm & Orchard, Spence Farm, Seedling, Vintage Prairie, Butternut Farms, Little Farm on the Prairie, Mick Klug Farms, and The Chefs Garden. We also have some fine purveyors who help us source the best—thank you to Regalis, Rare Tea Cellar, Testa Produce, and Market Produce.

I am blessed to have great Italian friends who simply live by a passion of food, health, and life's simple treasures. Alessandro Bellini, thank you. You have forever changed my life and food by introducing me to incredible artisans—balsamic makers, beekeepers, cheesemakers, olive oil producers, just to name a few. Now please enjoy life with Sara and Elena in Tuscany. Grazie mille to Elena and Francesca Paternoster, Luciano Galavotti, Gianni D'Amato, Fulvia Salvarani, Katia Amore, Alberto Giachi, Maria Nava Rondolino, Benito LaVecchia, Nadia Santini, Giovanni Sicilia and family, and Marina DeCarlo. Grazie to Trattoria Cognento, Dal Pescatore, Grano, and Il San Lorenzo for welcoming me into your kitchens. To my two Andreas—y'all have made an incredible impact on my understanding, knowledge, and love of regional Italian cuisine. Andrea Bezzecchi, you are a genius of balsamic vinegar and friendship. Thank you for sharing your country and cuisine with me. And to Andrea Paternoster, you will forever be missed while you are soaring high with the bees watching over us.

XO

INDEX